The O<!-- text cut off -->

Edited by

RONALD J. BURKE
SCHOOL OF BUSINESS,
YORK UNIVERSITY, CANADA

and **CARY L. COOPER**
UNIVERSITY OF MANCHESTER
INSTITUTE OF SCIENCE AND
TECHNOLOGY, UK

The Organization in Crisis

DOWNSIZING,

RESTRUCTURING,

AND PRIVATIZATION

BLACKWELL
Business

Copyright © Blackwell Publishers Ltd 2000
Editorial matter and organization copyright © Ronald J. Burke and Cary L. Cooper 2000

First published 2000

658.406 BUR

2 4 6 8 10 9 7 5 3 1

Blackwell Publishers Ltd
108 Cowley Road
Oxford OX4 1JF
UK

Blackwell Publishers Inc.
350 Main Street
Malden, Massachusetts 02148
USA

British Library Cataloguing in Publication Data

A CIP catalogue record for this book is available from the British Library.

Library of Congress Cataloging-in-Publication Data

The organization in crisis : restructuring, downsizing, and privatization / edited by Ronald J. Burke, Cary L. Cooper.
    p. cm.
  A collection of 17 papers by an international group of researchers.
  Includes bibliographical references and index.
  ISBN 0-631-21230-2 (hc : alk. paper) — ISBN 0-631-21231-0 (pb : alk. paper)
    1. Crisis management—Case studies. 2. Organizational change—Case studies. 3. Downsizing of organizations—Case studies. 4. Consolidation and merger of corporations—Case studies. 5. Privatization—Case studies. I. Title: Restructuring, downsizing, and privatization. II. Burke, Ronald J. III. Cooper, Cary L.

  HD49.073 2000
  658.4'056—dc21

00-025864

Typeset in 10 on 12pt Photina
by Graphicraft Limited, Hong Kong
Printed in Great Britain by TJ International, Padstow, Cornwall

This book is printed on acid-free paper.

Contents

List of contributors

Ronald J. Burke, School of Business, York University, Ontario

Cary L. Cooper, Manchester School of Management, UMIST

Marjorie Armstrong-Stassen, School of Business Administration, University of Windsor, Ontario

Fiona Campbell, Management Research Centre, Wolverhampton Business School

Susan Cartwright, Manchester School of Management, UMIST

Tom Cox, Department of Psychology, University of Nottingham

Rita Campos e Cunha, Faculty of Economics, Universidade Nova de Lisboa

Daniel C. Feldman, College of Business Administration, University of South Carolina

Esther R. Greenglass, Department of Psychology, York University, Ontario

Amanda Griffiths, Centre for Organizational Health, Department of Psychology, University of Nottingham

Douglas T. Hall, School of Management, Boston University

Sarah-Louise Hudson, Manchester School of Management, UMIST

Todd D. Jick, The Center for Executive Development, Cambridge, Massachusetts

Carrie R. Leana, Katz Graduate School of Business, University of Pittsburgh

Mika Kivimäki, Finnish Institute of Occupational Health, Department of Psychology, Vantaa

Craig R. Littler, Melbourne Institute of Applied Economic and Social Research, Melbourne University

John F. McCarthy, School of Management, Boston University

Aneil K. Mishra, Babcock Graduate School of Management, Wake Forest University

David Noer, Noer Consulting, Greensboro, North Carolina

Zehava Rosenblatt, Faculty of Education, University of Haifa

Zachary Schaeffer, Faculty of Education, University of Haifa

Paul Sparrow, Management School, University of Sheffield

Gretchen M. Spreitzer, Marshall School of Business, University of Southern California

Louise Thomson, Centre for Organizational Health, Department of Psychology, University of Nottingham

Jussi Vahtera, Finnish Institute of Occupational Health, Department of Health, Turku Regional Institute of Occupational Health, Turku

Harry J. Van Buren III, Katz Graduate School of Business, University of Pittsburgh

Mina Westman, Faculty of Management, Tel Aviv University

Les Worrall, Management Research Centre, Wolverhampton Business School

Preface

This collection was motivated by some disturbing trends we observed in an increasing number of organizations throughout the industrialized world. These trends also seemed to be consistent with and reflect broader changes in society as a whole.

The 1980s and 1990s saw considerable organizational restructuring, mergers and acquisitions, downsizing, and closures. These events first hit blue-collar workers in the manufacturing sector and later affected white-collar managers and professionals in all sectors. Organizations in both public and private sectors have similarly experienced these transitions.

Millions of workers have lost their jobs through no fault of their own; tens of millions of families have been directly or indirectly affected by these dislocations. Tens of millions of workers who survived these wrenching changes have had to cope with increased job insecurity, heightened levels of stress and increased feelings of anger, cynicism and alienation. There is evidence that levels of cynicism have also increased in the broader society in both North America and UK. The irony is that at least half of these organizational restructurings failed to realize the financial results that motivated them in the first place. Many were poorly planned and badly implemented, almost always producing emotional turmoil in staff.

Mergers and acquisitions continue to take place at an ever-accelerating pace. This phenomenon is not new; the 1980s saw an upsurge in merger and acquisition activity. What is new is the magnitude of the mergers, many exceeding US$50 billion in assets, and the international nature of the combinations and acquisitions.

The earliest restructurings and downsizings were carried out in companies that were unprofitable. Presently, companies that restructure and downsize are more likely to be profitable, the restructurings and downsizings undertaken to realize even greater short-term profits and favorable responses by the stock market. A firm that announces staff cuts one day is likely to be rewarded by the stock market the next day. The Canadian CEO of the year in 1998, while showing an increase in his company's profits, reduced staff by half.

Loyalty is now dead. Jobs are casual, part-time, temporary or contractual – you can have this job as long as you can contribute and the company needs you. The career is dead – or at least substantially altered.

The new technology has also served to intensify the work experiences of an increasing number of employees. This technology has quickened the pace at which individuals receive and can respond to others as well as increased the number of hours in the day that an individual can work and the places in which an individual can work. Related to these experiences is the myth that increasing use of technology will produce productivity increases. As a consequence, more attention has been paid to the technology at the expense of attention to the human element. A major reason for the failure of process re-engineering efforts in organizations has been the neglect of employees. When anticipated gains in productivity do not materialize, employee morale drops.

Recent events in Seattle, Washington, host city for the World Trade Organization meetings, highlight other international concerns. On the one hand demonstrators *outside* the WTO meetings were protesting – sometimes destructively – against what they perceived to be the exploitation of workers, the devastation of the physical environment and the undemocratic nature of the WTO, which, behind closed doors, develops policies that affect millions of people who have no voice in the debate. On the other hand, have-not countries *inside* the WTO refused to support policies advocated by the have countries which they believed would place their countries at an economic disadvantage.

Concerns were expressed several decades ago about the undue influence that the US, or the West more broadly, was having on the developing world. Fears of US imperialism and domination were common place. Such concerns are still being expressed today, but more often in a narrower sense to refer to the bottom line focus and intense work commitment seen in the US. Colleagues in some EU countries use the phrase "the Americanization" of their industries to capture this notion. France attempted to pass legislation reducing the work week but this legislation has been attacked by both employers and groups of workers.

There have also been efforts world-wide to apply a corporate or business model to the organization and management of both government and not-for-profit organizations. This has taken the form of privatization in most of the developed world. While there is some evidence that particular services may be delivered to tax payers with lower cost for a period of time, it is too early to tell whether there are costs related to privatization that are then borne by other publicly funded efforts.

The last decade has seen increasing interest in developing the high-involvement work organization. While a potentially positive initiative for individuals and organizations, at least as far as work experiences and job performance are concerned, there may be longer term individual well-being and family consequences. And when individuals prefer to be at work rather than at home who will take care of the children?

The new employment contract is an exciting concept to some employees. Taking responsibilities for one's own career, engaging in self-management of one's career, optimizing one's employability as a free-agent in an open market with potential employers bending over backwards to appeal to those high potential employees sounds idyllic. There is also a "dark" side to the new employment contract. Not all individuals are young, educated, computer literate, interpersonally skilled, flexible, adaptable and eager to learn. What about them?

There is also increasing tension on the work-family front. As women increase their participation in the workforce, and as more women move into more demanding managerial roles, women, men and families are increasingly challenged by these demands.

Technological advances have made it possible to work more hours per day, in more locations and at greater distances from home or office. Recent Canadian data have shown that increasing levels of employee absenteeism is costing firms billions of dollars per year in lost productivity as employees take time off work to take care of home and family needs.

The income disparity between the top and bottom organizational levels likewise continues to grow. Real income of most workers in the industrialized world has basically remained flat, or decreased in some cases, over the past decade. Although some organizations are doing better, many of their employees are not. It was recently reported that the richest individual in Mexico has as much wealth as the bottom 15 million Mexicans.

There is no doubt that developed countries have generally raised the standard of living of many of their citizens. Individuals are more likely to report greater income and more creature comforts now than 20 years ago. But has the increase in individual and social wealth brought about corresponding increases in happiness and well-being? The best available incidence suggests that the answer is no. "Doing better but feeling the same" summarizes much of the research findings.

A new organizational reality has emerged throughout the developed and developing world posing significant and potentially exciting challenges to company leaders. There is also a major role to be played by policy-makers in national governments in these countries. For example, policy makers in the European Union are grappling with some of these issues, while their North American counterparts seem to be oblivious to most of them.

While increasing awareness of the crises facing organizations has appeared in the academic literature, this awareness has not had much impact on the public debate. Well managed, leading-edge organizations have always had their antennae out and proactively responded to new demands and challenges. Most firms have done little or, at best, reacted passively. Policy makers have been relatively silent on these issues and have shown relatively little interest in them, particularly in North America. We are impressed by how much interest EU countries have shown in employee well-being and health matters, and quality of life more generally, and disappointed in how little concern and interest in these have been shown in Canada and the US.

Our objectives for this collection were to first lay out what we see as the major trends and challenges facing contemporary organizations – the new reality, and second, to indicate through the writings of leading international academics and practitioners, the latest thinking and research findings in key areas of challenge and examples of organizational best practice.

The collection has been organized into four parts, each part contributing to our understanding of the present state of organizational crisis and future prospects for renewal and revitalization.

The first part, consisting of five chapters, illustrates in a convincing way the impacts of restructuring and transition on employees and organizations. Up-to-date research findings indicate that the potentially devastating effects of these upheavals are present in all developed industrialized countries. These results are consistent with and add to the growing number of studies showing that most organizations implement and manage these change processes poorly.

The second part highlights new streams of research and thinking which supplement the more common efforts which examine the impact of these transitions on employees and employing organizations. This part, consisting of four chapters, exemplifies path-breaking research projects. Thus consideration is given to exploring the conditions under which some employees thrive during organizational restructuring and downsizing while others exhibit depression and alienation. The process of downsizing, while traumatic for both the implementers and victims, raises ethical concerns for those responsible for the initiative. Choices must be made in responsible and moral ways. The role played by gender has received scant research attention up to now since most restructurings and downsizings have impacted men. Finally, organizations involved in downsizing and restructuring sometimes simultaneously introduce other programs designed to improve effectiveness. Are these efforts likely to be successful under crisis conditions?

The third part, also consisting of four chapters, focuses specifically on the emerging employment contract in the new organizational reality. What will work look like under these conditions? What are the career prospects of middle-aged and older workers under this scenario? How will these changes impact on an individual's sense of identity? What new challenges does this raise for organizations striving to remain competitive while developing their human capital?

The fourth part, again consisting of four chapters, turns the spotlight on what we have learned about supporting individuals and organizations through these turbulent times. Contributions by both organizational consultants and academic researchers are included. Managing change and transition are demanding at the best of times. Fortunately, considerable understanding of what is required to better handle these transitions has emerged. It is possible to minimize the human and organizational costs during restructuring and downsizings, though it will never be painless. There *are* better ways. The application of these "lessons learned" by enlightened executive leadership will expedite the renewal and realization process.

There is some urgency for organizations to think about their reorganization and downsizing efforts in new ways. These initiatives show no signs of slowing down. In fact, there is evidence that the numbers of these transitions may be rising as contemporary organizations struggle to remain competitive in an increasingly unforgiving economic environment. There are indications that employees, their families and the larger communities in which these individuals live are now being taxed to a greater degree than ever. The time to act is now.

This volume offers the latest thinking and research findings on the new organizational reality. It describes ways in which the workplace has changed and reasons for these changes, implications of major organizational transitions such as restructuring, downsizing and privatization on the workforce, organizations and the broader society, and examples of best practice in implementing these complex and difficult changes.

Our contributors come from a number of countries (Australia, Canada, Finland, Israel, Portugal, UK, US) reflecting the world-wide nature of the new organizational reality. The chapters are similarly varied. They include empirical and conceptual contributions, quantitative and qualitative methodologies, case studies, country comparisons and a distillation of what research suggests as most effective ways to help individuals and organizations anticipate and respond to forces of change.

We believe that understanding and responding to the new organizational reality has both research and practical relevance (Gowing, Kraft and Quick, 1998). Because this area has only gained research attention within the past decade, many research and application questions remain unanswered or have been only partially addressed. In addition, transition and renewal processes will likely become more pervasive in organizations world-wide as we enter the new millennium.

We hope this book will serve to interest more organizational researchers to consider issues affecting individuals and organizations as they strive to be effective and productive in challenging times. We also hope it will encourage more organizations to embark on these transitions in a more planned, successful way. We are now beginning to identify more effective ways to support transition and revitalization efforts (Freeman and Cameron, 1993; Mishra, Spreitzer, and Mishra, 1998; Nelson and Burke, 1998).

REFERENCES

Freeman, S.J and Cameron, K.S. 1993: Organizational downsizing: a convergence and reorientation framework. *Organization Science*, 4, 10–29.

Gowing, M.K., Kraft, J.D., and Quick, J.C. 1998: A conceptual framework for coping with the new organizational reality. In M.K. Gowing, J.D. Kraft, and J.C. Quick (eds) *The New Organizational Reality: Downsizing, Restructuring, and Revitalization.* Washington DC: American Psychological Association, 259–68.

Mishra, K.E., Spreitzer, G.M., and Mishra, A.K. 1998: Preserving employee morale during downsizing. *Sloan Management Review*, 39, 83–95.

Nelson, D.L, and Burke, R.J. 1998: Lessons learned. *Canadian Journal of Administrative Sciences*, 15, 372–81.

Acknowledgments

My career journey has been influenced in significant ways by places and people. My graduate school days in the Department of Psychology, University of Michigan, afforded me an environment conducive to learning, personal development, meaningful teaching and research experiences and seeing a first-rate department up close. Important personal and career influences came from individuals in my family, my high school, my undergraduate and graduate schools, and men and women colleagues and friends. Thanks.

Ronald Burke
Toronto, Canada

I would like to acknowledge the support of my team of researchers and colleagues at UMIST, who have over the years helped me to develop the field of work and well being. These include Sue Cartwright, Lyn Davidson, Val Sutherland, Steve Williams, Les Worrall, Brian Faragher, Howard Kahn, Cheryl Travers, Carolyn Highley, Suzan Lewis and many more.

Cary Cooper
Manchester, England

part I

Impact of Restructuring on Employees and Organizations

1 The New Organizational Reality: Transition and Renewal[1]

Ronald J. Burke and Cary L. Cooper

Hardly a day goes by without stories about organizational restructuring, downsizing, merging or closing appearing in the popular press. These events are taking place throughout the industrialized world. Consider the following headlines in the *Financial Post*:

"Laidlaw's U.S. ambulance unit hit with job cuts" (April 19, 1999)

"Mitsubishi to cut 14,500 jobs in massive restructuring" (April 11, 1999)

"AOL to trim staff after Netscape deal" (March 25, 1999)

"Siemens to buy Redstone, cut jobs" (March 19, 1999)

"Olivetti proposes large job cuts in takeover bid" (March 18, 1999)

"Telecom Italia plans 40,000 job cuts" (March 15, 1999)

INTRODUCTION

More organizations are downsizing, restructuring and outsourcing, which means more workers in the future will be selling their services to organizations on short-term contract or freelance bases. What are the implications for the health of the individual, his/her family and future organizations? Can individuals commit to organizations that do not commit to them? Can families survive the conflicts surrounding the changing role of men and women? Will women become the main breadwinners, given their flexible approach to work? Will these developments create "virtual organizations" with more teleworkers? These are some of the issues addressed in this book.

The last half century has seen an enormous change in the nature of society and the workplace. The 1960s epitomized the limitless possibilities of change, as society confronted the horrors of the Vietnam War and the traditional and established lifestyles of the post-war period. It was an era that embraced new technology, some suggesting a leisure age of 20-hour weeks. This was followed by a period of industrial strife, conflict, and retrenchment in the 1970s. The workplace became the battleground between employers and workers, between the middle classes and the working classes, between liberal and conservative thinking.

Out of the turmoil of the 1970s came the "enterprise culture" of the 1980s, a decade of privatizations, statutory constraints on industrial relations, mergers and acquisitions, strategic alliances, joint ventures, process re-engineering and the like, transforming workplaces into free market, hot-house cultures. Although this entrepreneurial period improved the economic competitiveness of some countries domestically and in international markets, there were also the first signs of strain, as "stress" and "burn-out" became concepts in the everyday vocabulary of working people (Vahtera, Kivimäki, and Pentti, 1997).

By the end of the 1980s and into the early 1990s, the sustained recession, together with the privatizing mentality with regard to the public sector, laid the groundwork for potentially the most profound changes in the workplace since the Industrial Revolution. The early years of the 1990s were dominated by the effects of recession and efforts to get out of it, as organizations "downsized," "delayed," "flattened" or "right-sized." Whatever euphemism you care to use, the hard reality experienced by many was job loss and constant change (Lamertz and Baum, 1998). There were fewer people, doing more work, and feeling more insecure. The rapid expansion of information technology also meant the added burden of information overload and the accelerating pace of work, with people demanding more information, quicker and quicker. The mid-1980s through the 1990s, also saw the massive expansion in numbers of women in the workplace, with a noticeable pushing (not shattering) of the glass ceiling further upwards. The changing role of men and women at work and at home added another dimension to the enormity of change taking place in the offices, factory floors and techno-cultures of industry.

Three types of organizational transitions have received increasing attention during the past few years: mergers and acquisitions, restructurings and downsizings, and privatizations (Burke and Nelson, 1998). These three newly emerging sources of organizational change share some common features. First, they are interrelated since all represent the effects of the economic recession and attempts by organizations to survive and to increase productivity (Marks, 1994). Second, being fairly recent areas of research, relatively little empirical work has been completed (Kozlowski et al., 1993). Third, these changes have vast implications for both practice and intervention at both individual and organizational levels (Cameron, Freeman, and Mishra, 1991; Cascio, 1995; Martin and Freeman, 1998).

Some of the dramatic changes affecting work and organizations include increased global competition, the impact of information technology, the re-engineering of business processes, smaller companies that employ fewer people, the shift from making a product to providing a service and the increasing disappearance of the job as a fixed collection of tasks (Cascio, 1995; Martin and Freeman, 1998). These forces have produced wrenching changes to all industrialized economies. These changes have impacted most profoundly in terms of job losses.

In addition, companies were not downsizing simply because they were losing money. In a given year, 81 percent of companies that downsized were profitable in that year. Major reasons reported in the American Management Association's 1994 survey on downsizing were strategic or structural (to improve productivity, plant obsolescence, mergers and acquisitions, transfer of location, new technology).

The economic downturns of the 1980s highlighted the stress of not having a job. In the US, 10.8 million people lost their jobs between 1981 and 1988 (Fraze, 1988). Even in the growth periods from 1985–9, 4.3 million American workers lost their jobs (Herz, 1991). From June 1990 through July 1991, 1.6 million lost their jobs (Greenwald, 1991). In the European countries of France, Germany, Italy, the Netherlands and the UK, 2.1 million lost their jobs in 1989. In this same year, 320,000 Japanese, and 522,000 Canadians lost jobs (Sorrentino, 1993), and in Central and Eastern Europe, 3.7 million lost jobs (Organization for Economic Cooperation and Development, 1992). Global job loss is predicted to continue as organizational retrenchment and restructuring continue (Haugen and Meisenheimer, 1991).

Other studies have shown that anticipation or concern about job loss may be as damaging as job loss itself (Latack and Dozier, 1986). Job insecurity has been found to be associated with increased medical consultations for psychological distress (Catalano, Rook, and Dooley, 1986) and with increased disability claims for back pain (Volinn et al., 1988). Job insecurity of parents can also affect their children's work beliefs and attitudes (Barling, Dupre, and Hepburn, 1998).

Dekker and Schaufeli (1995) conducted a repeated measures study of the effects of job insecurity in a large Australian public transport organization undergoing significant change and downsizing. At the time of the study (1990–1), the organization employed about 20,000 people and provided train, streetcar and bus services to passengers in urban and rural areas. Although the public service in the Australian state in which this study was conducted did not typically terminate employees, recent events suggested that job insecurity was a real and justified concern. Four departments were identified as having an objective threat of having surplus workers or closure. Data were collected using questionnaires distributed twice, with an interval of two months. Job insecurity was associated with a deterioration of psychological health (psychological health and burnout) as well as job and organizational withdrawal. However, social support from colleagues, from management or from unions had no effect. Dekker and Schaufeli (1995) suggest that the job stressor itself (job insecurity/job loss) had to be directly addressed instead of trying to render its effects less harmful by providing more social support. Interestingly Dekker and Schaufeli (1995) found that being certain about the worst (those transport workers who knew they would lose their jobs) seemed to reduce symptoms of psychological stress and burnout, while prolonged job insecurity was associated with continued high levels of psychological stress and burnout.

In addition, most research has focused on actual or imminent job loss as opposed to job loss further in the future or loss of valued aspects of the job (salary increases, promotions, perks, working conditions). Roskies and Louis-Guerin (1990) examined perceptions of the reactions to job insecurity as a chronic ambiguous threat in a sample of 1,291 Canadian managers. Three companies participated in the study, each having multiple divisions and/or sites. Two high risk companies participated: one was a large manufacturing company in a traditional declining industry, that had undergone major restructuring and repositioning to address survival issues in the preceding five years; the second was in a high technology industry characterized by cyclical employment, dependent on the needs of projects in progress. The low risk company was engaged in high technology research and manufacturing and had rapidly expanded in the five years preceding the research.

Let us now consider some of their results. First, significantly more managers in the high risk companies saw themselves as insecure than in the low risk company. Second, substantial numbers of managers in the high risk companies felt insecure in their jobs. Third, various facets of insecurity showed different effects. Thus, less than 5 percent of all respondents reported high likelihood of termination or demotion in the short term; 15 percent reported high likelihood of deteriorating work conditions and over 40 percent reported a high likelihood of job loss in the long term. They also found significant relationships between the measures of insecurity and health problems: the higher the levels of perceived insecurity, the greater the number of health symptoms. A similar pattern was found on relationships between levels of job insecurity and work-related outcomes: the higher the level of perceived insecurity, the lower the job commitment and more negative the appraisal of one's career. Interestingly, subjective perceptions of job insecurity had significantly stronger relationships with the physical health measures than did the objective index.

Furthermore, laid-off workers who return to the job market often take pay cuts. Downward mobility is common (*Business Week*, 1994). Of approximately 2,000 workers terminated by RJR Nabisco, 72 percent eventually found jobs but at wages averaging about half their previous pay (Baumohl, 1993). And jobs that were lost were being lost permanently as a result of new technology, improved machinery and new ways of structuring work. They were not being lost temporarily because of a recession.

Organizations are becoming leaner and meaner. More and more are focusing on their core competencies and outsourcing everything else. Continental Bank Corporation, for example, has contracted its legal, audit, cafeteria and mailroom operations to outside companies. American Airlines is contracting out customer service jobs at 30 airports. There are no longer any guarantees to managers and workers. Flattened hierarchies also mean that there will be fewer managers in smaller remaining organizations.

Was there life after downsizing? Axmith (1995) surveyed the experiences of 1,034 Canadian organizations in 1994 with organizational restructuring and downsizing. Considering organizational outcomes, 85 percent of the surveyed organizations reported improved costs; 63 percent reported improved earnings; 58 percent reported improved productivity; and 36 percent reported improved customer service. Considering effects on remaining employees, 61 percent of surveyed organizations reported decreased morale; 50 percent reported decreased company loyalty; and 37 percent reported decreased job satisfaction. Respondents also indicated ways their companies would change their approach to future downsizings and restructurings: 43 percent of surveyed organizations would improve communications; 24 percent would plan more carefully the jobs to be eliminated and employees to be dismissed; 11 percent would move events more quickly; and 10 percent would increase managerial involvement and visibility.

Almost 90 percent of the organizations surveyed believed that organizations could no longer offer job security to employees. Forty percent of these organizations had implemented programs to help employees adjust to and manage this change. These involved: career management programs, skill-based training, change management seminars, communication of organization's current conditions and future prospects to employees and educating employees about the new employment contract – employment security versus job security.

Leana and Feldman (1992) focused on layoffs. Several institutions play a role in how layoffs are implemented: companies, unions, local and national regulatory bodies. Other people are affected besides those laid off: spouses, children, parents, friends, co-workers, communities. In the US, between 1980 and 1985, about 2.5 million jobs were lost each year, mainly blue collar. From 1985 to 1988, a different pattern occurred. Over one third of Fortune 1,000 companies reduced their workforces by 10 percent each year. They were reducing their workforces, not for economic reasons (losing money), but to increase productivity and cut costs. Hourly workers in manufacturing still are the hardest hit (about 50 percent of job losses); the rest are spread fairly evenly over other organizational levels.

Cascio (1993, p. 102) drew several conclusions from an exhaustive literature review and interviews with managers having downsizing experience.

1. Downsizing will continue as long as overhead costs remain noncompetitive with domestic and international rivals.
2. Firms with high debt will most likely downsize by aggressively cutting people.
3. Far too many companies were not well prepared for downsizing, having no retraining or redeployment policies in place, failing to anticipate the kinds of human resource problems that subsequently developed.
4. Six months to a year after a downsizing, key indicators, such as expense ratios, profits, return-on-investment to shareholders, and stock prices, often did not improve.
5. Survivors' syndrome was a common aftermath. Be prepared to manage it. Better yet, try to avoid it by actively involving employees in the planning phase of any downsizing effort.
6. Recognize that downsizing has exploded the myth of job security, and has accelerated employee mobility, especially among white-collar workers. It has fundamentally altered the terms of the psychological contract that binds workers to organizations.
7. Productivity and quality often suffered because there was no change in the way work was done. The same amount of work as before a downsizing was simply loaded onto the backs of fewer workers.

Many companies say they turn to layoffs only as a last resort. The facts indicate otherwise (Kets de Vries and Balazs, 1997). Right Associates, in surveys of 1,204 and 909 organizations that had downsized reported that only 6 percent of employers had tried cutting pay, 9 percent had shortened work weeks, 9 percent used vacations without pay and 14 percent had developed job sharing plans. Yet 80 percent of respondents in a Time/CNN survey indicated that they would rather see all employees of their firm take a 10 percent wage cut than lay off 10 percent of the workers to cut expenses to stay in business.

Similar initiatives have been undertaken in the public sector as governments attempt to reduce budget deficits and cut costs (Armstrong-Stassen, 1998). Privatization has been broadly defined as a strengthening of the market at the expense of the state. A narrower interpretation infers the conversion of public corporations into private ones, or at least hybrid ones in which the state has less than a 50 percent equity stake. There are several reasons for privatization: the goals underlying the formation of the public corporations no longer exist, or the goals are still valid but there are more efficient ways to achieve these goals.

Nelson, Cooper, and Jackson (1995) conducted a workforce study during the process of two major organizational transitions. The organization was a regional water authority about to move from public to private ownership as part of government policy to privatize the UK water industry. Two significant events took place during the period covering the research (October 1989 to July 1991): (1) privatization at the end of November 1989; and (2) structural reorganization in March 1991. These changes occurred in the context of previous changes including staff reductions. Between 1983 and 1989 the workforce had been reduced by 25 percent from 6,000 to 4,500, a reduction in levels of management and employees, with some changing jobs. The privatization plans called for a major restructuring and rationalization of the existing system of autonomous geographic regions, each with its own service functions. These service functions (for example, personnel, finance) were to be centralized at the head office. These changes would have significant effects on large numbers of employees (new reporting relationships, changes in jobs and responsibilities, relocation to other sites). The research examined the effects of these changes on employee morale and well-being. From a total workforce of 4,500, every third employee from each of the nine divisions of the organization was selected ($N = 1,500$). Data were collected from 332 employees (84 percent male) at three time periods: pre-privatization, November 1989; post-privatization, June 1990; post-reorganization, July 1991. Three dependent variables were included: job satisfaction, mental health symptoms, and physical health symptoms. Job satisfaction dropped following privatization and increased following reorganization. Mental health symptoms increased following privatization. There was also a significant increase in physical health symptoms following privatization.

Studies that examine survivors' attitudes in the aftermath of corporate layoffs consistently indicate that survivors' job attitudes such as job satisfaction, job involvement, organizational commitment, and intention to remain with the organization become more negative (Brockner et al., 1992; 1994; Hallier and Lyon, 1996). These negative reactions, combined with the fact that survivors must do more with less, make the aftermath of layoffs difficult to deal with.

Noer (1993) offered a vivid description of the state of layoff survivors. Individuals who survive cutbacks must deal with their own feelings as they develop a new relationship with the organization in which they are more empowered and less dependent. Managers must help other survivors through a painful but irrevocable change in the psychological contract between employees and employer. The need is to develop a more autonomous, less dependent link with the organization, not expecting job security.

Common symptoms among survivors are particularly strong in organizations that have historically taken great care of their employees. Employees often deny survivor symptoms. Noer (1993) uses the term "psychic numbing" to describe the denial, which is stronger the higher the organizational level and among those who plan and implement downsizing (human resource specialists). Survivor sickness has elements of psychic numbing. Some symptoms include denial, job insecurity, feelings of unfairness, depression, stress and fatigue, reduced risk taking and motivation, distrust and betrayal, lack of reciprocal commitment, wanting it to be over, dissatisfaction with planning and communication, anger at the layoff process, lack of strategic direction, lack of management credibility, short-term profit focus, and a sense of permanent change. There were also some unexpected findings with regard to survivors, including little survivor guilt, some optimism, lots of blaming others, and a thirst for information.

Interestingly, both survivors and victims shared common symptoms. Noer, in fact, believes the terms (survivors and victims) become reversed; that those who leave become survivors, and those who stay become victims (Wright and Barling, 1998). The organization typically provides resources to those who leave; however, they do not compensate survivors for the end to job security provided by organizations. The only way to have job security is to have up-to-date work experiences and skills. Rational decisions about non-human resources can be contrasted with the random decisions about human resources. Unlike discarding machines, discarding people has an effect on those who remain (Gottlieb and Conkling, 1995).

O'Neill and Lenn (1995) interviewed middle managers from one organization involved in a significant downsizing effort to hear their concerns. They found that emotions among middle managers ran high. Common among them were anger, anxiety, cynicism, resentment, resignation, desire for retribution, and hope. Anger seemed to be correlated with tenure and hierarchical level. Anger tended to be directed at two types of organizational activities: use of superficial slogans to rationalize the downsizing and condemnation of the past. Anxiety over not fully understanding the downsizing strategy was created in part by a lack of adequate communication. Cynicism stemmed from being victims and from senior executives who would not trust middle managers or who could not be trusted. Resentment illustrates the importance of equity of sacrifice by all employees – both real and symbolic.

THE CHANGING WORKPLACE

The downsizing and the rapidity of change has taken its toll in the 1990s. An Institute for Social Research (ISR) survey published in 1995, of 400 companies in 17 countries including 8 million workers throughout Europe, found that over the last 10 years the UK's employee satisfaction level dropped from 64 percent in 1985 to 53 percent by 1995, the biggest drop of any European country. In addition, the sickness absence rates rose during much of this period, recently hitting an all time high of a £12 billion cost to industry in one year. This had its effects on the family, as more and more two earner families/couples emerged in a climate which was anything but "family friendly". The BT Forum's report on *The Cost of Communication Breakdown* found that by 1991 the UK had the highest divorce rate in Europe with over 171,000 divorces, while the proportion of people living in one parent families increased four-fold between 1961 and 1991, with the prediction that over 3 million children and young people will grow up in step families by the year 2000.

This is in no small measure partly a result of a "long working hours" culture in most public and private sector organizations in the UK. DEMOS's report *Time Squeeze* in 1995 found that 25 percent of British male employees worked more than 48 hours a week; one-fifth of all manual workers worked more than 50 hours; one in eight managers worked more than 60-hour weeks and seven out of ten British workers want to work a 40-hour week but only three out of ten do.

This scenario is a cause for concern but the trend toward outsourcing is also leading toward a more insidious work environment, the short-term contract or freelance culture. This privatizing of the private sector no doubt stems from our insatiable appetite for privatizing the public sector in the 1980s. This has led to what employers refer to euphemistically as "the flexible workforce," although it is anything but flexible. The psychological contract between employer and employee in terms of "reasonably permanent employment for work well done" is being undermined, as more employees no longer regard their employment as secure and many more are engaged in part-time working. From 1984–94 the number of men working part-time doubled, the number of people employed by firms of more than 500 employees slumped to just over a third of the employed population and over one in eight British workers were self-employed.

There may be nothing inherently wrong with this trend but a recent *Quality of Working Life* survey by the Institute of Management and UMIST – which has and will continue to survey 5,000 managers each year over the next five years – found disturbing results among Britain's managers (Worrall and Cooper, 1997). Organizations at the end of the 1990s were found to be in a state of constant change, with 61 percent of this national sample of managers having undergone a major restructuring over the last 12 months. The consequences of this change, even among a group supposedly in control of events, were increased job insecurity, lowered morale, and the erosion of motivation and loyalty.

Most changes involved downsizing, cost reduction, delayering and outsourcing. Yet, although they led to an increase in profitability and productivity, decision-making was slower and, more importantly, the organization was deemed to have lost the right mix of human resource skills and experience in the process. In addition, the impact on working patterns, contract hours and evening and weekend working was penal. It was found that 82 percent of managers in the UK regularly work more than 40 hours a week, 38 percent report working over 50-hour weeks and 41 percent always or often work at weekends.

Poor communications and concern about future employability were some of the reasons for managers' insecurity: 60 percent feel they are in the dark about their organization's future strategies, while 48 percent say their biggest worry is financial security and employability in the wide job market. Due to outsourcing and intrinsic job insecurity, 89 percent of managers say they will need to develop new skills (for example IT, information management) over the next five years, presumably as they foresee the selling of their services to organizations on a freelance or short-term contract basis (Sparrow and Cooper, 1998).

This snapshot of corporate life from Britain's managers highlights the workplace of the future. Most organizations will have only a small core of full-time, permanent employees, working from a conventional office. They will buy most of the skills they need on a contract basis, either from individuals working at home and linked to the company by computers and modems (teleworking), or by hiring people on short-term contracts to do specific jobs or projects. In this way companies will maintain the flexibility they need to cope with a rapidly changing world. This change is already happening: BT claim that more than 2.5 million people are already working wholly or partly from home and predict this will rise to 4 million by the millennium. There is also a significant rise in the provision of interim management agencies to supply senior management on a project management basis to industry. All the trends are in the direction of what has been termed the "contingent workforce," an army of blue collar, white collar and managerial temps (Rousseau, 1996).

Organizational benefits

Restructuring and downsizing are expected to have economic as well as organizational benefits (Palmer, Kabanoff, and Dunford, 1997). The major economic benefit is increased value to shareholders. The rationale is that future costs are more predictable than future revenues; therefore cutting costs will improve profits. People can represent a high percentage of costs. Thus, cutting people seems to be a natural response. Other anticipated results are lower overheads, less bureaucracy, faster decision making, smoother communications, greater entrepreneurship, and increased productivity. Some organizations have seen benefits. As shown in the Canadian study by Axmith (1995), 85 percent of surveyed organizations cut costs, 63 percent improved earnings, 58 percent improved productivity, and 36 percent reported improvements in customer service. But other evidence suggests that most restructurings and downsizing fall short of objectives (Cascio, Young, and Morris, 1997).

Negative/unintended consequences for organizations

Many restructurings fail to reach anticipated financial objectives (Cascio, 1998). To understand why this happens, we must consider the impact of downsizing on organizational functioning. Most downsizing is done badly (Cascio, 1993; Folger and Skarlicki, 1998; Marks, 1994).

A recent survey of 1,142 firms conducted by the American Management Association (Greenberg, 1990) reported that more than half of them were unprepared for the downsizing, with no policies or programs in place to reduce the effects of the cutbacks (Rosenblatt and Mannheim, 1996). Surviving managers find themselves working in new and less-friendly environments, stretched thin managing more people and jobs, working longer. In addition, these companies sometimes replace staff functions with expensive consultants. Some severed employees will be hired back permanently while others will return to work part-time as consultants.

What about productivity? More than half of the 1,468 firms surveyed by the Society for Human Resources Management reported that productivity either stayed the same or deteriorated following downsizing. Similarly a study of 30 firms in the automobile industry indicated that in most of the firms productivity deteriorated relative to pre-downsizing levels.

Studies consistently show that after a downsizing, survivors become narrow-minded, self-absorbed and risk averse. Morale drops, productivity lessens. Survivors distrust management (Brockner, 1988). The long-term implications of survivor syndrome – lowered morale and commitment – are likely to be damaging for organizations. How likely are such employees to strive towards goals of high quality services and products?

Cascio (1993) reviewed the literature on the economic and organizational consequences on downsizing. He concluded that in many firms, expected economic benefits were not realized (for example, higher profits, lower expense ratios, higher stock prices, greater return on investment). Similarly, many expected organizational benefits were not achieved (such as better communication, greater productivity, lower overheads, greater entrepreneurship). Cascio attributed this failure to continued use of traditional structures and management practices. Instead, he advocated that downsizing be viewed as a process of continuous improvement that included restructuring, along with other initiatives to reduce waste, inefficiencies and redundancy.

Cameron, Whetten, and Kim (1987) identified 12 dysfunctional *organizational* consequences of any organization decline. These include: centralization, the absence of long-range planning, the curtailment of innovation, scapegoating, resistance to change, turnover, decreased morale, loss of slack, the emergence of special interest groups (politics), loss of credibility of top management, conflict and in fighting, and across-the-board rather than prioritized cuts.

Four out of ten companies that downsized had unintended business consequences (Marks, 1994). These included the need for retraining, more use of temporary workers, more overtime, increased retiree health costs, contracting out, loss of the wrong people, loss of too many people, and severance costs greater than anticipated (Bedeian and Armenakis, 1998).

Is there a healthy side to transition and change?

Marks (1994) contends that people are saturated with change and transition, and efforts must be made to help them deal with the pain of the past before they can move on to accept future changes. Most organizations in the 1980s and 1990s have gone through mergers, acquisitions, downsizing, restructuring, re-engineering, culture change and leadership succession. Many have had several of these and often overlapping. These events have not only changed organizational systems; they have had a major effect on workers in them – mostly negative (Ferrie et al., 1998; Kivimäki et al., 1997). Victims, survivors, destroyed careers and career paths; cynicism is up, trust in organizational leadership is down. Survivors work harder with fewer rewards. Multiple downsizings are seen over a few years (Armstrong-Stassen, 1997). Those who lost their jobs may in fact be better off – they can now get on with new things. And employees see no end to the changes, and feel powerless to influence them.

Yet organizations must continue to change to remain competitive (Nolan and Croson, 1995). New technology and increased competition will hasten the rate of change (Marks, 1994). Senior managers are excited about opportunities; middle managers are angry, depressed and tired. The negative psychological, behavioral and business consequences of these changes weigh heavily upon them.

There is a healthy side to transition and change. Some organizations were bloated: they needed to rightsize by eliminating unnecessary work (and people) and responding to the forces mentioned above. The point of Marks's book is the theme of using transitions such as mergers, acquisitions and downsizings to spur organizational renewal. This is easier said than done. Most organizations simply do not do this very well

(Baumohl, 1993). If organizations did not change they would stagnate and decline. Some restructurings, mergers and downsizings are wise business decisions. The merger of Molson's Breweries and Carling O'Keefe, is one Canadian example of such a decision. Many companies in the red may be wise to reduce their workforces. Companies can be revitalized and individuals can be renewed – if the emphasis is rightsizing rather than downsizing (Bruton, Keels, and Shook, 1996).

There are some opportunities following downsizing/change. It can re-energize tired workers and heighten their aspirations, shift the organization's focus to future possibilities, strengthen the pay-for-performance link, increase investment in training and development, encourage innovation, improve communication, and produce a clearer mission (Marks, 1994; Cascio, 1993).

Heckscher (1995) interviewed over 250 middle managers from 14 firms, each having gone through major changes, and having reduced their managerial workforces. Ten of the organizations were "troubled" and four "dynamic." In the troubled organizations, loyalty was racked with crisis. While supporting the need to downsize and restructure, over time these managers retreated into an inward looking paralysis. Three to five years after the changes had been undertaken, there was more bureaucracy than before. There was also inadequate communication from the top down. The loyalty in the troubled firms prevented managers from clearly seeing what the new situation demanded of them.

Traditional loyalty was rejected by managers in the dynamic companies. Instead they took time to re-evaluate their corporate values. They embodied what Heckscher termed "a community of purpose," a coming together of individuals with commitments and an organization with a mission. Individuals were committed to a personal set of skills, goals, interests and affiliations. This was also consistent with the emergence of a new employment contract. Individuals must build their own identities and careers without subordinating their needs to the organization; organizations must take responsibility for helping employees maintain employability (Noer, 1993). In addition, the government/societal infrastructure must change in ways supportive of the new employment contract (for example, service and insurance providers working to permit benefit continuity during workplace transitions, government consideration and scrutiny of private sector organizations). Heckscher suggests that the breakdown of the organization be seen as positive and necessary.

Consequences of change

As more people work from home, whether part-time or on a short-term contract, we will be increasingly creating "virtual organizations." How will this virtual organization of the future manage a dispersed workforce? Communications difficulties are already apparent in existing organizational structures, as found by the IM-UMIST survey (Worrall and Cooper, 1997).

With two out of three families/couples pursuing dual careers, how will working from home affect the delicate balance between home and work or indeed the roles between men and women? As employers increasingly look for and recruit "flexible workers," will women be preferred to men, given their history of flexibility? For example, there are currently five times as many women working part-time than men, and although twice as many men are now working part-time than a decade ago, women are historically more experienced at discontinuous career patterns, flowing in and out of the labour market, working part-time and on short-term contracts.

Since the Industrial Revolution, few white collar, managerial and professional workers have experienced high levels of job insecurity; even blue collar workers who were laid off in heavy manufacturing industries of the past, were frequently re-employed when times got better. The question that society has to ask is, "Can human beings cope with permanent job insecurity, without the safety and security of organizational structures, which in the past provided training, development and careers?" The European survey by ISR on employment security provides some cause for concern in this regard, showing the UK with the worst decline in employee satisfaction in terms of employment security of any of its competitors, from 70 percent satisfaction levels in 1985 to 48 percent by 1995, at a time when the UK has been moving faster toward a contingent workforce than all of its European counterparts.

Will this trend toward stable insecurity, freelance working and virtual organizations continue? More importantly, can organizations, virtual or otherwise, continue to demand commitment from employees to whom they do not commit? In comparative terms the UK economy is doing remarkably well but the levels of job insecurity and dissatisfaction are high. Developing and maintaining a "feel good" factor at work and in our economy generally is not just about bottom line factors, such as higher salaries, a penny off income tax or increased profitability; in a civilized society it should be about quality of life issues as well, like hours of work, family time, manageable workloads, control over one's career and some sense of job security.

WHAT ORGANIZATIONS CAN DO

Successfully managing transitions such as mergers and acquisitions, downsizing, and other restructurings requires considerable commitment from organizations. The research literature provides guidance for managers who are leading such transitions (Moser Illes, 1996).

Schweiger and DeNisi (1991) considered the impact of a realistic merger preview, a program of realistic information on employees of an organization that had just announced a merger. Employers from one plant received the merger preview while those in another plant received only limited information. Data were collected at four points in time: before the merger was announced, following the announcement but before the realistic merger preview program was introduced, and twice following the realistic merger program. The study extended for a five month period overall. Both objective and self-report data were obtained.

The following conclusions were drawn. First, the announcement of the merger was associated with significant increases in global stress, perceived uncertainty, and absenteeism and decreases in job satisfaction, commitment and perceptions of the company's trustworthiness, honesty and caring, and no change in self-reported performance. Second, the experimental plant was significantly lower on perceived uncertainty and significantly higher on job satisfaction, commitment and perceptions of the company's trustworthiness, honesty and caring following the realistic merger preview program. These same differences were also present three months later.

Noer (1993) offers a four-level process for handling layoffs and their effects. The first level of intervention addresses the lay-off process itself. Organizations that more effectively manage the layoff process will reduce (but not eliminate) layoff survivor sickness. The second level of intervention addresses the grieving process by providing an opportunity for catharsis in releasing repressed feelings and emotions. The third level of intervention helps survivors regain their sense of control, confidence, self-esteem and efficacy. The fourth level of intervention develops organizational policies, procedures and structures that will prevent future layoff survivor sickness. This includes the use of job enrichment and employee participation, employee autonomy, non-traditional career paths, short-term job planning, and the encouragement of employee independence and empowerment (Mishra and Spreitzer, 1998).

Government policies have been helpful, particularly advance notification provisions, extended unemployment benefits, and worker retraining programs. Advance notification gives workers more time to find new employment, decreasing the length of unemployment and emotional distress. Extended unemployment benefits lessen the economic distress. Retraining programs help the unemployed find new jobs. Company programs such as outplacement initiatives have also been of some help.

The large-scale survey of downsizing practices in Canada that was described earlier (Axmith, 1995) also investigated organizational efforts for survivors. Organizations that had downsized or restructured have undertaken a variety of initiatives to rebuild morale and commitment. These included:

- 60 percent conducted employee meetings or focus groups;
- 44 percent evaluated jobs to better reflect new responsibilities;
- 29 percent offered training programs to help employees adjust to the changes;
- 22 percent conducted employee surveys to identify their concerns;
- 9 percent developed new communication strategies, provided counselling and stress management assistance and held morale boosting events.

According to Cascio (1995) and Cameron, Freeman, and Mishra (1991), effective downsizing has some common characteristics, each an apparent contradiction.

- Downsizing was implemented by command from the top, with recommendations from lower-level employees, based on job and task analyses of how work was currently organized.
- Both short-term (workforce reduction) and long-term (organization redesign and systemic change in the organization's culture) strategies were used, together with across-the-board and targeted downsizing.
- Special attention was paid both to those employees who lost their jobs (for example, through outplacement, generous severance pay, retraining, family counselling), and to those who did not (by increasing information exchange among top managers and employees).

- Through internal data gathering and data monitoring, firms identified precisely where redundancy, excess cost, and inefficiency existed. They then attacked these areas specifically. They treated outside agents (suppliers, distributors) as involved partners as well as potential targets of their downsizing efforts.
- Reorganizations often produced small, semi-autonomous organizations within large, integrated ones. However, geographic or product reorganizations often produced larger, more centralized units (such as information processing) within decentralized parent companies.
- Downsizing was viewed as a means to an end (that is, as an aggressive strategy designed to enhance competitiveness), as well as the targeted end.

Cascio (1993) also offers some guidelines for managing downsizing effectively. First, to downsize effectively, be prepared to manage apparent contradictions – for example, between the use of top-down authority and bottom-up empowerment, between short-term strategies (headcount reduction) and long-term strategies (organization redesign and systemic changes in culture). To bring about sustained improvements in productivity, quality, and effectiveness, integrate reductions in headcount with planned changes in the way that work is designed. Downsizing is not a one-time, quick-fix solution to enhance competitiveness. Rather, it should be viewed as part of a process of continuous improvement.

We hope employers will reflect on where they are going and what that might mean for employees and society in the future, and try to act on their often espoused but rarely implemented belief: "Our most valuable resource is our human resource."

Note

1. Preparation of this chapter was supported in part by the School of Business, York University and the Manchester School of Management, UMIST. The comments of our colleagues Debra Nelson and Paul Sparrow are gratefully acknowledged.

References

Armstrong-Stassen, M. 1997: The effect of repeated management downsizing and surplus designation on remaining managers: an exploratory study. *Anxiety, Stress, and Coping*, 10, 377–84.

Armstrong-Stassen, M. 1998: Downsizing the Federal Government: a longitudinal study of managers' reactions. *Canadian Journal of Administrative Sciences*, 15, 310–21.

Axmith, M. 1995: *1995 Canadian Dismissal Practices Survey*. Toronto, Ontario, Canada: Author.

Barling, J., Dupre, K.E., and Hepburn, C.G. 1998: Effects of parents' job insecurity on children's work beliefs and attitudes. *Journal of Applied Psychology*, 83, 112–18.

Baumohl, B. 1993: When downsizing becomes dumbsizing. *Time*, March 15, 55.

Bedeian, A.G. and Armenakis, A.A. 1998: The cesspool syndrome: how dreck floats to the top of declining organizations. *Academy of Management Executive*, 12, 58–67.

Brockner, J. 1988: The effects of work layoffs on survivors: research, theory and practice. In B.M. Staw and L.L. Cummings (eds) *Research in Organizational Behavior* (Vol. 10). Greenwich, CT: JAI Press.

Brockner, J., Grover, S., Reed, T., and Dewitt, R. 1992: Layoffs, job insecurity, and survivors' work effort: evidence of an inverted-U relationship. *Academy of Management Journal*, 35, 413–25.

Brockner, J., Konovsky, M., Cooper-Schneider, R., Folger, R., Martin, C., and Bies, R. 1994: Interactive effects of procedural justice and outcome negativity on victims and survivors of job loss. *Academy of Management Journal*, 37, 397–409.

Bruton, G.D., Keels, J.K., and Shook, C.L. 1996: Downsizing the firm: answering the strategic questions. *Academy of Management Executive*, 10, 38–45.

Burke, R.J. and Nelson, D.L. 1998: Mergers and acquisitions, downsizing, and privatization: a North American perspective. In M.K. Gowing, J.D. Kraft, and J.C. Quick (eds) *The New Organizational Reality: Downsizing, Restructuring and Revitalization*. Washington DC: American Psychological Association, 21–54.

Business Week 1994: Downside to the jobs upturn. November 14, 26.

Cameron, K., Freeman, S.J., and Mishra, A.K. 1991: Best practices in white-collar downsizing: managing contradictions. *Academy of Management Executive*, 5, 57–73.

Cameron, K.S., Whetten, D.A., and Kim, M.U. 1987: Organizational dysfunctions of decline. *Academy of Management Journal*, 30, 126–37.

Cascio, W.F. 1993: Downsizing: what do we know? What have we learned? *Academy of Management Executive*, 7, 95–104.

Cascio, W.F. 1995: Whither industrial and organizational psychology in a changing world of work? *American Psychologist*, 50, 928–39.

Cascio, W.F. 1998: Learning from outcomes: financial experiences of 311 firms that have downsized. In M.K. Gowing, J.D. Kraft, and J.C. Quick (eds) *The New Organizational Reality: Downsizing, Restructuring and Revitalization*. Washington, DC: American Psychological Association, 55–70.

Cascio, W.F., Young, C.E., and Morris, J.R. 1997: Financial consequences of employment change decisions in major US corporations. *Academy of Management Journal*, 40, 1175–89.

Catalano, R., Rook, K., and Dooley, D. 1986: Labor markets and help seeking: a test of the employment security hypothesis. *Journal of Health and Social Behavior*, 27, 227–37.

Dekker, S.W.A. and Schaufeli, W.B. 1995: The effects of job insecurity on psychological health and withdrawal: a longitudinal study. *Australian Psychologist*, 30, 57–63.

Ferrie, J.E., Shipley, M.J., Marmot, M.G., Stansfeld, S., and Smith, G.D. 1998: The health effects of major organizational change and job insecurity. *Social Science and Medicine*, 46, 243–54.

Folger, R. and Skarlicki, D.P. 1998: When tough times make tough bosses: managerial distancing as a function of layoff blame. *Academy of Management Journal*, 41, 79–87.

Fraze, J. 1988: Displaced workers: Oakies of the 80s. *Personnel Administration*, 33, 42–51.

Gottlieb, M.R. and Conkling, L. 1995: *Managing the Workplace Survivors: Organizational Downsizing and the Commitment Gap*. New York: Quorum Books.

Greenberg, E.R. 1990: The latest AMA survey on downsizing. *Compensation and Benefits Review*, 22, 66–71.

Greenwald, J. 1991: Permanent pink slips. *Time*, September 9, 54–6.

Hallier, J. and Lyon, P. 1996: Job insecurity and employees' commitment: managers' reactions to the threat and outcomes of redundancy selection. *British Journal of Management*, 7, 107–23.

Haugen, S.E. and Meisenheimer, J.R. 1991: U.S. labor market weakened in 1990. *Monthly Labor Review*, 114, 3–16.

Heckscher, C. 1995: *White-Collar Blues: Management Loyalties in an Age of Corporate Restructuring*. New York: Basic Books.

Herz, D.E. 1991: Worker displacement still common in the late 1980s. *Monthly Labor Review*, 114, 3–9.

ISR 1995: *Employee Satisfaction: Tracking European Trends*. London: Institute for Social Research.

Kets de Vries, M.F.R. and Balazs, K. 1997: The downside of downsizing. *Human Relations*, 50, 11–50.

Kivimäki, M., Vahtera, J., Thomson, L., Griffiths, A., Cox, T., and Pentti, J. 1997: Psychosocial factors predicting employee sickness absence during economic decline. *Journal of Applied Psychology*, 82, 858–72.

Kozlowski, S.W.J., Chao, G.T., Smith, E.M., and Hedlund, J. 1993: Organizational downsizing: strategies, interventions, and research implications. In C.L. Cooper and I.T. Robertson (eds) *International Review of Industrial and Organizational Psychology*. New York: Wiley, 263–332.

Lamertz, K. and Baum, J.A.C. 1998: The legitimacy of organizational downsizing in Canada: an analysis of explanatory media accounts. *Canadian Journal of Administrative Sciences*, 15, 93–107.

Latack, J.C. and Dozier, J.B. 1986: After the axe falls: job loss as a career transition. *Academy of Management Review*, 11, 375–92.

Leana, C.R. and Feldman, D.C. 1992: *Coping with Job Loss: How Individuals, Organizations and Communities Respond to Layoffs*. New York: Macmillan/Lexington Books.

Marks, M.L. 1994: *From Turmoil to Triumph*. New York: Lexington Books.

Martin, R.E. and Freeman, S.J. 1998: The economic context of the new organizational reality. In M.K. Gowing, J.D. Kraft, and J.C. Quick (eds) *The New Organizational Reality: Downsizing, Restructuring and Revitalization*. Washington, DC: American Psychological Association, 5–20.

Mishra, A.K. and Spreitzer, G.M. 1998: Explaining how survivors respond to downsizing: the role of trust, empowerment, justice and work redesign. *Academy of Management Review*, 23, 567–88.

Moser Illes, L. 1996: *Sizing Down*. Ithaca, NY: Cornell University Press.

Nelson, A., Cooper, C.L., and Jackson, P.R. 1995: Uncertainty amidst change: the impact of privatization on employee job satisfaction and well-being. *Journal of Occupational and Organizational Psychology*, 68, 57–71.

Noer, D. 1993: *Healing the Wounds: Overcoming the Trauma of Layoffs and Revitalizing Downsized Organizations*. San Francisco: Jossey-Bass.

Nolan, R.L. and Croson, D.C. 1995: *Creative Destruction: A Six-Stage Process of Transforming the Organization*. Boston: Harvard Business School Press.

O'Neill, H.M. and Lenn, J. 1995: Voices of survivors: words that downsizing CEOs should hear. *Academy of Management Executive*, 9, 23–34.

Organization for Economic Cooperation and Development 1992: *Economic Outlook*. Paris: OECD Perspectives of Employment.

Palmer, I., Kabanoff, B., and Dunford, R. 1997: Managerial accounts of downsizing. *Journal of Organizational Behaviour*, 18, 623–40.

Rosenblatt, Z. and Mannheim, B. 1996: Workforce cutback decisions of Israeli managers: a test of a strategic model. *International Journal of Human Resources Management*, 7, 437–54.

Roskies, E. and Louis-Guerin, C. 1990: Job insecurity in managers: antecedents and consequences. *Journal of Organizational Behavior*, 11, 345–59.

Rousseau, D.M. 1996: Changing the deal while keeping the people. *Academy of Management Executive*, 10, 50–61.

Schweiger, D.M. and DeNisi, A.A. 1991: Communication with employees following a merger: a longitudinal field experiment. *Academy of Management Journal*, 34, 110–35.

Sorrentino, C. 1993: International comparisons of unemployment indicators. *Monthly Labor Review*, 116, 3–9.

Sparrow, P. and Cooper, C.L. 1998: New organizational forms: The strategic relevance of future psychological contract scenarios. *Canadian Journal of Administrative Sciences*, 15, 336–71.

Vahtera, J., Kivimäki, M., and Pentti, J. 1997: Effect of organizational downsizing on health of employees. *The Lancet*, 350, 1124–8.

Volinn, E., Lai, D., McKinney, S., and Loeser, J.D. 1988: When back pain becomes disabling: a regional analysis. *Pain*, 33, 33–9.

Walker, J. 1995: *The Cost of Communication Breakdown*. London: BT Forum.

Worrall, L. and Cooper, C.L. 1997: *IM-UMIST, Quality of Working Life Survey*. London: Institute of Management.

Wright, B. and Barling, J. 1998: "The executioner's song": Listening to downsizers reflect on their experiences. *Canadian Journal of Administrative Sciences*, 15, 339–55.

2 The Impact of Organizational Change on UK Managers' Perceptions of their Working Lives

Les Worrall, Cary Cooper, and Fiona Campbell

INTRODUCTION

The scale and nature of organizational change

In recent years, the pace and scale of organizational change has been considerable. The business press in the UK has been full of accounts of mergers, demergers, delayerings, redundancies, outsourcing, and rightsizing (usually downsizing). Perhaps not unrelated, the Greenbury, Hampel, Nolan and Cadbury Reports have explored issues of corporate governance and business ethics at a time when golden hellos, golden goodbyes, concern about standards in public and business life and concern about boardroom pay have all escalated to cause public disquiet about a new species of senior executives that the press have labeled "fat cats." Concern about boardroom pay, business practice and standards in public life has arisen at a time when reform of the industrial relations legislation in the UK under the 1979–97 Conservative administration had systematically brought about the large scale deregulation of business and the undermining of trade union power (Gallie et al., 1998) manifest in its most extreme form by the banning of trade unions in parts of central government.

The 1979–97 Conservative administration had also overseen the wholesale transformation of the public sector. This had taken the form of the privatization of the public utilities (Pendleton, 1994) and the introduction of market and quasi-market mechanisms in the National Health Service (Ferlie, 1992) signifying the rise of what has become known as the "new public management" (Ferlie et al., 1996; Osborne and Gaebler, 1993) under which the professions and managerialism clashed head to head. In the former public utilities, where organizations have moved from the relative shelter of the public sector into highly competitive markets, the extent and managerial impact of that translocation has been particularly pronounced (Worrall, Cooper, and Campbell, forthcoming).

While there was a clear political agenda to transform the UK from what was perceived to be an uncompetitive economy that was "controlled by the unions" and based on a "nanny state," the increasing globalization of capital markets, commodity markets, information markets and (to a much lesser extent) labor markets exposed UK business organizations to much more competitive pressure in the late 1990s than they had ever been exposed to before. Differentials in wage rates between the industrialized economies and the emerging economies have meant that many UK companies could no longer compete on price in what they perceived to be their traditional product or service markets. Consequently, companies have had to be more innovative in developing new products and adding value to older products. However, the main implication of increasing levels of competition is that firms, they would argue, have had to become far more brutal in how they manage their cost structures. Tiers of management perceived to be unnecessary from the viewing platform in the boardroom have become prime targets for cost cutting. This cost cutting has often taken place under the guise of "business process re-engineering" or "corporate transformation" assiduously carried out to comply with the received wisdom of the management guru of the moment and the prescriptions simplistically set out in their best selling management textbooks (Champy, 1995; Hamil and Prahalad, 1994; Hammer and Champy, 1993; Peters and Waterman, 1982). Perhaps MBA programs and the book shop at Heathrow airport – with its vast stock of plausible sophistry – have a lot to answer for.

As a result of these influences, our concepts of organization, management and work have been substantially redefined. Management has, for example, become far more "informational" with the rise of the knowledge worker and the increasing emphasis being placed on knowledge management (Nonaka and Takeuchi, 1995) and organizational learning (Moingeon and Edmondson, 1996). Organizational structures have changed radically in many cases from hierarchical, command and control structures to much flatter or even network organizations (Castells, 1996) which comprise "loosely coupled flotillas of smaller organizations" (Ferlie and Pettigrew, 1996). Kanter, Stein, and Jick (1992) defined their vision of the organization of the future based on the view that organizations would be flexible, adaptable, and concerned with stakeholders of all sorts. Kanter contrasts what she terms "corpocracies" – where there are clear hierarchies of command and control, with status being defined by position – with "post-entrepreneurial" organizations, which are more people-centered and where forms, structures and process are more fluid with managerial status being determined by knowledge and influence. It is clear that our notions of organization are changing radically but we shall find that many organizations in the UK fall short of Kanter's utopian ideal type.

The Royal Society of Arts has published research into the redefinition of work (RSA, 1998) and concluded that the patterns of people's daily working lives are changing fundamentally; that career structures are being redefined, that the way that organizations manage their workforces is changing and, most disturbingly, that while most people are learning to handle change "too many decision takers are behind the game." Other research (Gallie et al., 1998) has revealed that work has become more insecure, that the patterns of participation in the workplace have changed and that workers are redefining the way they think about issues such as loyalty, motivation, and commitment.

This review has revealed that work, organizations and organizational life are being redefined (Cooper, 1998a, b) and, if anything, the pace of change is quickening

(Worrall and Cooper, 1998). The fundamental nature of organizational change is evidenced by the array of new terms and concepts that have entered the field of organizational analysis in the recent past. These terms and concepts include delayering, outplacement, down-shifting, rightsizing, broad-banding and market testing with more recent additions being "presenteeism" and the metaphor of "the manager-as-mercenary."

While there have been a number of studies which have sought to develop frameworks with which to explore the nature of organizational change (Alvesson and Willmott, 1996; Hatch, 1997; Morgan, 1997) and studies which have explored the impact of organizational change among subsets of UK managers (Handy, 1998), there are relatively few cross-sectional and time-series studies which seek to assess how well these change management processes have been managed. Furthermore, what the impact of the (mis)management of these changes has had on managers' perceptions of managerial work and organizational life in different industrial sectors, different types of organization and, more important, what the differential impacts have been on managers at differing levels in the organizational hierarchy.

These issues will be addressed here using a unique database developed by researchers at UMIST in conjunction with the UK Institute of Management. This chapter is based on the first two years' research from a five-year research program (Worrall and Cooper, 1997; 1998) designed to paint a picture of the impact of organizational change on managers' experiences in order to provide a *more socially complete* view of the changes in organizational structures and working patterns that have affected corporate Britain (Lees, 1997). The essence of our research is to explore how well human resources are being managed within organizations; to assess the impacts of organizational change on managers in different sectors and levels in the organizational hierarchy; to assess how well change management processes are being managed and to assess how well the human resource base of UK organizations is being managed *as an asset and not as a cost.*

The underpinning value system which informs this research is that there is a need to view managers as a resource to be developed. In the natural environment, there has been much concern with developing environmentally friendly policies and with the concept of "sustainability." Sustainability requires us to move to a level of growth and a pattern of change that will not cause the long-term destruction or depletion of the world's natural resources. Perhaps there is a need to develop a more "manager-friendly" approach to human resource management geared less to making "the assets sweat" than to "keeping them fit" and not wearing out managers physically and/or mentally or causing them to make choices which undermine their out-of-work lives and their relationships with their partners and families (Lewis and Smithson, 1999; Worrall and Cooper, forthcoming).

The purpose of this chapter is, from the vantage point of the UK, to contribute to the debate on the changing nature of managerial work; to quantify the extent of change and to explore the recent impact of organizational change on managers' perceptions of work. In particular, the chapter will explore the impact of redundancy on UK managers' perceptions of working life in their organization. Essentially, we wish to contribute to developing a base of knowledge that will allow us to advise on the crafting and development of more informed and more socially complete human resource development strategies.

Table 2.1   The structure of the sample by managerial level in 1998

Management level	Number	Percentage
Chair	20	1.5
CEO/MD	152	11.6
Director	204	15.5
Senior manager	390	29.7
Middle manager	316	24.1
Junior manager	131	10.0
Other	65	5.0
Not stated	34	2.6

The research design

This chapter is based on a UMIST-Institute of Management research program labeled the "Quality of Working Life," which is conducted annually using the UK Institute of Management's membership database as a sampling frame. A questionnaire was designed based on our extensive prior research (Charlesworth, 1996; Cooper and Lewis, 1994; Institute of Management, 1996a, b, c; Liff, Worrall, and Cooper, 1997; Worrall and Cooper, 1995). The questionnaire was sent to a panel of 5,000 members of the Institute of Management who have been selected as a constant panel for the entire research period from 1997 to 2002. Where attrition of the panel has taken place, replacements to the panel are recruited with similar attributes to those managers who have left the panel.

The exercise generated 1,362 valid responses in 1997 and 1,313 responses in 1998 which represented a response rate of 27 percent and 26 percent respectively. (A detailed profile of the panel of respondents is contained in Worrall and Cooper, 1997; 1998.)

It is important to emphasize here that the sample reflects the structure of the membership of the Institute of Management particularly when exploring the distribution of respondents by management level. The profile of respondents by managerial level for 1998 is presented in table 2.1. Unfortunately, as there are no reliable and published estimates of the size and structure of the population of UK managers, it has not been possible to weight the survey data to give a more representative view.

The distribution by managerial level must be borne in mind when examining figures related to the total panel of respondents as the responses will reflect the profile of membership of the Institute of Management rather than the status profile of managers in UK businesses. Our panel tends to over-represent managers at more senior levels, and, as we shall see later on, there are significant differences in attitudes, behaviors and experiences by the respondent's level in the organizational hierarchy.

THE EXTENT OF ORGANIZATIONAL CHANGE AND THE DIMENSIONS OF RESTRUCTURING

The extent of organizational change in 1997 and 1998

In 1997 we highlighted the extent of organizational change in UK business organizations (Worrall and Cooper, 1997) by revealing that 59 percent of respondents had

Table 2.2 The changing extent of organizational change by type of organization

Has your organization carried out a restructuring in the last 12 months 1997 Base 1,361 1998 Base 1,312	% Yes 1997	% Yes 1998
Charity/not for profit	44	62
Family owned business	38	36
Partnership	38	30
Private limited company	58	61
Public limited company	71	75
Public sector	73	72
All	59	62

experienced some form of organizational change over the last year. By 1998, the rate had increased to 62 percent. It should be remembered that the respondents are drawn from the same panel, year on year. This reveals not only a considerable degree of dynamism in any one year but a degree of persistence, an increasing pace of change and, as we shall see later, an increasing level of employment instability and insecurity.

While there has been an overall increase in the number of managers affected by restructuring, there has not been an across-the-board change either by type of organization or by size of organization. Charity and not for profit organizations have had a significant increase in the amount of restructuring (see table 2.2). The extent of restructuring remained substantially higher in public limited companies (particularly the former public utilities) and public sector organizations than in any other type of organization. While the extent of restructuring remained roughly constant in the public sector, there was a 4 percent increase among PLCs. An analysis by firm size also revealed that there was a systematic relationship between size and the likelihood that restructuring had taken place. While 33 percent of respondents in organizations employing under 51 people had undergone some form of restructuring, this increased to 76 percent in organizations employing over 500 people: managers in large organizations were significantly more at risk of being affected by restructuring.

Different industrial sectors are affected by different pressures causing different forms of organizational adaptation in these sectors. The almost wholesale privatization of the former public utilities, the fragmentation of the National Health Service (NHS) into a myriad of health trusts, attempts to drive down local and national government costs through market testing and compulsory competitive tendering, the impact of information technology on the financial services sector and the impact of global competition on manufacturing have all caused massive – but differential – changes across industrial sectors. Elsewhere (Worrall, Cooper, and Campbell, forthcoming) we have commented in detail on the significant differences in the extent of restructuring and the form it has taken particularly in the public sector and among managers in the former public utilities. Table 2.3 reveals that the extent of change experienced by different industrial sectors varied considerably in 1998 from a high of 88 percent in the utilities sector to a low of 32 percent among consultancies.

It is clear that the extent of organizational restructuring is highest in the public sector and the former public sector (the utilities, public administration, education,

Table 2.3 The extent of organizational restructuring by industrial sector, 1998

Base 1,312	Respondents	Yes %	No %
All	1,311	62	36
Construction/engineering	113	54	45
Consultancy	130	32	68
Manufacturing/production	229	72	28
Distribution/transport	34	56	41
Retail/wholesale	36	53	42
Banking/insurance/finance	47	74	26
Utilities	49	88	12
Public administration/government	132	72	27
Education/training	146	64	34
Health services	78	69	31
Uniformed services/emergency	60	75	25
Business services	63	44	56

health and the emergency services all have rates over 64 percent) with manufacturing (72 percent) and the financial services sector (banking, insurance and finance) at 74 percent being the only private sector groups to have levels over the 62 percent global average.

Having established that there are significant differences in the extent of restructuring between industrial sectors, it is important to identify the extent to which these changes have been manifest in different ways across the sectors (see table 2.4). Subsequent tables relate only to those 818 (62 percent) of managers in 1998 who reported that their organization had experienced some form of restructuring over the last year.

The utilities sector stands out as having been most heavily affected by a wide range of forms of organizational restructuring. Over 60 percent of respondents from the utilities sector reported that the restructuring which affected their organizations had involved the use of contract staff, culture change programs, redundancies and cost reduction programs. The health, public administration, utilities and distribution sectors have been among the most affected by cost reduction programs and redundancies and by the increased use of temporary staff. In the manufacturing sector, given the impact of increasing global competitiveness, it is not surprising that the main emphasis has been on cost reduction and redundancies.

In this chapter, we have quantified the scale of the impact of organizational change and restructuring in the UK. In our surveys, we have shown that over 60 percent of managers were affected by organizational restructuring in 1998 and that the rate has increased over the two years of our research. We have demonstrated that the scale of change and the forms of change are variable across UK organizations. They have been shown to vary by type of organization, by industrial sector and by size of business. Perhaps more important than this, we have shown that the form of organizational change taken varies at the sectoral level. Having quantified the extent of change and analysed the differing forms that organization change and restructuring has taken, it now remains to assess the impact of this change on managers' working experiences.

Table 2.4 The nature of organizational restructuring by industrial sector (percentage of organizations deploying each form of restructuring)

	Closure of sites %	Cost reduction %	Culture change %	Delayering %	Outsourcing %	Redundancies %	Use of contract staff %	Use of temporary staff %
All	27	57	49	32	18	45	28	31
Construction/engineering	23	39	44	23	15	43	23	26
Consultancy	20	32	24	15	15	22	29	27
Manufacturing/production	27	62	55	34	21	48	29	33
Distribution/transport	21	68	37	32	11	58	16	32
Retail/wholesale	32	32	63	21	11	53	26	21
Banking/insurance/finance	29	57	43	26	23	40	29	34
Utilities	56	74	65	56	37	70	61	51
Public administration/government	28	66	49	44	23	54	26	40
Education/training	17	51	48	29	7	37	19	33
Health services	26	74	41	35	6	57	30	35
Uniformed services/emergency	38	58	49	24	20	27	42	20
Business services	21	57	25	11	11	29	21	18

This was a multi-choice question and the majority of organizations had used more than one form of adjustment.

Table 2.5 The effects of recent organizational change on perceived business performance (net agree score)[a]

Performance factor	All	Chair/ CEO/MD	Director	Senior manager	Middle manager	Junior manager
Accountability has increased	53	80	67	50	52	37
Decision making is faster	−1	48	24	−5	−7	−25
Participation has increased	11	60	34	6	4	−3
Flexibility has increased	18	65	35	11	15	−8
Key skills and knowledge have been lost	24	−24	2	24	43	27
Productivity has increased	21	70	47	16	12	−1
Profitability has increased	26	48	47	24	15	22

[a] The "net agree score" is the percentage of respondents agreeing with the proposition minus the percentage disagreeing with the proposition.

THE PERCEIVED IMPACT OF RESTRUCTURING ON ORGANIZATIONAL PERFORMANCE AND EMPLOYEE ATTITUDES

The impact of organizational change on business performance

Organizational change, according to the text books, is implemented to solve some organization problem and to yield business benefits. Among the expected benefits of downsizing are lower overheads, decreased bureaucracy, faster decision making, smoother decision making and in general greater efficiency (Kets de Vries and Balazs, 1997). Yet we are of the opinion that the change management programs are often not evaluated rigorously and often have unintended outcomes. Consequently, in our research program, we have set out to explore managers' views about the impact of the organizational change they had undergone on organizational performance measured in terms of accountability, faster decision making, knowledge and skills availability, productivity and profitability. The analysis presented here relates only to those respondents (814 in 1998) who reported that they had experienced organization restructuring in the last year.

Table 2.5 shows that evidence of organizations being perceived to win positive benefits from the significant amount of restructuring that has taken place is, at best, mixed. When all respondents are analyzed together, it would appear that some of the harder benefits of restructuring may have been won in the form of increased accountability, profitability, and productivity. However, it is noticeable, at the aggregate level, that the gains on some of the softer factors are less clear cut. For example, there appears not to have been any improvement in the speed of decision making as a result of organizational change, and, while participation and flexibility have been perceived to have increased, the improvement of these factors following restructuring is below that of the harder factors listed earlier.

There is a clear perception that the outcome of restructuring has been to leave organizations lacking the right mix of knowledge and skills. This measure increased from a net agree score of 14 in 1997 to 24 in 1998. While there is a degree of stability in the other measures used, the increase on this "now lacking knowledge and skills

Figure 2.1 Flexibility has increased by managerial level

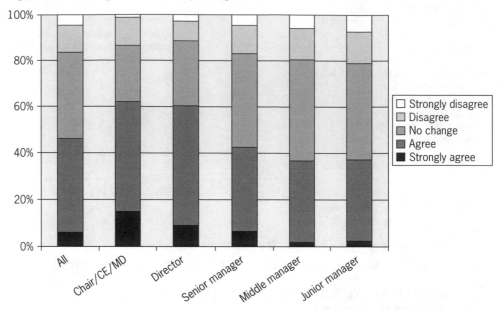

factor" is significant and is linked to our concern that the forms of occupational restructuring being used – such as outsourcing, delayering and the use of temporary
and contractual staff – are having a deleterious effect on the skills and knowledge
bases of organizations, perhaps indicating a greater willingness of organizations to
rely on a contingent workforce which, while it may be cheaper, does not possess
detailed organizational knowledge.

Table 2.5 explores the extent to which respondents from different levels in the management hierarchy have differing views about the effects of organizational restructuring.
The scale of differences between the highest and lowest levels of the hierarchy is stag-
gering and it is clear that perceptions of the organizational benefits of change and the
impact of change are viewed very differently depending on where one "sits" in the
managerial hierarchy. Those who inflict change from the top of the organization have
very different views of the impact of change than the recipients of change. The chairmen, CEOs and MDs group is the only group that thinks that key skills and knowledge
have not been lost and, with directors, are the only groups to think that decision
making has become faster as a result of organizational restructuring and change – an
issue which we shall discuss in more detail later.

While it is not surprising that junior managers have the least favourable impression
of the impact of change, the dissonance between their views and those at the top
managerial levels in organizations is considerable. Middle and junior managers are
much less likely to consider that the hard and soft objectives which underpinned
organizational restructuring have been achieved. For example, while chairman, CEOs
and MDs have net scores of 70 and 60 for increased productivity and participation,
junior managers recorded net scores of –1 and –3 respectively.

A more detailed analysis of two of the measures is shown in figure 2.1 (flexibility
has increased) and figure 2.2 (key skills and experience have been lost). For the most

Figure 2.2 Key skills and experience have been lost by managerial level

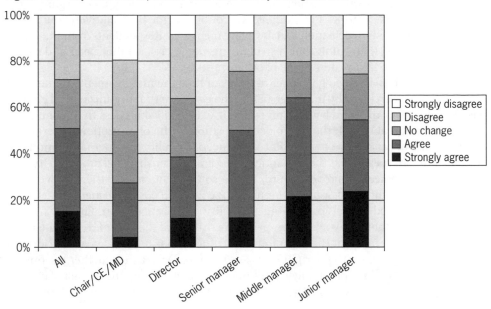

Table 2.6 The effects of recent organizational change on perceived business performance by type of organization (net agree score)[a]

Performance factor	All	Charity/ not for profit	Family owned business	Partnerships	Private limited company	Public limited company	Public sector
Accountability has increased	53	58	53	46	60	54	47
Decision making is faster	2	13	-7	-7	11	6	-11
Participation has increased	12	22	17	40	29	10	-3
Flexibility has increased	19	28	38	53	24	17	9
Key skills have been lost	23	2	-10	-40	-3	30	50
Productivity has increased	23	33	52	34	37	23	5
Profitability has increased	27	21	52	39	34	43	2

[a] The net agree score is defined in the note to table 2.5.

senior level of managers, the percentage agreeing with the proposition was in excess of 65 percent, declining to around 35 percent for both middle and junior managers. While 50 percent of chairmen, CEOs and MDs disagree that key skills and experience have been lost, this declines to 25 percent of junior managers.

Table 2.6 reveals that the perceived impact of organizational restructuring on both hard and soft measures of business performance is highly variable across different types of organization. It is noticeable, however, that in one aspect, there is a degree of consensus across different organizational types in that restructuring is viewed as having focused managerial accountability. Managers in all types of organization now appear to be much more aware of their own accountability. The broad similarity of views found on the accountability factor is not replicated elsewhere. Respondents from PLCs and the public sector were much more likely to feel that the impact of restructuring had been to reduce the skills and experience base of their organizations. In several instances, the public sector revealed sharp differences from other types of organization (Worrall and Cooper, 1998). For example, the public sector had relatively low scores on both the increased participation and flexibility measures. Respondents from the public sector are least likely to think that restructuring has increased the speed of decision making than those in any other type of organization.

The analysis has revealed a number of issues of how the management of change in organizations is perceived by managers. First, the evidence that organizational change has brought about the hard benefits on which it was justified are less than conclusive and vary considerably with the respondent's position in the organizational hierarchy. Second, there appears to be a view that while accountability has increased and been brought into sharper focus, there is much less of a consensus that productivity and profitability have been improved. Third, in the soft benefits arena, there is even less evidence that the impact of organizational change has had positive benefits in terms of increasing the speed of decision making, flexibility and participation. Finally, what is most noticeable is that many managers, particularly those at the lower levels of the management hierarchy feel that the main impact of change has been to leave their organizations lacking people with the right mix of skills. In order to assess further the impact of organizational change on managers, we now turn to exploring the impact of change on managers' perceptions of loyalty, motivation, morale and their sense of job security.

The impact of organizational change on employees' perceptions

After exploring the impact of change on organizational performance, attention was focused on examining how managers' perceptions of their loyalty to the organization, their morale, their motivation and their sense of job security had been affected by organizational change. Again, the analysis relates to the 814 respondents in the 1998 survey who had experienced some form of restructuring in the year prior to the survey. In both the 1997 and 1998 survey reports (Worrall and Cooper, 1997; 1998), we concluded that the impact of the considerable amount of restructuring in UK business organizations over the last 12 months had a considerably negative effect on employee loyalty, morale, motivation and, particularly, the perception of job security stimulating us to pose questions about the future of large organizations. Our research demonstrates that organizational restructuring has imposed considerable human and social costs on the recipients of change. In this section, we examine how the impact of organizational change has affected managers' perceptions by their level in the organization.

An analysis of the data by the respondent's level in the managerial hierarchy reveals large differences in the perceived impact of restructuring on the individual (see figure 2.3a–d). For three of our measures – loyalty, motivation, and morale – there are huge differences by level in the organization with a substantial proportion of chairmen, CEOs and MDs feeling that restructuring has increased their morale, motivation, and to a lesser extent, their loyalty. The effects have been perceived much more negatively by senior, junior and, particularly, middle managers. While responses from senior, middle, and junior managers are substantially negative for the loyalty, motivation, and morale measures, it is noticeable that the greatest negative impact has been on morale.

Figure 2.3 The impact of change on loyalty, morale, motivation and sense of job security by managerial level

(a) Loyalty

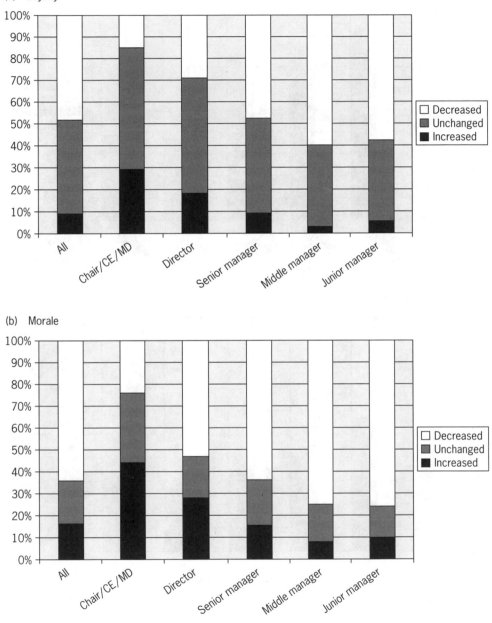

(b) Morale

Figure 2.3 (*cont'd*)

(c)   Motivation

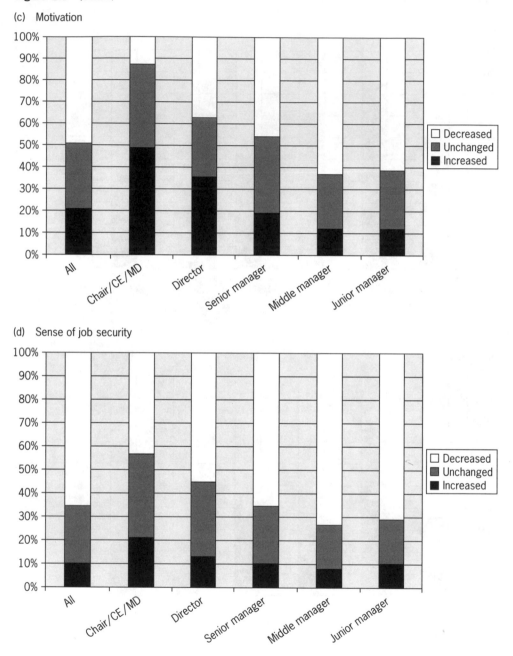

(d)   Sense of job security

Table 2.7 The impact of change on loyalty, morale, motivation and sense of job security by type of business

	All %	Charity/ not for profit %	Family owned business %	Partnership %	Private limited company %	Public limited company %	Public sector %
Effect on loyalty							
Increased	10	14	21	14	15	7	6
Unchanged	44	44	51	57	52	42	35
Decreased	46	42	28	29	33	51	59
Effect on morale							
Increased	17	20	36	40	26	15	8
Unchanged	21	20	28	7	24	26	13
Decreased	62	60	36	53	50	59	79
Effect on motivation							
Increased	22	28	25	33	30	21	14
Unchanged	30	23	39	20	36	34	23
Decreased	48	49	36	47	34	45	63
Effect on perceived job security							
Increased	11	9	14	13	19	10	5
Unchanged	25	29	32	40	30	25	19
Decreased	64	62	54	47	51	65	76

An examination of the perception of the job security measure shows that the majority view for all levels of management is that the impact of restructuring has significantly reduced their sense of job security. This finding provides clear evidence of the strength of the impact of organizational change on the nature of work and managers' perceptions of their own security of continuing employment.

Elsewhere (Worrall, Cooper, and Campbell, forthcoming), we identified that the impact of organizational change on our four measures varied considerably by industrial sector with respondents in the public and the former public utilities (now PLCs) recording much stronger levels of disaffection than respondents from, for example, private limited companies and family run businesses. In the 1997 report, we were led to hypothesize that there was a relationship between the governance style of an organization and, not only that the probability that organizational change would occur but also that when organizational change did occur, the perceived effect of that change by managers would also vary. Some of the analysis which led us to make that assertion is presented below.

Table 2.7 shows that the impact of organizational change on managers' sense of loyalty, morale, motivation and job security varies considerably by type of organization. The impact of change has generally been most detrimental in PLCs (particularly the former public utilities) and the public sector. Respondents from the public sector show the highest negative scores (labeled decreased in table 2.7) on all of the four factors listed. In 79 percent and 76 percent of cases in the public sector, restructuring had reduced the respondent's sense of job security and their morale respectively, compared to 54 percent and 36 percent among managers in family run businesses and 51 percent and 50 percent in managers from private limited companies.

It is also noticeable that the perceived negative impacts of restructuring are generally lower in family run businesses indicating, perhaps, the existence of different management styles in different organizational settings. This supports our assertions (Worrall and Cooper, 1997) that the impact and effect of restructuring is strongly mediated by the prevailing managerial and governance styles within organizations and the way that change is planned, communicated and implemented in different types of organization and the differing cultural settings.

We have identified some important outcomes of the processes of restructuring affecting UK organizations. First, there is a strong perception that restructuring is leaving many UK organizations – particularly very large organizations, PLCs and those in the public sector – with a depleted skills and experience base. Second, we have found that while there is wide variation on three of our measures (loyalty, morale, and motivation), all levels of management tend to consider that the impact of restructuring has been to make their jobs less secure. The main outcomes of organizational change would appear to be a sharpening of accountability but at the cost of decreased employee loyalty, reduced motivation, undermined morale and a reduced sense of job security, particularly for middle and junior managers, those in the public sector and former public utilities and those in organizations employing over 5,000 workers.

Perhaps most importantly, we have identified that the extent of change and its negative impact varies with type of organization, with the negative effects of restructuring being much less pronounced in family run firms and private limited companies than in PLCs and the public sector. A key finding is that there are strong concerns that organizational change is depleting the skills and experience base of organizations with this view having sharpened between the 1997 and 1998 surveys. This finding indicates a misalignment between organizations' human resource management strategies and their change management agendas and that senior managers have an insufficient understanding of the wider social, cultural, and personal impacts of their change agendas on their managerial workforce. This finding indicates strong support for the assertion made by the RSA (1998) quoted in the introduction that "most people are learning to handle change but too many decision takers are behind the game."

The extent to which the views of top managers and those at the lower levels of the organizational hierarchy conflict is a key finding and poses major questions about how well change is being managed, about the mix of stakeholder interests being reflected in the nature of the restructuring decisions made and about the effectiveness of organizational consultation and communications strategies. While a degree of change is inevitable, our findings pose questions about the need for such a high and quickening pace of change and about the way change is managed.

THE EFFECTS OF REDUNDANCY AS A FORM OF ORGANIZATIONAL RESTRUCTURING AND CHANGE ON MANAGERS' PERCEPTIONS

We have established that redundancy – linked to "downsizing" programs – has played a significant part in the overall process of restructuring that has affected many UK organizations (see table 2.4). Although, developed in the US, many UK companies have used downsizing-driven redundancy programs as a means of strategic transformation ostensibly in order to change organizations' corporate cultures. However, in many cases "downsizing" has been more cynically used as a corporate euphemism for mass sackings and redundancies (Vollmann and Brazas, 1993).

It has been suggested by previous research that redundancy affects survivors' emotions, attitudes, and behaviours (Brockner, 1990; Greenhalgh and Rosenblatt, 1984; Noer, 1993; Thornhill and Gibbons, 1995). Emotions synonymous with grieving such as shock, anger, denial, guilt, and fear have been noted alongside decreased motivation, decreased trust in management and decreased levels of organization commitment in subsequent jobs (Kozlowski et al., 1993). These emotions and attitudes have also been shown to affect the behaviors of survivors by making them indecisive, risk averse and less willing to go "that extra mile" (Smith and Vickers, 1994; Thornhill, Saunders, and Stead, 1997).

Reilly, Brett, and Stroh (1993) suggested that under redundancy, individuals become more loyal to their own personal development than to the organization, perhaps explaining the origin of the concept of "manager-as-mercenary" that has begun to appear in the literature (Handy, 1998). Reilly, Brett and Stroh (1993) also found that managers who had survived a turbulent corporate environment expressed more career loyalty (as opposed to organizational loyalty) than those in a more stable organization. This suggests that individuals are redefining and relocating their loyalty (away from organizations and towards themselves) and that they are now more inclined to build portfolios of portable skills and marketable experience than company-specific skills.

In support of Stroh, Brett and Reilly's (1994) findings, Robinson and Rousseau (1994) argued that employer violations of the psychological contract increases the probability of employee turnover while decreasing the satisfaction of those who remain: they also argued that redundancy (seen as a contract violation) will increase employee turnover, reduce job satisfaction, lessen organizational commitment and reduce morale and motivation. Such violations have caused employees to reduce their sense of obligation to employers and, at the same time, to increase their feelings of what they felt they were owed by their employers (Ebadan and Winstanley, 1997). In other instances, fear of redundancy may go some way to explain the increase in "presenteeism" (Handy, 1998) as managers attempt to demonstrate their indispensability by visibly working long hours.

Downsizing and redundancy are expected to improve productivity, effectiveness, efficiency and competitiveness and thus organizational performance (Cameron, 1994; Kets de Vries and Balzas, 1997; Shaw and Barrett-Power, 1997). However, our findings have called this into question with the main effect of much downsizing and redundancy appearing to be a sharpened sense of accountability amongst managers (table 2.5). There are a number of ways in which performance improvement through downsizing is alleged to be achieved (Fowler, 1993; Freeman and Cameron, 1993; Greenhalgh, Lawrence, and Sutton, 1988; Lewis, 1993; Turnball and Wass, 1997), yet, our research (Worrall and Cooper, 1997) suggests that the main consequence of redundancy on survivors is increased task overload and reduced role clarity as redundancy is far more effective at removing people from an organization than removing the tasks that they used to do, with residual, disembodied tasks being cascaded down the hierarchy. This view is supported by Tombaugh and White (1990) who found that redundancy survivors reported undergoing significant changes in daily operations, morale and workplace atmosphere as management expected managers to absorb increased responsibility and decision making at both the individual and work group levels. Surviving managers typically had wider spans of control (both in the number of workers and in the variety of tasks they had to manage). In many instances workers experienced difficulty in assuming their wider role and in undertaking the functions of their (former) immediate work group supervisor. It would appear commonplace that redundancy survivors are unprepared for the changes that result from downsizing and redundancy. In addition, our research (Worrall, Cooper, and Campbell, forthcoming) indicates that wholesale redundancy programs are effective in removing pockets of specialized organizational knowledge as entire levels of management are lost and the organization's reliance on temporary and contract staff increases.

Given the potentially widespread and damaging effects of redundancy and downsizing, an increasing number of management researchers have become interested in the phenomenon. The majority of literature concentrates on the technical or procedural issues associated with downsizing/redundancy strategies. While this field of research is important, such an approach pays insufficient attention to the psychological and emotional effects of downsizing on individual managers. Consequently, the analysis below focuses on seeking to identify differences in the perceptions of managers on issues such as loyalty, morale, motivation, and job security in organizations where there has been organizational change involving redundancy compared to managers in organizations where there has been restructuring without redundancy. At a second level of analysis we will contrast managers' responses on a number of perceptual measures in three different organizational settings: in organizations where there had been restructuring in the last year involving redundancy; in organizations where there had been restructuring without redundancy; and in organizations where there had been no restructuring in the last year.

Managers' perceptions of the impact of redundancies on aspects of their working life

Clearly, redundancy has serious and negative impacts not only on the victims but on the survivors. Below, we will analyze how redundancy has affected surviving managers' perceptions of loyalty, morale, motivation, and job security from our panel study. We also explore what effects redundancy has been perceived as having on business performance in terms of speed of decision making and on organizational knowledge and skills bases.

The first section refers to those organizations that reported experiencing organizational change. Respondents are divided into two groups: those working in organizations that used redundancy as a restructuring mechanism and those working in organizations that restructured but did not use redundancy. From table 2.8 it is evident that those organizations which implemented redundancy sustained a more negative impact on managerial perceptions of loyalty: where there had been redundancy, 60 percent of managers reported that their loyalty to the organization had decreased compared to 34 percent in organizations where restructuring had not involved redundancy. This finding reinforces that of Reilly, Brett, and Stroh (1993) who found that managers in

Table 2.8 The perceived impact of redundancy on loyalty

	(Base = 773)	Redundancy (364)	No Redundancy (409)
Increased	10.3	7.6	12.7
Unchanged	43.5	32.4	53.3
Decreased	46.2	60.0	34.0

Table 2.9 The perceived impact of redundancy on morale

	(Base = 778)	Redundancy (365)	No Redundancy (413)
Increased	17.2	9.8	23.7
Unchanged	20.4	14.2	25.9
Decreased	62.3	76.0	50.4

Table 2.10 The perceived impact of redundancy on motivation

	(Base = 777)	Redundancy (365)	No Redundancy (412)
Increased	22.1	16.2	27.4
Unchanged	30.1	25.8	34.6
Decreased	47.7	59.0	38.0

a post-redundancy setting had redirected their loyalty away from the organization. The results also support Robinson and Rousseau's (1994) finding that redundancy can be seen as a violation of the psychological contract which leads to a reduced sense of obligation to employers and hence a decrease in organizational loyalty.

The analysis revealed that it is not only loyalty which is affected negatively by organizational change involving redundancy. In particular, redundancy appears to reduce UK managers' morale (see table 2.9). Of the managers who experienced change involving redundancy, 76 percent of survivors felt their morale had decreased compared to 50 percent who experienced change not involving redundancy. Indeed, in almost 24 percent of cases where change had taken place without redundancy managers reported increased morale (compared to under 10 percent in cases where redundancy had occurred).

The negative effect of redundancy, over and above other forms of restructuring, was further apparent when questions were asked about managers' sense of motivation. Where change had involved redundancy, 59 percent of managers reported a reduced level of motivation compared to 38 percent in other instances (see table 2.10).

As expected, where redundancies have occurred, managers show a substantially reduced sense of job security even though they had survived previous rounds of redundancy. However, even in organizations where no redundancy had taken place almost 50 percent of managers reported a reduced sense of job security (see table 2.11). *Clearly, the primary outcome of organizational change on managers is an*

Table 2.11 The effect of redundancy on perceptions of job security

	(Base = 778)	Redundancy (367)	No Redundancy (411)
Increased	10.7	4.0	16.5
Unchanged	25.7	16.0	34.1
Decreased	63.6	80.0	49.4

Table 2.12 Impact on business performance: is decision making faster?

	(Base = 765)	Redundancy (361)	No Redundancy (404)
Strongly agree	3.8	4.2	3.5
Agree	26.3	23.8	28.5
No change	39.3	35.7	42.6
Disagree	18.2	21.9	14.9
Strongly disagree	10.3	12.7	8.2

Table 2.13 Impact on business performance: have key skills and knowledge been lost?

	(Base = 759)	Redundancy (359)	No Redundancy (400)
Strongly agree	15.7	24.8	7.5
Agree	34.1	40.7	28.3
No change	21.1	14.2	27.3
Disagree	19.2	14.8	23.3
Strongly disagree	8.4	4.7	11.8

increased sense of job insecurity but this is boosted – in our base by 21 percentage points – when redundancy is used as an instrument of adjustment.

In terms of the effects of redundancy on the operational aspects of the organization, our results indicate that while redundancies (often implemented to remove layers in the organizations) attempt to make an organization more effective (Kozlowski et al., 1993), decision making does not seem to have become any faster in the post-restructuring organization (see table 2.12). If anything, more managers in organizations where redundancy has been used tend to disagree that "decision making is faster" as a result of organizational change (34.6 percent disagree or disagree strongly, compared to 23.1 percent in organizations where redundancy has not occurred). This finding supports Thornhill, Saunders, and Stead (1997) who suggested that following a redundancy program, individuals are more likely to become indecisive and risk averse as spans of control and task overload increase and role clarity declines. More colloquially, managers seem less willing to "stick their neck out" following redundancies, which may explain why managers perceive decision making to have slowed down.

From table 2.13, there is strong evidence that the perceived impact of change generally is to cause the attrition of organizations' skills and knowledge bases. However, redundancy would seem to have a stronger impact on the process of knowledge and

Table 2.14 Morale is good overall in the organization

	Restructuring with Redundancy (372)	Restructuring No Redundancy (440)	No Restructuring (467)
Strongly agree	0.3	2.7	8.6
Agree	18.3	31.6	40.5
Neither	15.6	20.5	21.4
Disagree	47.3	33.6	23.8
Strongly disagree	18.5	11.6	5.8

skill loss. The implications of this perception by management suggests that the selection criteria being used by organizations to isolate individuals for redundancy may be ineffective and short-sighted and more geared to taking out high cost employees than ensuring the preservation and encapsulation of organizational knowledge. To ensure future success, it is essential for organizations to maintain their knowledge and skills bases yet the use of redundancy still remains an effective means of stripping out the knowledge base of many organizations. In instances where redundancy has been used, 65.5 percent of managers felt that key skills and knowledge had been lost, compared to 35.8 percent of managers in organizations where redundancy had not been deployed.

On each of our four measures which explore the personal impact of restructuring, the strong, negative impact of redundancy as a restructuring mechanism can be seen. While all forms of organization restructuring tend to reduce loyalty, motivation, morale, and sense of job security, the negative effects have been shown to be particularly pronounced when redundancy is used as a restructuring mechanism. Our research has also revealed that the impact of redundancy seems also to slow down decision making – in spite of the fact that it is often accompanied by delayering – and it is also perceived to substantially reduce the knowledge and skills bases of organizations. In order to explore the impact further, respondents' organizations were categorized into those where restructuring with redundancy had taken place, those where restructuring without redundancy had taken place and those where no restructuring had taken place. Here, managers were asked to rate the perceived level of morale in their organization. Table 2.14 shows a clear gradation across the three categories: while 68 percent of managers in organizations where redundancy has taken place do not agree that morale in their organization is good, this declines to 45 percent in organizations where change without redundancy occurred and to 30 percent where there was no organizational change.

Finally, in table 2.15, we reveal that managers who have experienced redundancy hold a substantially more negative view of their organization's priorities in terms of the importance of employees. While 42 percent of respondents in organizations not having restructured tend to agree that employees are the organization's greatest asset, this declines to 32 percent where there was restructuring but no redundancy and to 21 percent where redundancy occurred.

In summary, our results strongly support earlier research findings on the survivors of redundancy and on the impact of the use of redundancy – often used as a dimension of delayering – as an instrument of organizational restructuring. The analysis has

Table 2.15 Employees are the organization's most important asset

	Restructuring with Redundancy (372)	Restructuring No Redundancy (440)	No Restructuring (462)
Strongly agree	3.0	5.7	10.4
Agree	18.3	26.6	31.4
Neither	25.5	24.5	24.0
Disagree	35.8	31.4	26.2
Strongly disagree	17.2	11.8	8.0

shown that UK managers who experienced redundancy as part of organizational change and restructuring programs were far more likely to sustain a decrease in their loyalty, morale, motivation, and job security. Prior research (Campbell, Thornhill, and Saunders, 1997; Caulkin, 1996; Thornhill and Gibbons, 1995) has suggested that mismanaging change programs relying on the use of redundancy has led organizations into a spiral of decline where more emphasis is focused on internal politics and on managerial positioning in new structures rather than on products, markets, and customers. We have also revealed that the unintended impacts of redundancy and delayering – such as eroding the knowledge and skills bases of organizations coupled with the perceived slowing down of decision making – can be quite profound and damaging to the long-run success of businesses.

CONCLUSIONS

Change is increasingly becoming a major component of everyday organizational and managerial life. Change is inevitable and all organizations must adapt to change if they are to survive and to deliver high quality services and products to their customers. If change is endemic, then the ability to manage change effectively to achieve business objectives while simultaneously maintaining, if not enhancing, the quality of working life is a core managerial competence. If these tensions are not managed competently, then we are of the view that some of the traditional underpinnings of our concepts of organization and work will be eroded as managers become more committed to themselves than to their employing organizations; as managers cease to construct their futures in the context of their employing organizations; particularly as large organizations become increasingly fragmented into the "loosely coupled flotillas" of networked, smaller and – perhaps – more people-centered organizations that some authors have already identified (Ferlie and Pettigrew, 1996).

Our research has exposed a number of key concerns. First, the nature of organizations and the nature of managerial experiences within organizations are changing. Second, we have exposed a degree of "social incompleteness" in the way that change is being managed and implemented with the interests of one set of stakeholders (the board, the shareholders and the markets) clearly outweighing the interests of managers and other employees. Yet, at the same time that this imbalance is being perpetuated, the volume of managerial rhetoric about "people being our most important asset," which appears in most mission statements is exposing a clear lack of sincerity to the many managers who are being affected by organizational restructuring programs. Third, we have revealed that the pace, scale, and impact of organizational change varies systematically with firm size, industrial sector, type of organization and managers' position in the organizational hierarchy. Specifically, we have revealed that many of the business benefits of organizational change used to justify change are not being met and that the impact of change is triggering a set of adaptive behaviors among managers in which loyalty and commitment are being diverted from the organization to the individual. Finally, we have revealed that the impact of redundancy on organizations is considerable not only for the victims and the survivors but the organizational environment in which the survivors now reside.

Our analysis has also revealed that there is no clear consensus that the hard business benefits on which much change is justified are actually being won, apart from a sharpened sense of accountability. What limited business benefits it would appear have been gained are being won at the cost of dramatic decreases in managers' loyalty, motivation, morale, and sense of job security particularly at middle and junior management levels, in the public sector and the former public utilities and in large organizations. We have also identified a clear view that continuous organizational change, often involves the replacement of experienced but inflexible workers with more flexible contract and temporary staff. Perhaps our main finding is that the view from the top of the organization, and particularly from behind the boardroom door, on the business impact and human impact of change is radically different from that derived from the experiences of those at the base of the managerial hierarchy.

In this chapter, we have attempted to take a "pathological perspective" on organizational change, how it is managed in different organizational settings and how it is perceived to be being managed from different vantage points within the managerial hierarchy. It is our view that our findings give considerable cause for concern about how change is being managed indicating that many senior managers are overly influenced by gimmicks and fads; that they have limited understanding of the broader social impact of their actions; that many are lacking the ability to implement change management initiatives, and, most importantly, that many senior executives are taking too bounded a view of the impact of change. Organizational forms and structures are being redefined; managers are modifying their behavior in the light of the impact of organizational change: notions of organizational life and work are being substantially redefined. We hope that our research has cast some light on these complex and dynamic processes.

REFERENCES

Alvesson, M. and Willmott, H. 1996: *Making sense of management: a critical introduction*. London: Sage Publications.

Brockner, J. 1990: Scope of justice in the workplace: how survivors react to co-worker layoffs. *Journal of Social Issues*, 46 (1), 95–106.

Cameron, K.S. 1994: Investigating organizational downsizing – fundamental issues. *Human Resource Management*, 33 (2), 183–8.

Campbell, F.K., Thornhill, A., and Saunders, M.N.K. 1997: The development of a framework for survivors of downsizing. Paper presented at British Academy of Management Annual Conference, London Business School, London.

Castells, M. 1996: *The Rise of the Network Society:* volume 1. London: Blackwell.

Caulkin, S. 1996: Downsizers in spiral of decline. *The Observer,* June 16, 1996, 10.

Champy, J. 1995: *Reengineering Management.* London: Harper Collins.

Charlesworth, K. 1996: *Are Managers under Stress?* London: Institute of Management.

Cooper, C.L. 1998a: The psychological implications of the changing patterns of work. *Royal Society of Arts Journal,* 1 (4), 74–81.

Cooper, C.L. 1998b: The future of work: a strategy for managing the pressures. *Journal of Applied Management Studies,* 7 (2), 275–81.

Cooper, C.L. and Lewis, S. 1994: *Managing the New Work Force: The Challenge of Dual Income Families.* San Diego: Pfeiffer.

Ebadan, G. and Winstanley, D. 1997: Downsizing, delayering and careers – the survivors perspective. *Human Relations Journal,* 7 (1), 79–91.

Ferlie, E. 1992: The creation and evolution of quasi-markets in the public sector: a problem for strategic management. *Strategic Management Journal,* 13, 79–97.

Ferlie, E., Ashburner, L., Fitzgerald, L., and Pettigrew, A. 1996: *The New Public Management in Action.* Oxford: Oxford University Press.

Ferlie, E. and Pettigrew, A. 1996: Managing through networks: some issues and implications for the NHS. *British Journal of Management,* 7, s81–s89.

Fowler, A. 1993: *Redundancy.* London: Institute of Personnel Management.

Freeman, S.J. and Cameron, K.S. 1993: Organizational downsizing: a convergence and reorientation framework. *Organizational Science,* 4 (1), 10–28.

Gallie, D., White, M., Cheng, Y., and Tomlinson, M. 1998: *Restructuring the Employment Relationship.* Oxford: Clarendon Press.

Greenhalgh, L. and Rosenblatt, Z. 1984: Job insecurity: toward conceptual clarity. *Academy of Management Review,* 9, 438–48.

Greenhalgh, L., Lawrence, A., and Sutton, R. 1988: Determining workforce reduction strategies in declining organizations. *Academy of Management Review,* 13, 241–54.

Hamil, G. and Prahalad, C.K. 1994: *Competing for the Future.* Boston: Harvard Business School Press.

Hammer, M. and Champy, J. 1993: *Reengineering the Corporation: A Manifesto for Business Revolution.* London: Nicholas Brealey.

Handy, L. 1998: *The Ashridge Management Index.* Ashridge: Ashridge Management College.

Hatch, M.J. 1997: *Organization Theory: Modern, Symbolic and Postmodern Perspectives.* Oxford: Oxford University Press.

Institute of Management 1996a: *Survival of the Fittest.* London: Institute of Management.

Institute of Management 1996b: *Are Managers under Stress?* London: Institute of Management.

Institute of Management 1996c: *A Question of Balance.* London: Institute of Management.

Kanter, R.M., Stein, B., and Jick, T.D. 1992: *The Challenge of Organizational Change: How Companies Experience it and Leaders Guide it.* New York: Free Press.

Kets de Vries, M.F.R. and Balazs, K. 1997: The downside of downsizing. *Human Resources,* 50 (1), 11–50.

Kozlowski, S., Chao, G., Smith, E., and Hedlund, J. 1993: Organizational downsizing: strategies, interventions, and research implications. In C.L. Cooper and I.T. Robertson (eds) *International Review of Industrial and Organizational Psychology.* New York: John Wiley and Sons, 263–332.

Lees, D. 1997: The management of strategy. *Journal of Applied Management Studies,* 6 (2), 253–60.

Lewis, P. 1993: *The Successful Management of Redundancy.* Oxford: Blackwell.

Lewis, S. and Smithson, J. 1999: Young workers' perceptions of insecurity and work perceived implications of future management of work and family life. Paper presented at Plant Closures and Downsizing in Europe Conference, Leuven, Belgium.

Liff, S., Worrall, L., and Cooper, C.L. 1997: Attitudes to women in management: an analysis of West Midlands businesses. *Personnel Review,* 26 (3), 152–73.

Moingeon, B. and Edmondson, A. 1996: *Organization Learning and Competitive Advantage*. London: Sage.

Morgan, G. 1997: *Images of Organization*. London: Sage.

Noer, D. 1993: *Healing the Wounds: Overcoming the Trauma of Layoffs and Revitalizing Downsized Organizations*. San Francisco: Jossey Bass Publishers.

Nonaka, I. and Takeuchi, H. 1995: *The Knowledge-Creating Company*. Oxford: Oxford University Press.

Osborne, D. and Gaebler, T. 1993: *Reinventing Government*. New York: Addison-Wesley.

Pendleton, A. 1994: Structural reorganisation and labour management in public enterprise: a study of British Rail. *Journal of Management Studies*, 31, 33–54.

Peters, T.J. and Waterman, R.H. 1982: *In Search of Excellence*. New York: Harper Row.

Reilly, A.H., Brett, J.M., and Stroh, L.K. 1993: The impact of corporate turbulence on employee attitudes. *Strategic Management Journal*, 14, 167–79.

Robinson, S. and Rousseau, D.M. 1994: The psychological contract – not the exception but the norm. *Journal of Organizational Behavior*, 15 (3), 245–59.

RSA 1998: *Redefining Work*. London: Royal Society of Arts.

Shaw, J.B. and Barrett-Power, E. 1997: A conceptual framework for assessing organization, work group and individual effectiveness during and after downsizing. *Human Relations*, 50 (2), 109–27.

Smith, M. and Vickers, T. 1994: What about the survivors? *Training and Development*, 12 (1), 11, 13.

Stroh, L.K., Brett, J.M., and Reilly, A.H. 1994: A decade of change: managers' attachment to their organizations and their jobs. *Human Resource Management*, 33 (4), 531–48.

Thornhill, A. and Gibbons, A. 1995: "Could do better" is verdict of research. *People Management*, 1 (1), 31–5.

Thornhill, A. and Saunders, M.N.K. 1998: The meanings, consequences and implications of downsizing and redundancy: a review. *Personnel Review*, 27 (4), 271–95.

Thornhill, A., Saunders, M., and Stead, J. 1997: Downsizing, delayering – but where's the commitment? Development of a diagnostic tool to help manage survivors. *Personnel Review*, 26 (1/2), 81–98.

Tombaugh, J.R. and White, P.L. 1990: Downsizing: an empirical assessment of survivors' perceptions in a post layoff environment. *Organization Development Journal*, 8 (2), 32–43.

Turnbull, P. and Wass, V. 1997: Job insecurity and labour market lemons: the (mis)management of redundancy in steel making, coal mining and port transport. *Journal of Management Studies*, 34 (1), 27–51.

Vollman, T. and Brazas, M. 1993: Downsizing. *European Management Journal*, 11 (1), 18–29.

Worrall, L. and Cooper, C.L. 1995: Executive stress in different industrial sectors, structures and sizes of business. *Personnel Review*, 24 (7), 3–12.

Worrall, L. and Cooper, C.L. 1997: The quality of working life: the 1997 survey of managers' experiences. Institute of Management Research Report, Institute of Management, London.

Worrall, L. and Cooper, C.L. 1998: The quality of working life: the 1998 survey of managers' experiences. Institute of Management Research Report, Institute of Management, London.

Worrall, L. and Cooper, C.L. forthcoming: Working patterns and their impact on UK managers. *Leadership and Organizational Development* (forthcoming).

Worrall, L., Cooper, C.L., and Campbell, F.K. forthcoming: The impact of organizational change on the work experiences and attitudes of public sector managers. *Personnel Review* (forthcoming).

3 Impact of Privatization in Portugal

Rita Campos e Cunha

INTRODUCTION

Until World War I, either during the constitutional monarchy or the beginning of the Republic, the Portuguese State kept an ideal of non-intervention in the economy. However, the need to maintain vital enterprises which had financial difficulties, the intention to adopt new management practices for potentially profitable public services and the attempt to directly administer fiscal monopolies, led to the creation of a small sector of public enterprises.

After World War II, the public sector was enlarged to include naval transportation (since German ships were attributed as war reparation), social security and agriculture.

In May 1926, a revolution installed a military dictatorship, which adopted a policy of reduction of the state business sector; this policy was maintained by the authoritarian regime that followed. However, with time, the government started having shareholdings in several industrial sectors, like energy, transportation, steel, mass media, port authority, financial services and health care.

This regime was overthrown in 1974, by a military coup, which aimed at putting an end to the war with the African colonies, democratizing the political life and democratizing the economy, namely through the execution of a policy against the large private companies. In 1975, a nationalization program was approved whereby many economic activities were directly or indirectly nationalized, namely the financial, oil, transportation, steel, and energy sectors, the cement, paper pulp, tobacco, and chemical industries, as well as the ship construction, fishing, and mass media sectors.

Furthermore, the 1976 Constitution not only sanctioned the nationalization but also interdicted several sectors from private initiative: banking and insurance, production and distribution of electricity, gas and water for public consumption, basic sanitation, mail, telephone and telegraph, regular air and rail transportation, urban public transportation, operation of ports and airports, arms, oil refining, basic petrochemical, steel, fertilizers and cement.

Only in 1989 did the second Constitutional Revision change the socialist ideological character of the Constitution, to allow the privatizations and reprivatizations.

A large-scale process of privatization was then started, in the early 1990s, by the social-democratic government who had a majority in Parliament. The actual socialist government is continuing this process.

According to the *Financial Times* (1995), "sales of state-owned companies have to date raised a total of more than Es 1.3 trillion (£5.5 bn), representing about 9 percent of gross domestic product. This makes Portugal the third largest privatizing country in the western world after the UK and New Zealand, according to the Organization for Economic Co-operation and Development."

The transference of ownership has occurred in a great diversity of economic sectors, such as banking, insurance, transportation, cement, chemical, oil refining, paper pulp or telecommunications. Given the large number involved, a complete list of privatized companies would be tedious, but some examples may be cited: Banco Mello, Banco Português do Atlântico and Banco Espírito Santo (banking), Tranquilidade and Império (insurance), Rodoviária Nacional (transportation), Secil (cement), Quimigal (chemical), Petrogal (oil refining), Portucel Industrial (paper pulp) and Portugal Telecom (telecommunications).

The main objectives of the Portuguese privatization program were the efficiency enhancement of the national economy and entrepreneurial capacity, the strengthening of the capital market and the reduction of the state's presence in the economy, as well as the reduction of the state's liabilities (GAFEEP, 1995).

The privatization program has had a positive impact on the enhancement of productive and allocative efficiency, mainly because of the introduction of competition and market liberalization, coupled with the restructuring processes of the privatized companies that led to improvements in the internal incentive and monitoring systems. It has also contributed to the development of stronger economic groups, while, at the same time, bringing back to the national economic activity important financial resources and entrepreneurs (that left the country after 1974). There was a dramatic increase in the capitalization of the Lisbon Stock Exchange as well as a reduction of the public debt and state intervention in the economy (GAFEEP, 1995).

The impact of the privatization program in the organizational internal environment of privatized companies has not, however, been researched in a systematic fashion.

This chapter will focus on the less easily quantifiable results of the privatization, that is, the consequences in terms of organizational culture, human resource management practices and the well-being of individual employees, based on a study of four Portuguese companies (Cunha, 1997).

DESCRIPTION OF THE RESEARCH STUDY

This is a study of four industrial companies in the paper pulp, cement, and agricultural sectors, three of which have been privatized. In one company, the researcher was able to obtain one data collection before the privatization and two data collections after partial privatization. In the second company, there were two data collections after partial privatization and in the third one, there were two data collections after total privatization. The fourth one has not been privatized to date, although privatization was announced some years ago, with data collected in three different time periods.

The objective of the study was to evaluate the impact of privatization on organizational culture, human resource management practices and employees' well-being (perceived occupational stress, job satisfaction, mental and physical ill-health). It was hypothesized that privatization would have a major impact on these variables, although with different time horizons. While the period of preparation for privatization and immediately after privatization would affect human resource practices and employees' well-being, because of the companies' restructuring processes, changes in organizational culture were expected to take longer.

For these reasons, a longitudinal research design was justifiable and data were collected in either three or two time periods, so that an impact over time could be assessed.

Perceived occupational stress, locus of control, job satisfaction and mental and physical ill-health were assessed by the respective scales of the Occupational Stress Indicator (Cooper, Sloan, and Williams, 1988).

Organizational culture was assessed by a questionnaire which was developed for this study, with four cultural dimensions: *organizational integration*, reflecting openness of internal communication and co-operation between individuals and organizational units; *performance orientation*, concerning individual accountability for objectives and results as well as merit rewards; *people orientation*, dealing with the extent of concern the organization shows for its members and their development, as well as the individual feeling of belonging to a team; and *market orientation*, reflecting the company responsiveness to market opportunities and benchmarking.

The changes in human resource management practices were assessed by intensive semi-structured interviews with the human resource managers of these four companies.

Although, in theory, this research design was considered to be more adequate, in practice, several problems were encountered, the main one being missing data – subjects responded in one, or even two, of the data collection periods, but did not respond to all of them. Although randomness of missing data was ascertained, the sample size was too small for repeated-measures statistics.

For this reason, cross-sectional analyses were performed for the three companies that went through privatization, based on the first data collection period, with three levels of privatization: public, partially privatized and fully privatized. In the company with data collected both before privatization and after partial privatization, statistical analyses were performed based on independent samples of subjects (and not repeated-measures), in order to validate the results obtained in the cross-sectional analyses.

The company that has not yet been privatized was studied as a separate case and some remarks will also be presented, based on this case.

Some of the results from this study will be presented and discussed in the next sections. A major general finding was that organizational change processes were adopted, starting even before the privatization itself.

ORGANIZATIONAL CHANGE ASSOCIATED WITH PRIVATIZATION

Greater operational efficiency and greater attention to customer satisfaction are some of the objectives of a process of privatization.

Increased market exposure is a way of achieving this objective, by providing incentives for cost reduction, clear demand indicators, goals, performance measures and smaller constraints on incentives (like merit systems); but this also means that the change in the company's external environment, which derives mainly from duction of competition and transference of control to private investors, must panied by a change in the company's internal environment, starting in the preparation for privatization.

Some of these changes include:

1. *organizational goals*, since privatization is expected to create a shift towards profit and shareholder value maximization goals (Haskel and Szymanski, 1994);
2. *strategy*, in order to achieve the new organizational goals and also to promote a fit with the acquiring party's strategy;
3. *organizational structure*, emphasizing the core business, creating profit centers, commercially-focused departments and simplified management structures – in summary, creating more decentralized customer-focused or market-focused organizations;
4. *governance structure and management composition*, appointed by the new ownership – for example, the recruitment of senior management, with private sector experience, as well as marketing and finance executives, was reported in a study about privatization in the UK (United Research, 1990);
5. *human resource policies*, in order to motivate new work behaviors and contribute to attitudinal change. Reductions in the labor force and union influence (Bishop, Kay, and Mayer, 1994; Haskel and Szymanski, 1994), changes in compensation practices, towards an emphasis on performance pay (Bishop and Thompson, 1994; Cunha, 1997; Parker and Hartley, 1991; United Research, 1990), strong investments in training and development programs to achieve commercial and customer orientation (United Research, 1990), recruitment of new and younger employees and performance appraisal (Cunha, 1997) have been some of the reported changes in human resource practices, stemming from the privatization process.

All these changes in the company's internal environment, deriving from changes in the external environment of privatized companies, should fit together and work towards a change in organizational culture, which is needed to support the new strategic goals.

CHANGE IN ORGANIZATIONAL CULTURE

Organizational culture has been defined in the literature in many different ways, with different inherent emphases (Smircich, 1983). In this chapter, I will consider organizational culture as "the set of important assumptions (often unstated) that members of a community share in common" (Sathe, 1985, p. 10), and which include "beliefs" about the world and how it actually works and "values" or ideals worth striving for, with a pervasive influence in organizational life, in terms of seven basic processes that are central to any organization. These processes are "co-operation," or relative importance of individual versus group effort; "decision making," or who holds the power for it; "control," or the ability to take action to achieve planned results; "communication," that is, what goes without saying and how to interpret messages; "commitment," or level of identification and emotional attachment of the individual towards the organization; "perception," in the sense of shared interpretations of organizational members' experience; and "justification of behavior," which allows people to make sense of their actions.

This concept has the virtue of integrating the more intangible aspects of culture – beliefs and values – with the more visible facets of managerial practices – cooperation, decision making, control, etc. – making it possible to assess and manage corporate culture, in order to support strategy, which is especially useful in periods of deep change, such as the one generated by privatization.

On the other hand, the public attention that was given to the topic by a wave of books, such as Ouchi's *Theory Z* (1981) and Peters' and Waterman's *In Search of Excellence* (1982), raised the need for establishing the association between organizational culture and organizational effectiveness and financial performance. In fact, evidence from research articles demonstrates this association. Denison (1984) demonstrated the impact of culture on the financial performance of 34 companies, using two measures of culture – organization of work and decision making practices. These two facets had a significant positive impact on both return on investment and return on sales, which increased over a five-year period of time. In a study that investigated 904 college graduates hired in six public accounting firms over a six-year period Sheridan (1992) reported that individual perceptions of culture significantly influence personnel retention rates. The importance of culture has also been shown by the "negative", such as in the analysis of merger and acquisitions failures, because of cultural incompatibility (Cartwright and Cooper, 1993). Sheridan (1997) and Garmager and Shemmer (1998) provide examples of "best" organizations, where profitability is associated with the commitment to positive corporate cultures. These are some examples of empirical studies and articles reporting the impact of organizational culture on the company's bottom line. They stress that not only can culture either reinforce, or on the contrary, hinder the process of strategic change in organizations, but also that designing a high-performance culture can be an objective *per se*.

In Portugal, our study of companies in different stages of their privatization processes (Cunha, 1997; Cunha and Cooper, 1998) has revealed that privatization does lead to changes in the corporate culture. Both the cross-sectional and longitudinal companywise analyses pointed to the development of a more people-oriented culture in privatized companies.

As companies move from the public to the partially private and from the partially private to the fully private status, both performance orientation and people orientation get significantly higher. Organizational integration presented a significant increase from the public to the partially private status, but no significant differences were found in market orientation across stages of privatization.

These results demonstrate that corporate culture is affected by privatization. Privatized companies tend to present a more people-oriented culture, with stronger emphasis on internal co-ordination and communication, a higher concern for their human resources and the development of their competencies, as well as a commitment to the definition of individual objectives, making organizational members responsible for their achievement and rewarded accordingly.

On the other hand, the fact that market orientation did not present any significant differences across stages of privatization may be interpreted as a result of the change in organizational objectives and strategies that occur prior to the privatization, in order to start adapting the public companies to the new external environments, with a much larger market exposure, and thus, enhancing the market value of these companies for potential investors. Increased market responsiveness was, as pointed out above, to start well before privatization.

Besides these general changes, which are related to the creation of a commercial orientation and to the recognition of the impact of organizational members as sources of competitive advantage for the company, the more specific aspects of organizational culture, such as specific values, norms, rituals, folklore, etc., will depend on the idiosyncrasies of the particular privatization process. The acquisition of the whole privatized company by a sole owner or group is expected to lead to a different kind of acculturation than a privatization by flotation in the stock market with wide share dispersion. In the latter case, governance structures are less tied to a specific person or group. Culture change may thus be less dramatic than in the first case.

The question for companies lies in the processes that have to be implemented in order to achieve this cultural change. In the first place, it is important to recognize that changing organizational culture cannot be done quickly and painlessly, since beliefs, values and long-term behavioral patterns are at stake. There is a very strong probability that the recently privatized company has a culture shaped by frequently rotated leadership (who therefore did not have much time to establish and strengthen organizational values and norms), by conflicting objectives, since effectiveness and financial results may be surpassed by political and public good goals, by lack of individual accountability and emphasis on the production orientation instead of customer orientation, in summary the "no-owner company" syndrome.

The change of individual behaviors and attitudes has to be motivated through the use of both extrinsic and intrinsic sources. Extrinsic motivation, particularly the introduction of rewards and punishment, both tangible and symbolic, will induce compliance to new behaviors. Intrinsic motivation will result from the internalization of the need to change and from the feelings of satisfaction and personal growth that individual members of the organization may get from their jobs. Long-term change depends on the internalization of the new desired behaviors. Intrinsic motivation is, therefore, extremely important. However, since behaviors will affect beliefs and values, especially successful behaviors, the extrinsic inducement of new behaviors, coupled with the necessary support and opportunities to be successful, is also extremely important.

We may conclude, therefore, that the human resource management policies have a paramount role in the implementation of a strategic and cultural change. This will be the subject of the next section.

HUMAN RESOURCE MANAGEMENT POLICIES

Since Bem's self-perception theory (1967), which holds that people form attitudes on the basis of inferences drawn from observation of behavior (including their own), it is expected that new behaviors will originate new attitudes. Therefore, whenever human resource practices demonstrate the worth of new behaviors and help create the competencies for these new behaviors, it is directly and powerfully contributing to the attitudinal change that is necessary to achieve the organizational culture's change.

In Portugal, the human resource policies in companies that were privatized or were preparing for being privatized experienced substantial changes. Interviews with CEOs and human resource managers of privatized and to-be privatized companies demonstrated some common trends (Cunha, 1992, 1997). These changes covered the following areas.

1. *Mission, strategy and business policy*: written mission statements and strategic definitions were developed, sometimes with the help of external consultants, to replace the old ones. Personnel managers were usually involved in this process. Human resource strategies and annual/pluriannual plans were typically defined, as well as criteria to monitor the personnel function, such as number of workers, ratio of workers to production, personnel costs versus total production costs, productivity and absenteeism.

2. *Reduction of headcount, recruitment and selection*: the reduction of headcount has been reported as one of the major challenges in the preparation for the privatization. These reductions have basically been done by early retirement and negotiated terminations, coupled with a recruitment freeze and natural decruitment. Recruitment has only been made in terms of young high school and college graduates for manual and technical positions. In order to attract these young candidates, companies used several methods, such as an increase in compensation levels and enhancement of the company image. At the same time, investments in training actual employees have been made, in order to better align strategic plans and human skills. Some flexible work procedures have also increased, like flextime, outsourcing of maintenance and support services and part-time contracts. Job enlargement and job enrichment have been adopted for almost all job categories with an emphasis on functional flexibility, whereby employees are encouraged to perform tasks upstream and downstream. This philosophy has created some resistance and a negative reaction from the trade unions, but has nevertheless been maintained and even formalized in job descriptions.

3. *Training and development*: large investments in training and development activities accompany the process of privatization, covering the total set of employees. Functional flexibility (multiple skills), service to client, change management and quality are the areas that received the greater attention. Some kind of training evaluation started to be used, either in terms of the programs' structure and implementation, or in terms of job performance.

4. *Performance appraisal*: which usually was installed before privatization, although often lacking credibility and consistent usage, as well as strong commitment from top management. Performance appraisal systems have started being used as input for the introduction of merit pay systems, as well as for feedback and development purposes.

5. *Compensation practices*: refinements in the performance pay systems have been reported as well as an increase in the variable pay component. Merit rewards are usually in the form of individual bonuses, especially for managers and technical professional staff. Profit sharing is quite common, extending to all job categories. These incentive programs are usually linked to several criteria, which include company and organizational unit results (production and profit margins), individual performance and absenteeism.

6. *Labor relations and communication*: traditionally, public companies have had a very large proportion of unionized personnel. Although trade unions are still recognized for collective bargaining issues, it was felt that their influence has decreased.

Direct communication with employees increased dramatically, before and after privatization, with the use of several different media, from company bulletins and magazines to team briefings, from informal sessions with cross-sectional groups of employees to meetings with all members of a business unit. In one financial institution, for example, the day after privatization, all employees had a personalized letter with the strategic objectives and main action plans of the new owners, while, in another, a monthly luncheon in the outskirts, with a group of employees from different areas and categories, became a ritual. An increase in upwards communication was equally said to exist, both in informal ways, like meetings with superiors and informal gatherings, but also in formal ways, such as suggestion boxes and regularly scheduled meetings.

All of these changes and trends stress the pivotal role that human resource management practices have in the process of strategic and cultural change. A very significant sign of the growing importance of this function has been the appointment, in some companies, of new managers for the personnel/human resources departments, accompanied by a relative decentralization of many personnel decisions, such as recruitment, appraisal, development and merit rewards, to the line managers. This awareness is even reflected in the exponential increase in the demand for management development programs in interpersonal skills and human resource management.

Above all, these changes must be congruent with each other, so that employees have the whole picture, and not conflicting messages, coming from different sources. The sole announcement of privatization will create the anticipation of change and these expectations must be realistic. On the other hand, the processes implemented should correspond to these expectations, in a reasonably short period of time. The cognitive dissonance resulting from frustration or procrastination of expectations will be debated in a later section.

A consideration of the amount of change involved in the privatization leads us to the next section, which deals with the impact of this process on the individual employees, whose behaviors are expected to be different. It is reasonable to expect an increase in uncertainty, which is common to all major change processes, with several different individual consequences for mental and physical well-being and job satisfaction.

IMPACT OF PRIVATIZATION ON INDIVIDUAL EMPLOYEES

Privatization and preparation for privatization are associated with the restructuring of the company and, therefore, with heightened perceptions of uncertainty, with which individual employees will have to cope (Nelson, Cooper, and Jackson, 1995).

As such, one may expect that individual feelings of pressure will increase in the short term, while the restructuring is being designed and starts to be implemented. These feelings of pressure or occupational stress are qualitatively negative and personal, since the same situations may originate different perceptions by different people, as well as different coping strategies, which may be more or less effective in the removal of the source of pressure.

In companies undergoing privatization processes, several organizational conditions are present, deriving from the restructuring, which have been empirically demonstrated to be associated with perceptions of occupational stress. These conditions include *role ambiguity, role overload* or *role underload* (Beehr, 1981; Kelloway and Barling, 1991;

Kemery et al., 1985; Schuler, 1980) which may occur while alternative organizational objectives and task allocation are being considered and while new power structures are gaining weight; *new work relationships* (Cooper, Sloan, and Williams, 1988), that derive from new structural arrangements and job allocation; *job insecurity* (Roskies and Louis-Guerin, 1990; Roskies, Louis-Guerin, and Fournier, 1993; Sullivan, 1998; Williamson and Vine, 1998), since privatization has long been associated with job cuts, as well as the frustration of career expectations and deterioration of working conditions; *centralization and different decision making policies* (Cooper and Marshall, 1976; Parker and DeCotiis, 1983), which may be expected to happen, with the infusion of new leadership and governance bodies; *conflict of personal beliefs and company policies* (Marshall and Cooper, 1979), deriving from the cultural change that is aimed at.

Responses to the perceptions of occupational stress may be moderated by individual characteristics, such as "locus of control," but in general, they include symptoms of physical ill-health (from headaches to cardiovascular symptoms), symptoms of mental ill-health (from anxiety to depression and helplessness) and low job satisfaction (Schuler, 1980; Kahn and Byosiere, 1992).

In the previously cited study with Portuguese companies in different stages of privatization (Cunha, 1997; Cunha and Cooper, 1998), an increase in the perceptions of job stress was hypothesized, with the consequent negative results, in the short term, that is, while privatization was still being prepared or immediately after being carried out, and a decrease of these perceptions and consequent results, after privatization and company restructuring were implemented for a significant period of time.

The results from the cross-sectional and the longitudinal companywise analyses showed that perceptions of occupational stress increased for the companies going through privatization or preparing for it. As the process of privatization became consolidated, these perceptions decreased significantly. In fact, privatization may be considered to be a critical event in a company's life.

In what concerns individual differences, locus of control was found to significantly and negatively correlate with perceptions of stress, that is, individuals with internal locus of control reported lower levels of stress. Since locus of control refers to a generalized expectancy that we have some control over things that happen to us, we may derive some practical implications for the management of this kind of change processes, in terms of individual involvement in decision making, which will be explored in a later section.

Results obtained for the stress response variables pointed to the expected increase of job satisfaction, as companies moved from the public to the privatized status. However, the other two variables – physical and mental ill-health – did not behave as expected. In fact, the reverse was found. Mental and physical ill-health symptoms tended to increase in individual employees, as companies moved from the public to the private status. This apparently puzzling result may be explained, if we hypothesize that, while job satisfaction (or dissatisfaction) is immediately derived from the job performance and working conditions, mental and physical ill-health symptoms take longer to appear. These consequences are deferred on time. On the other hand, we can also argue that job demands are much greater in the private companies, presenting greater challenges and, therefore, with a larger potential for feelings of self-actualization and job satisfaction. The cost however, is physical and emotional exhaustion. This is a topic that deserves further investigation.

From this section, we may conclude that the process of privatization has a strong impact on the employees and their well-being.

As a side effect, the privatization will also be accompanied, especially in the early phases (announcement, preparation and immediately after privatization) by an inflation of rumors, the so-called "corridor radio!" These rumors are a response to the uncertainty and work as an escape, whereby people look for some social support from colleagues and start making "coalitions" in order to defend themselves from eventual threats that are anticipated.

Since these rumors are seldom based on realistic information, but rather on fear of losing acquired benefits (both tangible and intangible), they work as an anchor for individuals but have dysfunctional effects for the company, by increasing the ambiguities and the resistance to changes planned by top management.

It is top management's responsibility to deal with these expectations in the very early stages of the process.

THE MANAGEMENT OF EXPECTATIONS

The power of individual expectations is a well-known and accepted phenomenon in the psychological and economic literature. Behavior is determined by the expectations people have regarding the probability of achieving a certain level of performance and also on the probability that rewards will derive from this performance.

Starting with the announcement of privatization, these probabilities will be questioned, because of the ambiguity or uncertainty about the future and about the role that individual members will have to play in the company. Some individuals may anticipate the termination of a work relationship with the company, while others may anticipate functional changes that require different skills they do not feel able to acquire, while still others may aspire to job changes that are long desired.

Whatever the kind of expectations individual employees will develop, the fact is that they will develop them. They may or may not be realistic, and they may or may not be positive regarding the company and the willingness to be committed to the process.

For this reason, top management should take extra care in making sure that expectations correspond to the future (as they anticipate it!) and that the planned changes are implemented in a way that is consistent with the vision and strategic lines defined for the company. Their main purpose will be to help create expectations that motivate the intended work behaviors, making these desired work behaviors very clear and creating the conditions for these behaviors to develop, as well as identifying as early as possible who will not be able to adapt to the new business conditions.

Communication is necessary, but not sufficient in the management of change. Action is also necessary. Change processes are implemented because they are needed, so that the company may get out of a crisis situation or adapt to a new business context or grow.

As soon as the company mission and strategy are defined, implementation should start, that is, restructuring, allocation of new work roles, goal-setting for organizational units and individuals, training and development programs, contingent incentives, etc. It is extremely important that managers start behaving differently, so that conflicting messages are not sent and role models are presented.

Indefinitely delaying the implementation is dysfunctional, since the individual expectations do not materialize and employees develop a state of cognitive dissonance, which, over time, transforms into cynicism regarding any change at all. The same kind of reaction may be expected when the change process, by itself, is subject to frequent changes, that is, what has been changed in the recent past is not right in the present and has to be changed in the near future, towards a different direction.

An example from one Portuguese company may illustrate this point (Cunha, 1997). Privatization was announced and some action was started in terms of headcount reduction. However, privatization was never substantiated till now. The frustration of the internal change expectations, coupled with job insecurity, negatively affected employees, both in terms of job satisfaction and mental ill-health. The sense of ambiguity was reflected in remarks, made by individual employees, that the company was still looking for definition, that they were just expecting the salary at the end of the month, that there were no objectives to work for, and so on. It seems that there is a negative halo, which has been named the "wedge effect," that inhibits all future change plans to have any credibility and to have any success potential, like a wedge that blocks the opening of a door. This chronic uncertainty leads to the absence of expectation. As a consequence, people behave in a way where only individual interest is considered and all organizational objectives are discarded. This, of course, is a slow process that stems from continuous indeterminacy.

The objective of this section was to emphasize that individual expectations will naturally derive from the announcement of privatization (or any change process), and that these expectations must be considered and managed by change agents and top management, as well as by political officers.

The last section will try to point out some implications for practice stemming from the considerations and research findings reported above.

IMPLICATIONS FOR PRACTICE

The aim of this chapter was to provide some insights into the management of privatization processes, based on what privatization has meant for the human factor of the Portuguese organizations.

Privatization is associated with a deep change in the external economic and business environments, within which companies have to operate and adapt to. This change will inevitably lead to a change in the companies' internal environments, in order to become more efficient and more effective.

Changing the internal environment means, for instance, changing organizational objectives, strategies, structures, management composition, workforce, human resource practices and ultimately, organizational culture. This internal change may be more or less radical, according to the degree of market exposure that previously existed, the type of privatization process (acquisition or flotation with shareholder dispersion) and company leadership. Yet, an impact on individual employees will always be present. In the short term, the uncertainty associated with the change of status and restructuring will lead to increased individual perceptions of stress and lower job satisfaction. In the long run, however, as the organizational objectives and strategy, as well as the new rules of the game become clearer, occupational stress is expected to decrease and job satisfaction to increase, although symptoms of mental and physical ill-health may appear as a result of the early strain.

The indefinite postponing of privatization (after its announcement), or delaying the implementation of internal change action, is the worst possible outcome, since it will generate frustrated expectations and lead to the wedge effect, which will later on endanger the future potential change plans.

Some implications may be derived, the first one being the need for a careful planning of any process of profound change, the need for not stalling decisions which involve the well-being of many individuals and the need to draw an action plan and stick to it.

The second implication concerns the complexity of the process and the combination of interconnected activities, which present difficult challenges both for the public managers who have to prepare the company for the status change and for the private managers who have to continue the change program in a systematic and coherent fashion.

The main challenge for top management in the pre-privatization phase is to start the change process in terms of corporate culture. Public companies usually have a "weaker" culture, for several reasons, such as high rotation of top management, existence of objectives that do not always coincide with the company's profitability and market value maximization, lack of personal accountability for results and lack of commercial orientation. It is therefore extremely important that this period be focused on starting the cultural change.

Thirdly, the role of the human resource management practices is essential in the success of the change efforts and cannot be circumscribed to the personnel departments, but rather decentralized to line managers. These procedures include recruitment and selection, appraisal, training and development, compensation and communication.

Recruitment is a particularly sensitive issue, since this period is associated with headcount reduction. On the other hand, candidates for the particular jobs should have not only the required technical skills, but also the personal characteristics that help them be accepted by older employees. Placement should equally promote the integration of these individuals with the organizationally "more experienced" ones.

Credible and consistent performance appraisal systems have to be created and correctly implemented. Large investments in training and development programs have to be made, covering either specific needs or more general ones, such as functional flexibility. Compensation systems are certainly a powerful tool to motivate behavioral change, that may be internalized over time.

Communication with employees aims at conveying the new strategic objectives and the tactical programs to achieve them, the new desired behaviors and values, but also what employees may expect to gain and their opportunity costs. Opening and adapting communication channels to the different messages is essential.

The interconnected implementation of different human resource practices and the periodic monitoring of the progress achieved are a fourth implication. Change is slow and cannot be determined by internal memoranda; therefore results and feedback are necessary to reinforce the change process.

A fifth implication concerns employee involvement in the process. When employees feel some control over events that affect them, acceptance and commitment are greater. "Locus of control," as an individual characteristic, has been demonstrated to moderate the perceptions of stress; effective personal control should, therefore, be an essential ingredient in job redesign, through job enrichment and empowerment.

A final implication for the management of privatization processes concerns maintaining the momentum and knowing when new actions should occur, so that the wedge effect does not install in the company, acting as a vaccine against change. While considering that there may exist unforeseen problems that may slow down the process, governments should make a time schedule for privatizations and be concerned with keeping it.

As important as it is for companies to be efficient, they can only be so if their members contribute with their work behaviors and motivations. Organizations must satisfy the needs for achievement and psychological growth of their staff, needs which make up the essence of human beings and which determine the role of people as a source of sustainable competitive advantage, that is, being valuable, rare, hardly imitable and irreplaceable.

ACKNOWLEDGMENT

The author gratefully acknowledges the financial support of Junta Nacional de Investigação Científica e Tecnológica, JNICT, Portugal.

REFERENCES

Beehr, T. 1981: Work-role stress and attitudes toward co-workers. *Group and Organization Studies*, 6 (2), 201–10.

Bem, D.J. 1967: Self-perception: an alternative interpretation of cognitive dissonance phenomena. *Psychological Review*, 74, 183–200.

Bishop, M., Kay, J., and Mayer, C. 1994: Introduction: privatization in performance. In M. Bishop, J. Kay, and C. Mayer (eds) *Privatization and Economic Performance*. Oxford: Oxford University Press.

Bishop, M. and Thompson, D. 1994: Privatization in the UK: internal organization and productive efficiency. In M. Bishop, J. Kay, and C. Mayer (eds) *Privatization and Economic Performance*. Oxford: Oxford University Press.

Cartwright, S. and Cooper, C.L. 1993: The role of culture compatibility in successful organizational marriage. *Academy of Management Executive*, 7 (2), 57–70.

Cooper, C.L. and Marshall, J. 1976: Occupational sources of stress: a review of the literature relating to coronary heart disease and mental health. *Journal of Occupational Psychology*, 49, 11–28.

Cooper, C.L., Sloan, S.J., and Williams, S. 1988: *Occupational Stress Indicator Management Guide*. Windsor: NFER-NELSON Publishing Company Limited.

Cunha, R.C. 1992: Privatização: Uma Revolução Cultural. Conference paper presented at the Graduate School of Business, Universidade Nova de Lisboa, March 23, Lisbon, Portugal.

Cunha, R.C. 1997: *The Impact of Privatization on Organizational Culture, Human Resource Management and Individual Employees*. PhD dissertation, School of Management, University of Manchester Institute of Science and Technology, Manchester, UK.

Cunha, R.C. and Cooper, C.L. 1998: The impact of privatization on corporate culture and employee well-being. Manuscript submitted for review.

Denison, D.R. 1984: Bringing corporate culture to the bottom line, *Organizational Dynamics*, 12, 4–22.

Financial Times 1995: Privatisation programme: the rapid pace continues. Financial Times Survey: Portugal, November 8, 1–6.

GAFEEP 1995: *Privatizações em Portugal, Uma Reforma Estrutural*, Ministério das Finanças.

Garmager, T. and Shemmer, L. 1998: Rich in culture, rich in profits. *HR Focus*, October, 1–7.

Haskel, J. and Szymanski, S. 1994: Privatization and labor market: facts, theory and evidence. In M. Bishop, J. Kay, and C. Mayer (eds) *Privatization and Economic Performance*. Oxford: Oxford University Press.

Kahn, R.L. and Byosiere, P. 1992: Stress in organizations. In M.D. Dunnette and L.M. Hough (eds) *Handbook of Industrial and Organizational Psychology* (2nd edn.) Palo Alto, Ca: Consulting Psychologists Press, vol. 3, 571–650.

Kelloway, E.K. and Barling, J. 1991: Job characteristics, role stress and mental health. *Journal of Occupational Psychology*, 64, 291–304.

Kemery, E.R., Bedeian, A.G., Mossholder, K.W., and Touliatos, J. 1985: Outcomes of role stress: a multisample constructive replication. *Academy of Management Journal*, 28 (2), 363–75.

Marshall, J. and Cooper, C.L. 1979: Work experiences of middle and senior managers: the pressure and satisfaction. *International Management Review*, 19, 81–96.

Nelson, A., Cooper, C.L., and Jackson, P.R. 1995: Uncertainty amidst change: the impact of privatization on employee job satisfaction and well-being. *Journal of Occupational and Organizational Psychology*, 68, 57–71.

Ouchi, W.G. 1981: *Theory Z: How American business can meet the Japanese challenge*. Reading, MA: Addison-Wesley.

Parker, D. and Hartley, K. 1991: Do changes in organizational status affect financial performance? *Strategic Management Journal*, 12, 631–41.

Parker, D.F. and DeCotiis, T.H. 1983: Organizational determinants of job stress. *Organizational Behavior and Human Performance*, 32, 160–77.

Peters, T.J. and Waterman, R.H. 1982: *In Search of Excellence*. New York: Harper Row.

Roskies, E. and Louis-Guerin, C. 1990: Job insecurity in managers: antecedents and consequences. *Journal of Organizational Behavior*, 11, 345–59.

Roskies, E., Louis-Guerin, C., and Fournier, C. 1993: Coping with job insecurity: how does personality make a difference? *Journal of Organizational Behavior*, 14, 617–30.

Sathe, V. 1985: *Culture and Related Corporate Realities*. Homewood, IL: Richard D. Irwin.

Schuler, R. 1980: Definition and conceptualization of stress in organizations. *Organizational Behavior and Human Performance*, 25, 184–215.

Sheridan, J.E. 1992: Organizational culture and employee retention. *Academy of Management Journal*, 35 (5), 1036–56.

Sheridan, J. 1997: Culture-change lessons. *Industry Week*, February 17, 20–34.

Smircich, L. 1983: Concepts of culture and organizational analysis. *Administrative Science Quarterly*, 28 (3), 339–58.

Sullivan, T. 1998: Taking it to heart. *OH & S Canada*, 14 (6), 24–5.

United Research 1990: *Privatization: Implications for Cultural Change*. Morristown, NJ: United Research.

Williamson, J. and Vine, P. 1998: Run-down, stressed out. *The British Journal of Administrative Management*, January/February, 14–16.

4 Comparing the Downsizing Experiences of Three Countries: A Restructuring Cycle?

Craig R. Littler

INTRODUCTION

For many economies the 1990s have been a decade of downsizing. At the end of the 1970s organizational design and organizational culture theorists looked to the Japanese model for inspiration. Job security, long-term employment relationships, mutual dependency organizations were widely seen as the way forward (Dore, 1973, 1992). Reacting to Japanese competition, many US corporations created organizational cultures based on the opposite – flexibility, insecurity and temporary work contracts (Noer, 1993). These strategies of organizational change have become diffused across other economies as a major route to competitive success.

Given this process of diffusion of managerial strategies, I wanted to compare outcomes across similar economies. I chose three comparable countries – Australia, New Zealand, and South Africa – and conducted identical surveys in all three. In 1998 the Australian survey was repeated in order to enhance the longitudinal picture. This gave a database of 2,295 organizations across both the public and private sectors, manufacturing and services. This comparative survey data provides the major source for this chapter. In addition, I have built up a database of all private sector firms in Australia over the 1990s and conducted case studies in individual firms. The latter set of sources informs some of the conclusions of this chapter.

This chapter reviews the restructuring and downsizing experiences of three countries. It maps the degree to which downsizing and delayering have taken place. It then examines some of the consequences of downsizing especially in relation to the notion of survivor syndrome. The concept of a restructuring cycle is discussed as a means of understanding the differences between the three countries. Have these economies achieved a successful transition to new organizational forms and new job structures?

DEFINING ORGANIZATIONAL DOWNSIZING

The notion of corporate restructuring has been used in various ways in the literature and usually refers to one or more ways of re-configuring the firm. Bowman and Singh

(1993) distinguish between financial restructuring, asset or portfolio restructuring and organizational restructuring. This chapter is concerned with employment contraction, whatever form of corporate restructuring is the starting point.

There is no theoretically agreed way to define "downsizing". Downsizing is not equivalent to any and every form of workforce reduction. In general, researchers use the term to mean a deliberate organizational decision to reduce the workforce that is intended to improve organizational performance. It can be reactive or proactive. Some researchers have placed no minimum levels on the workforce reduction (for example Mentzer, 1996). The problem with such lack of specification is that a firm faced with sustained skill shortages may register as "downsized." Other researchers have specified numerical boundaries. For example, Cascio (1998, p. 59) "arbitrarily chose 3 % as the minimum level to be considered as significant downsizing." In our research "downsizing" was based on self-reporting by human resource and senior managers.

Most studies of downsizing have looked at it as a one-off event, downsizing versus no downsizing. Some studies have examined the extent, or depth, of downsizing; for example, Cascio (1998, p. 68) distinguishes between "high" and "low" downsizing companies. We also used depth as one measure of downsizing. In addition, we were concerned to examine the *frequency* of downsizing on the basis that it may affect the human resource outcomes, especially survivor syndrome.

We also examined the issue of delayering or flattening of the organizational hierarchy. Downsizing can occur without delayering (no surprise maybe) and delayering can occur without downsizing. The latter often causes surprise, because many think of "delayering" as managerial downsizing (for example Gordon, 1996). *Conceptually, delayering is an independent process.* Empirically, delayering may not result in downsizing because of managerial demotions, or re-location of managers laterally, possibly in new departments, without loss of status. Once we identify delayering as an independent factor, then we can conceptually raise the issue of the effects of delayering on downsizing processes.

DOWNSIZING TRENDS

What are the restructuring trends in the three focal countries of Australia, New Zealand, and South Africa? National statistical data provide us with some aggregate data on unemployment and lay-offs, but clear figures on organizational downsizing were not available for the workforce of these three countries. One of our major objectives was to remedy this gap and to provide an empirical picture of the extent of downsizing and delayering across firms, sectors and industries in Australia, New Zealand, and South Africa.

Given this objective, we conducted a series of surveys in all three target countries. The details of the various studies are set out in the Appendix. However, table 4.1 summarizes the basic information on sample frames, response rates, dates of the surveys and nature of the respondents.

Table 4.2 provides a picture of downsizing in Australia, New Zealand, and South Africa. The data in table 4.2 show that 57 percent of Australian organizations downsized between 1993–5. Just over 60 percent of South African firms indicated that they were involved in downsizing during 1994–6. There is a moderate difference compared

Table 4.1 Methodology of surveys

	Sample frame	Sample size	Response rate	Dates	Respondents
Australia	Australian Human Resources Institute (AHRI)	Census 1,722 orgs.	653 39.9% after sample loss	March/April 1995	1995: CEO/ Senior manager = 74% Middle manager = 26%
	AHRI and IBIS	Census 4,500 orgs.	1,222 orgs. 30% after sample loss	Repeated November 1998	1998: CEO/ Senior manager = 79% Middle manager = 17% Other = 4%
New Zealand	Institute of Personnel Management	Census 1,370 orgs.	668 48.8%	October 1995	CEO/Senior manager = 83% Middle manager = 17%
South Africa	South African Board for Personnel Practice	Random sample 1,200 orgs.	421 35.08%	May 1996	CEO/Senior manager = 70% Middle manager = 30%

Table 4.2 Downsizing trends in three countries, 1995–6; $N = 1,703$ organizations

	New Zealand %	Australia %	South Africa %
Downsized	48	57	60
Depth of downsizers			
1–10%	65.4	58	59.8
11–20%	19.8	24.9	24.5
21–30%	6.4	9.9	7.4
More than 30%	8.4	7.2	8.3
Frequency of downsizers			
Once	37	29.4	43.7
Twice	28.9	26.3	17
Three or more times	34.1	44.3	40.2

with New Zealand – 48 percent of New Zealand organizations have downsized during a similar period. However, across all three countries there is no statistically significant difference in relation to depth of workforce reductions (see table 4.2). Why has New Zealand apparently cut less? The major reason is that New Zealand has restructured for a longer period: the New Zealand economy has emerged from more than 12 years of restructuring having started in 1983/4.

Depth of downsizing is one dimension of change, but what about frequency of downsizing? Our case study data in Australian and New Zealand firms has indicated that frequency of downsizing might be a key factor in generating negative employee reactions. Over 44 percent of downsizing organizations in Australia have downsized three or more times over the two-year period 1993–5 and 71 percent twice or more. The South African data indicated that 40 percent of organizations had downsized three or more times over the two-year period 1994–6 and 57 percent twice or more. The New Zealand data show that 34 percent of organizations had downsized three or more times and 63 percent twice or more. This is significantly less than Australia, but still substantial. In general, downsizing tends to be followed by more downsizing (Burke and Nelson, 1998, p. 27).

Frequency of downsizing, as opposed to its extent, has been less in South Africa. This is because the restructuring cycle is still relatively new. The major events started in 1994 with President Mandela's accession. Many more South African firms are in the earlier stages of restructuring. However, in 1996 there was no sign of the process letting up – 44 percent of South African managers expected the restructuring cycle to continue over the next few years.

Many Australian managers also expect downsizing to continue. In 1995 43 percent of managers expected full-time employees to be cut in the foreseeable future. They were right. The 1998 Australian survey data shows that 62 percent of organizations had downsized in the past two years. For New Zealand, the downsizing cycle seems to be slowing down significantly and our studies in firms supports this interpretation. The Australian and South African economies are still in the midst of a downsizing cycle.

WHAT IS THE EXTENT OF DELAYERING?

Central to the new models of organization in the 1990s is a flatter structure, achieved by a reduction in the number of layers in the management hierarchy. Such organizational change has been advocated in order to push responsibility to the lowest organizational level ("empowerment"), to promote decision-making speed, to build shorter communication paths, and to cut bureaucracy (Kettley, 1995; Keuning and Opheij, 1994; Wissema, 1994). However, achieving such an organizational structure is not always a simple task. Prescriptions are one thing, but there is no agreement on the impact of restructuring on managers. On the one hand there is a delayering hypothesis to the effect that downsizing usually involves managerial cutting or delayering. In contrast, Levinson (1990) and Gordon (1996) have emphasized the problem of reconciling aggregate US data on the *growth* in managerial jobs with some accounts of middle manager decline. As Gordon puts it, there is a "myth of managerial downsizing." Given this debate, we were uncertain about the extent of delayering.

Our survey results indicated much more extensive delayering than we anticipated (see table 4.3): 42 percent of organizations across the entire three-country sample had delayered in the preceding two years. This consisted of 44 percent of organizations in Australia and 45.5 percent of South African organizations. The figures were slightly lower for New Zealand. For all three countries, middle managers were predominantly the target of these cuts. However, in the past ten years 50 percent of New Zealand organizations had delayered. Clearly, delayering has become a common managerial strategy and this is reflected across the three countries.

Table 4.3 Delayering trends, 1995–6; N = 1,703 organizations

	New Zealand %	Australia %	South Africa %
Percentage of delayered organizations	37.5	44	45.5
Percentage of delayerers reduced by:			
1 level	67.9	66.4	50.3
2 levels	26.0	28.2	34.9
3 or more	6.0	5.4	14.9

Another measure of delayering is the depth of delayering – stripping out one, two or three levels. In this respect, there were no statistically significant differences between Australia and New Zealand, but in South Africa there was a surprising depth of delayering (see table 4.3). Once we control for size differences between the samples, this difference vanishes. Therefore, we see a common pattern of restructuring across the three economies. By 1998 we found the same proportion of Australian organizations delayering (44 percent), but there was a significant reduction in the *depth* of delayering – perhaps not surprising; after all, firms run out of layers to cut, unless there is a cycle of delayering and relayering.

In relation to the argument that delayering is conceptually independent, then we can quantify this point. We found that in the Australian 1995 sample 10.7 percent of firms reported that they had delayered but *not* downsized. The figures are similar for the 1998 Australian sample.

Is delayering a one-way street? Or is there any evidence of a delayering–relayering cycle? Such a cycle may arise for several reasons. Unlike the scientific management movement, the current restructuring and organizational re-design movement lacks a clear set of measures. In attempting to find the appropriate organizational structure and size, senior managers, lacking clear guidelines, may over-react in a cyclical manner. In Australia we found that 10 percent of delayered firms had subsequently relayered. The figures for South Africa and New Zealand were similar – 11.6 percent and 11.4 percent respectively. The New Zealand figure represents a longer period of change and, therefore, a greater test of any relayering thesis. We can stretch the assessment forward in time by looking at the 1998 Australian survey: it shows that three years after the first survey and with longer experience of the delayered firm, only 11.9 percent of organizations are reporting relayering. These are not negligible figures, and one qualification should be noted. Managers might not always call relayering by such a name. Thus, Holbeche (1997) found that some firms in Britain were relayering, but not openly. She cites one example of a firm re-introducing new layers of senior management without explicit acknowledgement. Nevertheless, *at present, this does not appear to be a significant delayering–relayering cycle – for most firms delayering is a one-way street.*

The survey data indicate extensive downsizing and delayering across all three countries. Given this depth of organizational change, what have been the effects on firms?

Much of the research on post-downsizing consequences has been organized around the notion of "survivor syndrome" or "survivor sickness" (Noer, 1998). The focus of such work is on the organizational "survivors," in relation to the critical issues of managing the processes of the shrunken organization. This is because the performance outcomes depend on the people who remain, not the employees who exit.

COMPARATIVE EFFECTS

Measuring survivor syndrome

There are various definitions of the term "survivor syndrome." In general, survivor syndrome means "the negative effects the remaining workforce experiences after major organizational change". These effects on the workforce can include anxiety, guilt, apathy, disengagement, and other mental and emotional states that result in workplace impacts such as productivity loss, poor morale, decline in quality and increased workplace injuries. Survivor syndrome can result from downsizing, delayering, re-engineering, or any other method used to implement significant organizational change (Gottlieb and Conkling, 1995; Jackson, 1996). The work of Brockner and colleagues (1985, 1986, 1987, 1988) has been key in identifying this notion.

To date, the research in this field has not identified any hierarchy or cause-and-effect relations among the range of feelings apparently experienced by survivors. For any given set of emotions, it is difficult to agree on core emotional responses and common definitions. There is some argument that job insecurity is a key factor in relation to organizational commitment and job behavior (Burke and Nelson, 1998, pp. 34–6). However, there is no consensus on this.

Faced with these problems of definition, most survey researchers have opted for utilizing well-recognized scales of morale, commitment and so on. For example, the American Management Association (AMA) surveys of managers and workers still show very negative human resource outcomes post-downsizing – morale, commitment, job satisfaction, company loyalty are all down. This complex of damaged morale and crisis mentality has been labeled "survivor guilt," "survivor syndrome," "survivor sickness," "anxiety intensification through downsizing" (AIDS) or "post-downsizing stress syndrome" (PDSS) (Brockner, 1988; Caplan and Teese, 1997; Gottlieb and Conkling, 1995; Littler, Dunford, and Bramble, 1996; Noer, 1993; Shore, 1996).

We have not tried to study survivor syndrome as an individual phenomenon using clinical interview methodologies. Instead we were interested in it as an organizational phenomenon. Consequently, following the path of the US research, we utilized six key human resource variables:

- employee morale (decreased levels);
- employee motivation (decreased levels);
- employee commitment to the organization (decreased levels);
- employee job satisfaction (decreased levels);
- concern about job security (increased levels);
- perceived promotion opportunities within the organization (decreased expectations).

Strength of association within construct

These factors were used consistently across the survey questions in all three countries. Do these factors form a stable and consistent construct?

We have now built up a large number of survey sets at both national and company level using measures of survivor syndrome. We have conducted repeated factor analyses and reliability analyses on the results. On the basis of these analyses, it is clear that survivor syndrome involves core items referring to employee morale, motivation and commitment to the organization. Factor analysis repeatedly shows these components to be strongly associated together and the reliability coefficients have levels of 0.85 or above for such a construct. Job satisfaction is clearly associated with morale, motivation and commitment, but there are varying results from the analysis of some surveys. Perceived promotion opportunities and job insecurity appear to be broader factors with significant explanatory potential but not always tightly tied in with employee morale, motivation and commitment to the organization. Factor analysis often shows promotion opportunities to be a separate component. This is because perceived promotion opportunities are linked most strongly to delayering and there is overlap, not identity, between the two processes as we have seen.

Job security is also linked to morale, motivation and commitment to the organization, but tends to be a broader factor. Varimax rotation with three factors shows the strength of association (0.506), but Varimax rotation with five factors clearly indicates that a better solution has job security as a separate factor.[1] This is because job insecurity has at least two elements. Apart from personality factors that moderate both the perception of, and coping with, job insecurity (Roskies, Louis-Guerin, and Fournier, 1993), there are two key dimensions involved. First there is insecurity arising from the uncertainties within the organization – "will I survive the next downsizing?" Second, there is job insecurity arising from the perceived vulnerability to unemployment which is more of an external labor market issue. For example, post-redundancy occupational reemployability rates vary in Australia, from 74 percent (within three years) for managers and administrators to 43.5 percent for laborers. The average re-employability ratio is 55 percent compared to 76 percent in the USA (1995–7 data). Uncertainty of the labor market enhances or diminishes insecurity arising from the immediate organizational context.

In summary, the survivor syndrome construct measures significant aspects of post-downsizing and post-delayering outcomes with a core of three items – morale, motivation, and commitment – while job satisfaction, job security, and perceived promotion opportunities are more loosely linked to the core items.[2]

Post-downsizing human resource outcomes

Given the North American data on the effects of downsizing, then how do the Australian, New Zealand, and South African experiences fit? Our data indicated some surprising outcomes which are discussed below.

The survey results showed that South African organizations are the worst affected of all three countries by the negative effects of downsizing (see table 4.4). According to the national survey data, South Africa has caught a bad case of survivor syndrome. Employee morale has sunk in 75 percent of cases, commitment is down in 68.8 percent, and motivation in 70 percent of cases. These figures are the worst of all three countries.

Table 4.4 Post-downsizing human resource outcomes in three countries, 1993–6;
N = 1,703 organizations

	New Zealand		Australia		South Africa	
	Increase %	Decrease %	Increase %	Decrease %	Increase %	Decrease %
Employee morale	32.3	37.5	14.2	65.9	9.2	75.4
Motivation	37.7	25.3	19.1	50.0	12.6	70.8
Staff commitment to the organization	37.1	25.9	17.5	51.4	13.8	68.8
Perceived promotional opportunities within the firm	35.3	17.9	25.8	51.1	35.2	43.2
Job dissatisfaction	23.7	23.7	45.6	16.4	48.6	20.8
Concern about job security	56	15.4	71.9	6.2	80	7.6

One figure is against the trends in table 4.4 – perceived promotional opportunities. This is because such promotional opportunities are different for black and white workers in South Africa. Many black employees expect to be promoted and given a chance to become supervisors and managers. Due to affirmative action, many competent black managers find themselves in an enhanced position in relation to promotion. Many white managers find themselves more on a career plateau with restricted career opportunities. This policy of affirmative action explains the moderated effect of downsizing on promotions.

The Australian figures on survivor syndrome are not far behind the bleak South African scenario. The South African and Australian data appear to fit the broad range of US results very well. Though there are idiosyncratic factors (such as the affirmative action policy effects in South Africa), the data suggest a robust and consistent pattern to the human resource effects of downsizing. However, the New Zealand data suggests a different scenario – the workforce feel-good factors outweigh the feel-bad. For example, under the impact of downsizing the survivor syndrome indicators, such as motivation, morale, and commitment, only decline by half the Australian amounts in the New Zealand case (see table 4.4). But more significantly, the increased levels of workforce motivation, commitment and perceived promotion opportunities far outweigh any decreases. Compared to the Australian and South African cases, these positive outcomes are phenomenal.

What are the implications of the survivor syndrome data outlined in table 4.4? Our three-country research indicates several key conclusions:

- Negative human resource outcomes and survivor syndrome are difficult to avoid in a post-downsizing context.
- However, survivor syndrome is not inevitable and the processes can be managed.
- There are some signs of a "survivor syndrome cycle" across the three countries.

But what are the levers in relation to survivor syndrome effects? What factors make a difference? This issue is considered in the next section of the chapter.

EXPLANATIONS OF SURVIVOR SYNDROME

In the existing literature there are a few attempts to explain the variations in survivor syndrome. For example, Brockner and Weisenfeld (1993) found that the most negative reactions to layoffs occurred when:

- job insecurity increased;
- the process was perceived as unfair, distributionally and procedurally;
- intrinsic motivation of the job diminished.

We chose not to pursue the procedural justice issue in the context of national "mapping" surveys. We considered that it was unlikely that reliable data would be obtained. However, the extent of the database and the richness of the data allowed us to investigate other relationships.

Depth of workforce reductions

Many managers are concerned about the depth of workforce reductions at one time. Unionization and employee resistance tends to promote incremental downsizing – the salami-slice approach. Clearly, the extent of downsizing will have significant varying impacts in relation to the exiting employees, but does it matter in relation to the survivors? Some of the downsizing literature suggests that depth of workforce reduction (10 percent versus 20 percent for example) makes a difference to the human resource outcomes.

Table 4.2 makes it apparent that there was very little difference between Australia, South Africa, and New Zealand in relation to depth of cutting. In general, we found that depth of cutting explained very little. *We could find no significant correlations, either across countries or within countries, between depth of cutting and human resource outcomes.* Let us put this another way around. As the song puts it, "the first cut is the deepest" and it does not matter if the cut is 3 percent or 20 percent *in relation to the effects on the survivors.* Whetten (1997) also found that there were severe disproportionate outcomes in relation to the effects of small workforce reductions on survivors.

Frequency of workforce reductions

The depth of cutting is not the key factor in the survivor syndrome outcomes. Does frequency matter? There is some literature which argues for the importance of the frequency factor. For example, Shore (1996) argues that a series of downsizings is strongly related to what he calls "post-downsizing stress syndrome." The suggested mechanisms are "The human emotions of anxiety, fear, mistrust and paranoia [which] are all involved in a downsizing syndrome" (p. 7). These job stressors intensify over repeated downsizings.

At the management level, frequency of downsizing can create serious problems. The biggest management problem often is administering the process as a one-off event, when it is not likely to be so. For example, Stocks (1997) in discussing the downsizing

Table 4.5 Correlations between frequency of downsizing and survivor syndrome scale (within country data)

	Total sample	Australia	New Zealand	South Africa
Pearson correlation	0.156*	0.290*	−0.46	0.066
N	877	362	298	217

* Correlation is significant at the 0.01 level.

of the US airforce from 190,000 to 115,000 over the period 1992–5, made it clear that the process was managed successfully, but that senior airforce managers now had a credibility problem because earlier promises could not be kept without further downsizing.

As we have seen, 44 percent of downsizing firms in Australia have downsized three or more times over the two-year period 1993–5, and 71 percent twice or more. In New Zealand it is a significantly smaller proportion. *Within Australia, we found a significant correlation between a survivor syndrome scale and the frequency of downsizing.* Is this the key factor? Look at table 4.5.

For Australia, and the total sample, there is a weak positive correlation between frequency of downsizing and the survivor syndrome scale, but this association is not found for New Zealand or South Africa. New Zealand stands out as a continued exception – there the relation is *negative.* In other words, the higher the reported frequency, the more positive the human resource outcomes. Clearly, there is not a simple bivariate relationship between frequency of downsizing and survivor syndrome outcomes.

We have discussed elsewhere (Littler et al., 1997, pp. 74–5) the problem of confounding factors in relation to interpreting frequency. Survey respondents were asked: "Over the past 2 years, how often has your organization engaged in workforce reduction?" Consequently, high frequency responses are likely to involve a high recency factor. This means that the variable of frequency cannot be divorced from some contamination by a recency effect. This issue is discussed further below.

The downsizing/delayering hypothesis

To date, there has been limited research on the impact of downsizing on those who have to manage the process. However, it is quite evident that managers are not immune to survivor syndrome (Jones, 1998; Noer, 1993).

We surveyed respondents in relation to managers and the survivor syndrome scale. As one would expect, there were significant differences between the reports for employees in general, and managers, but the overall levels of survivor syndrome were surprisingly high. The levels of survivor syndrome in the Australian case hardly varied from the picture for the overall workforce. In contrast, the South African and the New Zealand pictures improved by significant margins. However, and this is the key to the situation, the perceived promotional opportunities of managers were reported as significantly worse ($p < 0.01$) in the Australian and New Zealand cases compared to

Table 4.6 The downsizing/delayering hypothesis

	No delayering	Delayering
Downsize once	Moderate effects	Increasing effects
	+	++
Downsize twice or more	Increasing effects across all Survivor syndrome variables +++	Maximum effects ++++

employees. Job satisfaction levels were also reported as being lower for managers in the Australian and New Zealand cases.

The main factor underlying the negative responses of managers to restructuring is that of delayering. Clearly the flattening of the managerial hierarchy affects promotional opportunities and career paths. Downsizing and delayering radically change the onward and upward view of careers. Organizational ceilings press harder and faster. The evidence also indicates that organizational commitment declines, requiring a new set of managing skills and also perhaps a new psychology of aspirations (Holbeche, 1997, 1998).

If we recognize that delayering is not the same as organizational downsizing, then there is one further effect of delayering that has not been explicitly investigated. What is the impact of delayering on the likely effects of downsizing? Are the effects positive or negative not just in relation to middle managers, but the entire workforce? Clearly, there is the empowerment thesis to the effect that delayering brings increases in job autonomy and responsibility to employees. On the other hand, it may lead to lower grades taking on additional responsibilities without skill transfers and with no increase in pay or grading. We tested this question across all three countries. In order to do so, we set out the following hypothesis:

> HY: Frequency of downsizing combined with the presence or absence of delayering negatively affects the survivor syndrome levels of non-managerial employees.

We can call the above hypothesis the "downsizing/delayering hypothesis." Table 4.6 sets out the downsizing/delayering hypothesis more explicitly.

Middle managers are themselves the sources of company information and facilitators of communication. Listen to one employee coping with downsizing:

> "My immediate manager. I can talk to him about what is going on . . . and he's more worried about his job than I am with mine. He's gone through six location changes, so he knows what it's all about. He's pretty open, pretty honest. He's even told me to polish up my resume . . . because things aren't looking good." (Noer, 1993, p. 78).

The key issue here is that delayering as a restructuring process exacerbates the tensions and uncertainties for managers. The dismantling of hierarchical structures results in loss of positions, titles and work responsibilities for many middle managers. Consequently, the planning, communication and the managing of change processes become disrupted or never take place. The result is heightened survivor syndrome outcomes for the rest of the workforce. Jones (1998, p. 186) found that the role of middle managers was critical in the success or failure of downsizing and restructuring in the US Federal Government. As Jones puts it, the less "middle managers buy-in" during downsizing the more likely the process of change will fail.

The Australian data show a very clear pattern lending support to the downsizing/delayering hypothesis. The South African picture is more mixed and the New Zealand case very mixed. Clearly, delayering has an independent effect that intensifies survivor syndrome in some cases, but not universally. Part of the problem here is that any relationship will depend on the initial conditions. In other words, it is important to understand the phase of downsizing and restructuring that the firm is going through. From our analysis of longitudinal data we know that contracting firms pass through several phases (see Littler and Innes, 1999). Do these phases at thc firm-level have significance at the national level? This is discussed below.

A restructuring cycle?

As we have indicated, underlying the frequency correlations may be recency effects. This may help to explain the organizational differences and some of the country differences. In other words, the more recent the downsizing program, the more widespread and intense the survivor syndrome emotions. This recency hypothesis implies that the New Zealand firms would be further along a restructuring cycle and that South Africa would be experiencing the pain of restructuring most intensely. In practice, the results fit a restructuring cycle model very well. This view is supported by the inclusion of South Africa in our study, a country which has restructured more recently than Australia. South Africa only started extensive downsizing and restructuring in 1993/4. Our results indicate that employee survivor syndrome outcomes are significantly worse in South Africa than Australia. This implies that a restructuring cycle involving a "cooling down" survivor syndrome process has a reality. But how does this work? What are the mechanisms involved? And what is the time-frame of change?

Brockner (1988, p. 244) raised the critical issue of the "time course of survivor reactions" as he called it, and argued that it is both theoretically and practically important to determine the nature of a restructuring cycle. Despite this importance, there has been little work done to advance the notion of such a cycle. Some research has been carried out by Noer (1993). This demonstrates that five years after post-downsizing effects were observed in individuals, most of the symptoms were still present; in fact, some were more pronounced and deep-rooted than ever. As Noer (1993, p. 83) puts it, "survivor symptoms do not automatically go away on their own, They remain, evolve, and often intensify over time."

Despite Noer's work, the mechanisms of a restructuring cycle have not been conceptualized. Part of the problem here is the confusion over levels of analysis. There are processes of crisis and change affecting individual's work-lives and careers. Second, there are the firm-level changes associated with labor turnover and changes in the population of firms. Finally there are macro-level changes pertaining to entire economies as they cope with globalization. These different transitions are summarized in table 4.7.

At the level of the individual, the work of Kubler-Ross (1969) has been applied derived from a general post-traumatic or grief model (for example Caplan and Teese,

Table 4.7 Levels involved in a restructuring cycle

Level	End-point
Personal transition	Psychological well-being and economic survival
Organizational transition	High productivity levels Organizational stability or growth
Societal transition	Coping with widespread job insecurities and new organizational forms

1997, pp. 146–9; Holbeche, 1998, pp. 25–8). The grief model assumes a transition process of three phases – "holding on," "letting go" and "reintegration." However, the grief model only tells us about individual adaptation or non-adaptation with the end-point assumed to be psychological well-being.

At the level of the firm, what we need to know is the *types of survivors*, and the processes of group adaptation over time. Here the work of Caplan and Teese (1997) is helpful, but theory is still embryonic. Our survey data were organization-based and did not involve process analysis. This is best conducted by means of systematic case studies across a range of firms and is an area for substantial future research. The notion of organizational transitions raises the issue of whether downsizing firms survive and grow. This issue has been discussed elsewhere (Littler et al., 1999).

As we have seen, the three country comparisons suggest a significant restructuring cycle effect – for *employees* South Africa has the worst case of survivor syndrome. However, if we examine the survivor syndrome scale for managers only, then this pattern does not persist. Australia comes out the worst, followed by South Africa and, then, New Zealand.[3] If a restructuring cycle is the driving factor, then why does this not carry through to managers? The lack of a consistent picture for managers suggests that a restructuring cycle cannot be the total explanation. The management of the change processes and of the dilemmas of change make a difference to the outcomes.

Trust relations and the societal context

Can inter-country differences be explained by industry differences or contextual differences, and how are these to be conceptualized? In brief, the answer is no, but this requires some elaboration. There were some uncontrollable differences in the samples between the three countries. The major factors were size and public/private sector distribution. For example, 51 percent of the Australian achieved sample consisted of organizations employing 500 plus; this compared to 14 percent in New Zealand because of the differing scale of the economies.

Given these sample differences, a log linear model was constructed with five factors – the set of survivor syndrome variables, country, size, sector, and nature of respondent. To test conditional independence of country, a reduced log-linear model was fitted where all interactions between country and survivor syndrome variables were removed. For each sub-question in relation to survivor syndrome the above method was used to test the hypothesis of conditional independence. The resulting model fitted well and the differences were significant at the 0.0001 level. Hence, there is very strong evidence that conditional independence of country does not hold. Inspection of the fitted parameters in the log-linear model indicates that for most survivor syndrome factors this lack of independence is due to opposing trends. For example, in New Zealand there is a tendency for positive effects to have increased following downsizing and delayering, whereas in Australia and South Africa the opposite is true.

Noer (1998) suggests that survivor syndrome can be explained by the sense of contract violation (using the language of the psychological contract) and that this in turn depends on the pre-existing levels of trust between employee and employer. These types of trust relations will depend on the degree of career structuring and internal labor markets that traditionally existed. Thus, much of the concern about downsizing has taken place in connection with the large banks, insurance companies, the public sector, and other areas of long-standing job security and career structuring. Certainly our data reflected this. We had no direct way of measuring employee/employer trust and did not attempt to do so. However, we found that the negative survivor syndrome outcomes were significantly worse in the public sector compared to the private sector, and in services compared to manufacturing. This was true for all three countries.

Noer's hypothesis, then, can help to explain inter-industry differences. However, they do not provide a simple explanation of the inter-country differences. The key notion involved in Noer's analysis is that of "trust in management." The more trust, the greater the sense of violation. The higher the sense of violation, the greater the probability of survivor syndrome symptoms (see also Whetten, 1997). The role of middle managers during the downsizing process reinforces or erodes this trust. Middle managers alienated by delayering and fearful of their own jobs reinforce distrust amongst employees. This is the downsizing/delayering hypothesis.

At the broader level the culture of the society and the polity may affect work relations. In Australia there has been no political consensus about the forces of change and restructuring. In South Africa the post-apartheid period has left a layer of distrust especially amongst the white managerial groups. In New Zealand there has been more of a consensus for change which served to underpin the restructuring of that society. This is now breaking down, but it is still reflected in our 1995 survey results.

CONCLUSIONS

"Employees now accept that employers intend to employ as few of them as possible, if you have a job, the new folklore says, it's because they haven't yet thought of a way of doing without you." (Hugh Mackay, *Sydney Morning Herald* August 22, 1998, p. 32).

Have these three economies achieved a successful transition to new organizational forms and new job structures? Have employees adapted to "organizations of insecurity"? To use Noer's phrase: "Have the wounds healed?"

Our data can only be one window into answering those questions, but the evidence so far is that after a decade of downsizing in Australia survivor syndrome effects are continuing and persistent. According to research done by the Melbourne Institute of Applied Economics and Social Research, only 56 percent of Australian workers in 1996/7 felt "fairly" or "very" secure in their jobs. This is down from 73 percent in 1989/90 (HR Report, 1998). In South Africa it is too early to make definitive judgments. In New Zealand the early successes appear to have turned into declining labor productivities. Labor productivity rates increased during the late 1980s but have since declined through the 1990s. In 1994 the economic value added (GDP) per hour worked in New Zealand was one of the lowest in the OECD countries.

The high levels of anxiety, job insecurity, and dislocation experienced by employees and managers in these countries may be necessary transition costs to achieve or maintain a competitive position. This is one view – the "it won't work, unless it hurts" perspective. The opposing view is that downsizing medicine is corrosive in small economy contexts, resulting in loss of skills, loss of research and development capacity, and erosion of an independent economic base. This is the economic autonomy perspective. Such a debate has figured significantly on the political scene in all three countries. Given the continuing processes of restructuring, such debates will no doubt persist and provide an emotive context for discussion on the directions of downsizing.

ACKNOWLEDGMENTS

This paper is part of a broader set of projects on organizational restructuring, downsizing, delayering, and managerial labor markets co-ordinated by Professor Craig R. Littler. I would like to thank my colleagues for their assistance and input, especially Professor Richard Dunford and Dr Retha Wiesner. The Australian survey was supported by the Australian Human Resources Institute (AHRI) which we would like to thank for their support. The 1998 Australian Survey was conducted through the Melbourne Institute of Applied Economic and Social Research, Melbourne University and we would like to thank them and Professor Peter Dawkins for their support. Apart from Peter Innes' dedicated work, The Australian Longitudinal Database has benefited from the assistance of Liz O'Brien (Australian Catholic University), Dr Tom Bramble (University of Queensland), Professor Andrew Hede (Sunshine Coast University College, Australia) and other colleagues.

NOTES

1. The following is a typical survivor syndrome factor analysis. It is based on the 1998 Australian survey data using 668 organizations.

Factor analysis: Rotated Component Matrix

	Component 1	Component 2	Component 3
Employee morale	0.823		
Employee motivation	0.819		
Employee commitment	0.808		
Employee job satisfaction	0.655		
Employee job security	0.506		
Managerial job satisfaction		0.804	
Managerial morale		0.704	
Managerial job security		0.702	
Managerial motivation		0.577	0.529
Managerial commitment	0.434	0.571	0.439
Managerial promotion opportunities			0.857
Employee promotion opportunities			0.809

Extraction method: principal component analysis with three factors
Rotation method: Varimax with Kaiser normalization
Rotation converged in five iterations. All correlations less than 0.4 in the coefficient display are suppressed.

2. We have measured other items in connection with a survivor syndrome construct, such as "level of stress in your job at that time." Factor analysis repeatedly shows *no* close association with morale, commitment or job satisfaction.
3. It should be noted that there are some differences in the question asked here and, therefore, the sub-sample of organizations.

REFERENCES

Ashford, S.J., Lee, C., and Bobko, P. 1989: Content, causes and consequences of job insecurity: a theory-based measure and substantive test. *Academy of Management Journal*, 32, 4, 803–29.

Australian Bureau of Statistics (ABS) 1998: *Retrenchment and Redundancy*. Cat.No.6266.0, ABS: Canberra, Australia.

Bowman, E.H. and Singh, H. 1993: Corporate restructuring: reconfiguring the firm. *Strategic Management Journal*, 14 (Special issue), 5–14.

Brockner, J. 1988: The effects of work layoffs on survivors: research theory and practice. *Research in Organizational Behaviour*, 10, 213–55.

Brockner, J., Davy, J., and Carter, C. 1985: Layoffs, self-esteem and survivor guilt: motivational, affective, and attitudinal consequences. *Organizational Behavior and Human Decision Processes*, 16, 229–44.

Brockner, J., Greenberg, J., Brockner, A., Bortz, J., Davy, J., and Carter, C. 1986: Layoffs, equity theory and work motivation: further evidence for the impact of survivor guilt. *Academy of Management Journal*, 29, 373–84.

Brockner, J., Greenberg, J., and Grover, S. 1988a: The impact of layoffs on survivors: insights from interpersonal and organizational justice theory. In J. Carrol (ed.) *Advances in Applied Social Psychology: Business Settings*. Hilldale, NJ: Erlbaum, 45–75.

Brockner, J., Grover, S., and Blonder, M. 1988b: Predictors of survivors' job involvement following layoffs: a field study. *Journal of Applied Psychology*, 73 (3), 436–42.

Brockner, J., Grover, S., Reed, T., DeWitt, R., and O'Malley, M. 1987: Survivors' reactions to layoffs: We get by with a little help for our friends, *Administrative Science Quarterly* 32, 526–41.

Brockner, J. and Weisenfeld, B.M. 1993: Living on the edge of social and organizational psychology: The effects of layoff on those who remain. In K. Murningham (ed.) *Social psychology in organizations: Advances in theory and research*. Englewood Cliffs, NJ: Prentice-Hall, 119–40.

Bultena, C.D. 1998: *Social Exchange under Fire: Direct and Moderated Effects of Job Insecurity on Social Exchange*. University of North Texas PhD, October 1998.

Burke, R.J. and Nelson, N. 1998: Mergers and acquisitions, downsizing, and privatization: a North American perspective. In M.K. Gowing, J.D. Kraft, and J. Campbell Quick *The New Organizational Reality*. Washington DC: American Psychological Association, 21–54.

Cameron, K., Freeman, S., and Mishra, A. 1991: Best practices in white-collar downsizing: managing contradictions. *Academy of Management Executive*, 5 (3), 57–73.

Cameron, K.S., Freeman, S.J., and Mishra, A.K. 1993: *Downsizing and Redesigning Organizations*. In G. Huber and W. Glick (eds) *Organizational Change and Redesign*. New York: Oxford University Press.

Caplan, G. and Teese, M. 1997: *Survivors: How to Keep Your Best People on Board After Downsizing*, Palo Alto, CA: Davies-Black Publishing.

Cascio, W.F. 1998: Learning from outcomes: financial experience of 311 firms that have downsized. In M.K. Gowing, J.D. Kraft, and J.C. Quick *The New Organizational Reality*. Washington DC: American Psychological Association, 55–70.

Dore, R.P. 1973: *British Factory/Japanese Factory*. London: Allen & Unwin.

Dore, R.P. 1992: Japan's version of managerial capitalism. In T.A. Kochan and M. Useem (eds) *Transforming Organizations*. New York: Oxford University Press, 17–27.

Downs, A. 1995: *Corporate Executions*. New York: AMACOM.

Elmuti-D. and Kathawala, Y. 1993: Rightsizing for industrial competitiveness: important thoughts to consider. *Business-Forum*, Fall, 18, 8–11.

Freeman, S.J. and Cameron, K.S. 1993: Organizational downsizing: a convergence and re-orientation framework. *Organization Science*, 4 (1), 10–29.

Gordon, D.M. 1996: *Fat and Mean: the Corporate Squeeze of Working Americans and the Myth of Managerial Downsizing*. New York: The Free Press.

Gottlieb, M.R. and Conkling, L. 1995: *Managing the Workplace Survivors*. Westport, CT: Quorum Books.

Gowing, M.K., Kraft, J.D., and Campbell-Quick, J. 1998: *The New Organizational Reality: Downsizing, Restructuring and Revitalization*. Washington DC: American Psychological Association.

Greenberg, E.R. 1989: The latest AMA survey on downsizing. *Personnel*, October, 38–44.

Greenhalgh, L. 1982: Maintaining organizational effectiveness during organizational retrenchment. *Journal of Applied Behavioral Science*, 18, 155–70.

Greenhalgh, L. and Jick, T.D. 1989: Survivor sense-making and reactions to organizational decline: effects of individual differences. *Management Communication Quarterly*, 2 (3), February.

Holbeche, L. 1997: *Career Development: The Impact of Flatter Structures on Careers*. Oxford: Butterworth-Heinemann.

Holbeche, L. 1998: *Motivating People in Lean Organizations*. Oxford: Butterworth-Heinemann.

HR Report 1998: Job security, Issue No. 184, p. 8. Australia.

Jackson, G.B. 1996: *Beyond Survivor Syndrome: Risks and Interventions*. Internet.

Kozlowski, S.W.J., Chao, G.T., Smith, E.M., and Hedlund, J. 1993: Organizational downsizing: strategies, interventions, and research implications. In C.L. Cooper and T. Robertson (eds) *International Review of Industrial and Organizational Psychology*. New York: John Wiley, 263–332.

Kettley, P. 1995: *Is Flatter Better? Delayering the Management Hierarchy*. Institute for Employment Studies, Brighton, UK.

Keuning, D. and Opheij, W. 1994: *Delayering Organizations: How to Beat Bureaucracy and Create a Flexible and Responsive Organization*. London: Financial Times/Pitman.

Kubler-Ross, E. 1969: *On Death and Dying*. New York: Macmillan.

Levinson, M. 1990: The myth of the missing manager. *Harvard Business Review*, November/December, 238–40.

Littler, C.R., Bramble, T., and MacDonald, J. 1994: *Organizational Restructuring: Downsizing, Delayering and Managing Change at Work*. Canberra: AGPS, ISBN 0 642 222452.

Littler, C.R. in association with Dunford, R. and Bramble, T. 1996: Downsizing: disease or cure? *HR Monthly*, lead article. August, 8–12. Reprinted in *The Professional*, October 1996, 1–10.

Littler, C.R., Dunford, R., Bramble, T., and Hede, A. 1997: The dynamics of downsizing in Australia and New Zealand. Invited Paper, *Asia Pacific Journal of Human Resources*, 35 (1) February, 65–79.

Littler, C.R., Kabanoff, B., Palmer, I., and Brown, S. 1999: Downsizing, stability and corporate performance. Paper for the American Academy of Management Conference, Chicago, USA, August.

Littler, C.R. and Innes, P. 1999: How firms contract – a longitudinal study of the effects of downsizing on firm employment structures. Paper for the American Academy of Management Conference, Chicago, USA, August.

Littler, C.R. and Wiesner, R. 1996: Restructuring in South Africa – Mandela's managers in crisis. *Financial Review*, Opinion page leading article, 6 December.

Manson, B.Y. 1998: *The Impact of Downsizing on Employee Morale and Productivity: Implications for Training*. Kansas State University PhD, November.

Maurer, Jeffrey S. 1996: Corporate restructuring in America. *Vital Speeches of the Day.* June, 62, 16, 505–8.

Mentzer, M. 1996: Corporate downsizing and profitability in Canada. *Canadian Journal of Administrative Sciences,* 13 (3), 237–50.

Noer, David M. 1993: *Healing the Wounds: Overcoming the Trauma of Layoffs and Revitalizing Downsized Organizations.* San Francisco: Jossey-Bass Publishers.

Noer, David M. 1998: Layoff survivor sickness: What it is and what to do about it. In M.K. Gowing, J.D. Kraft, and J. Campbell-Quick *The New Organizational Reality.* Washington DC: American Psychological Association, 207–20.

Roskies, E., Louis-Guerin, C., and Fournier, C. 1993: Coping with job insecurity: how does personality make a difference? *Journal of Organizational Behaviour,* 14, 617–30.

Shaw, M.D. 1994: *An Investigation into Strategies for Managing Rightsizing.* Master of Business Dissertation, University of Central Queensland, Australia.

Shore, Barry 1996: The legacy of downsizing: putting the pieces back together. *Business Forum,* 21 (3/4), Summer/Fall, 5–10.

Stocks, M. 1997: Downsizing air combat command: strategies used and lessons learned. Paper presented at the US Academy of Management Conference, Boston, 11 August, *mimeo.*

Whetten, D.A. 1997: Value conflicts and the demise of trust in the post-downsized organization. Paper presented at the US Academy of Management Conference, Boston, 11 August, *mimeo.*

Wissema, Hans 1994: *Flattened Organization: How to Reorganize for Maximum Productivity and Profitability.* Irwin Professional.

APPENDIX

Methodology

The primary focus of the investigation was directed at obtaining cross-cultural empirical data with regard to downsizing and delayering. The survey method was used to obtain the data. A questionnaire was developed by Littler et al. (1997) to measure downsizing and delayering in organizations. The questionnaire was standardized and applied in Australia, New Zealand, and South Africa. We utilized a virtually identical questionnaire in all three countries (three questions were added to the New Zealand questionaire to probe the longer period of restructuring).

The three target countries surveyed were chosen because of comparable industrial mixes and histories. However, one key factor of difference interested us, namely the three countries had started downsizing-restructuring at different times: New Zealand in 1983/4, Australia in 1989/90 and South Africa in 1993/4. Such dates can only be proximate and most economies are enduring processes of continual flux, but there was a *prima facie* case for the view that we could compare countries, with similar industry mixes, at different points on a restructuring cycle.

Reliability and validity

The questionnaire instrument was extensively piloted amongst managers and revised accordingly. Reliability of the samples was increased by their size relative to the population of larger firms in these economies. We attempted to achieve a census of all larger organizations in Australia and New Zealand and a large random sample in South Africa. Secondly, we had considerable information about the population from other sources. We are able to identify the companies by name, therefore it is possible to cross-check the survey data against our longitudinal data, employee survey data, and case study data.

In defining the limits of this study, it should be noted that the unit of analysis was the organization not the individual employee. Therefore, we asked HR managers and CEOs to assess a variety of employee attitudinal factors including morale and staff commitment. Can HR managers make such assessments? We checked the questionnaires for internal consistency (there were some overlapping questions deliberately inserted) and found high levels of consistency. A small number of questionnaires were rejected for lack of internal consistency. More generally, there may be a systematic bias because HR managers and CEOs under-report employee downturns in morale, commitment and so on. Some of the literature suggests this, though often without hard evidence. For example, Shore (1996, pp. 5–6) proposes that there may be a process of managerial denial. Manson (1998) found that there were discrepancies between employees' and managers' perceptions of morale and survivor job security post-downsizing, but that there were *similar* perceptions of trust in the workplace. However, while the discrepancies in perception should be borne in mind, our results indicate very high levels of survivor syndrome, not the opposite. In relation to the comparative trends, we know of no reason why there should be systematic bias of responses between the countries in this study. Across numerous variables where we had grounds to anticipate similar cross-country outcomes the results are remarkably similar.

Sampling frame

The rationale for the sampling in this study was to obtain a broad cross-section of larger organizations throughout Australia, New Zealand, and South Africa. We focused particularly on the larger organizations (employing 50 or more) and our sample is skewed towards these organizations. This size parameter was chosen because of the primary focus on downsizing and delayering. In relation to industry categories and the public/private sectors, there are no significant differences between the achieved sample and the larger firm population.

The timeframe of administering the questionnaire instrument has some relevance because of minor variations. The questionnaire was administered in Australia in March/April 1995, in New Zealand in October 1995, and in South Africa in May 1996. As several questions refer to "the past two years," it should be noted that this carries the meaning of 1993–5 for Australia and New Zealand, but means 1994–6 for South Africa.

Of the initial 1,722 in the Australian mailout, there was a sample loss of 30 comprising three whose organizations had been in existence for less than two years (as required for the key questions on change) and a further 27 who indicated that their organizations were too small for the questions to make sense. Some of the other non-responses may have been in this category such that the reported response rate is an underestimate. Consequently, there were 653 usable responses out of a possible 1,692 giving a response rate of 38.6 percent (this would increase to 40 percent if those who had left their organizations were treated as a sample loss).

In New Zealand questionnaires were sent to the 1,370 largest employing organizations and were personally addressed to the senior manager with HRM responsibilities. This generated a very similar sample to the Australian one. We obtained usable responses from 668 organizations. This represented a response rate of 48 percent.

In relation to South Africa, the sampling frame was derived from the professional register obtained from the South African Board for Personnel Practice. One thousand two hundred names were randomly picked from the register. This sample represents more organizations than those noted on the South African Stock Exchange. A questionnaire, accompanied by a covering letter, was mailed to each member of the sample. Of the questionnaires originally sent out, 421 responses were received. This represented a rate of 35.08 percent.

Statistical analysis

For the purposes of this paper, descriptive statistics were employed in order to demonstrate comparative trends and contrasts in the three-country data-set.

In addition we constructed the EMPDEC index as a measure of "survivor syndrome" in the three countries and across organizations. This consisted of the six items (morale among employees, employees' motivation, employees' commitment, job dissatisfaction; concern about job security; perceived promotional opportunities) which research had shown to have significance in a downsizing context. These items were added into a single score ranging from 0–6. The index is unweighted, so that the composite score is a sum of the multiple indicators. At the lower end (0,1) the score indicates low survivor syndrome. At the upper end (6,5) the score indicates serious levels of survivor syndrome. The causal linkage to downsizing arises from the nature of the question: "Consider the effects of workforce reduction over the past two years on staff generally in your organization. Please indicate for each [of the above factors] whether they have increased, decreased or remained unchanged" (C7).

t-tests were conducted to determine whether there are significant differences between Australia, New Zealand and South Africa across a range of variables. Multiple regression analysis was also used.

5 Sickness Absence and Organizational Downsizing

Mika Kivimäki, Jussi Vahtera, Amanda Griffiths, Tom Cox, and Louise Thomson

The evidence suggests that organizational downsizing may have both positive and negative impacts on the organization and on surviving employees (Mone, McKinley, and Barker, 1998; Parker, Chmiel, and Wall, 1997; Sutton and D'Aunno, 1989). The negative consequences of downsizing may last long after the time at which reductions in the workforce have been achieved and may reduce the anticipated gains from such reductions. One negative response among surviving employees is increased sickness absence with obvious costs to the organization and to society and with the implication of impaired employee health (Adams, 1987; Beale and Nethercott, 1988; Jones et al., 1998; Kivimäki et al., 1997b; Sargent, 1989; Vahtera, Kivimäki, and Pentti, 1997). This chapter considers sickness absence among survivors in relation to downsizing.

ECONOMIC IMPORTANCE

Reports from Finnish industry suggest that sickness absence accounts for over 5 percent of total working hours (Ministry of Labour, 1995). Somewhat similarly in Britain, the Confederation of British Industry noted that, in 1997, sickness absence represented about 3.7 percent of total working time (Confederation of British Industry, 1997). Such absence is of economic importance although it is not clear how much is attributable to the effects of downsizing.

Complex accounting models are required to determine the true costs of absence from work. Currently these must, by necessity, include many ill-defined and roughly estimated variables. Often at the core of such models are direct cost variables related to the fact and amount of paid sick leave, and costs attributable to the management response to absence such as provision of temporary cover, training and the reallocation of work tasks, the disruption to work systems, production and customer or client relations, the maintenance of absence monitoring and control systems, and the additional management work demanded by all of these activities. While several estimations have been made of the overall costs of sickness absence, both at the organizational and national levels, those specifically related to downsizing are somewhat rarer. A recent study by Vahtera, Kivimäki, and Pentti (1997) is an exception. It was focused on an organization which downsized the workforce from 1,237 person-years in 1991 to 1,064 person-years in 1993, that is, a 14 percent reduction in the workforce. Among other things, the authors reported that 8–13 percent of the immediate financial advantages of this reduction in workforce was lost because of an increase in sickness absence among survivors during the three years following downsizing.

Research suggests a number of other less direct cost variables that may be associated with downsizing and subsequent sickness absence. For example, it has been shown that perceived job insecurity, a possible mediating factor in the effects of downsizing on sickness absence (see later), may also be associated with the disruption of group performance (Kranz, 1985), with reduced productivity and increased labor turnover (Greenhalgh, 1982; Snyder, 1994; Sutton, 1984). Furthermore, the increased sickness absence related to downsizing may, in turn, reflect a deterioration in the health of the surviving employees (Marmot et al., 1995). All such factors should be included in the overall economic equation; as a result, the real costs of downsizing may be appreciable.

Whatever the economic realities, the relationship between downsizing, sickness absence, and health is of interest in itself, and this chapter explores what is known about this relationship within the framework of the "Raisio study" conducted in Finland. It first considers some of the methodological issues involved in the measurement of the key variables, and then it presents a brief overview of the study, pointing out its key findings in the context of the wider literature. Finally it explores the possible psychosocial mediation of the effects of downsizing on absence.

A QUESTION OF MEASUREMENT

What cannot be reliably and validly measured cannot be researched or managed. Therefore any discussion of the relationship between downsizing and sickness absence must be prefaced by careful consideration of measurement issues. The measurement of sickness absence and downsizing, and the analysis of such data, are discussed below as an introduction to the Raisio study.

Sickness absence

The validity of sickness absence as a measure of health and morbidity is the subject of discussion because of its multi-factorial nature and its sensitivity to a host of factors other than the health of the individual (Chadwick-Jones, Nicholson, and Brown, 1982; Folger and Belew, 1985; Hensing et al., 1998; Manning and Osland, 1989). It is important to distinguish between long and short spells of absence since clear differences exist in the relationships among these variables, correlates of health, and health outcomes.

In most industrialized countries, long spells of sickness absence typically require a physician's examination and formal certification, whereas shorter spells can be self-certified. Thus, short spells may reflect voluntary (non-health related) absence as well as that driven by illness. It has been suggested that the risk factors and decision processes for long and short spells of absence may significantly differ. For longer spells the influence of more severe illnesses, such as musculoskeletal and psychiatric disorders, and physical injury, appears to be substantial, while in shorter spells the influence of non-specific symptoms such as headache, nausea, and fatigue may prevail (Hensing et al., 1998). For longer spells, there may be less room for differences in medical diagnosis and advice, and in individual decision making on whether to be absent from work or not. Furthermore, the psychological and social processes which influence the recall of long and short spells of absence also differ (Griffiths et al., 1999).

The length of the sickness absence spell appears to be important when the associations between absence and other possible predictors of health are considered. Age correlates positively with long spells of absence, morbidity and mortality but the correlation is negative or lacking for age with short spells of absence (Ferris, Bergin, and Wayne, 1988; Johns, 1978; Leigh, 1986; Nicholson, Brown, and Chadwick-Jones, 1977; Schalk, 1987; Vahtera, Uutela, and Pentti, 1996). The socio-economic gradient for rates of long spells of absence resembles those for disease and mortality (Blaxter, 1987; Mackenbach et al., 1997; Marmot and Shipley, 1984; North et al., 1993; Smith et al., 1997; Vahtera et al., in press). Such a parallel cannot be found for short spells of absence (Vahtera et al., in press). Health risk behaviors such as regular smoking, a sedentary lifestyle and being overweight are strong predictors of long spells of absence (Kivimäki et al., 1997b; Vahtera et al., 1997), but little data has been published in relation to short spells of absence.

In addition to the distinction between long and short spells of absence, another distinction can be made between frequency-based (spells) and time-based (days) measures of absence. Although it has been argued that both types of measure can be used to demonstrate the relationship between absence and health (Chen and Spector, 1991; Cooper and Bramwell, 1992; Hammer and Landau, 1981; Ivancevich, 1986; Marmot et al., 1995; North et al., 1993; Smulders, 1983; Zaccaro, Craig, and Quinn, 1991), in large epidemiological studies, frequency-based measures are usually preferred. For example, measures based on spells of absence differentiated by length were used in Whitehall II studies, which are probably the most cited studies on sickness absence (for example, North et al., 1993). The Sick-leave Registration project, another major project in this field, also used frequency-based measures and focused exclusively on long spells of seven days or longer (see, for example, Alexanderson et al., 1994).

Frequency measures are effectively rate measures, and the denominator usually refers to the period during which a subject is thought to be at risk. Regarding permanent employees, this is approximately equal to their length of service during the study period (North et al., 1993; Alexanderson et al., 1994). A more precise denominator was used in the Raisio study (see below) in which days legitimately spent away from work (vacations, participation in external training events, maternity leave, etc.) were subtracted from the length of service (Kivimäki et al., 1997b; 1998; Vahtera, Uutela and Pentti, 1996; Vahtera, Kivimäki, and Pentti, 1997).

Downsizing

Although often used, the number of employees laid off is only a rough indicator of downsizing. Downsizing may include redundancies, temporary layoffs, not replacing those retiring or otherwise leaving, allowing temporary work contracts to expire without renewal, and not hiring of staff to cover for employees on sick leave, maternity leave, and so on (Mayfield, 1993). Many of these actions do not reduce the core staff complement. To reflect the degree of downsizing more accurately, one should not focus simply on the decrease in the number of employees but also consider the reduction in days worked. This measurement strategy was applied in the Raisio study.

To analyze the degree of downsizing in terms of working days, information was obtained from employers' records for all periods of employment in Raisio by occupation and by work unit. These data were also broken down by age, gender, and job status, and supplemented by questionnaire data. The sum of these periods represented the theoretical total number of contracted days worked. From this sum, the number of days legitimately spent away from work was subtracted. Thus, what remained was the number of contracted days worked which was, on the average, 15 percent less than the theoretical number of contracted days worked. The extent of downsizing was determined by the percentage reduction in the number of contracted days worked in 1993 (the worst year of the economic decline), compared with the number of contracted days worked in 1991 (the time before downsizing).

Data analysis

In the analysis of any sickness absence data, the nature of those data has to be considered. The distribution of sickness absence spells is not normal: it is usually strongly skewed with low values being the most frequent and high values being only rarely observed (Kivimäki et al., 1997b; North et al., 1993). The use of traditional regression models, based on normal distributions, may lead to underestimation of true predictive relationships. A more realistic estimation will be obtained by using Poisson regression models which are specifically developed to be used with skewed response variables and frequency data such as sickness absence spells (McCullagh and Nelder, 1989; North et al., 1993). Poisson regression was used with the data from the Raisio study.

THE RAISIO EXPERIENCE

According to Parker, Chmiel, and Wall (1997) there are at least two different forms of downsizing: strategic downsizing and reactive downsizing. The former, also called "rightsizing" (Hitt et al., 1994), refers to a process which is "well-articulated and designed to support the long-term organizational strategy" (Kozlowski et al., 1993, p. 268). It is often used in relation to organizational transformations such as moves towards lean production, total quality management or re-engineering (Kivimäki et al., 1997a; Womack, Jones, and Roos, 1990). The latter, reactive downsizing, usually refers to situations where staff reductions are undertaken in response to external events and short-term needs (Kozlowski et al., 1993). An example is an organization laying off employees as a result of diminishing needs, income or funds during a period of economic decline. The Raisio study is such a case, and relates to the experience of reactive downsizing by municipal workers in Finland. Reactive downsizing is more common than strategic downsizing and the related empirical evidence is more substantial (Parker, Chmiel, and Wall, 1997).

In 1991, 1,283 municipal employees worked in the service of the town of Raisio, in southwest Finland. During the following year, Finland faced its most severe economic decline since World War I. Unemployment rose from 3.4 percent in 1990 to 18.9 percent in 1993 (Statistics Finland, 1995b). The number of Finnish municipal personnel fell by 1.4 percent in 1990–1, by 2.7 percent in 1991–2, by 7.8 percent in 1992–3, and by 2.7 percent in 1993–4. In Raisio, the number of municipal employees in 1993, the worst year of the decline, was 1,083, 15.6 percent lower than in 1991.

What was the effect of this reactive downsizing in Raisio on sickness absence and health among the surviving municipal workers, and what mediated this effect?

Downsizing and contracted days worked

The effects of downsizing on the number of contracted days actually worked were interesting and strongly moderated by factors related to job status and age. As shown in figure 5.1, actual days worked by the temporary employees, who were generally younger than the permanent staff, decreased. This was largely because their contracts were not extended and because extra staff were not hired to cover for those on sick leave. Consequently, a relatively higher proportion of work was done by the permanent

Figure 5.1 Contracted days worked among permanent and temporary staff and employees aged over 50 years

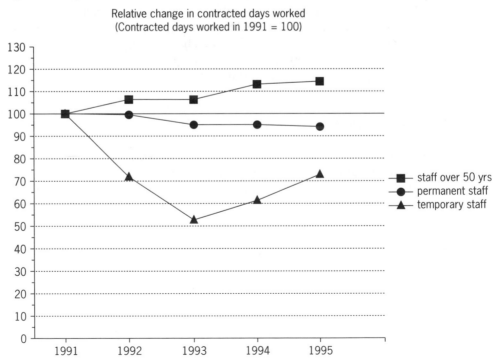

Relative change in contracted days worked
(Contracted days worked in 1991 = 100)

staff over 50 yrs
permanent staff
temporary staff

employees who were also older (cf. Corzine, Buntzman, and Busch, 1994). Before the decline, almost a third of the total days were worked by employees aged 35 years or younger. In 1993, less than a fifth of the total days were worked by this age group. In contrast, the actual number of days worked by individuals older than 50 years increased.

Ignoring the strong age effect, the actual number of days worked by permanent employees decreased slightly. Since none were laid off during the study period, this reduction reflected a freeze on vacancies and the influence of short-term temporary layoffs in 1993.

Such patterns in the effects of downsizing on actual number of days worked appear to vary across organizations as well as within organizations across types of worker. In the town of Raisio, considerable variation in downsizing was observed from a mean reduction of 14 percent in actual number of days worked. For example, in horticultural and building workers, the reduction in working days was more than 35 percent, whereas among technicians the days worked actually increased by 4 percent between 1991 and 1993 (figure 5.2).

Downsizing and sickness absence

The findings of the Raisio study show that an increase in long spells of absence, irrespective of cause, was related to the degree of downsizing (figure 5.3). Comparing groups, the risk of long periods of absence was 1.9 to 6.9 times greater after major downsizing (reduction of actual working hours by over 18 percent) than after minor downsizing (reduction of less than 8 percent). Adjustment for employees' demographic characteristics, including annual income, and their sickness absence before downsizing did not significantly affect the results. In this study, a medical doctor had certified all these sick leaves, and these findings suggest that downsizing represented a substantial health risk.

In other studies, job control has proved to be among the most consistent psychosocial predictors of morbidity and mortality (Bosma et al., 1997; Johnson et al., 1996; Kivimäki et al., 1997b; Marmot, 1994; Theorell and Karasek, 1996; Theorell et al., 1998). One way to estimate the significance of downsizing in relation to absence is to compare its influence with the effects of well-known psychosocial factors such as job control (see Griffiths, 1999a). In female employees in the service of Raisio, the association between downsizing and subsequent long spells of absence was slightly higher than that between job control and later absence (Kivimäki et al., 1997b). In male employees, the opposite was true. Continuing this analysis, downsizing was a stronger predictor of absence, in both sexes, than job insecurity, social support and negative life events (Kivimäki et al., 1997b).

As expected, there were striking differences in the prediction of long- and short-term sickness absence. While the relationship between the degree of downsizing and long spells of absence was linear and positive, that with short spells was linear but negative (figure 5.3). Interestingly, this latter effect did not depend on other individual and organizational variables such as sex, baseline health status, age, length of service,

Figure 5.2 Degree of downsizing in different occupational groups in the town of Raisio

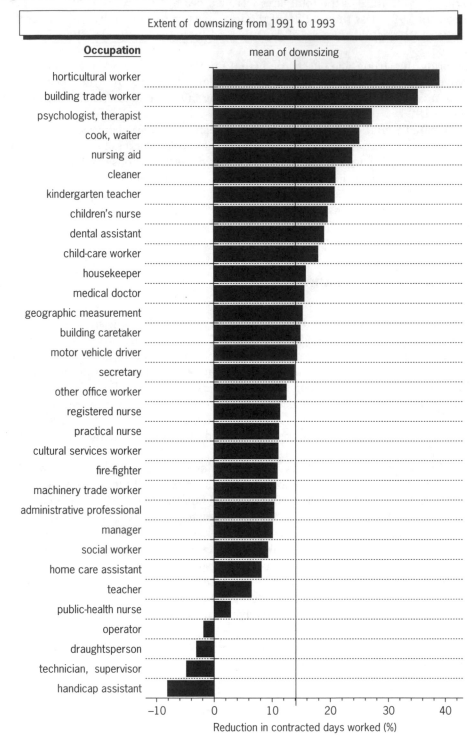

Figure 5.3 Rate ratios for short and long sick leaves associated with downsizing (reproduced from Vahtera, Kivimäki, and Pentti, 1997, © *The Lancet*)

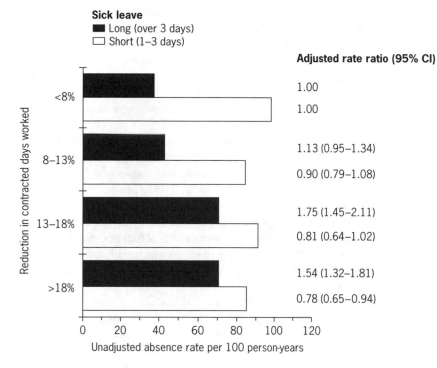

income level, marital status, number of dependent children, change in occupation/ work unit, or size and age structure of work units.

Since short spells can be more voluntary in nature than long spells and may not be as related to illness, the effects of downsizing on job involvement may be more obvious there. An observed decrease in the frequency of short spells of absence did not support the hypothesis of demoralization or loosening of the psychological contract in this particular case (Leiter, 1991). In contrast, in work units facing major downsizing, employees seemed to avoid short-term absences. Several explanations may be advanced. First, increased job insecurity during a period of growing unemployment may change the absenteeism culture. Employees may be afraid of being frequently absent because such behavior might be assumed to increase their likelihood of being laid off in the future. Second, the absenteeism culture may alter because of the changes in work demands as a result of downsizing. Because the number of employees available for a given amount of work is reduced, there may be increased demands on those remaining (Parker, Chmiel, and Wall, 1997). In such a situation, anticipation that absence will badly affect colleagues may lead to psychological and social pressure to be present at work even when not completely well.

It is important to note that the reduced frequency of short-term absences did not compensate for the increase in long-term absences. On average, the number of days involved in short periods of absence fell by 14 percent but those involved in long sick leaves rose by 16–31 percent.

At-risk groups

While downsizing seems to increase long spells of absence, this risk appears to vary according to both organizational and individual factors. In the Raisio study, the risk of long-term sick leave after downsizing was especially high in older employees, employees with a tendency to hostile reactions, employees with a higher income, in large work units and in those units in which the mean age of the employees was high (see figure 5.4; Kivimäki et al., 1998; Vahtera, Kivimäki, and Pentti, 1997).

The moderating effect of age is important because reactive downsizing strategies can sometimes increase the number of older employees in the organization and the number of work units with a high proportion of older staff (cf. figure 5.1). In work units with older employees, the adverse effects of downsizing seemed particularly clear with regard to musculoskeletal disorders, the most common cause of disability in workers (Jones et al., 1998; Klaukka, Sievers, and Takala, 1982; Martin, Meltzer, and Elliot, 1988). Major downsizing led to a ten-fold increase in the risk of an individual developing musculoskeletal disorders compared with minor downsizing (Vahtera, Kivimäki, and Pentti, 1997). In work units with a low proportion of older employees, downsizing did not significantly increase the overall risks to employee health (figure 5.4). Thus, by raising the mean age of the personnel, reactive strategies may paradoxically increase the vulnerability of the survivor group to the adverse health effects of downsizing. We call this phenomenon "the reactive downsizing dilemma." These data also serve to reinforce the increasing concern for age-related factors in our understanding and management of the relationship between work and health (Griffiths, 1998, 1999b).

The personality of survivors may also play a role in the effects of downsizing (Armstrong-Stassen, 1994; Kivimäki et al., 1998; Mone, 1994). In research on disease-prone personality traits, tendency to hostility has received particular attention (Friedman and Booth-Kewley, 1987). It has been reported that hostility independently contributes to various health problems and diseases including coronary heart disease (Barefoot, Dahlström, and Williams, 1983; Chen and Spector, 1991; Dembroski et al., 1989; Julkunen et al., 1994; Kivimäki, Kalimo, and Julkunen, 1996; Koskenvuo et al., 1988; Miller et al., 1996; Romanov et al., 1994; Siegler et al., 1992; Vahtera et al., 1997). Several explanations of the mechanisms which underpin the relationship between hostility and health have been advanced. The "psychosocial vulnerability model" suggests that the health of hostile individuals is at greater risk than that of others, partly because the coping strategies that they employ in stressful situations are ineffective, and partly because they lack good social support (Miller et al., 1996; Smith, 1992, 1994; Smith and Christensen, 1992).

Since downsizing is a significant stressor, hostile employees may be hypothesized to be more vulnerable to its adverse effects than other employees. Findings on women belonging to the most hostile third of the Raisio employees support this hypothesis (Kivimäki et al., 1998). Among this group, major downsizing was associated with a greater risk of long spells of absence, irrespective of cause, than among other female employees. The risk of long spells of absence did not differ between hostile and non-hostile women in conditions of minor downsizing. These results remained unaltered when the effects of confounding factors such as baseline sickness, socio-economic background, health-risk behavior and biological risks were partialled out.

Figure 5.4 Interaction between downsizing and other predictors of sick leave (reproduced from Vahtera, Kivimäki, and Pentti, 1997, © *The Lancet*)

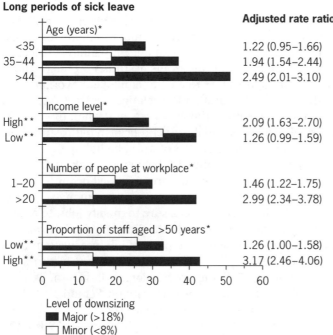

Long periods of sick leave

Age (years)*

	Adjusted rate ratio (95% CI)
<35	1.22 (0.95–1.66)
35–44	1.94 (1.54–2.44)
>44	2.49 (2.01–3.10)

Income level*

| High** | 2.09 (1.63–2.70) |
| Low** | 1.26 (0.99–1.59) |

Number of people at workplace*

| 1–20 | 1.46 (1.22–1.75) |
| >20 | 2.99 (2.34–3.78) |

Proportion of staff aged >50 years*

| Low** | 1.26 (1.00–1.58) |
| High** | 3.17 (2.46–4.06) |

0 10 20 30 40 50 60

Level of downsizing
■ Major (>18%)
□ Minor (<8%)

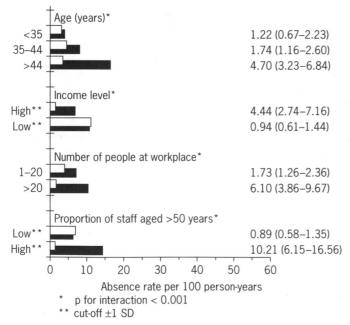

Sick leave due to musculosceletal disorders

Age (years)*

<35	1.22 (0.67–2.23)
35–44	1.74 (1.16–2.60)
>44	4.70 (3.23–6.84)

Income level*

| High** | 4.44 (2.74–7.16) |
| Low** | 0.94 (0.61–1.44) |

Number of people at workplace*

| 1–20 | 1.73 (1.26–2.36) |
| >20 | 6.10 (3.86–9.67) |

Proportion of staff aged >50 years*

| Low** | 0.89 (0.58–1.35) |
| High** | 10.21 (6.15–16.56) |

0 10 20 30 40 50 60

Absence rate per 100 person-years
*****   p for interaction < 0.001
** cut-off ±1 SD

DOWNSIZING AND SICKNESS ABSENCE: PSYCHOSOCIAL MEDIATION

Although the association between downsizing and long sickness absence spells has been demonstrated both in the Raisio study and elsewhere, much remains to be discovered about the mechanisms underpinning this association. Only indirect evidence is available. This evidence is to be found, first, in the results of studies on the relationships between downsizing and changes in factors related to employees' working and private lives and, second, in the results of studies on the relationships between such factors and health outcomes. From the results of these two sets of studies, three mediating mechanisms are hypothesized – all are essentially psychosocial in nature (Griffiths, 1999a): (1) changes in the stress-related characteristics of work, including (2) adverse effects on social support, and (3) changes in health risk behaviors, such as smoking and excessive alcohol consumption. These mechanisms are discussed below.

As organizations downsize, feelings of job insecurity may increase among surviving employees. These employees may also be faced with pressure to modify jobs, to accept different employment conditions, and even to relocate. In the Raisio study, for example, the degree of downsizing correlated with subsequent reports of job insecurity in both sexes (Kivimäki et al., 1997b). Job insecurity or anticipation of job loss, in turn, is a health risk for a wide range of conditions, including psychological ill-health, psychological distress, burnout, organizational withdrawal (Dekker and Schaufeli, 1995), impaired self-reported health status, physical symptomalogy (Ferrie et al., 1995; Heaney, Israel, and House, 1994), lowered quality of sleep (Beale and Nethercott, 1988), the occurrence of ischemic heart disease (Siegrist et al., 1990), and heightened rates of sickness absence (Beale and Nethercott, 1988; Kivimäki et al., 1997b). It may be an important mediating factor in the relationships among downsizing, long spells of absence and employee health. It may also be important for short-term sickness absence but may operate in a different way (see earlier).

Increased role and task demand – job demands – may also be a mediating factor. In an examination of 236 employees who survived downsizing, Tombaugh and White (1990) found that participants reported increases in role overload and role ambiguity, and that these sources of stress were related to dissatisfaction and intention to leave the organization. In a labor-process analysis of developments in mill and mine operations, Russell (1995) concluded that one of the main outcomes of downsizing was job expansion. Consistent with this, Parker, Chmiel, and Wall (1997) reported an increase in job demands after downsizing in a chemical processing company. Finally, the results of the Raisio study showed that the degree of downsizing predicted lowered levels of job control in both sexes (Kivimäki et al., 1997b). Both these stressors – job demands and control – have been shown elsewhere to have adverse effects on sickness absence and employee health (Cox, 1993; Dwyer and Ganster, 1991; Farrell and Stamm, 1988; Ferrie, 1997; Karasek, 1979; Karasek and Theorell, 1990; Marmot et al., 1993; North et al., 1996).

According to Mayfield (1993), downsizing often increases the risk of conflict with co-workers, upper management, and other groups of employees (see also Tombaugh and White, 1990). This can result in the deterioration of social interaction, the restriction of social networks and a high prevalence of rumor, all of which effectively reduce social support. Reduced social support, in turn, has been shown to predict heightened rates of sick leave (Rael et al., 1995; Unden, 1994).

Taking these findings together, it is clear that, among other things, downsizing may exacerbate the "classic" equation for stressful working conditions (Cox, 1993; Karasek and Theorell, 1990) – increased job demands, decreased job control, and decreased social support – and it is entirely possible that such an effect may partly mediate its other effects on absence and health. For example, the experience of stress can also increase alcohol consumption and smoking – as an emotion-focused coping strategy (Cox, 1993) – and such health risk behavior, particularly in men, has been found to be associated with sickness absence (Altchiler and Motta, 1994; Bush and Wooden, 1995; French et al., 1995; Gill, 1994; Jeffery et al., 1993; Jones, Casswell, and Zhang, 1995; Kirkcaldy et al., 1994; Leigh, 1995; Marmot et al., 1993; Wooden and Bush, 1995).

CONCLUSIONS

In summary, the data discussed in this chapter led to at least four conclusions. First, the effects of downsizing may vary considerably within organizations. This variation should not be ignored when studying the association between downsizing and health. Second, downsizing may have a negative effect on long spells of absence in survivors reflecting a detrimental effect on their health. Third, the risks of downsizing to long spells of absence and to health are partially moderated by organizational and individual factors such as employees' age, the structure and size of their work units, their job status and personality. Age effects may be particularly important. Fourth, some aspects of the relationships among downsizing, long-term sickness absence and health may be mediated by psychosocial factors related to stress such as perceived job insecurity, increased work demands, decreased job control and social support, and increased health risk behaviors.

It is likely that downsizing will continue to be a significant trend within industrialized countries for the foreseeable future. Considering this, it is important to increase understanding about the factors that mediate and moderate the adverse effects of downsizing on employee health. Such an understanding may help in the planning of better organizational strategies and associated management actions. Moreover, if the effectiveness of downsizing depends largely on the reactions and age of the employees, then these variables should be a central feature of those planning and subsequent actions and of related research.

ACKNOWLEDGMENTS

Preparation of this paper was supported, in part, by grants from the Emil Aaltonen Foundation, from the Finnish Work Environment Fund, and from the British Health and Safety Executive.

REFERENCES

Adams, G.T. 1987: Preventive law trends and compensation payments for stress-disabled workers. In J.C. Quick, R.S. Bhagat, J.E. Dalton, and J.D. Quick (eds) *Work Stress: Health Care Systems in the Workplace*. New York: Praeger.

Alexanderson, K., Leijon, M., Åkerlind, I., Rydh, H., and Bjurulf, P. 1994: Epidemiology of sickness absence in a Swedish county in 1985, 1986 and 1987. *Scandinavian Journal of Social Medicine*, 22, 27–34.

Altchiler, L. and Motta, R. 1994: Effects of aerobic and non-aerobic exercise on anxiety, absenteeism, and job satisfaction. *Journal of Clinical Psychology*, 50, 829–40.

Armstrong-Stassen, M. 1994: Coping with transition – a study of layoff survivors. *Journal of Organizational Behavior*, 15, 597–621.

Barefoot, J.C., Dahlström, W.G., and Williams, J.B. Jr. 1983: Hostility, CHD incidence, and total mortality: a 25-year follow-up study of 255 physicians. *Psychosomatic Medicine*, 45, 59–63.

Beale, N. and Nethercott, S. 1988: Certificated sickness absence in industrial employees threatened with redundancy. *British Medical Journal of Clinical Research and Education*, 296, 1508–10.

Blaxter, M. 1987: Evidence on inequality in health from a national survey. *Lancet*, 333, 30–3.

Bosma, H., Marmot, M.G., Hemingway, H., Nicholson, A.C., Brunner, E., and Stansfeld, S.A. 1997: Low control and risk of coronary heart disease in Whitehall II (prospective cohort) study. *British Medical Journal*, 314, 558–64.

Brockner, J. 1988: The effects of work layoff on survivors: research, theory, and practice. In B.M. Straw and L.L. Cummings (eds) *Research in Organizational Behavior*. Greenwich, CT: JAI Press, 213–56.

Brockner, J., Davy, J., and Carter, C. 1985: Layoffs, self-esteem, and survivor guilt: motivational, affective and attitudinal consequences. *Organizational Behavior and Human Decision Processes*, 36, 229–44.

Bush, R. and Wooden, M. 1995: Smoking and absence from work: Australian evidence. *Social Science and Medicine*, 41, 437–46.

Chadwick-Jones, J.K., Nicholson, N., and Brown, C. 1982: *Social Psychology of Absenteeism*. New York: Praeger.

Chen, P.J. and Spector, P.E. 1991: Negative affectivity as the underlying cause of correlations between stressors and straints. *Journal of Applied Psychology*, 76, 398–407.

Confederation of British Industry 1997: *1996 Absence and Labour Turnover Survey*. London: CBI Publications.

Cooper, C.L. and Bramwell, R.S. 1992: Predictive validity of the strain components of the Occupational Stress Indicator. *Stress Medicine*, 8, 57–66.

Corzine, J.B., Buntzman, G.F., and Busch, E.T. 1994: Mentoring, downsizing, gender and career outcomes. *Journal of Social Behavior and Personality*, 9, 517–28.

Cox, T. 1993: *Stress Research and Stress Management: Putting Theory to Work.* (res. rep. no. 61/1993). Health and Safety Executive, London.

Dekker, S.W.A. and Schaufeli, W.B. 1995: The effects of job insecurity on psychological health and withdrawal: A longitudinal study. *Australian Psychologist*, 30, 514–22.

Dembroski, T.M., MacDougall, J.M., Costa, P.T. Jr., and Grandits, G.A. 1989: Components of hostility as predictors of sudden death and myocardial infarction in the Multiple Risk Factor Intervention Trial. *Psychosomatic Medicine*, 51, 514–22.

Dwyer, D.J. and Ganster, D.C. 1991: The effects of job demands and control on employee attendance and satisfaction. *Journal of Organizational Behavior*, 12, 595–608.

Farrell, D. and Stamm, C.L. 1988: Meta-analysis of the correlates of employee absence. *Human Relations*, 41, 211–27.

Ferrie, J.E. 1997: Labour market status, insecurity and health. *Journal of Health Psychology*, 2, 373–97.

Ferrie, J.E., Shipley, M.J., Marmot, M.G., Stansfeld, S., and Smith, G.D. 1995: Health effects of anticipation of job change and non-employment: Longitudinal data from the Whitehall II study. *British Medical Journal*, 331, 1264–9.

Ferris, G.R., Bergin, T.G., and Wayne, S.J. 1988: Personal characteristics, job performance, and absenteeism of public school teachers. *Journal of Applied Social Psychology*, 62, 55–9.

Folger, R. and Belew, J. 1985: Nonreactive measurement. A focus for research on absenteeism and occupational stress. *Research in Organizational Behaviour*, 7, 129–70.

French, M.T., Zarkin, G.A., Hartwell, T.D., and Bray, J.W. 1995: Prevalence and consequences of smoking, alcohol-use, and illicit drug-use at five worksites. *Public Health Reports*, 110, 593–9.

Friedman, H.S. and Booth-Kewley, S. 1987: The "disease-prone personality": a meta-analytic view of the construct. *American Psychologist*, 42, 539–55.

Gill, J. 1994: Alcohol problems in employment: epidemiology and responses. *Alcohol and Alcoholism*, 29, 233–48.

Greenhalgh, L. 1982: Maintaining organizational effectiveness during organizational retrenchment. *Journal of Applied Behavioral Science*, 18, 155–70.

Griffiths, A.J. 1998: Work-related ill-health in Great Britain. *Work and Stress*, 12, 1–5.

Griffiths, A.J. 1999a: The psychosocial work environment. In R.C. McCaig and M.J. Harrington (eds) *The Changing Nature of Occupational Health*. Sudbury: Health & Safety Executive Books. Thomas Legge, 213–32.

Griffiths, A.J. 1999b: Work design and management – a lifespan perspective. *Experimental Aging Research* (in press).

Griffiths, A.J., Thomson, L., Cox, T., and Kivimäki, M. 1999: The validity and accuracy of self reported absence data. Manuscript submitted for publication.

Hammer, T.H. and Landau, J.C. 1981: Methodological issues in the use of absence data. *Journal of Applied Psychology*, 66, 574–81.

Heaney, C.A. and Clemans, J. 1995: Occupational stress, physician-excused absences, and absences not excused by a physician. *American Journal of Health Promotion*, 10, 117–24.

Heaney, C.A., Israel, B.A., and House, J.S. 1994: Chronic job insecurity among automobile workers: effects on job satisfaction and health. *Social Science and Medicine*, 38, 1431–7.

Hensing, G., Alexanderson, K., Allebeck, P., and Bjurulf, P. 1998: How to measure sickness absence? Literature review and suggestion of five basic measures. *Scandinavian Journal of Social Medicine*, 26, 133–44.

Hitt, M.A., Keats, B.W., Harback, H.F., and Nixon, R.D. 1994: Rightsizing – building and maintaining strategic leadership: a long-term competitiveness. *Organizational Dynamics*, 23, 18–32.

Ivancevich, J.R. 1986: Life events and hassles as predictors of health symptoms, job performance, and absenteeism. *Journal of Occupational Behavior*, 7, 39–51.

Jeffery, R.W., Forster, J.L., Dunn, B.V., French, S.A., McGovern, P.G., and Lando, H.A. 1993: Effects of work-site health promotion on illness-related absenteeism. *Journal of Occupational Medicine*, 35, 1142–6.

Johns, G. 1978: Attitudinal and non-attitudinal predictors of two forms of absence from work. *Organizational Behaviour and Human Performance*, 22, 431–44.

Johnson, J.V., Steward, W., Hall, E.M., Fredlind, P., and Theorell, T. 1996: Long-term psychosocial work environment and cardiovaascular mortality among Swedish men. *American Journal of Public Health*, 86, 324–31.

Jones, J.R., Hodgson, J.T., Clegg, T.A., and Elliot, R.C. 1998: *Self-reported Working Conditions in 1995: Results from a Household Survey*. Sudbury: HSE Books.

Jones, S., Casswell, S., and Zhang, J.F. 1995: The economic costs of alcohol-related absenteeism and reduced productivity among the working population of New Zealand. *Addiction*, 90, 1455–61.

Julkunen, J., Salonen, R., Kaplan, G.A., and Salonen, J.T. 1994: Hostility and the progression of carotid atherosclerosis. *Psychosomatic Medicine*, 56, 519–25.

Karasek, R.A. 1979: Job demands, job decision latitude and mental strain: implications for job redesign. *Administrative Science Quarterly*, 24, 285–308.

Karasek, R.A. and Theorell, T. 1990: *Stress, Productivity, and Reconstruction of Working Life*. New York: Basic Books.

Kirkcaldy, B.D., Cooper, C.L., Brown, J.M., and Athanasou, J.A. 1994: Job stress and health profiles of smokers, ex-smokers and nonsmokers. *Stress Medicine*, 10, 159–66.

Kivimäki, M., Kalimo, R., and Julkunen, J. 1996: Components of type A behavior pattern and occupational stressor-strain relationship: testing different models in a sample of industrial managers. *Behavioral Medicine*, 22, 67–76.

Kivimäki, M., Mäki, E., Lindström, K., Alanko, A., Seitsonen, S., and Järvinen, K. 1997a: Does the implementation of total quality management (TQM) change the wellbeing and work-related attitudes of health care personnel? Study of a TQM prize-winning surgical clinic. *Journal of Change Management*, 10, 456–70.

Kivimäki, M., Vahtera, J., Koskenvuo, M., Uutela, A., and Pentti, J. 1998: Response of hostile individuals to stressful change in their working lives: test of a psychosocial vulnerability model. *Psychological Medicine*, 28, 903–13.

Kivimäki, M., Vahtera, J., Thomson, L., Griffiths, A., Cox, T., and Pentti, J. 1997b: Psychosocial factors predicting employee sickness absence during economic decline. *Journal of Applied Psychology*, 82, 858–972.

Klaukka, T., Sievers, K., and Takala, J. 1982: Epidemiology of rheumatic disease in Finland in 1964–76. *Scandinavian Journal of Rheumatology*, 47, 5–13 (Suppl.).

Koskenvuo, M., Kaprio, J., Rose, R.J., Kesäniemi, A., Sarna, S., Heikkilä, K., and Langinvainio, H. 1988: Hostility as a risk factor for mortality and ischemic heart disease in men. *Psychosomatic Medicine*, 50, 330–40.

Kozlowski, S.W.J., Chao, G.T., Smith, E., and Hedlund, J. 1993: Organizational downsizing: strategies, interventions, and research implications. In C.L. Cooper and I.T. Robertson (eds) *International Review of Industrial and Organizational Psychology*. London: Wiley, 264–332.

Kranz, J. 1985: Group processes under conditions of organizational decline. *Journal of Applied Behavioral Science*, 21, 1–17.

Leigh, J.P. 1986: Correlates of absence from work due to illness. *Human Relations*, 39, 81–100.

Leigh, J.P. 1995: Smoking, self-selection and absenteeism. *Quarterly Review of Economics and Finance*, 35, 365–86.

Leiter, M.P. 1991: The dream denied: professional burnout and the constraints of service organizations. *Canadian Psychology*, 32, 547–61.

Mackenbach, J.P., Kunst, A.E., Cavelaars, A.E., Groenhof, F., and Geurts, J.J. 1997: Socioeconomic inequalities in morbidity and mortality in Western Europe. The EU Working Group on Socioeconomic Inequalities in Health. *Lancet*, 349, 1655–9.

Manning, M.R. and Osland, J.S. 1989: The relationship between absenteeism and stress. *Work and Stress*, 3, 223–35.

Marmot, M. 1994: Work and other factors influencing coronary health and sickness absence. *Work and Stress*, 8, 191–201.

Marmot, M., Feeney, A., Shipley, M., North, F., and Syme, S.L. 1995: Sickness absence as a measure of health status and functioning: from the UK Whitehall II study. *Journal of Epidemiology and Community Health*, 49, 124–30.

Marmot, M., North, F., Feeney, A., and Head, J. 1993: Alcohol consumption and sickness absence: from the Whitehall II study. *Addiction*, 88, 369–82.

Marmot, M.G. and Shipley, M.J. 1984: Inequalities in death – specific explanations of a general pattern? *Lancet*, 330, 1003–6.

Martin, J., Melzer, H., and Elliot, D. 1988: Office of population censuses and surveys. Surveys of disability in Great Britain, rep. 1 (the prevalence of disability among adults). London: HM Stationery Office.

Martocchio, J.J. 1994: The effects of absence culture on individual absence. *Human Relations*, 47, 243–62.

Mayfield, D.L. 1993: Downsizing as a mode of organizational change. In R.T. Golembiewski (ed.) *Handbook of Organizational Consultation*. New York: Marcel Dekker, 559–66.

McCullagh, P. and Nelder, J.A. 1989: *Generalized Linear Models*. London: Chapman and Hall.

Miller, T.Q., Smith, T.W., Turner, C.W., Guijarro, M.L., and Hallet, A.J. 1996: A meta-analytic review of research on hostility and physical health. *Psychological Bulletin*, 119, 322–48.

Ministry of Labour 1995: *Mitä sairauspoissaolot maksavat (What sickness absence costs)*. Tampere: Pirkan Painotuote.

Mone, M.A. 1994: Relationships between self-concepts, aspirations, emotional responses, and intent to leave a downsizing organization. *Human Resource Management*, 33, 281–98.

Mone, M.A., McKinley, W., and Barker, V.I. III 1998: Organizational decline and innovation: a contingency framework. *Academy of Management Review*, 23, 115–32.

Nicholson, N., Brown, C., and Chadwick-Jones, J. 1977: Absence from work and personal characteristics. *Journal of Applied Psychology*, 62, 319–407.

North, F., Syme, S.L., Feeney, A., Head, J., Shipley, M.J., and Marmot, M.G. 1993: Explaining socioeconomic differences in sickness absence: the Whitehall study. *British Medical Journal*, 306, 361–6.

North, F., Syme, S.L., Feeney, A., Head, J., Shipley, M.J., and Marmot, M.G. 1996: Psychosocial work environment and sickness absence among British civil servants: The Whitehall II study. *American Journal of Public Health*, 86, 332–40.

Parker, S.K., Chmiel, N., and Wall, T.D. 1997: Work characteristics and employee well-being within a context of strategic downsizing. *Journal of Occupational Health Psychology*, 2, 289–303.

Rael, E.G.S., Stansfeld, S.A., Shipley, M., Head, J., Feeney, A., and Marmot, M. 1995: Sickness absence in the Whitehall II study, London: the role of social support and material problems. *Journal of Epidemiology and Community Health*, 49, 474–81.

Romanov, K., Hatakka, M., Keskinen, E., Laaksonen, H., Kaprio, J., Rose, R.J., and Koskenvuo, M. 1994: Self-reported hostility and suicidal acts, accidents, and accidental deaths: a prospective study of 21,433 adults aged 25 to 59. *Psychosomatic Medicine*, 56, 328–36.

Russell, B. 1995: The subtle labor process and the great skill debate – evidence from a potash mine-mill operation. *Canadian Journal of Sociology*, 20, 359–85.

Sargent, A. 1989: *The Missing Workforce: Managing Absenteeism*. London: IPM.

Schalk, M.J.D. 1987: *A Challenge to Occupational Psychologists: Are We Able to Influence Short-term Absenteeism*. Tilburg: Tilburg University.

Siegler, I.C., Peterson, P.L., Barefoot, J.C., and Williams, R.B. 1992: Hostility during late adolescence predicts coronary risk factors at mid-life. *American Journal of Epidemiology*, 136, 146–54.

Siegrist, J., Peter, R., Junge, A., Kremer, P. et al. 1990: Low status control, high effort at work and ischemic heart disease: prospective evidence from blue-collar men. *Social Science and Medicine*, 31, 1127–34.

Smith, G., Hart, C., Blane, D., Gillis, C., and Hawthorne, V. 1997: Lifetime socioeconomic position and mortality: prospective observational study. *British Medical Journal*, 314, 541–6.

Smith, T.W. 1992: Hostility and health: current status of a psychosomatic hypothesis. *Health Psychology*, 11, 139–50.

Smith, T.W. 1994: Concepts and methods in the study of anger, hostility and health. In A.W. Siegman and T.W. Smith (eds) *Anger, Hostility and the Heart*. Hillsdale, NJ: Erlbaum, 23–42.

Smith, T.W. and Christensen, A.J. 1992: Hostility, health and social contexts. In H.S. Friedman (ed.) *Hostility, Coping, and Health*. Washington, DC: American Psychological Association, 33–48.

Smulders, P.G.W. 1983: Personal, nonwork and work characteristics in male and female absence behavior. *Journal of Occupational Behavior*, 4, 285–95.

Snyder, W. 1994: Hospital downsizing and increased frequency of assaults on staff. *Hospital and Community Psychiatry*, 45, 378–80.

Statistics Finland 1995a: Kuolemansyyt 1993 (Causes of death 1993). *Terveys*, 1, 32–47.

Statistics Finland 1995b: *Tilastollinen vuosikirja tuotannossa* (Statistical Yearbook of Finland). Helsinki: Statistics Finland.

Sutton, R.I. 1984: Managing organizational death. *Human Resource Management*, 22, 391–412.

Sutton, R.I. and D'Aunno, T. 1989: Decreasing organizational size: untangling the effects of money and people. *Academy of Management Review*, 14, 194–212.

Theorell, T. and Karasek, R.A. 1996: Current issues relating to psychosocial job strain and cardiovascular disease research. *Journal of Occupational Health Psychology*, 1, 9–26.

Theorell, T., Tsutsumi, A., Hallquist, J., Reuterwall, C., Hogstedt, C., Fredlund, P., Emlund, N., Johnson, J.V., and the SHEEP Study Group 1998: Decision latitude, job strain, and myocardial infarction: a study of working men in Stockholm. *American Journal of Public Health*, 88, 382–8.

Tombaugh, J.R. and White, L.P. 1990: Downsizing: an empirical assessment of survivors' perceptions in a post-layoff environment. *Organizational Development Journal*, 8, 32–43.

Unden, A.L. 1994: Social support at work. *Homeostasis in Health and Disease*, 35, 63–70.

Vahtera, J., Kivimäki, M., Koskenvuo, M., and Pentti, J. 1997: Hostility and registered sickness absence: a prospective study of municipal employees. *Psychological Medicine*, 27, 693–701.

Vahtera, J., Kivimäki, M., and Pentti, J. 1997: Effect of organizational downsizing on health of employees. *Lancet*, 350, 1124–8.

Vahtera, J., Uutela, A., and Pentti, J. 1996: The effects of objective job demands on registered sickness absence spells: do personal, social and job-related resources act as moderators?. *Work and Stress*, 10, 286–308.

Vahtera, J., Virtanen, P., Kivimäki, M., and Pentti, J. in press: Workplace as an origin of health inequalities. *Journal of Epidemiology and Community Health*.

Womack, J.P., Jones, D.T., and Roos, D. 1990: *The Machine that Changed the World*. New York: Rawson Associates.

Wong, L. and McNally, J. 1994: Downsizing the army: some policy implications affecting the survivors. *Armed Forces and Society*, 20, 199–216.

Wooden, M. and Bush, R. 1995: Smoking cessation and absence from work. *Preventive Medicine*, 24, 535–40.

World Health Organization 1992: *World Health Statistics Annual, 1991*. Geneva: WHO.

World Health Organization 1993: *World Health Statistics Annual, 1992*. Geneva: WHO.

Zaccaro, S.J., Craig, B., and Quinn, J. 1991: Prior absenteeism, supervisory style, job satisfaction, and personal characteristics: An investigation of some mediated and moderated linkages to work absenteeism. *Organizational Behavior and Human Decision Processes*, 50, 24–44.

Zapf, D., Dormann, C., and Frese, M. 1996: Longitudinal studies in organizational stress research: a review of the literature with reference to methodological issues. *Journal of Occupational Health Psychology*, 1, 145–69.

part II New Research Directions

6 An Empirical Examination of a Stress-Based Framework of Survivor Responses to Downsizing

Gretchen M. Spreitzer and Aneil K. Mishra

INTRODUCTION

During the last decade, downsizing has become the strategy favored by many companies attempting to cope with fundamental structural changes in the world economy. Although the price paid by laid-off workers has been high, the costs to employees who survive downsizing have been substantial as well (Cascio, 1993; Elshtain, 1996; Fisher, 1991). However, some survivors also report benefits from downsizing – some are energized and see an opportunity for personal growth (Emshoff, 1994; Henkoff, 1994; Isabella, 1989). Indeed, researchers have documented a range of seemingly contradictory survivor responses to downsizing. A recent theoretical paper by Mishra and Spreitzer (1998) synthesized previous research on survivor responses to downsizing and identified four general archetypes of survivor responses – cynical, fearful, obliging, and hopeful. They then developed a stress-based theoretical framework specifying the key factors that influence these four survivor archetypes. The purpose of this paper is to provide a first empirical examination of the Mishra and Spreitzer (1998) framework of survivor responses to downsizing.

The paper is organized as follows. After defining downsizing, we introduce our typology of survivor archetypes, which begins to synthesize the growing body of research on survivor responses to downsizing. We then provide an overview of our stress-based framework of survivor responses. We draw on the primary and secondary appraisal processes central to the Lazarus theory to develop our propositions, which explain how trust, empowerment, justice, and work redesign affect the range of survivor responses to downsizing delineated in our typology. We then describe our research design, discuss our results, and provide some implications for the theoretical framework.

SURVIVOR ARCHETYPES

Downsizing is defined as a purposeful reduction in the size of an organization's workforce (Cameron, Freeman, and Mishra, 1991; Cascio, 1993). Survivors can have a wide variety of responses to organizational downsizing. We draw on Farrell's (1983) exit,

Figure 6.1   Archetypes of survivor response

	Constructive	
Obliging Responses Calm, relief Committed, loyal Following orders, routine behavior "Faithful Followers"		**Hopeful Responses** Hope, excitement Optimism Solving problems, taking initiative "Active Advocates"
Passive		**Active**
Fearful Responses Worry, fear Anxiety, helplessness Withdrawing, procrastinating "Walking Wounded"		**Cynical Responses** Anger, disgust Cynicism, blaming others Badmouthing, retaliating "Carping Critics"
	Destructive	

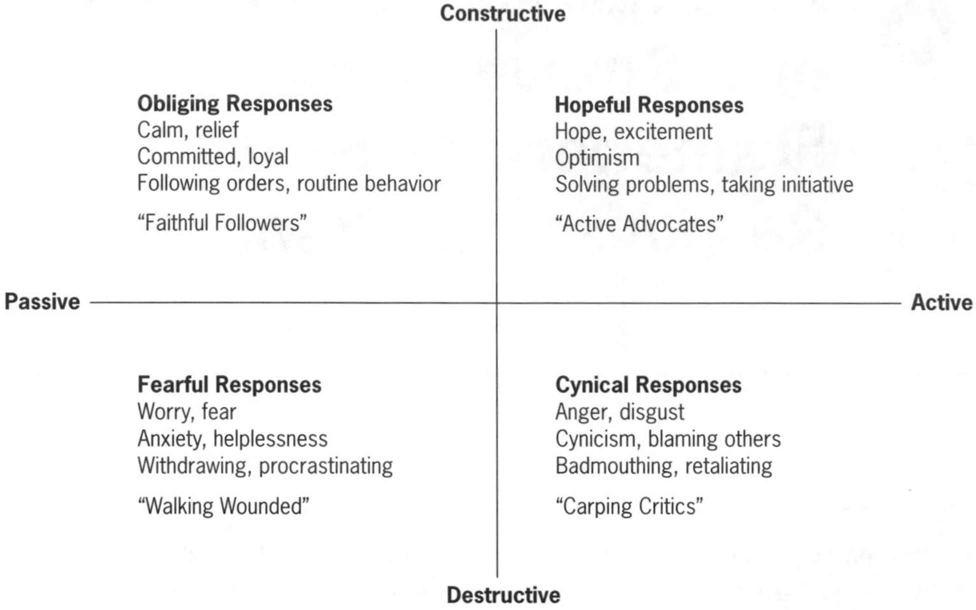

voice, loyalty, and neglect (EVLN) framework in building our typology of survivor responses. Building on Hirschman (1970), Farrell (1983) argued that responses to job dissatisfaction could be aligned along two separate dimensions: constructive/destructive and active/passive (see figure 6.1). *Constructive* survivors do not view significant threat or harm from the downsizing and are thus willing to cooperate with top management in implementing the downsizing. *Destructive* survivors feel more threatened or evaluate more potential for harm from the downsizing and are less willing to cooperate in implementing the downsizing. An *active* survivor response reflects a belief that the survivor can cope with the downsizing and is manifest in an assertive response. *Passive* survivors evaluate themselves as having less ability to cope with the downsizing and tend to take little personal initiative in responding to the downsizing.

The juxtaposition of these two dimensions results in four archetypes of survivor responses to downsizing: *fearful, obliging, cynical,* and *hopeful.* Our survivor archetypes capture the emotions, cognitions, and behaviors that survivors use to cope with the stress of downsizing (Kets de Vries and Balazs, 1997) – they are affective, cognitive, and behavioral composites. Each is described below.

The fearful response: "walking wounded"

Fearful survivors consider the downsizing as having potential for harm and believe that they have few resources to cope with the downsizing. Consequently, these survivors are destructive and passive in their response (see figure 6.1). Those manifesting a fearful response might be labeled the "walking wounded" of the organization.

Common emotions experienced by fearful survivors include fright, depression, and worry. Typical cognitive responses associated with this archetype might be anxiety (Astrachan, 1995), reduced concentration (Kets de Vries and Balazs, 1997), a sense of being out of control (cf. Folkman, 1984; Lazarus and Folkman, 1984), and helplessness (Seligman, 1975). These survivors may reduce their level of commitment to the organization, because they identify with respected co-workers and friends who have lost their jobs (Brockner et al., 1987). Behaviorally, these survivors tend to withdraw from work (Brockner, 1988) and procrastinate about decision making (Kets de Vries and Balazs, 1997). Because they believe that they have few resources to cope with the downsizing, they may attempt to "escape" through absenteeism and lateness (Robinson, 1992) or by focusing on non-work interests and activities (Withey and Cooper, 1989).

The obliging response: "faithful followers"

Similar to fearful survivors, obliging survivors, or "faithful followers," do not believe that they have the personal resources to adequately cope with the downsizing. However, unlike fearful survivors, obliging survivors view the downsizing as less threatening with less potential for personal harm. Fearful survivors believe that a downsizing effort is inimical to their interests and that nothing can be done about it. In contrast, obliging survivors believe that downsizing is basically benign, and they are willing to go along with what is expected of them because it isn't expected to lead to harm. Consequently, obliging survivors are constructive, yet passive in their responses (see figure 6.1). Emotionally, obliging survivors are not highly aroused and are likely to feel calmness or relief that they have not lost their jobs. Cognitively, these survivors are likely to be committed and loyal to the organization, in spite of the problems it may be experiencing. Behaviorally, instead of withdrawing from the organization or procrastinating, as was the case for fearful survivors, obliging survivors tend to respond by obediently following orders. Because they believe they have few personal resources for coping, these survivors are apt to willingly wait for conditions to improve and stick with the job through good times and bad (Robinson, 1992; Rusbult et al., 1988). Though they cooperate in the implementation of the downsizing, obliging survivors are mainly compliant and accommodating, accepting the goals and objectives given to them by management (Rusbult et al., 1988).

The cynical response: "carping critics"

Unlike obliging survivors discussed above, cynical survivors, or "carping critics," believe that they have the personal resources to cope with the downsizing. Like fearful survivors, cynical survivors feel personally threatened. Thus, they are active and destructive in their response (see figure 6.1). Emotionally, these survivors are highly aroused and are likely to feel anger, disgust, and resentment because they see significant potential for personal harm. This survivor archetype is cognitively manifested in a sense of moral outrage (Bies, 1987), cynicism, or blaming others (Smith et al., 1996). Cynical survivors may perceive a blatant violation of their psychological contract (Rousseau, 1995). Because they believe that they have the personal resources to cope with the downsizing, the cynical survivor's behavioral response is proactive, more so than that of the fearful or obliging survivor described above. Cynical survivors have a voice, but that voice tends to be destructive – they militate against the downsizing process rather than support it. They may challenge or "badmouth" management during the downsizing (Cameron, Freeman, and Mishra, 1993), and at the extreme, may engage in acts of vandalism, retaliation, or sabotage (Kets de Vries and Balazs, 1997; Robinson, 1992).

The hopeful response: "active advocates"

The hopeful response is the opposite of the fearful response; survivors in this quadrant believe they have the resources to cope with the downsizing and do not feel threatened by the potential for harm from the downsizing. Thus, hopeful survivors, or "active advocates," are both active and constructive (see figure 6.1). Because they do not feel particularly threatened, this archetype is manifest emotionally in terms of excitement about the future and hope that things will get better with time. Cognitively, because hopeful survivors believe they have the resources to effectively cope with the downsizing, they tend to be optimistic about what can come from the downsizing (Smith et al., 1996). They experience a sense of ownership in helping to enhance the performance of the organization (O'Neill and Lenn, 1995; Robinson, 1992). Behaviorally, this quadrant reflects active and constructive efforts of survivors to improve conditions by discussing problems or taking actions to solve problems (Rusbult et al., 1988). Rather than just following orders, as is the case with obliging survivors, hopeful survivors are not afraid to take risks or develop novel ways to improve the organization's competitiveness. Such hopeful responses have been documented in the downsizing literature as good citizenship behavior (Bies, Martin, and Brockner, 1993) and job involvement (Brockner, Grover, and Blonder, 1988).

Thus, our synthesis of the literature suggests that there are four archetypes of survivor responses to downsizing.

Hypothesis 1.   Survivor responses to downsizing can be organized into four archetypes.

A STRESS-BASED FRAMEWORK OF SURVIVORS' RESPONSES

The purpose of our theoretical framework is to explain the factors that influence the different survivor responses identified in our typology. We draw on the Lazarus theory of stress (Lazarus and Folkman, 1984) and its focus on cognitive appraisal. Through primary appraisal, survivors evaluate the potential threat of the downsizing. We posit that trust in management and a perceived just implementation of the downsizing reduce threat assessments and in turn lead to more cooperative survivor responses. Through secondary appraisal, survivors evaluate their capability for coping with the downsizing. We posit that survivor empowerment and the redesign of work will influence secondary appraisal by increasing survivors' sense that they have the capability to cope with the downsizing and in turn lead to more active responses to the downsizing. The theoretical framework is illustrated in figure 6.2.

Figure 6.2 Stress-based theoretical framework

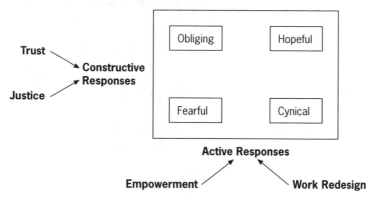

Factors shaping primary appraisal

Two factors shape the primary appraisal process by reducing the perceived threat inherent in the downsizing that in turn facilitates more constructive survivor responses. First, trust in top management minimizes the categorization of threat by helping survivors to understand and believe in management's intentions and expected behavior. Second, the perceived justness of the downsizing implementation will reduce the degree to which the downsizing is evaluated as threatening by reducing the ambiguity of the expected outcome from the encounter (cf. Folkman, 1984). Because trust in management and a perceived just implementation of downsizing both work to reduce the appraised threat inherent in downsizing, we argue that they will lead to more constructive survivor responses.

Trust in top management

Trust is defined as a willingness to be vulnerable to others (Granovetter, 1985; Lewis and Weigert, 1985) based on the prior belief that they are trustworthy (Mayer, Davis, and Schoorman, 1995; Mishra, 1996; Sitkin and Roth, 1993). Being vulnerable means that a significant potential for loss exists (Deutsch, 1973; Luhmann, 1979; Zand, 1972). Several key dimensions of trustworthiness have been documented in the management literature, including a concern for others' interests, competence, openness or honesty, and reliability (Hart and Saunders, 1997; Mayer, Davis, and Schoorman, 1995; Mishra, 1996). Each dimension additively contributes to a party's trustworthiness. A belief that management is *concerned* about the best interests of survivors leads to less threatening appraisals because survivors believe that top management is acting in the interests of survivors as well as themselves. Survivors who believe that management is *competent* may also appraise the downsizing as less threatening because they view top management as capable of enhancing the organization's competitive position. Survivors who believe that top management is *reliable* may also be less threatened because they believe that top managers will keep their promises. Finally, survivors who believe that top management is being *open and honest* about what is happening (O'Neill and Lenn, 1995) may be less threatened because uncertainty is reduced. Nevertheless, that fact that trust may be violated in each of these instances (that is, management may be self-interested, lack the skills to lead the organization through the restructuring, break its promises, or withhold important information) reflects the vulnerability of trust.

Because trust facilitates less threatening appraisals, it is likely to foster more constructive survivor responses. In general, trust allows individuals to cooperate with others because it minimizes the threat of malfeasance (Fukuyama, 1995; Golembiewski and McConkie, 1975). More specifically, a belief that top management is *concerned* about the interests of employees enhances constructive responses because survivors presumably are willing to further their own interests. When top management is *reliable* in keeping its promises and open in sharing information, uncertainty and ambiguity are reduced for survivors. Lower ambiguity and uncertainty allow individuals to work together more easily to deal with a stressful encounter (Lazarus and Folkman, 1984). A belief that top management is *competent* may also lead to constructive responses because individuals feel comfortable supporting management's vision of the future. For these reasons, higher levels of trust prior to the downsizing are likely to lead to constructive survivor responses during the downsizing process.

Hypothesis 2.   Survivors who trust top management will be likely to exhibit constructive responses.

Justice

Brockner and his colleagues have produced a significant body of research showing that perceptions of justice or fairness have a strong influence on survivors' responses to a downsizing activity (for example, Brockner et al., 1992; 1993). We discuss three kinds of justice.

Distributive justice reflects the fairness of the *outcomes* resulting from the downsizing (Brockner and Greenberg, 1990). Because distributive justice facilitates less threatening appraisals, we suggest that it will lead to more constructive survivor responses. Thus, if survivors believe that the victims of the downsizing receive fair outcomes, they will be less likely to consider top management as adversarial but rather as helpful in easing the transition for victims, and thus will respond more constructively. Furthermore, if the burdens shouldered by downsizing survivors are distributed fairly (for example, across-the-board pay cuts, budget reductions based on equality or need), survivors will feel less need to defend scarce resources and will be more likely to work constructively with management in implementing the downsizing. Sharing the burden across levels of the hierarchy creates the perception that everyone is "in this together," thus reducing defensiveness and increasing survivors' constructive behavior.

Hypothesis 3.   Survivors who appraise the downsizing as distributively just will be likely to exhibit constructive responses.

Procedural justice reflects the fairness of the *processes* used to implement the downsizing (Brockner and Greenberg, 1990). When the decision rule to determine whom to lay off is based on merit, a survivor is more likely to appraise the downsizing as predictable and hence less threatening; thus, in such cases, we expect survivors to respond more constructively. In contrast, when survivors perceive the decision rule to be politically based or random, they are less likely to see the implementation as fair and are more likely to retaliate against the injustice of the system rather than working constructively to implement the downsizing. Advance notice, another component of procedural justice (Brockner et al., 1994; Kozlowski et al., 1993), allows individuals to respond constructively because the probability of an unannounced downsizing has been minimized. Rather than feeling incapacitated by anxiety about future downsizing, if they have the assurances of advance notice, survivors can lower their defenses because they know they will be given adequate time to prepare for downsizing in the future.

> Hypothesis 4.   Survivors who appraise the downsizing as procedurally just will be likely to exhibit constructive responses.

Recent formulations of interactional justice focus on at last three types of social accounts, or verbal strategies, used to minimize the apparent severity of the encounter (Bies, 1987; Brockner and Greenberg, 1990; Tyler and Bies, 1990): (1) causal accounts that focus on credible mitigating circumstances for the downsizing (for example, "We had to lay off workers because of an economic recession that was beyond our control"); (2) ideological accounts that link the downsizing to a vision of the organization's future (for example, "Laying off workers will help improve our company's competitive advantage in the future"); and (3) penitential accounts that focus on the interpersonal treatment of those who are affected by the downsizing (for example, "We are really sorry to have had to resort to layoffs"). Research has shown that offering explanations of why the unpopular events must happen ameliorates negative reactions and promotes the belief that decision makers' actions were fair and the result of good judgment (Bies, 1987). Each of these social accounts reduces the inherent threat in the downsizing and can contribute to more constructive survivor responses.

> Hypothesis 5.   Survivors who appraise the downsizing as interactionally just will be likely to exhibit constructive responses.

Factors shaping secondary appraisal

Through secondary appraisal, individuals evaluate what, if anything, can be done to overcome or prevent harm. Beliefs about the kinds of resources available to the individual to cope with the potentially stressful encounter influence the secondary appraisal process and will lead to more active survivor responses. In this section, we describe two factors, personal beliefs about empowerment in the work role and work redesign, that we suggest will enhance survivors' evaluations that they can cope with the downsizing and in turn lead to more active survivor responses.

Empowerment

Empowerment reflects a personal sense of control in the workplace as manifested in four beliefs about the person–work relationship: meaning, competence, self-determination, and impact (Spreitzer, 1995; Thomas and Velthouse, 1990). *Meaning* reflects a sense of purpose or personal connection about work. *Competence* indicates that individuals believe they have the skills and abilities necessary to perform their work well. *Self-determination* reflects a sense of freedom about how individuals do their own work. *Impact* describes a belief that individuals can influence the system in which they are embedded. Layoffs are likely to threaten a survivor's sense of control; therefore, factors that affect a sense of control before and during downsizing are likely to be important in mitigating the helplessness often experienced by survivors during downsizing (Brockner, 1988).

We suggest that such empowered survivors will be more likely to become active participants in implementing the downsizing rather than passive recipients of a top management mandate. "People fear and tend to avoid . . . situations they believe exceed their skills whereas they get involved in activities and behave assuredly when they judge themselves capable of handling situations that would otherwise be intimidating" (Lazarus and Folkman, 1984, p. 70). Without having some sense of control over a stressful situation, individuals will withdraw into an utter state of helplessness (Greenberger and Strasser, 1986). Indeed, those who have less control over their work environment, as measured by influence over work content, deadlines, and the people they work with in accomplishing assignments exhibited greater stress as measured by coronary heart disease symptoms (Marmot, 1997). When empowered, however, employees do not feel as though they are mere "cogs" in a machine but more active shapers of the organization (Bell and Staw, 1989). Thus, we argue that the four dimensions of empowerment should help survivors feel more in control, should help them to cope with the demands of the downsizing, and hence should increase their propensity to respond more actively.

Hypothesis 6.   Survivors who feel empowered will be likely to exhibit active responses.

Work redesign

Work design changes which enhance the intrinsic quality of the survivors' work (Brockner et al., 1992) are likely to help survivors to feel more able to cope with the downsizing and thus increase the likelihood of more active responses. If the intrinsic quality of work has increased or remained constant as a result of the downsizing, survivors can focus their attention on coping with the downsizing rather than being distracted with how they can return the design of their work to previous levels of intrinsic quality (Brockner et al., 1993). Survivors may be asked to take on the responsibilities of their former co-workers, thereby increasing the perceived variety of their work (Brockner et al., 1993). Survivors may consider the use or development of the additional skills needed for the enhanced job variety as resources that can be used to help them cope with the downsizing. These newly developed skills and abilities may reduce the survivors' sense of job insecurity and thus facilitate assessments of coping ability. Hackman and Oldham (1980) have shown that more job variety can increase individual motivation about the job and in turn facilitate more flexibility and initiative, which are consistent with active survivor responses.

Hypothesis 7.   Changes in the design of work during the downsizing that increase job variety will increase the likelihood of active responses.

Survivors may also experience role overload as they struggle to complete the work formerly assigned to the victims of the downsizing (Cameron, Freeman, and Mishra, 1993; Cascio, 1993; Kozlowski et al., 1993). If these new tasks require skills and competencies that survivors have not been trained for, then survivors may be less confident in their ability to cope with the downsizing. This is not atypical, as top management rarely conducts systemic analysis of tasks and personnel before downsizing (Cameron, Freeman, and Mishra, 1993). To the extent that work demands exceed survivors' physical resources (for example, stamina) or psychological resources (for example, skills), survivors are likely to appraise their coping resources as limited (Folkman, 1984, p. 842). Believing that they have fewer resources for coping, when survivors experience role overload, they are likely to respond more passively.

Hypothesis 8.   Changes in the design of work during the downsizing that increase role overload will enhance the likelihood of passive survivor responses.

RESEARCH DESIGN

Sample and data collection procedures

In late 1996, surveys were administered to a sample of 731 aerospace workers at a plant that had recently announced a downsizing. The downsizing announcement was made approximately one month before the surveys were distributed. At this time, approximately 10 percent of the site's contract workers were laid off, and remaining employees were told that a substantial number of additional employees were going to be laid off within the next year. Some employees would be eligible for a transfer to another facility. At the time the survey was distributed, the specific non-contract employees who were to be laid off had not yet been completely identified by management. Thus, the employees who were surveyed were initial survivors of the downsizing of the contract workers.

A total of 350 workers responded for a response rate of 48 percent. Respondents were assured of the confidentiality of their response. All surveys were mailed back directly to the researchers. The population of employees sampled were 69 percent male with an average age of 42 years, 10 years of service at the company, and some college education. Analysis of the demographic data suggests that the characteristics of those responding to the surveys were virtually identical to those who did not return the survey; thus, there is little evidence of response bias.

Measures

All survey measures were assessed with seven-point Likert scales ranging from very strongly disagree to very strongly agree. To the extent possible, we used already validated scales of each variable in the model.

Independent variables

We used Mishra and Mishra's (1994) 16-item measure of trust ($\alpha = 0.97$). A sample item for each of the four dimensions include: "I believe that site management tells the truth" (openness); ". . . provides capable and competent leadership" (competence); ". . . does not try to get out of its commitments" (reliable), and ". . . would make personal sacrifices for our organization" (concern).

Our measures of distributive and procedural justice were adapted from Niehoff and Moorman (1993) measures of justice. We changed the wording to fit a downsizing context. We also created our own measure of interactional justice as no appropriate measure was available at the time the data were collected. A sample item measuring distributive justice (four items in total) is "Separated employees are being taken care of by the company." A sample item for procedural justice (three items in total) is "Decisions on who is going to be separated are being made in an unbiased manner." A sample item for interactional justice (six items in total) is "In implementing the downsizing, [this company] is offering explanations that make sense." Because many of the justice items were new or reworded, we conducted an exploratory factor analysis to make sure we were tapping three distinct constructs. The factor analysis suggested that the distributive and procedural items tapped a single construct. Thus, we created one scale to measure distributive/procedural justice ($\alpha = 0.90$) and one scale to measure interactional justice ($\alpha = 0.86$).

We used Spreitzer's (1995) 12-item measure of empowerment ($\alpha = 0.85$). Sample items for each of the four dimensions include: "The work I do is very important to me" (meaning); "I am confident about my ability to do my job" (competence); "My impact on what happens in my department is large" (impact); "I have significant autonomy in determining how I do my job" (self-determination).

As theorized, we measured two elements of job design: task variety and role overload. The measure of task variety was drawn from three items from Hackman and Oldham's (1980) job characteristics measure ($\alpha = 0.90$). A sample item is "My job allows me to do a number of different things." Role overload was drawn from the Rizzo, House, and Lirtzman (1970) scale of role characteristics ($\alpha = 0.48$). A sample item is "The performance standards for my job are too high."

Dependent variables

To measure the archetypes of survivor responses to downsizing we had to create our own measures. We asked survivors for their response to the downsizing. The hopeful response was measured by four items: "optimistic," "involved," "hopeful," and "assertive." The obliging response was measured with four items: "guilty," "relieved," "obliging," and "accommodating." The cynical response was measured with four items: "resentful," "angry," "cynical," and "bitter." The fearful response was measured with four items: "fearful," "helpless," "numb", and "paralyzed." Because these measures are new, their reliability will be discussed in the results section.

Control variables

Several additional variables were included as controls in the analyses because they may also have effects on the dependent variable. For example, a single survey item asked whether the respondent "was the primary source of income for your family." Those survivors who are the primary breadwinners in their families may feel more vulnerable in a downsizing situation and thus may respond more fearfully. An item assessing employees' educational level (measured as a seven-category scale ranging from less than high school to doctoral degree) was also included in the survey. Survivors with higher levels of education may have more employment options and thus may have more hopeful responses. The age of the employee (measured as number of years) was collected from archival sources. Older workers may believe they have fewer options in the labor market and may thus have more fearful responses. Length of service or company tenure (measured as years of employment at the organization) and gender were also collected from archival sources. Those survivors with longer tenures at the organization may have greater attachment to the firm because of their longevity and thus may have more constructive responses (Dunham, Grube, and Castaneda, 1994). Gender was also included as some research suggests that female downsizing survivors do differ from male survivors in how much they perceive threat of job loss following a downsizing (Armstrong-Stassen, 1994).

Analyses

Hypothesis 1 was assessed with a factor analysis of the 16 items developed to measure survivor responses to downsizing. Hypotheses 2 through 8 were assessed with a series of regression analyses, one for each of different survivor responses.

RESULTS

Table 6.1 contains the results of the factor analysis of the items measuring the four survivor responses to downsizing. A principal components analysis with an oblique rotation (because the archetypes were expected to be related to each other) was conducted. General support for hypothesis 1 was achieved. The results indicate that a five-factor solution emerged. As expected, clean factors emerged for the hopeful, fearful, and cynical archetypes. What was unexpected was that the items created to measure the obliging archetype split into two factors. One factor included the "obliging" and "accommodating" items. The other factor included the "guilty" and "relieved" items. This breakout suggests that survivors see guilt and relief as somewhat distinct from being obliging and accommodating. Thus, future work must focus on refining the obliging archetype. Nevertheless, the loadings for the fourth factor (made up of the guilty and relieved items) were not strong, and the resulting scale did not achieve an acceptable level of reliability (all of the other four scales achieved reliabilities in excess of 0.80). A second factor analysis without the guilty and relieved items yielded a four-factor solution with hypothesized items loading on their respective factors (see table 6.2). Thus, for the next set of analyses, only the four scales with acceptable reliability were retained.

Table 6.3 contains the means, standard deviations, and correlations for the variables in the analyses. Table 6.4 includes the regression analyses that are used to examine hypotheses 2–8. No support was found for hypothesis 2 – that trust in management would be related to more constructive survivor responses. However, this lack of support should be interpreted with caution. Trust was highly correlated with both of the justice scales. It may be that trust is an important antecedent of justice, which in turn predicts constructive survivor responses (as hypothesis 3 indicates). Indeed, in

Table 6.1 Factor analysis results: principal components with oblique rotation

	Factor 1	Factor 2	Factor 3	Factor 4	Factor 5
Cynical					
Resentful	**0.86**	−0.02	−0.05	−0.21	−0.05
Angry	**0.85**	−0.08	−0.07	−0.11	−0.07
Bitter	**0.83**	−0.00	−0.11	0.07	0.00
Cynical	**0.77**	0.08	0.10	0.23	0.11
Obliging					
Obliging	0.03	**0.90**	0.04	0.10	0.03
Accommodating	−0.04	**0.87**	0.04	−0.03	−0.08
Fearful					
Paralyzed	0.06	−0.16	**−0.81**	0.25	−0.02
Numb	0.08	−0.09	**−0.80**	0.06	−0.03
Fearful	0.08	0.05	**−0.73**	−0.31	−0.07
Helpless	0.08	0.09	**−0.63**	−0.22	0.23
Relieved					
Relieved	0.03	0.02	0.09	**0.75**	−0.23
Guilty	−0.04	0.30	−0.44	0.44	0.11
Hopeful					
Hopeful	−0.04	−0.05	−0.08	0.08	**−0.90**
Optimistic	−0.02	−0.06	0.06	0.20	**−0.86**
Assertive	0.06	0.31	0.09	−0.15	**−0.66**
Involved	−0.12	0.44	−0.01	−0.12	**−0.48**
Cronbach alpha	0.86	0.85	0.80	0.12	0.80

Table 6.2 Revised factor analysis results: principal components with oblique rotation

	Factor 1	Factor 2	Factor 3	Factor 4
Cynical				
Resentful	**0.87**	0.02	0.03	0.01
Angry	**0.86**	0.06	0.05	0.07
Bitter	**0.83**	0.02	0.09	0.01
Cynical	**0.77**	−0.05	−0.09	−0.05
Hopeful				
Hopeful	−0.05	**0.91**	0.09	0.03
Optimistic	−0.01	**0.89**	−0.06	0.07
Assertive	0.08	**0.61**	−0.11	−0.32
Involved	−0.09	**0.46**	−0.02	−0.42
Fearful				
Numb	0.03	0.06	**0.84**	0.06
Paralyzed	0.02	0.10	**0.83**	0.17
Fearful	0.04	−0.01	**0.74**	−0.14
Helpless	0.03	−0.30	**0.68**	−0.18
Obliging				
Obliging	0.01	−0.03	0.02	**−0.90**
Accommodating	−0.06	0.07	0.00	**−0.88**
Cronbach alpha	**0.86**	**0.80**	**0.80**	**0.80**

Table 6.3 Means, standard deviations, and correlations

Variable	Mean (SD)	1	2	3	4	5	6	7	8	9	10	11	12	13	14	15
Educational level	3.65 (1.18)	1.0														
Breadwinner status	0.734 (0.444)	0.12*	1.0													
Sex	1.69 (0.46)	0.14*	0.33***	1.0												
Age	42.1 (8.92)	−0.02	0.00	−0.09*	1.0											
Service	10.0 (5.8)	−0.05	0.02	0.09*	0.47***	1.0										
Procedural/distributive justice	3.83 (1.10)	0.09	0.00	−0.07	−0.02	−0.02	1.0									
Interactional justice	3.23 (1.27)	0.00	0.03	−0.07	−0.09	−0.13*	0.67***	1.0								
Trust in management	3.91 (1.47)	0.06	0.04	−0.04	0.04	0.02	0.72***	0.62***	1.0							
Empowerment	5.27 (0.793)	−0.09	−0.03	−0.07	0.13*	0.14*	0.19**	0.15**	0.26***	1.0						
Task variety	5.21 (1.26)	−0.09	0.01	0.06	0.08	0.26***	0.21***	0.29***	0.55***		1.0					
Role overload	3.96 (0.97)	−0.06	−0.01	0.09	−0.10	−0.02	0.18**	0.09	0.10	0.21**	0.16**	1.0				
Hopeful	4.42 (1.32)	0.08	−0.11*	0.00	−0.08	0.05	0.26***	0.19***	0.24***	0.26***	0.19***	0.06	1.0			
Obliging	3.83 (1.44)	−0.04	−0.06	−0.04	0.12*	0.06	0.29**	0.23***	0.20***	0.10	0.06	−0.02	0.42***	1.0		
Fearful	2.97 (1.42)	−0.21***	−0.01	0.04	0.05	0.07	−0.22***	−0.16*	−0.16**	−0.05	−0.10	0.15**	−0.25***	−0.03	1.0	
Cynical	3.49 (1.56)	−0.08	−0.02	0.10	−0.04	0.07	−0.40***	−0.34***	−0.32***	−0.14**	−0.24***	0.03	−0.23***	−0.16***	0.46***	1.0

Table 6.4 Results of regression analyses

Variable	Hopeful	Obliging	Fearful	Cynical
Controls				
Education	0.10	−0.08	−0.24***	−0.10
Primary breadwinner	0.15**	0.05	0.03	0.03
Sex	0.05	0.00	0.04	0.07
Age	−0.16**	0.09	0.07	−0.06
Years of service	0.10+	0.03	0.03	0.07
Independent variables				
Distributive/procedural justice	0.14*	0.22**	−0.06	−0.28**
Interactional justice	0.01	0.08	−0.03	−0.15*
Trust in management	0.03	0.01	0.01	0.07
Empowerment	0.20**	0.10	−0.08	−0.01
Task variety	0.05	−0.07	−0.07	−0.17**
Role overload	−0.08	−0.01	0.14*	0.10
R^2	0.16	0.10	0.10	0.23
F	5.11***	2.97***	3.06***	7.93***

Significance levels:
*** $p < 0.001$
** $p < 0.01$
* $p < 0.05$

regressions without the justice variables, trust in management was a significant predictor of each of the four survivor responses (at the 0.01 level or better for the hopeful, cynical, and obliging responses and at the 0.10 level for the fearful response). Subsequent hierarchical regression analysis revealed that the justice variables mediated trust in management in its effect on the four survivor responses.

This finding is contrary to previous research by Brockner and his colleagues who found that trust may mediate the relationship between justice and outcomes such as organizational commitment (Brockner and Siegal, 1996; Brockner et al., 1997). In our study, procedural justice, rather than trust, appears to be the mediating factor. Without the justice scales in our model, trust was a significant predictor of the survivor responses. But when justice was entered into the equation, the direct effect of trust disappeared. Clearly, understanding the relationship between trust and justice is a particularly important area to be addressed in future research.

Support was found for hypotheses 3 and 4 – that distributive (that is, fair outcomes) and procedural (that is, fair process) justice would be related to more constructive survivor responses. Because the individual scales of distributive and procedural justice were so strongly correlated, they were combined into a single scale; thus, we cannot assess their independent effects on survivor responses. However, their joint effect was found to be significantly related to the two most constructive survivor responses, the hopeful and obliging responses, and negatively related to the cynical response. This finding supports a significant amount of prior research by Brockner and colleagues indicating the importance of procedural and distributive justice in moderating survivor responses.

Modest support was found hypothesis 5 – that interactional justice would be related to constructive survivor responses. This element of justice has received much less focus in prior research on survivor responses. The findings indicate that interactional justice (that is, credible social accounts for the downsizing) is negatively related to the most destructive survivor response, the cynical archetype. In other words, if survivors do not find the rationale for the downsizing to be well thought out, well communicated, and credible, they will be more likely to respond cynically. Thus, these results indicate that interactional justice does have an important effect on survivor responses, above and beyond the effects of the well-studied distributive and procedural elements of justice.

Modest support was also found for hypothesis 6 – that empowerment would be related to active survivor responses. Empowerment was found to be related to the hopeful archetype, one of the two active responses. The more that survivors feel empowered, the more likely it was that they responded in a hopeful way. However, empowerment was not found to have an effect on the other three archetypes, even the active cynical response.

No support was found for hypothesis 7 – that task variety would be related to more active survivor responses. Task variety was found to be negatively related to the cynical survivor response, which is an active type of survivor response. In other words, the more task variety an individual experiences following a downsizing, the less cynical the individual is likely to be. The task variety likely increases the intrinsic value of the job, and thus, survivors feel less need to complain or to work actively against the goals of the downsizing. In this way, it appears that the task variety dimension of task variety influences a more constructive than active response – this is why we see a negative influence of task variety on the cynical archetype.

Modest support was found for hypothesis 8 – that role overload would be related to more passive survivor responses. Role overload was found to be significantly related to the fearful survivor response, which is very passive. In other words, the more overloaded survivors feel following a downsizing, the more passive their response.

Thus, in summary, strong support was found for hypotheses 1 (existence of four archetypes), 3 (distributive justice leading to constructive responses) and 4 (procedural justice leading to constructive responses), modest support was found for hypotheses 5 (interactional justice leading to constructive responses), 6 (empowerment leading to active responses), and 8 (role overload leading to passive responses), and no support for hypotheses 2 (trust in management leading to constructive responses) and 7 (task variety leading to active responses).

DISCUSSION

The results do indicate support for our stress-based framework of survivor responses to downsizing. Strong support was found for the existence of the four archetypes of survivor responses to downsizing: hopeful, obliging, cynical, and fearful. The three elements of justice were found to reduce the threat inherent in downsizing, facilitating more constructive survivor responses, specifically the hopeful and obliging archetypes, and discouraging the more destructive response of cynicism. Empowerment was found to be helpful in increasing survivors' perceptions that they could cope with the downsizing, facilitating the more active survivor archetype – the hopeful response. In terms of the design of work, role overload was found to increase the probability of a fearful survivor response through a reduction in an individual's perception that they can cope with the downsizing. Task variety reduced the cynical survivor response. Thus, general support was found for most of the key elements of our theoretical model.

Although we hypothesized that trust would be directly related to survivor responses, we found trust to be completely mediated by justice in its effect on survivor responses. When justice was not included in the regression equation, trust had a direct effect on survivor responses, but this effect disappeared when the justice variables were entered in the model. One possible explanation for this is that our study surveyed the survivors at the very beginning of the downsizing, when justice perceptions of the downsizing effort were initially forming and may have been influenced by trust levels that are presumably more stable. A survivor's trust level then may have shaped justice assessments that then influenced their stress responses. Future research will be necessary to test this assertion.

To gain a better understanding of the four survivor archetypes, we profile what we have learned from the analyses about each in turn.

The hopeful response

The results indicate that distributive/procedural justice and empowerment are important predictors of the hopeful archetype. The hopeful archetype is a combination of a constructive and active response so it is not surprising that variables that predict both constructive and active outcomes would come out significant. The control variables also suggest some important information about the characteristics of hopeful survivors. The hopeful survivors tend to be the primary breadwinner in their family and tend to be younger than those in other archetypes. Because they are younger, hopeful survivors may have less invested in the company and thus have less at risk in the company. Since they are younger, they also have more up-to-date skills, which would allow them to move to another employer if the need should arise. The ability to be mobile, if desired, can increase a sense of hopefulness.

The obliging response

We can say much less about the obliging response from our results. All that we know is that distributive/procedural justice increases the obliging response. It makes sense that because the obliging response is both constructive and passive that only constructive independent variables would be significant. None of the other predictors or controls was significant. Thus, future research should begin to investigate what other sorts of variables influence the obliging response. For example, individuals with certain personality traits such as high external locus of control or high self-monitoring may be more obliging as they may be prone to external cues from their superiors. At this point, however, the analyses provide little information about obliging survivors.

The fearful response

We also do not know very much about the fearful response from our results. The results indicate that role overload increases the probability of a fearful response. Those who have too many different things going on in their work are likely to be overwhelmed by a downsizing and thus may respond in a fearful way. We also know that those with less education are likely to respond fearfully. Individuals with less education may feel more vulnerable in a downsizing – that they may have limited options for employment outside of their current employer.

The cynical response

Our stress-based framework does the best job of predicting the cynical archetype. The results indicate that cynical survivors tend to see less distributive/procedural justice, less interactional justice, and less task variety. Thus, they appear to experience the downsizing as unfair and overwhelming in terms of work. They respond actively but destructively to the downsizing. However, none of the control variables was a significant predictor of the cynical survivor, so we know little else about the characteristics of the cynical survivor.

LIMITATIONS AND DIRECTIONS FOR FUTURE RESEARCH

One limitation of this research is the potential for common method bias. Survivors provided data on both the independent and dependent variables. While it would be preferable to have different referents provide different pieces of data to minimize the potential for common method bias, it is not clear conceptually who the appropriate referents would be for this research. Clearly, the survivor responses are affective variables that are most appropriately assessed by the survivors themselves. Similarly, trust and empowerment are both perceptual variables that must be self-assessed. Justice and job design may be variables that might be assessed by an appropriate other, perhaps a close co-worker, but we know from research on individual differences that different individuals differentially perceive even "objective" sorts of variables such as work design. So it is not clear how to avoid the problem of common method bias when the variables are examined from a conceptual basis.

A second limitation of the study was that the data used to test our model were cross-sectional in nature. In order to ascertain the real effects of trust, justice, empowerment, and job design, we must have longitudinal research designs. Researchers can best capture the dynamic nature of the downsizing process on survivor responses through longitudinal data collection methods. Ideally, data on the trust and empowerment of survivors should be collected prior to the downsizing announcement. Data on survivors' perceptions of justice and job redesign as well as subsequent levels of trust and empowerment should be collected as the downsizing is being implemented. Finally, data on survivors' responses should be collected after the downsizing has been implemented. Longitudinal designs will enable researchers to assess the sequence of events contributing to downsizing outcomes. Such data are also necessary for assessing causality. However, collecting longitudinal data presents a formidable challenge for researchers, because it requires that they enter the firm prior to the downsizing announcement. Many organizations, by necessity, keep their strategic plans secret prior to announcing a downsizing, making it extremely difficult to identify a study site before an announcement is made.

One particularly important step for future research is to begin to assess the effectiveness of the different survivor responses for the individuals. At first glance, the *hopeful* response may appear to be the most effective survivor response. Clearly, the hopeful response appears to be effective from an individual career perspective, because the survivor takes an active and constructive role in implementing the downsizing. However, hopeful survivors who exert a great deal of effort to help the organization may experience burnout over time and even exit the organization if management is not vigilant in identifying signs of excessive stress. As Brockner, Tyler, and Cooper-Schneider (1992) found, individuals who are the most supportive can be the most damaged by a downsizing if they are not treated fairly. Under other circumstances, a *fearful* response may provide some psychological protection for the survivor and facilitate coping. For 60-year-old employees who know they have few job alternatives and know they will eventually be laid off, a fearful response, where they can begin to psychologically withdraw from the situation, may be an effective response for their mental health (cf. Folkman, 1984). This disassociation can protect survivors against the pain of downsizing (Kets de Vries and Balazs, 1997). The *cynical* response may have mixed effects for survivors. It can help survivors feel better in the short run by allowing them to let off steam, but it may derail the survivor's career in the future. The *obliging* response may result in survivors passively responding to the wishes of management and failing to take initiative on their own. Such survivor responses increase the susceptibility for conformity and groupthink. Following these ideas, researchers could expand the theoretical framework to address and empirically examine the individual effectiveness outcomes of the survivor response typology.

Researchers also could address the effect that personality dispositions have on survivor responses. Lazarus and Folkman (1984) suggested that generalized beliefs (or personality traits) also affect primary and secondary appraisal. We focus on specific beliefs such as trust and empowerment rather than personality traits, because such beliefs are more malleable to the influence of the organization. Nevertheless, personality traits may be important moderating variables for the relationships specified in our framework. For example, Brockner, Davy and Carter (1985) and Brockner and colleagues (1993) found self-esteem to be an important moderator on survivor responses to downsizing. Moreover, Kets de Vries and Balazs (1997) suggested that hardiness can mitigate the stressful aspects of downsizing and result in more proactive and constructive survivor responses.

IMPLICATIONS FOR PRACTICE

Our theoretical framework suggests a number of strategies for managers to implement during a downsizing that may evoke more hopeful survivor responses. First, facilitating perceptions of fairness is critical for influencing the hoped for, but often elusive, outcomes of downsizing. Researchers have shown that if the downsizing is not implemented fairly, employees who are more committed will actually respond to the downsizing in more dysfunctional ways than employees who are less committed (Brockner, Tyler, and Cooper-Schneider, 1992). Thus, organizations may antagonize the employees who have the most to offer during a downsizing. Second, the framework emphasizes the importance of empowering survivors in terms of meaning, competence, self-determination, and impact during a downsizing. Empowerment provides a buffer against the threat inherent in a downsizing initiative by helping survivors feel better able to cope. However, empowerment is often eroded during downsizing efforts as job security becomes more tenuous and survivors come to see themselves more as independent contractors than valued members of the firm. Empowerment may further erode as management takes on more control, which is typical during a crisis situation (D'Aunno and Sutton, 1989; O'Neill and Lenn; 1995; Staw, Sandelands, and Dutton, 1981). The irony, then, is that downsizing may destroy the empowerment that is necessary to make or keep the organization competitive in the future. Finally, the framework does emphasize the importance of keeping the workload manageable as a downsizing is implemented. If employees feel overwhelmed, they are more likely to feel unable to cope and in turn will become fearful. At the same time, maintaining some variety in the work of survivors will help them from becoming cynical. Although the way in which the downsizing is implemented does make a difference, our framework highlights the importance of good long-term managerial relationships with employees beginning long before an announcement to downsize. In this way, effective downsizing is not a short-term fix, but rather a long-term investment in the human resources of the organization.

REFERENCES

Armstrong-Stassen, M. 1994: Coping with transition: a study of layoff survivors. *Journal of Organizational Behavior*, 15, 597–621.

Astrachan, J.H. 1995: Organizational departures: the impact of separation anxiety as studied in a mergers and acquisitions simulation. *Journal of Applied Behavioral Science*, 31, 31–50.

Bell, N.E. and Staw, B.M. 1989: People as sculptors versus sculpture. In M.B. Arthur, D.T. Hall, and B.S. Lawrence (eds) *Handbook of Career Theory*. New York: Cambridge University Press.

Bies, R.J. 1987: The predicament of injustice: the management of moral outrage. In B.M. Staw and L.L. Cummings (eds) *Research in Organizational Behavior*, vol. 9. Greenwich, CT: JAI Press, 289–319.

Bies, R., Martin, C., and Brockner, J. 1993: Just laid off, but still a good citizen? Only if the process is fair. *Employee Rights and Responsibilities Journal*, 6, 227–38.

Brockner, J. 1988: The effects of work layoffs on survivors: Research, theory, and practice. *Research in Organizational Behavior*, vol. 10. Greenwich, CT: JAI Press, 213–55.

Brockner, J., Davy, J., and Carter, C. 1985: Layoffs, self-esteem, and survivor guilt: motivational, affective, and attitudinal consequences. *Organizational Behavior and Human Decision Processes*, 36, 229–44.

Brockner, J. and Greenberg, J. 1990: The impact of layoffs on survivors: an organizational justice perspective. In J.S. Carroll (ed.) *Applied Social Psychology and Organizational Settings*. Hillsdale, NJ: Erlbaum, 45–75.

Brockner, J., Grover, S.L., and Blonder, M.D. 1988: Predictors of survivors' job involvement following layoffs: a field study. *Journal of Applied Psychology*, 73, 436–42.

Brockner, J., Grover, S.L., Reed, T.F., and DeWitt, R.L. 1992: Layoffs, job insecurity, and survivors' work effort: evidence of an inverted-U relationship. *Academy of Management Journal*, 35, 413–25.

Brockner, J., Grover, S.L., Reed, T.F., DeWitt, R.L., and O'Malley, M.N. 1987: Survivors' reactions to layoffs: we get by with a little help for our friends. *Administrative Science Quarterly*, 32, 526–41.

Brockner, J., Konovsky, M., Cooper-Schneider, R., Folger, R., Martin, C., and Bies, R. 1994: Interactive effects of procedural justice and outcome negativity and survivors of job loss. *Academy of Management Journal*, 37, 397–409.

Brockner, J. and Siegel, P.A. 1996: Understanding the interaction between procedural and distributive justice: the role of trust. In R.M. Kramer and T.R. Tyler (eds) *Trust in Organizations: Frontiers of Theory and Research*. Thousand Oaks, CA: Sage, 390–413.

Brockner, J., Siegel, P.A., Daly, J.P., Tyler, T., and Martin, C. 1997: When trust matters: the moderating effects of outcome favorability. *Administrative Science Quarterly*, 42, 558–83.

Brockner, J., Tyler, T.R., and Cooper-Schneider, R. 1992: The influence of prior commitment to an institution on reactions to perceived fairness: the higher they are, the harder they fall. *Administrative Science Quarterly*, 37, 241–61.

Brockner, J., Wiesenfeld, B.M., and Martin, C.L. 1995: Decision frame, procedural justice, and survivors' reactions to job layoffs. *Organizational Behavior and Human Decision Processes*, 63, 59–68.

Brockner, J., Wiesenfeld, B.M., Reed, T.F., Grover, S., and Martin, C. 1993: Interactive effect of job content and context on the reactions of layoff survivors. *Journal of Personality and Social Psychology*, 64, 187–97.

Cameron, K.S., Freeman, S.J., and Mishra, A.K. 1991: Best practices in white-collar downsizing: managing contradictions. *Academy of Management Executive*, 5 (3), 57–73.

Cameron, K.S., Freeman, S.J., and Mishra, A.K. 1993: Organizational downsizing. In G. Huber and W. Glick (eds) *Organizational Change and Redesign: Ideas and Insights for Improving Performance*. New York: Oxford University Press, 19–65.

Cascio, W.F. 1993: Downsizing: What do we know? What have we learned? *Academy of Management Executive*, 7 (1), 95–104.

D'Aunno, T. and Sutton, R.I. 1989: The responses of drug abuse treatment centers to financial adversity: a partial test of the threat-rigidity thesis. *Journal of Management*, 18, 117–32.

Deutsch, M. 1973: *The Resolution of Conflict: Constructive and Destructive Processes*. New Haven, CT: Yale University Press.

Dunham, R.B., Grube, J.A., and Castaneda, M.B. 1994: Organizational commitment: the utility of an integrative definition. *Journal of Applied Psychology*, 79, 370–80.

Elshtain, C. 1996: Trust me. *Training*, January, 28–33.

Emshoff, J.R. 1994: How to increase employee loyalty while you downsize. *Business Horizons*, March–April, 49–57.

Farrell, D. 1983: Exit, voice, loyalty, and neglect as responses to job dissatisfaction: a multidimensional scaling study. *Academy of Management Journal*, 26, 596–607.

Fisher, A.B. 1991: Morale crisis. *Fortune*, June 6, 70–80.

Folkman, S. 1984: Personal control and stress and coping processes: a theoretical analysis. *Journal of Personality and Social Psychology*, 46, 839–52.

Fukuyama, F. 1995: *Trust: The Social Virtues and the Creation of Prosperity*. New York: Free Press.

Golembiewski, R.T. and McConkie, M. 1975: The centrality of interpersonal trust in group processes. In C.L. Cooper (ed.) *Series of Group Processes*. New York: Wiley, 131–85.

Granovetter, M. 1985: Economic action and social structure: the problem of embeddedness. *American Journal of Sociology*, 91 (3), 481–510.

Greenberger, D.B. and Strasser, S. 1986: Development and application of a model of personal control in organizations. *Academy of Management Review*, 11, 164–77.

Hackman, J.R. and Oldham, G.R. 1980: *Work Redesign*. Reading, MA: Addison-Wesley.

Hart, P. and Saunders, C. 1997: Power and trust: critical factors in the adoption and use of electronic data exchange. *Organization Science*, 8 (1), 23–42.

Henkoff, R. 1994: Getting beyond downsizing. *Fortune*, January 10, 58–64.

Hirshman, A.O. 1970: *Exit, Voice, and Loyalty: Responses to Decline in Firms, Organizations, and States*. Cambridge, MA: Harvard University Press.

Isabella, L.A. 1989: Downsizing: survivors' assessments. *Business Horizons*, May–June, 35–41.

Kets de Vries, M.F.R. and Balazs, K. 1997: The downside of downsiding. *Human Relations*, 50, 11–50.

Kozlowski, S.W.J., Chao, G.T., Smith, E.M., and Hedlund, J. 1993: Organizational downsizing: strategies, interventions, and research implications. In C.L. Cooper and I.T. Robertson (eds) *International Review of Industrial and Organizational Psychology*, vol. 8. New York: Wiley, 263–332.

Lazarus, R.S. and Folkman, S. 1984: *Stress, Appraisal, and Coping*. New York: Springer Publishing Company.

Lewis, J.D. and Weigert, A. 1985: Trust as a social reality. *Social Forces*, 63, 967–85.

Luhmann, N. 1979: *Trust and Power*. New York: Wiley.

Marmot, M.G. 1997: Just the job for heart disease. *The Lancet*, 350, 231–2, 235–9.

Mayer, R.C., Davis, J.H., and Schoorman, F.D. 1995: An integrative model of organizational trust. *Academy of Management Review*, 20, 709–34.

Mishra, A.K. 1996: Organizational responses to crisis: the centrality of trust. In R.M. Kramer and T.R. Tyler (eds) *Trust in Organizations: Frontiers of Theory and Research*. Thousand Oaks, CA: Sage, 261–87.

Mishra, A.K. and Mishra, K.E. 1994: The role of mutual trust in effective downsizing strategies. *Human Resource Management*, 33 (2), 261–79.

Mishra, A.K. and Spreitzer, G.M. 1998: Explaining how survivors respond to downsizing: the roles of trust, empowerment, justice, and work redesign. *Academy of Management Review*, 23, 567–88.

Niehoff, B.P. and Moorman, R.H. 1993: Justice as a mediator of the relationship between methods of monitoring and organizational citizenship behavior. *Academy of Management Journal*, 36, 527–56.

O'Neill, H.M. and Lenn, D.J. 1995: Voices of survivors: words that downsizing CEOs should hear. *Academy of Management Executive*, 9 (4), 23–33.

Rizzo, J.R., House, R.J., and Lirtzman, S.I. 1970: Role conflict and ambiguity in complex organizations. *Administrative Science Quarterly*, 15, 150–63.

Robinson, S.L. 1992: Retreat, voice, silence, and destruction: A typology of behavioral responses to organizational dissatisfaction and an examination of their contextual predictors. Unpublished doctoral dissertation. Northwestern University.

Rousseau, D.M. 1995: *Psychological Contracts in Organizations: Understanding Written and Unwritten Agreements*. Thousand Oaks, CA: Sage.

Rousseau, D.M. and Anton, R.J. 1988: Fairness and implied contract obligations in termination: a policy capturing study. *Human Performance*, 1, 273–89.

Rusbult, C.E., Farrell, D., Rogers, G., and Mainous, A.G. 1988: Impact of exchange variables on exit, voice, loyalty, and neglect: an integrative model of responses to declining job satisfaction. *Academy of Management Journal*, 31, 599–627.

Seligman, M.E.P. 1975: *Helplessness*. San Francisco: Freeman.

Sitkin, S.B. and Roth, N.L. 1993: Explaining the limited effectiveness of legalistic "remedies" for trust/distrust. *Organization Science*, 4, 367–92.

Smith, C.A., Haynes, K.N., Lazarus, R.S., and Pope, L.K. 1996: In search of the "hot" cognitions: attributions, appraisals, and their relation to emotion. *Journal of Personality and Social Psychology*, 65, 916–29.

Spreitzer, G.M. 1995: Psychological empowerment in the workplace: dimensions, measurement, and validation. *Academy of Management Journal*, 38, 1442–65.

Staw, B.M., Sandelands, L.E., and Dutton, J.E. 1981: Threat-rigidity effects in organizational behavior. *Administrative Science Quarterly*, 26, 501–24.

Thomas, K. and Velthouse, B. 1990: Cognitive elements of empowerment: An "interpretive" model of intrinsic task motivation. *Academy of Management Review*, 15, 666–81.

Tyler, T.R. and Bies, R.J. 1990: Beyond formal procedures: the interpersonal context of procedural justice. In J. Carroll (ed.) *Applied Social Psychology and Organizational Settings*. Hillsdale, NJ: Erlbaum, 77–98.

Withey, M.J. and Cooper, W.H. 1989: Predicting exit, voice, loyalty, and neglect. *Administrative Science Quarterly*, 34, 521–39.

Zand, D.E. 1972: Trust and managerial problem solving. *Administrative Science Quarterly*, 17, 229–39.

7 Gender and Job Insecurity

Mina Westman

INTRODUCTION

Feelings of job insecurity may arise from changes in the organizational environment, adverse emerging trends in the labor markets, and mergers and acquisitions that result in downsizing. Marks (1994) coined the term "organizational MADness" to denote the impact of mergers, acquisitions, and downsizing, which all have vast implications and psychological costs including job insecurity. Similarly, Meyer (1995) found that mergers, acquisitions and downsizing have many consequences for individuals, including job insecurity and symptoms of strain.

Greenhalgh and Rosenblatt (1984) conceptualized job insecurity as a source of stress involving fear, potential loss, and anxiety. They defined it as an experience of being "powerless to maintain desired continuity in a threatened job situation" (p. 438). Jacobson (1987) defined the experience of job insecurity as "a perceptual phenomenon resting entirely on the individual's subjective evaluations that there is a potential threat to his or her job security" (p. 143). It is generally agreed that job insecurity is a subjective, perceptual phenomenon (Ashford, Lee, and Bobko, 1989; Greenhalgh and Rosenblatt, 1984; Hartley et al., 1991; Roskies and Louis-Guerin, 1990).

The purpose of this chapter is to examine gender differences in job insecurity research. First we will survey some of the antecedents and outcomes of job insecurity. Then we will examine the relationship between gender and job insecurity and the impact of gender on the relationship between job insecurity and outcomes. Finally, we will discuss some problems caused by job insecurity affecting women, and offer some concluding remarks. The original plan for this chapter was a review of the literature followed by suggestions for further research. The literature review revealed a dearth of information on the relationship between gender and job insecurity. Therefore this chapter draws on research into gender and stress, and gender and unemployment, and extrapolates to the relationship between gender and job insecurity.

JOB INSECURITY, STRESS AND STRAIN

Because job insecurity is considered by most researchers as a stressor or perceived stress, it is adequate to rely on stress theories to analyze this phenomenon. Lazarus and Folkman (1984) defined stress as a "relationship between the person and the environment that is appraised by the person as taxing or exceeding his or her resources and endangering his or her well-being" (p. 19). The stress aroused by such stressors as MAD is hypothesized to cause strain. Strains are reactions or outcomes resulting from the experience of stressors (Jex and Beehr, 1991). These include job insecurity and work overload.

Job insecurity originates in a critical organizational event, such as a decision to merge or to downsize, that elicits rumors about layoffs and other threatening organizational changes. This uncertainty becomes a source of chronic stress and leads to psychological strain. Now, there is another way to look at the predicted relationship between job insecurity and psychological strain – as an outcome of chronic misfit between personal characteristics and environmental characteristics (Etzion, 1988; Etzion and Westman, 1994; Maslach and Leiter, 1997; Shirom, 1989). Similarly, Hartley et al. (1991) suggested that job insecurity arises from a misfit between the level of job security that the individual experiences and the level he or she desires. Thus, job insecurity may lead to psychological strain.

According to Hobfoll (1989), stress occurs when individuals are threatened with resource loss, actually lose resources, or fail to gain resources following resource investment. A situation of continual downsizing poses a threat of resource loss to the remaining employees (for example, loss of money, self-esteem), actual loss of friends who have been laid off, and though the employees may continue to invest resources (by increasing their efforts at work) they are still uncertain as to their job security.

Utilizing Lazarus's theory of stress, appraisal and coping (Lazarus and Folkman, 1984) we claim that whereas most people perceive downsizing as an external stressor, they respond differently. Individuals' experience of job insecurity is shaped by how threatening they appraise the situation to be for them, and their expectation of other occupational opportunities opening up for them in case of a layoff.

ANTECEDENTS OF JOB INSECURITY

Previous work addressing the antecedents of job insecurity has been restricted to direct exposure to major organizational change as the cause of job insecurity. In presenting a theoretical framework of job insecurity, Greenhalgh and Rosenblatt (1984) listed restructuring, mergers, and downsizing as examples of threats that could act as antecedents. Ashford, Lee, and Bobko (1989) found a positive relationship between anticipated organizational changes and perceived job insecurity. Schweiger and Ivancevich (1985) and Buono and Bowditch (1989) argued that mergers create uncertainty and insecurity. These kinds of changes cause employees to experience anxiety and a lack of control. A major antecedent of job insecurity is downsizing. Shaw and Barrett-Power (1997) define downsizing as "a constellation of stressor events centering around pressures toward work force reductions which place demands upon the organization, work groups, and individual employees, and require a process of coping and adaptation" (p. 109). Downsizing has been found to result in feelings of job insecurity, anger, job stress, decreased organizational commitment, and lowered motivation and productivity (Brockner, 1988; Greenhalgh and Rosenblatt, 1984). Greenhalgh (1983) suggests that during downsizing, employees' sense of job security is undermined by seeing loyal co-workers dismissed. Similarly, Brockner (1988) suggests that layoffs have the potential to generate a variety of psychological states in survivors, including job insecurity and fear of additional downsizing.

OUTCOMES OF JOB INSECURITY

Job insecurity has been empirically linked to a variety of individual outcomes that can negatively impact organizations including lower levels of commitment (Ashford, Lee, and Bobko, 1989; Hartley et al., 1991; Roskies and Louis-Guerin, 1990), higher stress (Roskies and Louis-Guerin, 1990; Roskies, Louis-Guerin, and Fournier, 1993) and elevated job search behavior (Lim, 1996). Furthermore, findings show that job insecurity is related to physical and psychological strains such as somatic complaints (Greenhalgh and Rosenblatt, 1984), health problems (McGugan, 1989), job dissatisfaction (Oldham et al., 1986) and anxiety, depression, and burnout (Dekker and Schaufeli, 1995; McGugan, 1989; Westman and Etzion, 1995).

Two additional consequences of job insecurity that have not been investigated until recently are longer working hours (Lewis and Cooper, in press) and the impact of job insecurity on family members. Job insecurity has exacerbated the tendency toward long hours, as employees feel pressure to be visible in the workplace for long hours to display commitment lest they jeopardize their jobs (Bailyn, 1993; Hochschild, 1997; Lewis and Taylor, 1996). Long working hours reflect increased workloads and unrealistic deadlines as a consequence of downsizing (Worrall and Cooper, 1998).

An important different issue is the impact of job insecurity on others. When layoffs occur, other people are affected besides those laid off and the survivors who witness job insecurity: spouses, children, parents, co-workers, and friends. Findings show that the stress of job insecurity and job loss can spill over to affect other family members (Barling and Mendelson, 1999; Westman, Etzion, and Danon, 1998; Wilson, Larson, and Stone, 1993). Westman, Etzion, and Danon (1998) and Wilson, Larson, and Stone (1993) found that wives' psychological strain had increased as a result of their husbands' job insecurity. Barling and Mendelson (1999) investigated the impacts of parents' job insecurity on children. They found that parents' reported job insecurity affected children's grades at school indirectly through their beliefs in an unjust world and negative mood.

GENDER DIFFERENCES

The last twenty years have seen organizations undergo sweeping changes. Traditionally secure jobs have become insecure. The participation of women in the labor market has increased dramatically, and so has the range of occupations in which women are employed. Women are now found at all levels. Nevertheless, only a few researchers have focused exclusively on the gender differences in job insecurity and their outcomes. Some researchers have investigated the impact of unemployment and job insecurity on wives of male employees – but rarely on female employees.

Gender in stress research

This field deals with the gender differences in stress, strain, and the relationship between them. This section begins with the general impact of gender in stress research and moves on to the unique role of gender in job insecurity research. Reviewing stress research in organizations, some researchers have found little evidence of gender influences in perception of job stress and stress-strain relationships (Beehr and Schuler, 1980; Di Salvo et al., 1994; Martocchio and O'Leary, 1989). On the other hand, Jick and Mitz (1985) have suggested that the difficulty in identifying gender-related differences in workplace stress may be due to sampling bias: men are over-represented in managerial positions and women are more to be found in clerical and service jobs. This is well illustrated in Spielberger and Reheiser's (1994) finding that even though the number of men and women in their sample was similar, there were nearly twice as many men in the higher occupational level group, and more than twice as many women in the lower group. Jick and Mitz (1985) found evidence that women reported more symptoms of psychological stress than men did. They concluded from the research review that gender acts "not only as a direct predictor of the source of stress, but also as a moderator affecting how stress is perceived, what coping skills are called upon, and how stress is manifest" (p. 409). Furthermore, they pointed out that gender differences might be due either to main effects of stress or to moderating effects of gender. In the same vein, Nelson and Quick (1995) concluded from their review that women experience more occupational stress than men do because of the unique sources of stress they face (such as, lower salaries, sexual harassment). Spielberger and Reheiser (1994) found that gender-related differences in occupational stress are determined by differences in the perceived severity of specific stressors, and in the frequency that these stressors are experienced by men and women. They concluded that gender is extremely important in determining how different workplace stressors are perceived, and that men and women experience a different frequency of various stressors, depending to some extent on their occupational level. It has not been established that women are more vulnerable to stress than men, but it does appear that the family acts more strongly as a direct source of stress for women than for men.

Utilizing and giving social support is another variable that may cause gender differences in the effect of stress on outcomes. Kessler and McLeod (1984) showed that events happening to significant others are more distressing for women than for men. They suggested that because of their greater involvement in family affairs, women become more sensitive not only to the stressful events that they experience themselves, but also to those that affect other family members. Furthermore, research on social support has increasingly characterized support seeking, giving, and utilization of various sources of support as processes that involve men and women differently (Etzion, 1984).

Unemployment and job insecurity

Research into the relationships between gender and workplace stress has been incon-sistent, and the effects of globalization, downsizing, and flexible job markets on these relationships are vague. With regard to job insecurity, the effect of gender has hardly been investigated at all, so we must fall back on studies of unemployment. The data indicate that the effects of job insecurity, that is, anticipation or concern about job loss, may be as damaging as actual job loss (Latack and Dozier, 1986, among others). Depolo and Sarchielli (1987) found no differences in emotional well-being between individuals who had lost their jobs and survivors in the same organization. Cobb and Kasl (1977) reported a longitudinal study in which they found that the distress of workers was even greater when they were anticipating job loss than after they had actually lost their jobs. Dekker and Schaufeli (1995) conducted a repeated measures study of the effect of job insecurity; they found that workers who knew they would lose their job suffered fewer psychological symptoms than the survivors, who felt prolonged job insecurity. This might be due to the fact that chronic stress has been characterized as generally more persistent and intractable than acute stress regardless of the personal qualities of the individual (Frone and McFarlin, 1989). Gender is one such personal quality.

Gender and unemployment

Gender differences may play a moderating role with regard to the experience of being unemployed. Kozlowski et al. (1993) suggested that the dearth of findings on women is due to the limited number of women in the samples of studies of unemployment. Unemployed women have been found to be less affected by unemployment in compar-ison with men, because even today the traditional role of full-time housewife remains open to women (Stokes and Cochrane, 1984; Warr and Parry, 1982; Winefield and Tiggerman, 1985).

In a sample of unemployed, educated, married white-collar workers, Shamir (1985) found that men experienced more psychological difficulties than did women. This dif-ference resulted from greater financial hardship rather than from differences in the meaning and the function of work and family roles. Shamir concluded that when women did not have to provide for the family, the psychological impact of unemploy-ment was lower. Bartel and Bartel (1985) explained the differential response of men and women to unemployment in terms of gender role identity. It may be that women identify more with home and community, and less with individual careers, but this explanation remains untested.

From another angle, Conger et al. (1993) found different responses to financial stress in the form of greater hostility among men. Increasing hostility carries the potential for undermining of the spouse, thereby increasing depressive symptoms in her. Harding and Sewel (1992) found gender differences in the relationship between employment status and psychological health. In comparison with employed men in the sample, unemployed men were less psychologically healthy, reported a higher number of doctor visits, experienced greater financial stress and were less satisfied with their life. Among women, no systematic differences between the employed and the unemployed emerged other than a difference in financial stress. These findings are in contrast with those of Gallie and Vogler (1989) who reported that the relationship between employment status and psychological health was very similar for men and women.

Perrucci, Perrucci, and Targ (1997) investigated the impact of plant closing on men and women, shortly after the closing and twelve months after the closing. They found no gender differences in psychological effects and family relations. Similarly, in a study of Dutch technical college graduates, Schaufeli and van Yperen (1992) found that the association between employment status and psychological distress was similar for men and women. They attributed this result to the high correlation among women between level of education and egalitarian sex-role attitudes.

Gender and job insecurity

Little research exists on the differential impact on men and women of unemployment and even less on the impact of job insecurity. Hartley et al. (1991) stated that most of the studies on job insecurity "have focused almost exclusively on male workers" adding that "the pattern of full employment without interruption is predominantly a male pattern and, for example, it could be that males as a group react to and cope with job insecurity differently from women" (p. 202). Investigating the impact of job insecurity on managers, Roskies and Louis-Guerin (1990) found that sex bore no significant relationship to perceived job insecurity.

Concerning the importance of job insecurity, Harpaz (1990) and Scozzaro and Subich (1990) found no gender differences in the importance attributed to job insecurity. A few researchers (Bridges, 1989; Elizur, 1994; Tolbert and Moen, 1998), have found gender differences in the importance of job insecurity – but in opposite directions. Whereas Elizur (1994) showed that females ranked the importance of job insecurity higher than males did, Bridges (1989) and Tolbert and Moen (1998) found that males attributed higher importance to job insecurity than females did. The divergent results may be explained by differences in the definitions of job insecurity and the populations investigated.

Looking at coping among employees six months after a merger, Cartwright and Cooper (1993) found gender differences in managers' coping patterns. Women used more maladaptive coping strategies (increased smoking, drinking, and eating) than men. Further, whereas women tended to use more "home-based" coping strategies (exercises, sports, etc.), men used social support, and talking with spouse or friend more than did women. The authors suggested that two-career couples did not take sufficient time for the woman to talk about her career because the male's career remained dominant. Vingerhoets and Van Heck (1990) have also explored gender differences in coping and found that men engaged more in problem-focused coping strategies such as planned and rational actions, positive thinking, and personal growth. Women engaged more in emotion-focused coping strategies such as seeking social support, self-blame, expression of emotions and wishful thinking. Therefore, the impact of gender on the outcomes of unemployment and job insecurity may be mediated by the coping strategies.

Two recent studies using similar definitions of job insecurity but different samples investigated the impact of gender on perceived job insecurity and on the relationships between job insecurity and outcomes (Rosenblatt, Talmud, and Ruvio, 1999; Westman, Etzion, and Danon, 1998). Rosenblatt, Talmud, and Ruvio (1999) investigated gender effects on job insecurity in a sample of 385 Israeli schoolteachers (263 women and 112 men). They found that gender affected both the experience of job insecurity and its impact on work attitudes. Men were more insecure than females. Gender differences were also found in the profile of job insecurity: men emphasized financial concerns and making significant impact, whereas women expressed concerns about intrinsic facets of their jobs such as work content and work schedule. Furthermore, job insecurity affected work attitudes differently for men and women: for women, all the investigated job attitudes (commitment, tendency to quit, resistance to change, perceived performance and perceived organizational support) were adversely affected by job insecurity, whereas for men, only commitment, intention to leave, and resistance to change were affected. The authors related their conclusions to three sociological gender theories – the patriarchy theory, theories of gendered occupations and jobs, and a theory of gendered organizations – and suggested that research into job insecurity be based on sociological theories as well as stress theories.

Westman, Etzion, and Danon (1998) examined 98 married couples working in the same organization and facing the same stressful events and threats of job insecurity. They investigated the impact of job insecurity on burnout at the time when the organization was undergoing a continuous downsizing process. Some employees had already been laid off, and the organization was facing further cuts. Job analysis showed that in 46 percent of the couples, husband and wife held jobs of the same status, in 35 percent of couples the husband's job was of higher status than the wife's, and in 19 percent the wife's job was higher status than the husband's. Harris (1988) found a similar pattern: female respondents had, on average, less education and reported lower income than did male respondents.

Whereas Harris (1988) focused on women, and a few studies have investigated the contribution of gender to prediction of the outcomes of job insecurity, Westman, Etzion, and Danon (1998) compared the same number of husbands and wives with regard to their perception of job insecurity and the impact of gender on the relationship between job insecurity and burnout. Wives were found to be significantly more burned out than their husbands, although there was no difference in perceived *job* insecurity between husbands and wives. Positive correlations were found between husbands' and wives' job insecurity, indicating that job insecurity presented a common stressor to the couple. Structural equation modeling (SEM) showed, as predicted, that the husband's job insecurity increased his own burnout whereas the wife's job insecurity did not have a significant impact on her own burnout. Though both partners experienced a similar level of job insecurity due to the frequent downsizing in the organization for which both of them worked, job insecurity had a significant effect only on husbands' burnout.

The absence of an adverse impact of job insecurity on the wives may be due to differences in the ways men and women react to economic hardships. Conger et al. (1993) found that whereas for the most part, men's reports on undesirable life events concerned work and financial status, wives related mainly to events in the arena of family and friends. The authors concluded that women might still consider family and friends to be their primary responsibility, and financial matters only a secondary responsibility. Furthermore, despite social changes in family roles many men still regard themselves as "good providers" (Bernard, 1981), perceiving the importance of bread-winning to their identity. Loscocco (1997) as well as Gerson (1993) depicted men who subscribe to the ideal type of traditional manhood, claiming the breadwinner role to themselves, downplaying their wives' economic contributions, and securing the privilege and power of traditional manhood. The importance of the breadwinner role to men's consciousness might have caused their elevated burnout when faced with job insecurity.

It is worth mentioning that in the Westman, Etzion, and Danon (1998) study, wives reported higher initial levels of burnout than their husbands, and wives were mostly lower in the organizational hierarchy than their husbands. Thus, women may have found their jobs to be less involving and less central to their self-image (Bailyn, 1993; Etzion and Bailyn, 1994). Kuhnert and Palmer (1991) found that employees who define themselves mostly by their job had more difficulty handling perceived job insecurity because not only their income was threatened but also their identity. In general, defining oneself by a job is more typical of men than of women.

However, in previous studies (Etzion, 1987, 1988) when job levels of men and women were carefully controlled, women managers were still found to be more burned out than their male counterparts, and women's burnout was highly correlated with home pressures and career-family conflict. Although wives' burnout was not affected by their own job insecurity, they may have been burning out from other job stressors and from stressors in family and social life (Etzion, 1988). Furthermore, Westman, Etzion, and Danon (1998) found that wives' burnout was directly affected by their husbands' burnout, a crossover effect. This is in accord with the conclusion by Rook, Doodley, and Catalano (1991) that an increase in wives' symptomatology in response to their husbands' job stressors was related to wives' emotional investment in their husbands. This corroborates the findings of crossover of burnout (Westman and Etzion, 1995) and depression (Westman and Vinokur, 1998) from husbands to wives. Thus we may conclude that in Westman, Etzion, and Danon's study job insecurity had an indirect effect on wives through their husbands' burnout.

Another plausible explanation of the divergent findings relates to the outcome measures. Rosenblatt, Talmud, and Ruvio (1999) found that job insecurity affected various outcomes differently for males and females, but Westman, Etzion, and Danon (1998) measured only a single possible outcome; perhaps wives' job insecurity affected outcomes not measured in the study.

CONCLUSIONS

The proposition that job insecurity does not affect all individuals uniformly (Ashford, Lee, and Bobko, 1989; Greenhalgh and Rosenblatt, 1984) has rarely been tested empirically. Neither theory nor empirical evidence gives adequate guidance on how gender differences may be expected to affect the impact of job insecurity. Research results concerning the relationships between gender and job insecurity are contradicting and inconclusive.

The major social change driving research in the last several decades has been the growth of women's participation in all areas of the labor market, and associated changes in families; the most significant recent development has been the erosion of job security. A secure income is one of the most fundamental needs of a family but research on the impact of gender on job insecurity is scarce and inconclusive. However, the available findings indicate that gender differences do exist, and that gender may be a crucial issue in the job insecurity domain.

There are three aspects of the relationship between gender and job insecurity that merit further research because of its societal implications: the impact of job insecurity on gender roles; the impact of long working hours on women; and the impact of job insecurity on the family.

The impact of job insecurity on gender roles

A possible positive outcome of the erosion of job security may be a challenge to the implicit contract that men will provide economically for their family in return for domestic services (Pateman, 1997). Widespread job insecurity may bring about changes that women's participation in the labor force could not achieve. According to Lewis and Cooper (1999), the men's role as family provider is already being challenged to some extent, as men can no longer count on a lifelong secure income. One possibility then, is that as non-permanent jobs become the norm, it will no longer be possible to ascribe priority to one partner's job. More women will perceive themselves as sole or co-providers. Rising long-term job insecurity may force families to reassess gender identities and roles in relation to family and work.

The impact of long working hours on gender occupational roles

Traditionally it has been less legitimate for mothers of young children to work long hours than it has been for fathers, but increasingly, in order to compete, mothers as well as fathers appear to be working long hours. Earnshaw, Amunson and Borgen (1990) found that, in comparison with men, professional women who experienced job insecurity reported working harder at their jobs in order to keep them. This is an important issue that may exacerbate work-home conflict.

The impact of job insecurity on family members

Another consequence of job insecurity that has not been investigated until recently is the impact of job insecurity on family members. As research suggests that men's stress may be more contagious than women's stress (Johnson and Jackson, 1998; Jones and Fletcher, 1993), women will be disproportionately affected by husbands' job insecurity. More research is needed on the impact of job insecurity on family members.

Information about the contribution of gender will enrich our knowledge of job insecurity. The prevalence of mergers and downsizing in the recent past, and the prospect that this will continue (Cooper, 1998; Freeman and Cameron, 1993), makes understanding its impact an important research objective. Furthermore, as the experience of job insecurity becomes prevalent, and the number of women affected increases, the need for a thorough study of its effects becomes urgent. Following Rosenblatt, Talmud, and Ruvio (1999), we suggest that one possible implication of these studies is that occupational stress theories that provide the basis for job insecurity research are not sufficient for a full understanding of the impact of job insecurity and that sociological theories (such as gender theory) are needed as well.

For a better understanding of the impact of job insecurity on outcomes, we need more research, including more variables, especially from the non-work spheres of life, that might shed light on the processes. Furthermore, we recommend that future research employ a longitudinal design in order to better elucidate the dynamics of the impact of gender on perceived job insecurity and its consequences.

REFERENCES

Ashford, S.J., Lee, C., and Bobko, P. 1989: Control, causes, and consequences of job insecurity: a theory-based measure and substantive test. *Academy of Management Journal*, 4, 803–29.

Bailyn, L. 1993: *Breaking the Mold: Women, Men, and Time in the New Corporate World*. New York: Free Press.

Barling, J. and Mendelson, M.B. 1999: Parents' job insecurity affects children's grade performance via the mediating effects of beliefs in an unjust world and negative mood. *Journal of Occupational Health Psychology*, 4, 347–55.

Bartel, M. and Bartel, R. 1985: An integrative perspective on the psychological response of women and men to unemployment. *Journal of Economic Psychology*, 27–49.

Beehr, T.A. and Schuler, R. 1980: Stress in organizations. In K. Rowland and G. Ferris (eds) *Personnel Management*. Boston: Allen and Bacon, 390–419.

Bernard, J. 1981: The good provider role: its rise and fall. *American Psychologist*, 36, 1–12.

Bridges, J. 1989: Sex differences in occupational values. *Sex Roles*, 20, 205–11.

Brockner, J. 1988: The effects of work layoffs on survivors: research, theory, and practice. *Research in Organizational Behavior*, 10, 213–55.

Buono, A.F. and Bowditch, J.L. 1989: *The Human Side of Mergers and Acquisitions: Managing Collisions between People, Cultures, and Organizations*. San Francisco, CA: Jossey-Bass.

Cartwright, S. and Cooper, C.L. 1993: The psychological impact of mergers and acquisition on the individual: a study of building society managers. *Human Relations*, 46, 327–47.

Cobb, S. and Kasl, S.V. 1977: *Termination: The Consequences of Job Loss*. Cincinnati: NIOSH.

Conger, R.D., Lorenz, R.O., Edler, G.H., Simons, R.L., and Xiaojia, G.E. 1993: Husband and wife differences in response to undesirable life events. *Journal of Health and Social Behavior*, 34, 71–88.

Cooper, C.L. 1998: The psychological implications of the changing pattern of work. *RSA Journal*, 1 (4), 74–8.

Dekker, S.W. and Schaufeli, W.B. 1995: The effect of job insecurity on psychological health and withdrawal: a longitudinal study. *Australian Psychologist*, 30, 57–63.

Depolo, M. and Sarchielli, G. 1987: Job insecurity, psychological well-being, and social representation: a case of cost sharing. In H.W. Schroiff and G. Debus (eds) *Proceedings of the West European Conference on the Psychology of Work and Organizations*. Amsterdam: Elsevier.

Di Salvo, V., Lubbers, C., Rossi, A.M., and Lewis, J. 1994: The impact of gender on work-related stress. In P.L. Perrewe and R. Crandall (eds) *Occupational Stress: A Handbook*. New York: Taylor & Francis, 39–50.

Earnshaw, A.R., Amundson, N.E., and Borgen, W.A. 1990: The experience of job insecurity for professional women. *Journal of Employment Counseling*, 27, 3–18.

Elizur, D. 1994: Gender and work values: a comparative analysis. *Journal of Social Psychology*, 2, 201–12.

Etzion, D. 1984: Moderating effect of social support on the stress-burnout relationship. *Journal of Applied Psychology*, 69, 615–22.

Etzion, D. 1987: Burning out in management: a comparison of women and in matched organ-positions. *Israel Social Science Research Journal*, 5, 147–63.

Etzion, D. 1988: The experience of burnout and work/non-work success in male and female engineers: a matched-pairs comparison. *Human Resource Management*, 27, 163–79.

Etzion, D. and Bailyn, L. 1994: Patterns of adjustment to the career/family conflict of technologically trained women in the US and Israel. *Journal of Applied Social Psychology*, 24, 1520–49.

Etzion, D. and Westman, M. 1994: Social support and sense of control as moderators of the stress-burnout relationship in military careers. *Journal of Social Behavior and Personality*, 9, 639–56.

Freeman, S.J. and Cameron, K.S. 1993: Organizational downsizing: a convergence and reorientation framework. *Organization Science*, 4, 10–29.

Frone, M.R. and McFarlin, D.B. 1989: Chronic occupational stressors, self focused attention and well-being: testing a cybernetic model of stress. *Journal of Applied Psychology*, 74, 876–993.

Gallie, D., and Vogler, C. 1989: Labor market deprivation, welfare and collectivism: the social change and economic life initiative. Working Paper 7, Economic and Social Research Council.

Gerson, K. 1993: *No Man's Land: Men's Changing Commitment to Work and Family*. New York: Basic Books.

Greenhalgh, L. 1983: Managing the job insecurity crisis during organizational retrenchment. *Journal of Applied Behavioral Science*, 18, 155–70.

Greenhalgh, L. and Rosenblatt, Z. 1984: Job insecurity: toward conceptual clarity. *Academy of Management Review*, 9, 438–48.

Harding, L. and Sewel, J. 1992: Psychological health and employment status in an island community. *Journal of Occupational and Organizational Psychology*, 65, 269–75.

Harris, M.M. 1988: Sex differences in psychological well-being during a facility closure. *Journal of Management*, 14, 391–402.

Harpaz, I. 1990: The importance of work goals: an international perspective. *Journal of International Business Studies*, 21, 75–93.

Hartley, J., Jacobson, D., Klandermans, B., and Van Vuuren, T. 1991: *Job Insecurity: Coping with Job at Risk*. London: Saga.

Hobfoll, S.E. 1989: Conservation of resources: a new attempt at conceptualizing stress. *American Psychologist*, 44, 513–24.

Hochschild, A. 1997: *The Time Bind: When Work becomes Home and Home becomes Work*. New York: Holt.

Jacobson, D. 1987: A personological study of the job insecurity experience. *Social Behavior: An International Journal of Social Psychology*, 2, 143–55.

Jex, S.M. and Beehr, T.H. 1991: Emerging theoretical and methodological issues in the study of work-related stress. *Research in Personnel and Human Resources Management*, 9, 311–65.

Jick, T.D. and Mitz, L.E. 1985: Sex differences in work stress. *Academy of Management Review*, 10, 408–20.

Johnson, A. and Jackson, P. 1998: A longitudinal investigation into the experience of male managers who have re-entered the workforce after redundancy, and their families. *Proceedings of the International Work Psychology Conference*, Sheffield, July.

Jones, E. and Fletcher, B. 1993: An empirical study of occupational stress transmission in working couples. *Human Relations*, 46, 881–902.

Kessler, R.C. and McLeod, J.D. 1984: Sex differences in vulnerability to undesirable life events. *American Sociological Review*, 49, 620–31.

Kozlowski, W.J., Chao, G.T., Smith, E.M., and Hedlund, J. 1993: Organizational downsizing: strategies, interventions, and research implications. In C.L. Cooper and I.T. Robertson (eds) *International Review of Organizational Psychology*. New York: Wiley, 8, 263–332.

Kuhnert, K.W. and Palmer, D.R. 1991: Job security, health, and the intrinsic and extrinsic characteristics of work. *Group and Organizational Studies*, 16, 178–92.

Latack, J.C. and Dozier, J.B. 1986: After the ax falls: job loss as a career transition. *Academy of Management Review*, 11, 375–92.

Lazarus, R. and Folkman, S. 1984: *Stress, Appraisal, and Coping*. New York: Springer.

Lewis, S. and Cooper, C. 1999: The work-family research agenda in changing contexts. *Journal of Occupational Health Psychology*, 4, 382–93.

Lewis, S. and Taylor, K. 1996: Evaluating the impact of friendly employment policies: a case study. In S. Lewis and J. Lewis (eds) *The Work Family Challenge: Rethinking Employment*. London: Sage, 112–27.

Lim, V.K.G. 1996: Job insecurity and its outcomes: moderating effects of work-based and non-work-based social support. *Human Relations*, 49, 171–93.

Loscocco, K.A. 1997: Work-family linkages among self-employed women and men. *Journal of Vocational Behavior*, 50, 204–26.

Marks, M.L. 1994: *From Turmoil to Triumph*. New York: Lexington.

Martocchio, J.J. and O'Leary, A.M. 1989: Sex differences in occupational stress: a meta-analytical review. *Journal of Applied Psychology*, 74, 495–501.

Maslach, C. and Leiter, M.P. 1997: *The Truth about Burnout*. San Francisco, CA: Jossey-Bass.

McGugan, P. 1989: *Beating Burnout: The Survival Guide for the 90's*. London, ON: Potentials Press.

Meyer, G.J. 1995: *Executive Blues: Down and Out in Corporate America*. New York: Franklin Square Press.

Nelson, D.L. and Quick, J.C. 1985: Professional women: are distress and disease inevitable? *Academy of Management Review*, 10, 206–13.

Oldham, G.R., Julik, C.T., Ambrose, M.I., Stepina, L.P., and Brand, J.F. 1986: Relations between job facet comparisons and employee relations. *Organizational Behavior and Human Decision Processes*, 38, 28–47.

Pateman, C. 1997: Beyond the sexual contract. In G. Dench (ed.) *Rewriting the Sexual Contract*. London: Institute of Community Studies.

Perrucci, C.C., Perrucci, R., and Targ, D.B. 1997: Gender in the economic, psychological and social effects of plant closing in an expanding economy. *The Social Science Journal*, 34, 217–33.

Rook, S.K., Doodley, D., and Catalano, R. 1991: Stress transmission: the effects of husbands' job stressors on emotional health of their wives. *Journal of Marriage and the Family*, 53, 165–77.

Rosenblatt, Z., Talmud, I., and Ruvio, A. 1999: The gender-based framework of the experience of job insecurity and its effects on work attitudes. *European Journal of Work and Organizational Psychology*, 8, 197–217.

Roskies, E. and Louis-Guerin, C. 1990: Job insecurity in managers: antecedents and consequences. *Journal of Organizational Behavior*, 11, 345–9.

Roskies, E., Louis-Guerin, C., and Fournier, C. 1993: Coping with job insecurity: how does personality make a difference? *Journal of Organizational Behavior*, 14, 617–30.

Schaufeli, W.B. and Van Yperen, N.W. 1992: Unemployment and psychological distress among graduates: a longitudinal study. *Journal of Occupational and Organizational Psychology*, 65, 291–305.

Schweiger, D.L. and Ivancevich, J.M. 1985: Human resources: the forgotten factor in mergers and acquisitions. *Personnel Administrator*, 47–61.

Scozzaro, P.P. and Subich, L.M. 1990: Gender and occupational sex-type differences in job outcome factor perceptions. *Journal of Vocational Behavior*, 36, 109–19.

Shamir, B. 1985: Sex differences in psychological adjustment to unemployment and reemployment: a question of commitment, alternatives or finance? *Social Problems*, 33, 67–79.

Shaw, J.B. and Barrett-Power, E. 1997: A conceptual framework for assessing organization, work group, and individual effectiveness during and after downsizing. *Human Relations*, 50, 109–27.

Shirom, A. 1989: Burnout in work organizations. In C.L. Cooper and I. Robertson (eds) *International Review of Industrial and Organizational Psychology*. New York: Wiley, 26–48.

Spielberger, C.D. and Reheiser, E.C. 1994: The job stress survey: measuring gender differences in occupational stress. *Journal of Social Behavior and Personality*, 9, 199–218.

Stokes, G. and Cochrane, R. 1984: A study of the psychological effects of redundancy and unemployment. *Journal of Occupational Psychology*, 57, 309–22.

Tolbert, P.S. and Moen, P. 1998: Men's and women's definitions of "good" jobs: similarities and differences by age and across time. *Work and Occupations*, 25, 168–94.

Vingerhoets, A.J. and Van Heck, G. 1990: Gender, coping and psychosomatic symptoms. *Psychological Medicine*, 20, 125–35.

Voydanoff, P. 1990: Economic distress and family relations: a review of the eighties. *Journal of Marriage and the Family*, 52, 1099–115.

Warr, P.B. and Parry, G. 1987: Paid employment and women's psychological well-being. *Psychological Bulletin*, 91, 498–516.

Westman, M. and Etzion, D. 1995: Crossover of stress, strain and resources from one spouse to another. *Journal of Organizational Behavior*, 16, 169–81.

Westman, M. and Vinokur, A. 1998: Unraveling the relationship of distress levels within couples: common stressors, emphatic reactions, or crossover via social interactions? *Human Relations*, 51, 137–56.

Westman, M., Etzion, D., and Danon, E. 1998: Downsizing and the crossover of burnout in married couples employed by the same organization. Working Paper 1/98. The Israel Institute of Business Research.

Wilson, M.S., Larson, J.H., and Stone, K.L. 1993: Stress among job insecure workers and their spouses. *Family Relations*, 42, 74–80.

Winefield, A.H. and Tiggerman, M. 1985: Psychological correlates of employment and unemployment: effects, predisposition factors, and sex differences. *Journal of Occupational Psychology*, 58, 229–42.

Worrall, L. and Cooper, C.L. 1998: *The Quality of Working Life: 1998 Survey of Managers' Changing Experiences*. London: Institute of Management.

8 Ethical Problems in Downsizing

Zehava Rosenblatt and Zachary Schaeffer

INTRODUCTION

Like most other human behaviors, organizational management involves ethical aspects. Effectively managing social contexts requires that not only laws and regulations be effectuated but values and ethical principles as well. Yet even when endorsed ethical tenets are perceived as universal, a variety of situations exist where these ethical principles are particularly problematic.

Organizational downsizing is a notable example. Hosmer (1987) has listed downsizing (in addition to plant closing and job exporting) as one of the most dramatic and most complex ethical issues in human resource management. Downsizing is often a stressful event where resources diminish and various interests of potential stakeholders are in direct conflict. As a result of the fight over scarce resources, the more powerful interests – not necessarily the more *just* ones – prevail, while others are belittled and crushed. Such processes represent ethical problems, that is, as "the harm caused to other people in ways outside their own control" (Hosmer, 1994, p. 18).

In addition, ethical problems might be linked to inconsistencies and paradoxes characterizing declining organizations. In contrast to traditional organizational theorists, recent authors acknowledged that there is much inconsistency in the way organizations operate (for example, Quinn and Cameron, 1988). Authors contend that organizations do more than one thing at a time, employing a large arsenal of surviving strategies, which are not necessarily mutually complementary.

During decline-triggered downsizing, it is expected that these discrepancies will surface more conspicuously owing to increased ambiguity, uncertainty, job insecurity and heightened infighting (Rosenblatt and Nord, 1999). It is likely, therefore, that during downsizing executives will act less consistently and systematically than during routine times. Miller and Friesen (1980; 1983), for example, showed that while organizations adapt to environmental changes by shifting back and forth between periods of momentum and revolution, during decline executives exhibit more extreme responses, alternating between innovation and stagnation.

These seemingly extreme behavioral patterns and inconsistencies are best captured in terms of paradoxes characterizing downsizing as listed by Levine (1979). These include (1) *the participation paradox*, where employees partake in decision-making processes that are liable to entail the elimination of their own jobs, and (2) *the tooth fairy syndrome*, where employees refuse to face reality as is evident in their optimism that the situation will be restored in which laid off workers will be rehired.

Likewise, Cameron, Freeman, and Mishra (1991) describe organizational downsizing paradoxes within the context of downsizing strategies. Following downsizing in the American automotive industry they concluded that the most effective downsizing strategy entailed internal self-contradiction, as captured in the following assertions: (1) downsizing initiatives ought to emanate from the top but also from lower organizational echelons; (2) downsizing stresses short-term across-the-board cutbacks, but also long-term and selective; (3) downsizing strategy accentuates the plight of laid-off employees and simultaneously emphasizes survivors' unique needs; (4) downsizing strategy aims at cutting through the organization but it also brings about cutbacks in institutions extraneous to the organization; (5) downsizing strategies aim at generating small, semi-autonomous, and leaner organizations but seek to generate large integrative organizations; (6) downsizing eliminates mid-range management and facilitates decentralized decision-making flow – successful organizations, however, tend to also merge units, hence become larger and not the least centralized; (7) successful downsizing means carrying through goals, but often this means is perceived as an end unto itself.

The above-listed paradoxes explicitly clarify the way in which contradictory forces constitute the backdrop against which ethical dilemmas counteract with a multitude of interests during downsizing. These dilemmas mirror the myriad of conflicting interests whose magnitude increases chiefly during decline and downsizing. Consequently, stakeholders' proneness to adversity becomes apparent.

This present article addresses ethical problems involved in organizational downsizing. First, the downsizing phenomenon is briefly described in respect of its proneness to ethical problems. Second, the adverse effects of downsizing on ethics in organizations are illustrated. Third, downsizing-generated ethical dilemmas are presented; and fourth, their managerial implications are discussed. Finally, conclusions pertaining to conditions under which ethical principles can be upheld during downsizing are proposed.

PRONENESS OF DOWNSIZING TO ETHICAL PROBLEMS

Organizational downsizing is defined as an intended and systematic reduction in the workforce with a view to enhancing performance (Kozlowski et al., 1993), fulfilling shareholders' profit-maximizing expectations (De Meuse, Vanderheiden, and Bergmann, 1994; Lee, 1997), or being in vogue by way of organizational mimicking or cloning (McKinley, Sanchez, and Schick, 1995). A wider perspective perceives downsizing as a planned elimination of roles or jobs, abrogation of entire units, and flattening organizational structures or reducing costs, all of which engender downscaling of organizational activities (Cascio, 1993).

Whether downsizing is generated by reactive response to decline or by proactive restructuring, it is often associated with ethical violation and abuse. Powell (1998, p. 95) describes an abusive organization as one that "operates with callous disregard for its employees, not even displaying what might be considered a minimum amount of concern for their human needs." He also contends that the number of abusive organizations is increasing. This is evidenced by the sheer number of organizations subject to pressures from competitors, financiers, or governments, resulting in downsizing, rightsizing, re-engineering, etc. From the employees' perspective, the acute need to stay, notably in the framework of often depressed labor markets and recessed economies, fuels a variety of abusive and unethical behaviors.

The above description of crisis-triggered organizational abuse points to an assumed association between organizational *failure* and ethical problems. Ingredients of this association are extrapolated from research findings linking corporate *success* with adherence to ethics. Deshpande (1996), for example, notes that executives associate business success with a conducive ethical climate. Likewise, Willa (1994) has shown that ethical behavior is related to productivity at work in public-sector organizations. Further, in a study on top management of multinational subsidiaries, extra-role behavior was shown to be affected by executives' perception of procedural justice (Kim and Mauborgne, 1996). Although there is some evidence of success-derived ethical breaching (for example, the "Bathsheba Syndrome," see Ludwig and Longenecker, 1993), most linkages between corporate performance and ethical violations refer to business failures, not successes. Taken together, these findings raise a question regarding the unique characteristics inherent in the downsizing phenomenon that elicits ethical problems. Next we will identify and discuss some of these downsizing characteristics, including high stress, rigidity in response to threat, faulty decision making, and the dissolution of the psychological contract.

High stress

Downsizing organizations often operate under heightened stress levels. First, stress might be induced by decision-makers' frustrations. Despite emerging trends in organization theory advocating shrinkage via externalization of workforces (Barry and Crant, 1994; Matusik and Hill, 1998), downsizing might be still viewed by growth-biased practitioners as a business failure. In this vein, Bluedorn (1993) emphasizes prevalent organizational suppositions holding that bigger organizations are necessarily better. It follows that involvement in organizational downsizing might inherently elicit disillusionment and frustration on the part of decision makers.

Second, it has been widely documented that during downsizing the best performers, who are essential for the continuation of the organization, often leave voluntarily and thus gravely impair accumulative human and social capital (Pennings, Lee, and Witteloostuijn, 1998; Rosenblatt and Sheaffer, 1997). Consequently, as observed by Fisher and White (1997), crucial skills inherent in human resources disappear, and organizational memory is disrupted or completely lost. Third, existing organizational structures are shifted around during downsizing, often resulting in unbalanced workloads (Marks, 1994) that aggravate pressures on the already stressed employees. Fourth, clinical observation of the victims of downsizing attests that their experiences of loss and separation signify that downsizing is an extremely traumatic event (Kets de Vries and Balazs, 1996).

Rigidity in response to threat

A number of studies have indicated that in the face of threat organizations and individuals tend to react rigidly. The most notable work in this line of research is Staw, Sandelands, and Dutton's (1981) threat-rigidity model. This model maintains that organizations respond to threat rigidly with respect to information, control, and efficiency. With regard to information, rigidity is reflected in restriction of information processing characterized by overloaded communication channels, reliance on prior knowledge, and reduction in communication complexity. As for control, rigidity is mirrored by constriction in control, illustrated by centralization of authority and increased formalization. Regarding efficiency, rigidity is manifested in conservation of resources. Despite some evidence that innovative and flexible responses to organizational threat prevail (Rosenblatt and Nord, 1999; Rosenblatt, Rogers, and Nord, 1993), empirical findings generally support the basic tenets of the threat-rigidity model (D'Aunno and Sutton, 1992; Gladstein and Reilly, 1985).

The association between rigidity and ethical problems is seemingly straightforward. The organizational characteristics delineated above might infringe upon employees' rights to relevant information and curtail opportunities to utilize higher level skills. During downsizing, rigid managerial response often means the use of layoffs instead of exhausting alternative means of cost reduction, thus severely taxing employees' well-being, motivation, and commitment.

Faulty decision making

Organizational situations characterized by threats and stress tend to amplify faulty decision making. Landau and Chisholm (1995) use the term "arrogant optimism" to illustrate the tendency of failing managers to overemphasize efficiency and to analyze information wrongly. Similarly, Weitzel and Jonsson (1989) contend that during the "blinded" phase of decline, decision-makers tend to ignore early warning signals. This point is illustrated in the Barings crisis: Sheaffer, Richardson, and Rosenblatt (1998) show how early warning signals were sidetracked by various cognitive syndromes. As critical situations proceed and persist, faulty decisions might lead directly to the breach of ethical principles. Street, Robertson, and Geiger (1997) noted that in escalating situations decision makers were more likely to choose unethical alternatives. Likewise, in "groupthink" contexts (Janis, 1972), participants often develop such cognitive defenses as misjudgment of relevant warnings and failure to further explore information. These tendencies, according to Sims (1994), lead to "groupthinker" weighting of only few ethical alternatives. Faulty decision making characterizing organizational decline and crisis, then, might lead to unethical outcomes.

More specifically, Messick and Bazerman (1996) showed how typical biases and weaknesses in decision-making processes (for example, ignoring low probability events, faulty judgment of risk, stereotyping) result in unethical business decisions in regard to downsizing. Drawing on Kahneman and Tversky (1979), they use an example of hypothetically downsizing firms, where saving jobs was contingent not on trade-off evaluations between ethics and profits but on risk framing. If the problem was framed in terms of losing jobs and plants, executives tended to take risks to avoid losses. By contrast, if the problem was perceived in terms of savings, executives tended to take the sure "gain" (meaning, hasty layoffs with minimal consideration of alternative strategies).

Evidence supporting the differential framing effect in negative versus positive circumstances was provided by Elster (1992). According to him, distribution of such negative outcomes as layoffs is associated with a "fairness" connotation, while distribution of positive outcomes such as hiring is associated with a "productivity" connotation. Similarly, in a study addressing positive and negative justice judgments, Sabbagh and Schmitt (forthcoming) argue that justice judgments of negative outcome distribution are expressed in a higher emotional intensity than are justice judgments of positive outcome distributions.

To summarize, such stressful events as downsizing tend to intensify typical decision-makers' biases by further transgressing ethical principles.

Dissolution of the psychological contract

A psychological contract refers to "an individual's beliefs regarding the terms and conditions of a reciprocal exchange agreement between that focal person and another party" (Rousseau, 1989, p. 123). Fairness and good faith are implied in psychological contracts, and violations have strong implications on employees' trust in the organization (Robinson, 1996), performance (Robinson and Wolfe-Morrison, 1995), and behavior (Nicholson and Johns, 1985).

A typical issue in a psychological contract is the promise of job security by the organization (Herriot, Manning, and Kidd, 1997; McLean Parks and Schmedemann, 1994). Employees feel a sense of ownership and entitlement about their jobs, and they tend to expect their employment to be guaranteed. However, psychological contracts are dynamic in nature (Robinson, Kraatz, and Rousseau, 1994), and employers' obligations in regard to job security tend to change, subject to environmental and business constrictions.

An employer's withdrawal from a former guaranteed employment policy (as well as any other obligation) is viewed as a contract violation. This is likely to lead to feelings of injustice, since the unfulfilled promise of job security is perceived as depriving the employee of desired outcomes. As repeatedly stated (Robinson, Kraatz, and Rousseau, 1994; Robinson and Rousseau, 1994; Rousseau, 1989), failure to honor a contract leads to a sense of deception and betrayal in employees. It is likely, then, that downsizing situations are prone to ethical problems, being perceived as violations of employees' rights and expectations. Only a change in the subjective perception of the psychological contract in regard to the promise of job security (Baruch and Hind, 1999) might change such perceptions.

The organizational characteristics of downsizing listed above, namely high stress, rigidity in response to threat, faulty decision making, and the dissolution of the psychological contract, provide a theoretical background against which the repercussions of downsizing on ethics can be interpreted. Proneness and vulnerability alone, however, are not sufficient to establish a conceptual framework for ethical issues. To establish that ethical principles are violated during downsizing, some evidence of downsizing-generated harm has to be shown. The following section outlines specific and adverse effects inflicted by downsizing on organizational members. Ethical perspectives ascribed to these effects from the victims' point of view are highlighted.

ADVERSE EFFECTS OF DOWNSIZING AND ETHICAL IMPLICATIONS

The negative impact of downsizing on individual employees (and indirectly on the organization) has been extensively acknowledged with regard to a plethora of indicators. Studies addressing downsizing effects distinguish four types of potentially affected individuals. The first group is laid-off employees, or those who suffer job loss as a consequence of downsizing. The second group is job-insecure employees, whose jobs are under real or perceived threat. The third group is "survivors," whose jobs stayed intact within a downsizing environment (while survivors might be viewed as a sub-group of the second group, the job-insecure, they have been the center of extensive and independent research, and therefore are reported separately here). Finally, the fourth group constitutes "downsizers," the executives who make the downsizing-related decisions. Findings concerning the effect and ethical implications of downsizing on the four predicaments are presented next.

Downsizing effects on laid-off employees

The experience of job loss has been described by Jacobson (1991) as an objective feeling, involving inter-role transition, active threat, and social visibility. Literature on job loss consistently points to the negative personal effects of downsizing. In an exhaustive survey conducted by Kozlowski et al. (1993) the following life domains were found to be affected by job loss: financial position (income loss), well-being (for example, cognitive functioning, psychosomatic symptoms), attitudes (for example, life dissatisfaction), and family relationships (such as familial conflicts, increased divorce rate). In fact, as concluded by Latack, Kinicki, and Prussia (1994), the impact of job loss is detrimental to individuals by virtually any criteria a researcher chooses to examine.

However, the potential harm of job loss is moderated by the coping mechanisms used by the afflicted individuals. Latack, Kinicki, and Prussia (1994) show that individuals differ in the coping resources they elect to employ. Coping strategies can be *problem-focused*, where individuals assume control of their lives and search for a new job, or *escape-oriented*, where individuals might take to short-term stress-relief actions such as drinking. The latter case further magnifies the harm inflicted on the individual by the original act of job termination.

Indeed, some individuals might experience job loss as an opportunity for growth and career transition, not as a personal crisis (Feldman, 1996; Latack and Dozier, 1986). This line of research is based on the assumption that organizations can so structure the downsizing process as to turn it into a positive experience for the dismissed individual. The transition from job loss into career growth is, however, contingent on a host of moderators, such as financial resources, social support, and activity level. It follows that the potential benefit of job loss is likely to affect some employees while bypassing others, since individuals differ in their opportunities for acquiring supporting resources. For example, women may enjoy more social support than men (Mallinckrodt and Fretz, 1988).

Downsizing effects on the job-insecure employees

As distinct from the experience of job loss, the experience of job insecurity has been described by Jacobson (1991) as subjective rather than objective, involving intra-role rather than inter-role transition, potential rather than real threat, and little, if any, social visibility. Greenhalgh and Rosenblatt (1984) proposed a model that attempted to explain the link between the organizational predicament of downsizing and the individual experience of employment uncertainty. Their model predicts that perceived threat to the continuation of one's job leads to adverse reactions on the job (in terms of effort, propensity to leave, and resistance to change), which in turn lead to reduced organizational effectiveness (in terms of productivity, turnover, and adaptability). These relationships are moderated by such psychological and social factors as individual differences and dependency (for example, occupational mobility and economic security). This job insecurity model has been content-validated by Hartley et al. (1991, p. 72) and construct-validated by Ashford, Lee, and Bobko (1989). Its predictive validity was tested and confirmed by Ashford, Lee, and Bobko (1989) and by Rosenblatt and Ruvio (1996). These authors showed that in addition to the variables specified in the model, job insecurity also affects organizational commitment, perceived organizational support, intra-organizational trust, and satisfaction.

The relationships between job insecurity and employees' attitudes and behaviors were found to be moderated by several work-related and non work-related factors. Lim (1996) found that work-based support buffered individuals against job dissatisfaction, proactive job search, and non-compliant job behaviors when their job security was at stake. In addition, Davy, Kinicki, and Scheck (1997) assert that job satisfaction and organizational commitment mediate job insecurity effects on withdrawal cognition in a downsizing organization.

In addition to direct and indirect (mediated) effects of job insecurity on work attitudes and behaviors, effects on health and family relationships were also detected. Kuhnert and Vance (1992), Kuhnert and Palmer (1991), and Kuhnert, Sims, and Lahey (1989) showed that job insecurity affects physical and psychological well-being symptoms, including somatization, anxiety, depression, obsessive/compulsive behavior, hostility, and interpersonal sensitivity. Following this line of research, Hartley et al. (1991, p. 80) showed that job insecurity in both The Netherlands and Israel contributed to poorer mental health. Roskies, Louis-Guerin, and Fournier (1993) found the effects of job insecurity on employees to be moderated by personality attributes.

Within the framework of family relationships, job insecurity is believed to have both a direct and a spilling-over effect. Hughes and Galinski (1994) reported that job insecurity affects marital stability. Westman, Etzion, and Danon (forthcoming) found that job insecurity influences work burnout among husbands. This effect spills over to wives sharing their husbands' workplace. Further, it was found that fathers' job insecurity influences children's behavior (Stewart and Barling, 1996) and children's work beliefs and attitudes (Barling, Dupre, and Hepburn, 1998). Finally, Ruvio and Rosenblatt (1999) and Rosenblatt, Talmud, and Ruvio (1999) report that the effects of job insecurity on work attitudes are moderated by structural (sector) and demographic (gender) variables.

Several recent studies focus on the effects of job insecurity on the managerial segment of the workforce. Hallier and Lyon (1996), for instance, assert that threats to managers' positions and careers result in decreased trust and diminished organizational commitment. Roskies and Louis-Guerin (1990) report that the exposure to downsizing environment leads to decreased personal well-being and to deterioration of work climate and attitudes among executives. Similarly, Wiesenfeld and Thibault (1997) report that managers experience an unfair downsizing as a threat to the self more than non-managers, and that perceived unfairness leads to less effective managerial practices. Moreover, authors (Kets de Vries and Balazs, 1996; O'Neill and Lenn, 1995) underscore such emotional responses of threatened executives as depression, anger, anxiety, cynicism, resentment, and retribution.

Downsizing effects on survivors

Studies focusing on survivors of downsizing report work-related symptoms including increases in work-related stress, dissatisfaction, and intent to leave the organization, and decreases in guilt, morale, and productivity (Brockner, 1988; Tombaugh and White, 1990).

Research on survivors, led by Joel Brockner of Columbia University and his associates, focused on the notion of perceived justice as a central theme in employees' reactions. In two exhaustive surveys of this literature, Brockner (1988) and Brockner and Greenberg (1990) summarized the results of previous studies showing that survivors' attitudes and behaviors (the "survivors syndrome") are consistently negative when perceived justice is observed to be low. These relationships are dependent on such variables as attachment to layoff victims and the degree of perceived injustice in the layoff procedure. Later studies corroborated these findings. Reporting on the results of three studies, Brockner et al. (1994) reported that when perceived justice was low, organizational trust and support were highly related to perceived outcome negativity (layoff-related). Also, Davy, Kinicki, and Scheck (1991) found that fairness of the layoffs had a direct effect on job satisfaction. Finally, Mishra and Spreitzer (1998) suggested that perceived justice led to constructive (hopeful and obliging) behavior.

Downsizing effects on downsizers

Some reports exist as to downsizing's stressful effects on executives. In in-depth interviews Wright and Barling (1997) found that downsizers ("executioners") suffered from work overload, search for meaning, social and organizational isolation, and a decline in personal well-being. The reactions of "executioners" responsible for the implementation of downsizing may become clinically extreme. Kets de Vries and Balazs (1996) described the following patterns: compulsive/ritualistic behavior, hostility and aggression toward colleagues and subordinates, profound detachment, difficulty in experiencing affect, withdrawal, and depression.

These reactions might be dependent on subjective framework perception. Folger and Skarlicki (1998) reported that downsizers' attitudes towards victims was often contingent on the perceived reason for downsizing: when downsizing was perceived as caused by mismanagement (as opposed to external reasons) managers reacted with a "tough" distancing attitude.

Taken together, these studies point overwhelmingly to the detrimental effect of job insecurity on employees' well-being in both rank-and-file and managerial echelons. As will be shown next, this effect depends chiefly on the justice perception of all parties involved, most notably that of victims.

ETHICAL DILEMMAS IN DOWNSIZING

Here we illustrate typical problems in downsizing decisions, reflecting ethical principles. In order to analyze downsizing problems by means of an ethical framework, key justice-related concepts need to be delineated.

Brockner and Greenberg (1990) proposed a useful framework of organizational justice, applying it to layoffs. They distinguished three types of organizational justice: *distributive*, *procedural*, and *interactional*. Distributive justice relates to the normative rules used to make decisions about the allocations of outcomes. The differential likelihood of organizational units being downsized or of individuals losing their jobs, and the selection criteria employed by decision-makers, reflect facets of distributive justice. Procedural justice focuses on the fairness of the processes involved in outcome allocations. For example, the extent to which employees are involved in decisions related to the continuation of their own employment, or the extent to which an executive enjoys downsizing-derived payoffs, reflect procedural justice. Finally, interactional justice is the fairness of the interpersonal treatment of people during the implementation of the outcome allocation. The way downsizing-related information is transmitted and interpreted is an example of interactional downsizing.

Combined, these three forms of justice (sometimes viewed as variations of distributive justice) might be considered one ethical system of beliefs. Hosmer (1987) lists, in addition to distributive justice, three other systems that help in understanding the dilemmas and problems in human resource management decisions. The first is the utilitarian (consequentialist) theory, which represents the principle that everyone should act to generate the greatest benefits for the largest number of people. The second ethical system is the universalist theory, representing the principle that everyone should act to ensure that similar decisions will be reached by others, given similar circumstances. The third is personal liberty, stating that everyone should act to ensure greater freedom of choice. These ethical belief systems reflect different principles that do not perfectly complement each other; indeed, the primacy of the values they represent might be in conflict.

Next, typical downsizing dilemmas, representing the above types of organizational justice and illustrating the different ethical belief systems, are discussed, grouped into the following issues: downsizing strategic decisions, treatment of afflicted employees, and downsizing communication.

Ethical dilemmas in downsizing strategic decisions

Several ethical dilemmas befall decision makers during deliberations concerning dismissals. First, the very decision to layoff might reflect a biased decision-making process, representing a poor assessment of a policy's consequences. For example, layoff decisions might be characterized by a bias such as limiting the search for stakeholders (Messick and Bazerman, 1996), thus magnifying the will of shareholders and other interest groups and minimizing employees' needs. Studies show that cutback strategies often operate within non-rational, political paradigms (Rosenblatt and Mannheim, 1996b; Rosenblatt, Rogers, and Nord, 1993), driven by utilitarian considerations (maximizing profits for most stakeholders).

A typical example of a strategic downsizing decision is the choice between employing across-the-board redundancies and prioritized layoffs, for example, dismissals tailored to organizational needs. While the latter strategies are organizationally logical they are likely to result in indiscriminate layoffs, thus infringing the ethical principle of distributive justice. Across-the-board layoffs, however, are perceived as fair from the point of view of the individual but they are organizationally unreasonable. Moreover, they hardly satisfy the ethical requirement of the utilitarian approach, that is, satisfaction of most stakeholders' interests.

Another ethical problem related to downsizing selection results is the differential likelihood of employment guarantee faced by various groups within the internal workforce. Atkinson's flexible firm model (1987) shows that modern organizations aspire to flexibility in two major domains: functional and numerical. Only workers with whom organizations can exercise functional flexibility, that is, redeploy them quickly and smoothly between tasks, are granted job security. External workers, who are relatively more replaceable and rigid, are deprived of job security. This problem is also raised by Hartley et al. (1991) in their thorough study of job insecurity. They describe three unique groups vulnerable to job discrimination. The first group includes the secondary labor market such as new emigrants, ethnic minorities, aging workers, and women. The second is freelancers and short-term contractors, and the third is newly appointed workers. Employees in the three groups are most likely to be the first to be made redundant irrespective of qualifications and performance. This human resources approach engenders discrimination among groups. Moreover, it monumentalizes disparity of opportunities, namely the ethical principle of distributive justice is retracted.

On a personal level, different ethical principles determine different selection criteria. For example, using seniority as a major selection criterion represents a distributive principle of *equality*, while selection based on employees' unique circumstances (for example, the job is the sole income source of a one-parent family) represents the distributive principle of *need*. These two selection criteria, however, hardly satisfy the utilitarian principle of maintaining economic efficiency.

Cutback strategies that offer alternatives to layoffs are considered more oriented to employee welfare (Greenhalgh, Lawrence, and Sutton, 1988), but even these might be unethical. Often management resorts to differential retrenchment whereby employees are accorded an opportunity to exit voluntarily. While this strategy offers personal liberty, it also violates the ethical principle of distributive justice, and more, it works against the best organizational interests (utilitarian approach) of keeping the more valuable employees in.

Ethical dilemmas in treatment of afflicted employees

Even when dismissals are inevitable, the way they are effectuated can influence employees' lives no less than the act itself. This aspect of downsizing is termed procedural justice. Several practices that are specifically intended to alleviate the impact of layoffs include reparations, outplacement, and counseling. However, while these and other measures are aimed at mitigating the personal loss, they often impose a substantial financial burden on both crisis-beset and proactively retrenching firms. We assume that the motivation to activate assistance measures is not particularly high, as these are not rewarding in the short run. Often, assistance is extended following union pressure. The notion of layoffs as a useless expenditure, however, is somewhat shortsighted since organizational reputation and turnaround prospects following retrenchment are often determined by policies intended to assist survivors and laid-off workers. In this regard, Feldman and Leana (1994) found that successful organizations are characterized by extending comprehensive assistance to redundant workers. The presumed assumption about catering to the public good, or to the good of most stakeholders, then, is unsubstantiated. Moreover, this issue is ethically problematic since redundant employees require financial resources whereas the already financially reduced organization is necessarily more inclined to bolster its commitment to survivors.

Another procedural justice form that can be employed in downsizing is participative decision making. While this, as mentioned above, might be viewed as a paradoxical idea (Levine, 1979), there is some evidence in organizational literature on the employment of participative decision making in declining and downsizing organizations (Rosenblatt and Nord, 1999). For example, Kochan, MacDuffie, and Osterman (1988) report on cutbacks in the Digital Equipment Corporation, where the transition process was decentralized and employees participated in plant-level decisions. Subject to its level, participative decision making constitutes taking control over one's life, hence represents the ethical principles of universality (treating employees with dignity and respect) and personal liberty (letting individuals make informed choices about their welfare).

Ethical dilemmas in downsizing communication

Information dissemination is an ethically charged topic. It is argued that management in conventional organizations tends to use and abuse information as a power source (Munson, Rosenblatt, and Rosenblatt, 1999). This tendency is exacerbated under stress conditions. Managerial tendency for informational secrecy during downsizing (Gilmore and Hirschhorn, 1983), decline (Rosenblatt and Mannheim, 1996a;

Weitzel and Jonsson, 1991), crisis (Abrahamson and Park, 1994), and general business failures (D'Aveni and MacMillan, 1990; Page, 1984; Sutton and Callahan, 1987) is a well-documented aspect of downturn management. This phenomenon is partially explained by the above-mentioned threat-rigidity theory (Staw, Sandelands, and Dutton, 1981) and by psychological inhibitors (Sheaffer, Richardson, and Rosenblatt, 1998).

Noteworthy is dissemination of disinformation, such as the distortion of information to shareholders regarding the genuine situation of the distressed firm (Abrahamson and Park, 1994; D'Aveni and MacMillan, 1990). Another manifestation of disinformation is the release of management-interpreted information to stakeholders. This interpretation, labeled "impression management," is often characterized by such strategies as concealment of information regarding the true situation, relinquishing responsibility (evading acknowledgment concerning crisis or denying guilt), prettifying grave circumstances, and retreat (disengaging from suspecting partners) (Sutton, 1990; Sutton and Callahan, 1987). These tendencies create ethical problems since they impinge on the right to relevant information of such stakeholders as employees, worried financiers, customers, and distributors interested in continuing services and productions.

The tendency to conceal information from individuals concerning their impending dismissal is also a widely documented phenomenon. The case study of Atari (Sutton, Eisenhardt, and Jucker, 1986) reports a variety of instances where the downsizing firm manipulated vital information, employees were kept uninformed about their future jobs, layoffs were belatedly announced, and management disseminated slanders, aimed, paradoxically, to encourage survivors. Pompa (1992) shows that withholding information about layoffs is harmful to employees from both a consequentialist (financial and psychological damage) and a universal (deception) approach. Despite frequent managerial justifications such as potential loss of employees' productivity, sabotage to company property, and fear of morale problems, Pompa concludes that withholding information is unethical. It is noteworthy that managerial proclivity to information concealment is not without cause. De Meuse, Vanderheiden, and Bergmann (1994) point to the declining performance of firms after expected redundancies were made public. Moreover, Kaufman, Kesner, and Hazen (1994) note that releasing superfluous information is liable to put highly leveraged firms at risk.

An interesting communication expression for manipulating information during downsizing is the rampant use of euphemisms. Frequent downsizing metaphors are layoffs or labor force cutbacks, as well as deliberately ambivalent terms such as rightsizing, dismissals, terminations, and retrenchment. Lately, academic as well as business literature abounds with alternative expressions, none of which seems to differ meaningfully from the others. These include vocational relocation, skill-mix adjustment, resizing, streamlining, career assignment, relocation, and workforce rebalance (Cameron, 1994; Haley, 1997; O'Neill, 1994). While these terms imply a certain strategic orientation, the common denominator is simply human resource cutbacks. It is postulated that some of the above expressions are merely cosmetic, aiming at distracting vulnerable stakeholders' attention from unpopular managerial policies.

To sum up, ethical principles such as utilitarian benefits and economic efficiency on one hand, and universal rules, individual rights, and contributive justice (Hosmer, 1994) on the other, seem to be in conflict in downsizing-related communication.

MANAGERIAL IMPLICATIONS OF ETHICAL DILEMMAS IN DOWNSIZING

The above review shows that the ethical principles guiding downsizers are often different from employees'. While their subordinates are mostly concerned about their rights (such as job security, true information), managers are typically expected to take a utilitarian cost-benefit stance aimed at maximizing the organization's profits. Greenhalgh, Lawrence, and Sutton (1988) advance a proactive model featuring a synch between organizational and personal needs. According to their model, downsizing strategies are scaled subject to values pertaining to individuals' welfare on the one hand and organizational utility on the other. For example, natural attrition would be least hard on personal welfare but financially the dearest. Likewise, nil assistance to redundant employees will be least expensive for the firm but hardest on workers' welfare. The ultimate model addresses criteria for managerial decision making including organizational (employees' skills) and contextual (formal labor relations) constraints. These criteria determine which downsizing strategy organizations should start with and at what stage ethics will be impinged upon. Greenhalgh, Lawrence, and Sutton's (1988) hierarchy can be used to characterize ethical considerations of downsizing. While such a strategy as natural attrition requires no managerial ethical compromise, negligible assistance to dismissed employees would be considered as the harshest according to both natural duty and fairness principles, let alone employees' right to job security.

Regardless of the principles directing managers' decisions, morality has been strongly advocated as an inherent part of strategic planning. Hosmer (1994, p. 25) argues that "it is essential in any competitive sense to be moral." He claims that competitive companies are dependent upon a wide range of stakeholders, and that for these stakeholders to be innovative and cooperative, ethical principles need to be included in the strategic decision processes of the firm, thus building trust, commitment, and effort. He further suggests the addition of ethics to the business curriculum (Hosmer, 1988), thus raising managers' awareness of and sensitivity to moral issues. Ethics programs, such as formal ethics codes, ethics officers, and ethics training are increasingly part of organizations. Weaver, Treviño, and Cochran (1999) show that the scope of these programs is dependent, in addition to environmental influences, on executives' commitment to ethics.

CONCLUSIONS

Organizational literature shows overwhelmingly that downsizing has negative effects on individuals: economically, psychologically, socially, and health-wise. Naturally, the most affected employees are the ones whose work is discontinued, but studies reveal that survivors, and even the "executioners" themselves, are adversely affected by workforce cutbacks as well. If we believe that ethical problems involve harm caused to individuals in ways beyond their control, we accept that downsizing is liable to inherently infringe upon ethical principles. This notion is reinforced by the characterization of downsizing organizations in terms of inner inconsistencies and high stress, and the tendency of executives resorting to downsizing to favor sub-optimal decisions. It is also corroborated by research results showing persistently that employees tend to evaluate downsizing processes in terms of distributive, procedural, and interactional justice. To complicate things further, applied ethics shows that ethical principles are often contradictory, so that the harm inflicted on one party may seem as a benefit to the other.

Clearly, organizations need to downsize, either as a reactive measure to cope with decline and crisis, or as a proactive management strategy designed to economize, to streamline obese structures, and advantageously to reposition firms in circumstances of accelerated competition. The corporate challenge is to avoid or minimize circumstances where ethical principles either clash or are impinged upon. To start with, a useful way would be to enhance executives' sensitivity and awareness of the personal costs incurred by implementing ill-planned and hastily executed downsizing. Business schools' curricula can draw substantially on research findings regarding potential pitfalls inherent in downsizing. Second, such carefully practiced measures as outplacement and counseling can alleviate adverse symptoms and likewise prevent corporate image failures. These measures are likely to reduce the likelihood of having to clash with ethical principles. Third, no counter measures help when executives do not internalize the need to lead by example, notably during decline and crisis. By internalizing, they are likely to evade ethical pitfalls and contradictions, and to ascend to a higher moral plane to demand cutbacks.

It should be borne in mind that ethical analysis of downsizing decisions is dependent, among other things, on the perceptual framing of the situation. Organizational changes involving new psychological contracts, specifically alternative expectations of job security, might alter the view of employees' welfare, hence redefine ethical problems. It appears essential, therefore, to further study the unique organizational and managerial characteristics that might lead to ethical problems.

Finally, the study of ethics during downsizing should have implications for other organizational situations sharing similar attributes and characteristics. Recent theorists agree that inner inconsistencies and paradoxes characterize complex organization. Also, in hypercompetitive, and uncertain business environments, more and more organizations tend to feature stressful behaviors, so decisions are made in sub-optimal conditions. As shown in the present study, these and other organizational characteristics make organizations prone to ethical violations. The study of ethical implications of specific organizational characteristics in a variety of circumstances, chiefly during crises and decline, might help further our understanding of organizational ethical problems.

REFERENCES

Abrahamson, E. and Park, C. 1994: Concealment of negative organizational outcomes: an agency theory perspective. *Academy of Management Journal*, 37 (5), 1302–34.

Ashford, S.J., Lee, C., and Bobko, P. 1989: Content, causes, and consequences of job insecurity: a theory-based measure and substantive test. *Academy of Management Journal*, 32 (4), 803–29.

Atkinson, J. 1987: Flexibility or fragmentation? The United Kingdom labour market in the eighties. *Labour and Society*, 12 (1), 87–105.

Barling, J., Dupre, K.E., and Hepburn, C.G. 1998: Effects of parents' job insecurity on children's work beliefs and attitudes. *Journal of Applied Psychology*, 83 (1), 112–18.

Barry, B. and Crant, J.M. 1994: Labor force externalization in growing firms. *The International Journal of Organizational Analysis*, 2 (4), 361–83.

Baruch, Y. and Hind, P. 1999: Perceptual motion in organizations: effective management and the impact of the new psychological contracts on "survivor syndrome". *European Journal of Work and Organizational Psychology*, 8 (2), 295–306.

Bluedorn, A.C. 1993: Pilgrim's progress: trends and convergence in research on organizational size and environments. *Journal of Management*, 19 (2), 163–91.

Brockner, J. 1988: The effects of work layoffs on survivors: research, theory, and practice. *Research in Organizational Behavior*, 10, 213–55.

Brockner, J. and Greenberg, J. 1990: The impact of layoffs on survivors: an organizational justice perspective. In J.S. Carroll (ed.) *Applied Social Psychology and Organizational Settings*. Hillsdale, NJ: Lawrence Erlbaum Associates, Chapter 3, 45–75.

Brockner, J., Konovsky, M., Cooper-Schneider, R., Folger, R., Martin, C., and Bies, R.J. 1994: Interactive effects of procedural justice and outcome negativity on victims and survivors of job loss. *Academy of Management Journal*, 37 (2), 397–409.

Cameron, K.S. 1994: Strategies for successful organizational downsizing. *Human Resource Management*, 33 (2), 189–211.

Cameron, K.S., Freeman, S.J., and Mishra, A.K. 1991: Best practices in white collar downsizing: managing contradictions. *Academy of Management Executive*, 5 (3), 57–73.

Cascio, W.F. 1993: Downsizing: What do we know? What have we learned? *Academy of Management Executive*, 7 (1), 95–103.

D'Aunno, T. and Sutton, R.I. 1992: The responses of drug abuse treatment organizations to financial adversity: a partial test of the threat-rigidity thesis. *Journal of Management*, 18, 117–31.

D'Aveni, R.A. and MacMillan, I.C. 1990: Crisis and the content of managerial communications: a study of the focus of attention of top managers in surviving and failing. *Administrative Science Quarterly*, 35, 634–57.

Davy, J.A., Kinicki, A.J., and Scheck, C.L. 1991: Developing and testing a model of survivor responses to layoffs. *Journal of Vocational Behavior*, 38, 302–17.

Davy, J.A., Kinicki, A.J., and Scheck, C.L. 1997: A test of job security's direct and mediated effects on withdrawal cognitions. *Journal of Organizational Behavior*, 18, 323–49.

De Meuse, K.P., Vanderheiden, P.A., and Bergmann, T.J. 1994: Announced layoffs: their effect on corporate financial performance. *Human Resource Management*, 33 (4), 509–30.

Deshpande, S.P. 1996: Ethical climate and the link between success and ethical behavior: an empirical investigation of a non-profit organization. *Journal of Business Ethics*, 15, 315–20.

Elster, J. 1992: *Local Justice: How Institutions Allocate Scarce Goods and Necessary Burdens*. New York: Russell Sage Foundation.

Feldman, D.C. 1996: Managing careers in downsizing firms. *Human Resource Management*, 35 (2), 145–61.

Feldman, D.C. and Leana, C.R. 1994: Better practices in managing layoffs. *Human Resource Management*, 33, 239–60.

Fisher, S.R. and White, M.A. 1997: Downsizing and organizational learning: a question of compatibility. Paper presented at the Academy of Management Annual Meeting, Boston.

Folger, R. and Skarlicki, D.P. 1998: When tough times make tough bosses: managerial distancing as a function of layoff blame. *Academy of Management Journal*, 41 (1), 79–87.

Gilmore, T.N. and Hirschhorn, L. 1983: Management challenges under conditions of retrenchment. *Human Resource Management*, 22 (4), 341–57.

Gladstein, D.L. and Reilly, N.P. 1985: Group decision making under threat: the tycoon game. *Academy of Management Journal*, 25, 613–27.

Greenhalgh, L., Lawrence, A.T., and Sutton, R.I. 1988: Determinants of work force reduction strategies in declining organizations. *Academy of Management Review*, 13 (2), 241–54.

Greenhalgh, L. and Rosenblatt, Z. 1984: Job insecurity: toward conceptual clarity. *Academy of Management Review*, 9 (3), 438–48.

Haley, A.A. 1997: *Downsizing Glossary,* Alliance for redesigning government, National Academy of Public Administration, http://www.clearlake.ibm.com/alliance/clusters/rs/glossary.html.

Hallier, J. and Lyon, P. 1996: Job insecurity and employee commitment: managers' reactions to the threat and outcomes of redundancy selection. *British Journal of Management,* 7, 107–23.

Hartley, J., Jacobson, D., Klandermans, B., and Van Vuuren, T. 1991: *Job Insecurity: Coping with Jobs at Risk.* London: Sage.

Herriot, P., Manning, W.E.G., and Kidd, J.M. 1997: The content of the psychological contract. *British Journal of Management,* 8, 151–62.

Hosmer, L.T. 1987: Ethical analysis and human resource management. *Human Resource Management,* 26 (3), 313–30.

Hosmer, L.T. 1988: Adding ethics to the business curriculum. *Business Horizons,* 31 (4), 9–15.

Hosmer, L.T. 1994: Strategic planning as if ethics mattered. *Strategic Management Journal,* 15, 17–34.

Hughes, D. and Galinsky, E. 1994: Work experiences and marital interactions: elaborating the complexity of work. *Journal of Organizational Behavior,* 15, 423–38.

Jacobson, D. 1991: Toward a theoretical distinction between the stress components of the job insecurity and job loss experiences. *Research in the Sociology of Organizations.* Greenwich, CT: JAI Press Inc, vol. 9, 1–19.

Janis, I.L. 1972: *Victims of Groupthink.* Boston: Houghton Mifflin.

Kahneman, D. and Tversky, A. 1979: Prospect theory: an analysis of decision under risk. *Econometrica,* 47, 263–91.

Kaufman, J.B., Kesner, I.F., and Hazen, T.L. 1994: The myth of full disclosure: a look at organizational communications during crises. *Business Horizons,* July–August.

Kets de Vries, M. and Balazs, K. 1996: The human side of downsizing. *European Management Journal,* 14 (2), 111–20.

Kim, W.C. and Mauborgne, R.A. 1996: Procedural justice and managers' in-role and extra-role behavior: the case of the multinational. *Management Science,* 42 (4), 499–515.

Kochan, T.A., MacDuffie, J.P., and Osterman, P. 1988: Employment security at DEC: Sustaining values amid environmental change. *Human Resource Management,* 27 (2), 121–43.

Kozlowski, S.W., Chao, G.T., Smith, E.M., and Hedlund, J. 1993: Organizational downsizing: strategies, interventions and research implications. *International Review of Industrial and Organizational Psychology.* New York: Wiley.

Kuhnert, K.W. and Palmer, D.R. 1991: Job security, health, and the intrinsic and extrinsic characteristics of work. *Group and Organizational Studies,* 16 (2), 178–92.

Kuhnert, K.W., Sims, R.R., and Lahey, M.A. 1989: The relationship between job security and employee health. *Group and Organizational Studies,* 14 (4), 399–410.

Kuhnert, K.W. and Vance, R.J. 1992: Job insecurity and moderators of the relation between job insecurity and employee adjustment. In J.C. Quick, L.R. Murphy, and J.J. Hurrell Jr. (eds) *Stress and Well-Being at Work.* Washington, DC: APA, Chapter 4, 48–63.

Landau, M. and Chisholm, D. 1995: The arrogance of optimism: notes on failure-avoidance management. *Journal of Contingencies and Crisis Management,* 3 (2), 67–79.

Latack, J.C. and Dozier, J.B. 1986: After the ax falls: job loss as a career transition. *Academy of Management Review,* 11 (2), 375–92.

Latack, J.C., Kinicki, A.J., and Prussia, G.E. 1994: An integrative process model of coping with job loss. *Academy of Management Review,* 19 (2), 311–42.

Lee, P.M. 1997: A comparative analysis of layoff announcement and stock price reactions in the United States and Japan. *Strategic Management Journal,* 18, 879–94.

Levine, C.H. 1979: More on cutback management: hard questions for hard times. *Public Administration Review,* March–April, 179–83.

Lim, V.K.G. 1996: Job insecurity and its outcomes: moderating effects of work-based and nonwork-based social support. *Human Relations,* 49 (2), 171–94.

Ludwig, D.C. and Longenecker, C.O. 1993: The Bathsheba syndrome: the ethical failure of successful leaders. *Journal of Business Ethics*, 12 (4), 265–76.

Mallinckrodt, B. and Fretz, B.R. 1988: Social support and the impact of job loss on older professionals. *Journal of Counseling Psychology*, 35, 281–6.

Marks, M.L. 1994: Regrouping after downsizing. In A.K. Orman (ed.) *Human Dilemmas in Working Organizations*. New York: The Guilford Press, Chapter 5.

Matusik, S.F. and Hill, C.W.L. 1998: The utilization of contingent work, knowledge creation and competitive advantage. *Academy of Management Review*, 23 (4), 680–700.

McKinley, W., Sanchez, C.M., and Schick, A.G. 1995: Organizational downsizing: constraining, cloning, learning. *Academy of Management Executive*, 9 (3), 32–43.

McLean Parks, J. and Schmedemann, D.A. 1994: When promises become contracts: implied contracts and handbook provisions on job security. *Human Resource Management*, 33 (3), 403–23.

Messick, D.M. and Bazerman, M.H. 1996: Ethical leadership and the psychology of decision making. *Sloan Management Review*, Winter, 9–22.

Miller, D. and Friesen, P.H. 1980: Momentum and revolution in organizational adaptation. *Academy of Management Journal*, 23 (4), 591–614.

Miller, D. and Friesen, P.H. 1983: Successful and unsuccessful phases of the corporate life cycle. *Organization Studies*, 4 (4), 339–56.

Mishra, A.K. and Spreitzer, G.M. 1998: Explaining how survivors respond to downsizing: the roles of trust, empowerment, justice, and work redesign. *Academy of Management Review*, 23 (3), 567–88.

Munson, C.L., Rosenblatt, M., and Rosenblatt, Z. 1999: The use and abuse of power in supply chains. *Business Horizons*, January–February, 55–65.

Nicholson, N. and Johns, G. 1985: The absence culture and the psychological contract: who's in control of absence? *The Academy of Management Review*, 10 (3), 397–408.

O'Neill, H.M. 1994: Restructuring, re-engineering, and rightsizing: do the metaphors make sense? *Academy of Management Executive*, 8 (4), 96–104.

O'Neill, H.M. and Lenn, D.J. 1995: Voices of survivors: words that downsizing CEOs should hear. *Academy of Management Executive*, 9 (4), 23–34.

Page, R.M. 1984: *Stigma*. London: Routledge and Kegan Paul.

Pennings, J.M., Lee, K., and Van Witteloostuijn, A. 1998: Human capital, social capital, and firm dissolution. *Academy of Management Journal*, 41 (4), 425–40.

Pompa, V. 1992: Managerial secrecy: an ethical examination. *Journal of Business Ethics*, 11, 147–56.

Powell, G.N. 1998: The abusive organization. *Academy of Management Executive*, 12 (2), 95–6.

Quinn, R.E. and Cameron, K.S. 1988: *Paradox and Transformation: Toward a Theory of Change in Organization and Management*. Cambridge, MA: Ballinger.

Robinson, S.L. 1996: Trust and breach of the psychological contract. *Administrative Science Quarterly*, 41, 574–99.

Robinson, S., Kraatz, M.S., and Rousseau, D. 1994: Changing obligations and the psychological contract: a longitudinal study. *Academy of Management Journal*, 37 (1), 137–52.

Robinson, S. and Rousseau, D. 1994: Violating the psychological contract: not the exception but the norm. *Journal of Organizational Behavior*, 15, 245–59.

Robinson, S.L. and Wolfe-Morrison, E. 1995: Psychological contracts and OCB: the effect of unfulfilled obligations on civic virtue behavior. *Journal of Organizational Behavior*, 16 (3), 289–99.

Rosenblatt, Z. and Mannheim, B. 1996a: Organizational response to decline in the Israeli electronics industry. *Organization Studies*, 17 (6), 953–84.

Rosenblatt, Z. and Mannheim, B. 1996b: Work-force cutback decisions of Israeli managers: a test of a strategic model. *The International Journal of Human Resource Management*, 7 (2), 437–54.

Rosenblatt, Z. and Nord, W.R. 1999: Participative decision making as a strategic response to decline: flexibility, rigidity, or a mixture? *Journal of Contingencies and Crisis Management*, 7 (2), 63–75.

Rosenblatt, Z., Rogers, K.S., and Nord, W.R. 1993: Toward a political framework for flexible management of decline. *Organization Science*, 4 (1), 76–91.

Rosenblatt, Z. and Ruvio, A. 1996: A test of a multidimensional model of job insecurity: the case of Israeli teachers. *Journal of Organizational Behavior*, 17, 587–605.

Rosenblatt, Z. and Schaeffer, Z. 1997: Brain drain in declining organizations. The Sixth Annual Conference of the Eastern Academy of Management, Dublin, Ireland.

Rosenblatt, Z., Talmud, I., and Ruvio, A. (1999): A gender-based framework of the experience of job insecurity and its effects on work attitudes. *European Journal of Work and Organizational Psychology*, 8 (2), 197–218.

Roskies, E. and Louis-Guerin, C. 1990: Job insecurity in managers: antecedents and consequences. *Journal of Organizational Behavior*, 11, 345–59.

Roskies, E., Louis-Guerin, C., and Fournier, C. 1993: Coping with job insecurity: how does personality make a difference? *Journal of Organizational Behavior*, 14, 617–30.

Rousseau, D. 1989: Psychological and implied contracts in organizations. *Employee Responsibilities and Rights Journal*, 2 (2), 121–39.

Ruvio, A. and Rosenblatt, Z. 1999: Job insecurity among Israeli schoolteachers: sectoral profiles and organizational implications. *Journal of Educational Administration*, 37 (2), 139–58.

Sabbagh, C. and Schmitt, M. forthcoming: Exploring the structure of positive and negative justice judgements. *Social Justice Research*, 4 (11).

Sheaffer, Z., Richardson, B., and Rosenblatt, Z. 1998: Early-warning-signals management: a lesson from the Barings crisis. *Journal of Contingencies and Crisis Management*, 6 (1), 1–22.

Sims, R.R. 1994: The relationship between groupthink and unethical behavior in organizations. In *Ethics and Organizational Decision Making: A Call For Renewal*. Westport, CT: Quorum Books, Chapter 4.

Staw, B.M., Sandelands, L.E., and Dutton, J.E. 1981: Threat-rigidity effects in organizational behavior: a multi-level analysis. *Administrative Science Quarterly*, 26, 501–24.

Stewart, W. and Barling, J. 1996: Fathers' work experiences effect children's behaviors via job-related affect and *parenting* behaviors. *Journal of Organizational Behavior*, 17, 221–32.

Street, M.D., Robertson, C., and Geiger, S.W. 1997: Ethical decision making: the effects of escalating commitment. *Journal of Business Ethics*, 16, 1153–61.

Sutton, R.I. 1990: Organizational decline processes: a social psychological perspective. In L.L. Cummings and B.M. Staw (eds) *Research in Organizational Behavior*. Greenwich, CT: JAI Press, 12, 205–53.

Sutton, R.I. and Callahan, A.L. 1987: The stigma of bankruptcy: spoiled organizational image and its management. *Academy of Management Journal*, 30 (3), 405–36.

Sutton, R.I., Eisenhardt, K.M., and Jucker, J.V. 1986: Managing organizational decline: lessons from Atari. *Organizational Dynamics*, Spring, 17–29.

Tombaugh, J.R. and White, L.P. 1990: Downsizing: an empirical assessment of survivors' perceptions in a postlayoff environment. *Organizational Development Journal*, 8, 32–43.

Weaver, G.R., Treviño, L.K., and Cochran, P.L. 1999: Corporate ethics programs as control systems: influences of executive commitment and environmental factors. *Academy of Management Journal*, 42 (1), 41–57.

Weitzel, W. and Jonsson, E. 1989: Decline in organizations: a literature integration and extension. *Administrative Science Quarterly*, 34, 91–109.

Weitzel, W. and Jonsson, E. 1991: Reversing the downward spiral: lessons from WT Grant and Sears Roebuck. *Academy of Management Executive*, 5 (3), 7–22.

Westman, M., Etzion, D., and Danon, E. forthcoming: Job insecurity and burnout in married couples employed by an organization undergoing downsizing. *Journal of Occupational Health Psychology*.

Wiesenfeld, B.M. and Thibault, V. 1997: Managers are employees too: exploring the relation-ships between procedural fairness, managers' self-perceptions, and managerial behaviors following a layoff. Proceedings of the Academy of Management Meeting.

Willa, B. 1994: Ethical people are productive people. *Public Productivity and Management Review*, 17 (3), 241–51.

Wright, B. and Barling, J. 1997: "The executioners' song": listening to downsizers reflect on their experiences. Academy of Management annual meeting, Boston.

9 Total Quality Management during Downsizing

Marjorie Armstrong-Stassen

"There has to come a time when doing a massive reorganization that things like continuous improvement and upward feedback become a problem when people are leaving. We continue to use the tools of TQM but the fact was when the axe came down all these principles went out the window. Employees felt a certain amount of betrayal. In terms of priority, the staff are not receptive to hearing about TQM. They want to hear whether or not they have a job." (Armstrong-Stassen, 1997).

"The downsizing has made it [the TQM initiative] a joke. It's a contradiction in terms. Everyone understands the initiative, but it's really hard to deploy when your staff wonders when they'll be hit or how the job will change. It's difficult to manage with quality efforts. The two just don't fit." (Armstrong-Stassen, 1997).

Two strategic initiatives have been dominant in the 1990s: total quality management (TQM) and organizational downsizing. The question is what happens when a firm that has implemented a total quality management initiative is faced with downsizing its workforce? In other words, can TQM continue to exist in a downsizing context? This is the issue that this chapter addresses. In the first section, the basic premises underlying TQM and downsizing are briefly outlined. In the second section, the arguments why TQM and organizational downsizing cannot coexist are presented. In the third section, the case for the coexistence of TQM and downsizing is made. In the fourth section, the empirical evidence, especially from the organizational downsizing and layoff survivor literatures, is reviewed in relation to the basic principles of TQM.

UNDERLYING PREMISES OF TQM AND DOWNSIZING

Although total quality management is widely practiced, there is little agreement on how TQM should be defined (Boaden, 1997), and there is no single theoretical formulation of the TQM approach (Lawler, 1994). However, there does appear to be a general consensus that the premises underlying TQM are mutual trust, commitment and respect (Bassi and Van Buren, 1997). TQM is characterized by a focus on customer satisfaction and the convergence of the interests of employees, shareholders, and customers (Grant, Shani, and Krishnan, 1994).

The driving force behind organizational downsizing is cost reduction and this is generally accomplished through the reduction of the number of employees (Scott, 1995). Underlying this strategic initiative is an economic model based upon the principles of profit maximization (Grant, Shani, and Krishnan, 1994). The key goal is to maximize shareholder wealth. In the economic model, conflict is inherent because individuals are driven by their own self-interests to maximize their economic welfare. Downsizing engenders distrust, individualism, and a lack of commitment on the part of the organization to its employees and, in turn, employees lack commitment to the organization (Krishnan et al., 1993). The mutual trust, commitment, and respect that are an integral part of TQM are thus undermined by organizational downsizing.

THE ARGUMENT AGAINST THE COEXISTENCE OF TQM AND ORGANIZATIONAL DOWNSIZING

Many experts argue that downsizing poses a serious challenge to the practice of TQM. These experts contend that the underlying premises of TQM and downsizing are inherently incompatible and that attempting to combine the two will result in the inevitable failure of one or both initiatives (Grant, Shani, and Krishnan, 1994). Cameron (1995) argued that the attributes of downsizing are antithetical to the principles of TQM. These attributes include centralization of decision making, loss of trust, increased conflict, restricted communication, and lack of teamwork. Cameron concluded that the impact of downsizing on quality and performance "has been lamentable" (p. 94). Hubiak and O'Donnell (1997) provided this scathing assessment of combining TQM and organizational downsizing: "W. Edwards Deming, father of the worldwide quality movement, recognized that an essential element to unleashing the human potential in any organization was to drive out fear. Downsizing achieves the exact opposite. Consequently, it can be considered organizational suicide" (p. 35).

Supporting empirical evidence against the coexistence of TQM and downsizing

Although much of the TQM literature consists of anecdotal case studies, there is some empirical evidence to support the argument against the successful coexistence of TQM and downsizing. In a study conducted by the American Society for Training and Development, downsized companies had less improvement in product and service quality, work-life quality, employee satisfaction, and overall performance than similar, but undownsized, companies (Bassi and Van Buren, 1997). Powell (1993) examined the effect of downsizing on TQM by interviewing 36 quality executives. Powell reported that team development was disrupted by downsizing and senior management commitment to TQM was weakened. In a study involving 241 managers, Armstrong-Stassen (1997) found that downsizing had a negative effect on the organization's TQM program, teamwork, and the quality of client service. The quotes at the beginning of this chapter were taken from the interview portion of the study. Two-thirds of the managers who were interviewed said that the downsizing had negatively affected the organization's total quality management efforts. In a survey of 254 companies conducted by

Buch (1992), over half of the companies reported that downsizing had an overall negative effect on their employee involvement activities including reduced motivation and morale, cynicism towards the employee involvement efforts, and a decline in the quality and quantity of employee involvement activities. Buch concluded that downsizing is a serious threat to the health and survival of employee involvement. In a study examining the impact of TQM on the financial performance of 108 firms, Easton and Jarrell (1998) found a positive impact of TQM on performance only for those firms that did not downsize. Thus, the empirical evidence would appear to support the argument that downsizing is detrimental to total quality management initiatives.

THE ARGUMENT FOR THE COEXISTENCE OF TQM AND ORGANIZATIONAL DOWNSIZING

Some experts, however, believe that TQM can continue to exist in a downsizing context and there are certainly examples of companies where this has been achieved. In fact, some argue that a TQM program can actually assist a company in its downsizing endeavours (Bassi and Van Buren, 1997). Hyde (1993) argued that TQM and downsizing must be seen as complementary and concurrent, rather than as incompatible and antithetical processes, and that "TQM can help insure that downsizing does things right, [and] downsizing can insure that TQM does the right things" (p. 37). Cameron (1995) concluded from his research that a successful quality program implies successful downsizing and, in turn, successful downsizing implies a successful quality program. Moreover, several authors (Hill and Wilkinson, 1995; Stowell, 1994) point out that, because of the prevalence of organizational downsizing, companies will need to learn how to introduce and maintain TQM initiatives while undergoing downsizing if they are to survive in the current business environment.

Supporting empirical evidence for the coexistence of TQM and downsizing

The empirical evidence to support the case for the coexistence of TQM and organizational downsizing is meager at best. However, one of the most rigorous studies examining the relationship between TQM and organizational downsizing conducted to date provides support for the coexistence of TQM and downsizing. Cameron (1998) conducted a large-scale longitudinal study of the impact of the downsizing of a US Army Command unit. Cameron gathered data in three different forms: objective indicators of organizational performance which included measures of quality, customer service, customer complaints, and costs; interviews conducted in 1992, 1993, and 1995 with senior officers and teams of organization members; surveys administered to a stratified random sample of 500 personnel representing all hierarchical levels, all functions, and all subunits in 1992 and again in 1995. Cameron found an increase in product quality, an increase in customer satisfaction, a decrease in the number of customer complaints, and increased cost savings. Employees rated organizational effectiveness significantly higher in 1995 compared to 1992. Cameron concluded that not only had downsizing not been detrimental to the performance of this Army Command unit but that the downsizing may have in fact contributed to organizational effectiveness.

Cameron attributed the effective downsizing to several factors – leadership, preparation, and implementation. The highest performing sub-units had leaders who were accessible, motivational, and visionary and who communicated broadly and consistently with everyone affected by the downsizing. The preparation stage was critical to effective downsizing and consisted of having anticipated the mandate to downsize thus allowing time for advanced planning and preparation, articulating a vision for the future, identifying core competencies, determining where to target downsizing (after ranking the importance of each unit and every activity within each unit), and identifying resource requirements. How the downsizing was implemented was also important. The implementation phase consisted of designing as much flexibility into the downsizing process as possible, communicating openly and fully about the downsizing with employees through multiple media, investing in human resources by making training a priority, involving employees from all levels in the development and implementation processes, and maintaining a customer focus. The approach to downsizing that the Command unit took differed dramatically from the "downsize first – ask questions later" approach identified by Burke and Nelson (1998) as the typical practice. Cameron argues that the Command unit was successful in implementing downsizing because it used a reorientation approach, an approach involving large-scale organizational changes, rather than just merely focusing on reducing its head count.

THE BASIC PRINCIPLES OF TQM

The TQM literature offers a myriad of basic principles associated with total quality management (see for example Boaden, 1997; Dean and Bowen, 1994; Eskildson, 1995; Hill and Wilkinson, 1995; Howes, Citera, and Cropanzano, 1995; Richardson, 1997). However, three of the primary principles are continuous process improvement, teamwork, and a customer focus (Dean and Bowen, 1994). In this section, how a TQM initiative may be affected by organizational downsizing is addressed by examining the empirical evidence as it relates to these three primary principles of total quality management.

Continuous improvement

The evidence suggests that quality and productivity often decline following downsizing, although this is not always the case (see Cameron, 1998). The American Management Association (1996) conducted a survey of 1,441 firms and found that fewer than one-third of the companies that had downsized reported improved productivity and only 35 percent reported quality improvements following job cuts. Hitt et al. (1994) interviewed executives of 65 major US corporations that had recently downsized and less than a quarter indicated increased productivity. Similarly, the American Society for Training and Development study of over 200 companies found that downsized companies had less improvement in quality and overall performance than did companies that had not downsized (Bassi and Van Buren, 1997).

Following a downsizing, it is the remaining employees who will determine to a large extent the level of quality and productivity and, ultimately, the organization's survival (Armstrong-Stassen, 1994; Mone, 1997). The impact of organizational downsizing on the job performance of the survivors is somewhat unclear at this time. There is evidence that work effort and job performance decline following downsizing (Armstrong-Stassen, 1998; Davy et al., 1988; Jalajas and Bommer, 1996; Jick, 1979). However, Brockner and his colleagues (1986; 1992) found an increase in performance. Brockner and Wiesenfeld (1993) suggested that some survivors may work harder because they see this as a way of preserving their job. Brockner et al. (1992) found that a moderate amount of job insecurity was associated with increased work effort, but as job insecurity increased from moderate to high, there was a decrease in work effort. DeFrank and Ivancevich (1986) proposed that layoff survivors will initially show an increase in productivity after a downsizing due to job insecurity, but productivity will decrease over time because of the increased workload, the anxiety and stress created by the downsizing, and reduced commitment to the organization.

Whether or not downsizing has a detrimental effect on continuous improvement is determined to a large extent by the impact that downsizing has on those factors that influence survivors' work effort and job performance: workload demands, job security, organizational commitment, and trust in the organization. Heavy workload demands have been found to be related to lower work effort (Jex and Beehr, 1991) and reduced job performance and productivity (Fox, Dwyer, and Ganster, 1993; Remondet and Hansson, 1991). There is evidence of an increase in workload demands following organizational downsizing as most organizations strive to accomplish the same amount of work with fewer workers (Solomon, 1993). Ganster and Dwyer (1995) found that groups that were understaffed had lower levels of group performance than groups that were adequately staffed.

One of the core responses to organizational downsizing is insecurity (Noer, 1993). Konovsky and Brockner (1993) proposed that job insecurity may ultimately affect organizational functioning through its negative effect on survivors' productivity. Job insecurity has been found to be associated with reduced work effort and productivity (Greenhalgh, 1982; Roskies and Louis-Guerin, 1990). There is some empirical support that job insecurity negatively affects survivors' performance. In a study of production workers in a manufacturing firm undergoing downsizing, Armstrong-Stassen (1993a) found that job insecurity was negatively related to job performance. In another study of 200 technicians in a downsizing company, Armstrong-Stassen (1994) reported a negative relationship between perceived job insecurity and self-rated job performance.

A key element in the success of TQM programs is employee commitment to the organization (Hill and Wilkinson, 1995; Krishnan et al., 1993). Meyer and Allen (1997) claim that employees with strong affective commitment work harder at their jobs and perform them better than do employees with weak affective commitment. Meyer and Allen suggest that committed employees direct their attention to those aspects of their work performance that are valued by and valuable to the organization. Survivors' commitment to the organization has been shown to decrease significantly following downsizing (Armstrong-Stassen, 1998; Cameron, Freeman, and Mishra, 1993; Davy et al., 1988). Although studies investigating the relationship between organizational commitment and job performance have yielded inconsistent findings, organizational commitment has been found to be a significant predictor of job performance and productivity (DeCotiis and Summers, 1987; Galunic and Anderson, 1997; Meyer et al., 1989). Armstrong-Stassen (1993a; 1994) found a significant positive relationship between organizational commitment and job performance for layoff survivors following organizational downsizing.

TQM programs require a high level of trust – trust is central to the long-term success of any TQM initiative (Hill and Wilkinson, 1995; Petrick and Furr, 1995). Employee trust is often seriously undermined in the process of downsizing. Mone (1997) contends that the deterioration in trust following downsizing will result in detrimental effects for both organizations and employees including reduced productivity, lower quality, customer dissatisfaction, and reduced organizational growth and profits. Mone proposed that reduced trust affects these organizational and individual outcomes indirectly through its effects on such factors as job security and organizational commitment. Mone argues that whether or not organizational downsizing will be beneficial or detrimental to an organization and its employees depends upon how well employee trust is preserved. Despite the fact that trust has been identified in both the practitioner and the theoretical literature as playing a key role in survivors' adaptation to organizational downsizing, there has been little empirical research conducted on the role that trust plays in downsizing (Mishra and Spreitzer, 1998). Armstrong-Stassen (1993a; 1993b) found that layoff survivors who expressed greater trust in the company following downsizing reported higher levels of job performance and were more likely to engage in action coping (working harder, putting more effort into doing one's job, and working longer hours) than survivors with less trust.

I am proposing that continuous improvement following downsizing will be impaired to the extent that the downsizing results in excessive workload demands, increased job insecurity, reduced commitment to the organization, and a deterioration in trust in the organization. A detrimental effect on any one of these factors has the potential to disrupt productivity and quality. A downsizing that adversely affects all four factors could be disastrous for an organization's total quality management initiative.

Teamwork

Teamwork, another essential component of TQM, requires a supportive climate in which trust and commitment prevail (Al-Kazemi and Zajac, 1998; Howes, Citera, and Cropanzano, 1995). As noted above, organizational trust and commitment are often seriously undermined by organizational downsizing. The specific factors that are important for successful teamwork include employee empowerment and involvement, cooperation amongst team members and between teams, and organizational support. Unfortunately, there has been much less attention given to the impact of organizational downsizing on the workgroup or team than on the individual layoff survivor.

Employee empowerment is shared decision making which allows members of a team to make decisions on how to improve performance (Richardson, 1997). Eskildson (1995) argued that the strategies that accompany organizational downsizing de-emphasize TQM efforts and result in a much different and more limited role for employee involvement and empowerment. Richardson (1997) noted that honest, open communication is an extremely important component of TQM. Communication has also been identified as a key element in determining survivors' reactions to downsizing (Brockner and Greenberg, 1990). According to Right Associates (1993), "Well-planned and executed communications are as important in a downsizing situation as a musical score is to an orchestra" (p. 4). Unfortunately, there tends to be much less sharing of information during and following downsizing (Cameron, 1995; Kets de Vries and Balazs, 1997). Although much of the focus has been on the decrease in communication from top management, there is also a reduction in the sharing of information among employees. Downsizing disrupts interpersonal connections within the organization. Reynolds Fisher and White (1997) showed that a 20 percent downsizing translates into a 58 percent loss of network connections.

The restriction of communication during and following organizational downsizing has been shown to result in increased job insecurity (Casey, Miller, and Johnson, 1997; Dunlap, 1994). Thorlakson and Murray (1996) contend that it is difficult to create a sense of empowerment in employees who believe that the continuity of their employment is being threatened. Hill and Wilkinson (1995) argue that the insecurity created by downsizing results in a hostile climate, characterized by low trust, that works against TQM. In a study of management-level layoff survivors, Armstrong-Stassen (1997) found that communication quality related to the downsizing was significantly negatively related to perceived threat of job loss and positively related to cooperation between work groups. Managers who felt that the communication they had received during the downsizing was useful and informative were more likely to feel secure about their job and to perceive greater cooperation between their workgroup and other workgroups than managers who felt communication was lacking. Moreover, managers who reported lower communication quality perceived a more negative effect of the downsizing on the organization's TQM program, on teamwork, and on the quality of client service provided by the manager's workgroup.

Teamwork requires cooperation among the team members. However, downsizing tends to create competition and conflict within groups as well as between groups (Cameron, 1995; Davy et al., 1988; Jick and Murray, 1982). Mone (1997) suggests that, given the individualistic nature of layoffs, survivors will feel greater pressure to demonstrate to the organization how their own individual efforts make a difference to the organization. The impact of downsizing on the effectiveness of teams is, however, another area that has been largely ignored by researchers (Leatt et al., 1997; Shaw and Barrett-Power, 1997). The speculation is that downsizing has a negative effect on teamwork by creating a climate characterized by mistrust, suspicion, backstabbing, scapegoating, unwillingness to share information, and turf protection. Such a climate is not conducive to the development and maintenance of effective teams.

According to Howes, Citera, and Cropanzano (1995), one of the key determinants of the success of total quality teams is perceived organizational support. They argue that organizational support is absolutely crucial for effective team performance. Perceived organizational support reflects employees' beliefs that the organization is committed to them, values their contribution, and cares about their well-being (Eisenberger et al., 1986). A downsizing organization that is seen as lacking commitment to its employees will find that its employees are unwilling to make sacrifices on behalf of the organization (Shore and Shore, 1995). The research findings suggest that perceived organizational support is an important determinant of employees' attitudes and behaviors including helping co-workers in their jobs, conscientiousness in carrying out job responsibilities, and attendance (Eisenberger et al., 1997; Eisenberger, Fasolo, and Davis-LaMastro, 1990). All of these are important for effective teamwork. In a longitudinal study of layoff survivors, Armstrong-Stassen (1998) found that perceived organizational support at the beginning of the downsizing was significantly positively related to job satisfaction, organizational morale and trust in the organization, and negatively related to job insecurity two years later. Moreover, managers who perceived greater organizational support reported a less negative effect of the downsizing on the TQM program, on teamwork, and on the quality of client service (Armstrong-Stassen, 1997).

Teamwork can be disrupted by downsizing because of the potentially negative effects that downsizing has on employee empowerment and involvement, on cooperation within the team as well as between teams, and on perceived organizational support. It is difficult to maintain effective teams in a climate characterized by restricted opportunity for making decisions, little sharing of information, diminished cooperation amongst team members and between teams, and limited support on the part of the organization.

Customer Focus

For many people, total quality management initiatives are synonymous with providing high-quality customer service and ensuring customer satisfaction. The downsizing and layoff survivor literatures have rarely addressed the impact of organizational downsizing on the organization's customers, especially its external customers. The one exception is the study by Cameron (1998). Cameron found a decrease in customer complaints and an increase in customer satisfaction following downsizing. However, the practitioner literature suggests that downsizing has a negative impact on customer service and satisfaction (Anderson, Fornell, and Rust, 1997; Miller, 1993; Struebing, 1997). Whether or not organizational downsizing will have a detrimental effect will depend upon the impact of the downsizing on the remaining employees for it is the remaining employees who will be responsible for maintaining high-quality customer service and ensuring high-level customer satisfaction during and following downsizing. The factors that are most likely to influence the quality of service provided by the survivors, and hence customer satisfaction, are organizational morale and a willingness to engage in extra-role behaviors.

Morale reflects individual group members' sense of common purpose and is reflected in the enthusiasm that the group members have to attain group goals (Hershey, 1985; Locke, 1976). Organ (1997) posits that morale is a general factor, similar to the "g" factor of intelligence, underlying such attitudes as job satisfaction, job involvement, alienation, burnout, organizational commitment, group cohesion, and trust in management. Researchers have found a dramatic deterioration in morale following downsizing (Cameron, Freeman, and Mishra, 1993; Jalajas and Bommer, 1996; Jick, 1979). The American Management Association (1996) found that 86 percent of the firms in their study that engaged in downsizing reported a negative impact on employee morale. Armstrong-Stassen (1997) found that organizational morale assessed during the initial stages of downsizing was significantly related to the perceived impact of the downsizing on the organization's TQM initiative. Managers who reported lower levels of organizational morale during the initial stages of the downsizing were significantly more likely to perceive a more negative impact of the downsizing on the TQM program, on teamwork, on quality of client service, and on their own job performance a year later than managers who reported higher morale initially.

Morrison (1996) proposed that organizational citizenship behavior (OCB) has a positive impact on an organization's level of service quality. Organ (1988) defines organizational citizenship behavior as representing "individual behavior that is discretionary, not directly or explicitly recognized by the formal reward system, and that in the aggregate promotes the effective functioning of the organization" (p. 4). Organ (1997) argues that organizational morale directly leads to organizational citizenship behavior. Therefore, if downsizing has a detrimental effect on morale, we would expect that organizational citizenship behavior will be adversely affected as well. Moreover, because downsizing encourages individualism, we would also expect a deterioration in such citizenship behaviors as helping others, civic virtue, and sportsmanship. Moorman and Blakely (1995) found that individuals who are oriented more towards self-interest and reaching their own goals are much less likely to engage in organizational citizenship behaviors than employees who are oriented to the well-being of the collective. Although most of the research focus has been on determining the antecedents of organizational citizenship behavior, OCB has been shown to be related to improved organizational effectiveness (Podsakoff and MacKenzie, 1997), workgroup performance (Podsakoff, Ahearne, and MacKenzie, 1997), and individual performance (Van Dyne and LePine, 1998).

Organ (1988) identified perceived justice as an important determinant of organizational citizenship behavior. People who believe that they have been treated fairly by the organization will be more likely to perform OCBs. Conversely, people who believe that they have been treated unfairly may not be able to respond by reducing their performance because of organizational sanctions so they withhold discretionary behaviors such as citizenship behaviors. Perceived justice has been the focus of much of the research conducted on layoff survivors by Brockner and his colleagues (see, for example, Brockner and Greenberg, 1990; Brockner et al., 1994; Brockner, Wiesenfeld, and Martin, 1995). Brockner and his colleagues have shown that layoffs are frequently characterized by perceived unfairness and that perceived unfairness has negative consequences for layoff survivors and, ultimately, for the organization. An organization that is characterized by poor morale and an unwillingness on the part of its employees to "go the extra mile" is unlikely to provide high service quality to its customers.

The focus of this chapter was on the reactions of the remaining employees to downsizing and the implications of these reactions for a TQM initiative. The empirical evidence from the downsizing and layoff survivor literatures suggests that many TQM initiatives will encounter formidable, but not insurmountable, challenges during downsizing. Of the three key TQM principles examined, there is evidence that the reactions of remaining employees to downsizing will have potentially negative consequences for continuous improvement. The impact of downsizing on teamwork and customer orientation is speculative at this time given the lack of empirical research in these two areas. In conclusion, if TQM and downsizing are to coexist, then management must attempt to limit as much as possible the detrimental effects on those factors that contribute to continuous improvement, teamwork, and customer service and satisfaction. As Cameron (1998) has shown, there are ways to accomplish this.

REFERENCES

Al-Kazemi, A. and Zajac, G. 1998: The self-managed team and tori theory. *International Journal of Commerce and Management*, 8 (1), 70–87.

American Management Association. 1996: *1996 AMA Survey on Downsizing, Job Elimination and Job Creation*. New York: Author.

Anderson, E.W., Fornell, C., and Rust, R.T. 1997: Customer satisfaction, productivity, and profitability: differences between goods and services. *Marketing Science*, 16 (2), 129–45.

Armstrong-Stassen, M. 1993a: Production workers' reactions to a plant closing: the role of transfer, stress, and support. *Anxiety, Stress, and Coping*, 6, 201–14.

Armstrong-Stassen, M. 1993b: Survivors' reactions to a workforce reduction: a comparison of blue-collar workers and their supervisors. *Canadian Journal of Administrative Sciences*, 10, 334–43.

Armstrong-Stassen, M. 1994: Coping with transition: a study of layoff survivors. *Journal of Organizational Behavior*, 15, 597–621.

Armstrong-Stassen, M. 1997: *Organizational downsizing and quality management programs: Can they co-exist?* Paper presented at the annual meeting of the Academy of Management, Boston.

Armstrong-Stassen, M. 1998: Downsizing the federal government: a longitudinal study of managers' reactions. *Canadian Journal of Administrative Sciences*, 15, 310–21.

Bassi, L.J. and Van Buren, M.E. 1997: Sustaining high performance in bad times. *Training and Development*, 51, June, 32–41.

Boaden, R.J. 1997: What is total quality management . . . and does it matter? *Total Quality Mangement*, 8, 153–72.

Brockner, J. and Greenberg, J. 1990: The impact of layoffs on survivors: an organizational justice perspective. In J.S. Carroll (ed.) *Applied Social Psychology and Organizational Settings*. Hillsdale, NJ: Erlbaum, 45–75.

Brockner, J., Greenberg, J., Brockner, A., Bortz, J., Davy, J., and Carter, C. 1986: Layoffs, equity theory, and work performance: further evidence of the impact of survivor guilt. *Academy of Management Journal*, 29, 373–84.

Brockner, J., Grover, S., Reed, T.F., and DeWitt, R.L. 1992: Layoffs, job insecurity, and survivors' work effort: evidence of an inverted-U relationship. *Academy of Management Journal*, 35, 413–25.

Brockner, J., Konovsky, M., Cooper-Schneider, R., Folger, R., Martin, C., and Bies, R.J. 1994: Interactive effects of procedural justice and outcome negativity on victims and survivors of job loss. *Academy of Management Journal*, 37, 397–409.

Brockner, J. and Wiesenfeld, B. 1993: Living on the edge (of social and organizational psychology): the effects of job layoffs on those who remain. In J.K. Murnighan (ed.) *Social Psychology in Organizations: Advances in Theory and Research*. Englewood Cliffs, NJ: Prentice-Hall, 119–40.

Brockner, J., Wiesenfeld, B.M., and Martin, C.L. 1995: Decision frame, procedural justice, and survivors' reactions to job layoffs. *Organizational Behavior and Human Decision Processes*, 63, 59–68.

Buch, K. 1992: How does downsizing affect employee involvement? *Journal for Quality and Participation*, 15, 74–7.

Burke, R.J. and Nelson, D. 1998: Downsizing, restructuring and privatization: a North American perspective. In M.K. Gowing, J.D. Kraft, and J.C. Quick (eds) *The New Organizational Reality: Downsizing, Restructuring, and Revitalization*. Washington, DC: American Psychological Association, 21–54.

Cameron, K.S. 1995: Downsizing, quality, and performance. In R.E. Cole (ed.) *The Death and Life of the American Quality Movement*, New York: Oxford University Press, 93–114.

Cameron, K.S. 1998: Strategic organizational downsizing: an extreme case. *Trends in Organizational Behavior*. New York: John Wiley, 5, 185–229.

Cameron, K.S., Freeman, S.J., and Mishra, A.K. 1993: Organizational downsizing. In G.P. Huber and W.H. Blick (eds) *Organizational Change and Redesign: Ideas and Insights for Improving Performance.* New York: Oxford University Press, 19–65.

Casey, M.K., Miller, V.D., and Johnson, J.R. 1997: Survivors' information seeking following a reduction in workforce. *Communication Research,* 24, 755–81.

Davy, J.A., Kinicki, A., Kilroy, J., and Scheck, C. 1988: After the merger: dealing with people's uncertainty. *Training and Development Journal,* 42 (11), 57–61.

Dean, J.W. Jr. and Bowen, D.E. 1994: Management theory and total quality: improving research and practice through theory development. *Academy of Management Review,* 19, 392–418.

DeCotiis, T.A. and Summers, T.P. 1987: A path analysis of a model of the antecedents and consequences of organizational commitment. *Human Relations,* 40, 445–70.

DeFrank, R.S. and Ivancevich, J.M. 1986: Job loss: an individual level review and model. *Journal of Vocational Behavior,* 28, 1–20.

Dunlap, J.C. 1994: Surviving layoffs: a qualitative study of factors affecting retained employees after downsizing. *Performance Improvement Quarterly,* 7 (4), 89–113.

Easton, G.S. and Jarrell, S.L. 1998: The effects of total quality management on corporate performance: an empirical investigation. *Journal of Business,* 71, 253–307.

Eisenberger, R., Cummings, J., Armeli, S., and Lynch, P. 1997: Perceived organizational support, discretionary treatment, and job satisfaction. *Journal of Applied Psychology,* 82, 812–20.

Eisenberger, R., Fasolo, P., and Davis-LaMastro, V. 1990: Perceived organizational support and employee diligence, commitment, and innovation. *Journal of Applied Psychology,* 75, 51–9.

Eisenberger, R., Huntington, R., Hutchison, S., and Sowa, D. 1986: Perceived organizational support. *Journal of Applied Psychology,* 71, 500–7.

Eskildson, L. 1995: TQM's role in corporate success: analyzing the evidence. *National Productivity Review,* 14 (4), 25–38.

Fox, M.L., Dwyer, D.J., and Ganster, D.C. 1993: Effects of stressful job demands and control on physiological and attitudinal outcomes in a hospital setting. *Academy of Management Journal,* 36, 289–318.

Galunic, D.C. and Anderson, E. 1997: *From Security to Mobility: Generalized Investments in Human Assets and Agent Commitment.* Paper presented at the annual meeting of the Academy of Management, Boston.

Ganster, D.C. and Dwyer, D.J. 1995: The effects of understaffing on individual and group performance in professional and trade organizations. *Journal of Management,* 21, 175–90.

Grant, R.M., Shani, R., and Krishnan, R. 1994: TQM's challenge to management theory and practice. *Sloan Management Review,* Winter, 25–35.

Greenhalgh, L. 1982: Maintaining organizational effectiveness during organizational retrenchment. *The Journal of Applied Behavioral Science,* 18, 155–70.

Hershey, R. 1985: *Organizational Morale.* Kings Point, NY: Kings Point Press.

Hill, S. and Wilkinson, A. 1995: In search of TQM. *Employee Relations,* 17 (3), 8–25.

Hitt, M.A., Keats, B.W., Harback, H.F., and Nixon, R.D. 1994: Rightsizing: building and maintaining strategic leadership and long-term competitiveness. *Organizational Dynamics,* 23 (2), 18–32.

Howes, J.C., Citera, M., and Cropanzano, R.S. 1995: Total quality teams: how organizational politics and support impact the effectiveness of quality improvement teams. In R. Cropanzano and K.M. Kacmar (eds) *Organizational Politics, Justice, and Support: Managing Social Climate at Work.* Westport, CT: Quorum Press, 165–84.

Hubiak, W.A. and O'Donnell, S.J. 1997: Downsizing: a pervasive form of organizational suicide. *National Productivity Review,* 16 (2), 31–6.

Hyde, A.C. 1993: Barriers in implementing quality management. *Public Manager,* 22 (1), 33, 36.

Jalajas, D.S. and Bommer, M. 1996: The effect of downsizing on the behaviors and motivations of survivors. *Organization Development Journal,* 14 (2), 45–54.

Jex, S. and Beehr, T. 1991: Emerging theoretical and methodological issues in the study of work-related stress. *Research in Personnel and Human Resources Management*, 9, 311–65.

Jick, T.D. 1979: Process and Impacts of a Merger: Individual and Organizational Perspectives. Unpublished doctoral dissertation, Cornell University, Ithaca, New York.

Jick, T.D. and Murray, V.V. 1982: The management of hard times: budget cutbacks in public sector organizations. *Organization Studies*, 3, 141–69.

Kets de Vries, M.F.R. and Balazs, K. 1997: The downside of downsizing. *Human Relations*, 50, 11–50.

Konovsky, M.A. and Brockner, J. 1993: Managing victim and survivor layoff reactions: a procedural justice perspective. In R. Cropanzano (ed.) *Justice in the Workplace: Approaching Fairness in Human Resource Management*. Hillsdale, NJ: Lawrence Erlbaum Associates, Inc., 133–53.

Krishnan, A.B., Shani, R.M., Grant, R.B., and Bear, R. 1993: In search of quality improvement: problems of design and implementation. *Academy of Management Executive*, 7 (4), 7–20.

Lawler, E.E. III. 1994: Total quality management and employee involvement: are they compatible? *Academy of Management Executive*, 8, 68–76.

Leatt, P., Baker, G.R., Halverson, P.K., and Aird, C. 1997: Downsizing, reengineering, and restructuring: long-term implications for healthcare organizations. *Frontiers of Health Services Management*, 13 (4), 3–37.

Locke, E.A. 1976: The nature and causes of job satisfaction. In M.D. Dunnette (ed.) *Handbook of Industrial and Organizational Psychology*. Chicago: Rand McNally, 1297–1349.

Meyer, J.P. and Allen, N.J. 1997: *Commitment in the Workplace: Theory, Research, and Application*. Thousand Oaks, CA: Sage Publications, Inc.

Meyer, J.P., Paunonen, S.V., Gellatly, I.R., Goffin, R.D., and Jackson, D.N. 1989: Organizational commitment and job performance: it's the nature of the commitment that counts. *Journal of Applied Psychology*, 74, 152–6.

Miller, C. 1993: In their efforts to cut costs, companies also cut service. *Marketing News*, 27, February 15, 9–10.

Mishra, A.K. and Spreitzer, G.M. 1998: Explaining how survivors respond to downsizing: the roles of trust, empowerment, justice, and work redesign. *Academy of Management Review*, 23, 567–88.

Mone, M.A. 1997: How we got along after the downsizing: post-downsizing trust as a double-edged sword. *Public Administration Quarterly*, 21, 309–36.

Moorman, R.H. and Blakely, G.L. 1995: Individualism-collectivism as an individual difference predictor of organizational citizenship behavior. *Journal of Organizational Behavior*, 16, 127–42.

Morrison, E.W. 1996: Organization citizenship behavior as a critical link between HRM practices and service quality. *Human Resource Management*, 35, 493–512.

Noer, D.M. 1993: *Healing the Wounds: Overcoming the Trauma of Layoffs and Revitalizing Downsized Organizations*. San Francisco: Jossey-Bass Publishers.

Organ, D.W. 1997: Toward an explication of "Morale": In search of the *m* factor. In C.L. Cooper and S.E. Jackson (eds.) *Creating Tomorrow's Organizations: A Handbook for Future Research in Organizational Behavior*. New York: John Wiley and Sons, 493–503.

Organ, D.W. 1988: *Organizational Citizenship Behavior: The Good Soldier Syndrome*. Lexington, MA: D.C. Heath and Company.

Petrick, J.A. and Furr, D.S. 1995: *Total Quality in Managing Human Resources*. Delray Beach, FA: St. Lucie Press.

Podsakoff, P.M., Ahearne, M., and MacKenzie, S.B. 1997: Organizational citizenship behavior and the quantity and quality of work group performance. *Journal of Applied Psychology*, 82, 262–70.

Podsakoff, P.M. and MacKenzie, S.B. 1997: Impact of organizational citizenship behavior on organizational performance: a review and suggestions for future research. *Human Performance*, 10, 133–51.

Powell, A.S. 1993: *Sustaining the Deployment of TQM in an Era of Downsizing*. New York: The Conference Board.

Remondet, J.H. and Hansson, R.O. 1991: Job-related threats to control among older employees. *Journal of Social Issues*, 47, 129–41.

Reynolds Fisher, M. and White, M.A. 1997: *Downsizing and Organizational Learning: A Question of Compatibility*. Paper presented at the annual meeting of the Academy of Management, Boston.

Richardson, T. 1997: *Total Quality Management*. Albany, NY: Delmar Publishers.

Right Associates 1993: *Lessons Learned: When Canadian Organizations Downsize*. Philadelphia: Right Associates.

Roskies, E. and Louis-Guerin, C. 1990: Job insecurity in managers: antecedents and consequences. *Journal of Organizational Behavior*, 11, 345–59.

Scott, G.M. 1995: Downsizing, business process reengineering, and quality improvement plans: how are they related? *Information Strategy*, 11, Spring, 18–34.

Shaw, J.B. and Barrett-Power, E. 1997: A conceptual framework for assessing organization, work group, and individual effectiveness during and after downsizing. *Human Relations*, 50, 109–27.

Shore, L.M. and Shore, T.H. 1995: Perceived organizational support and organizational justice. In R. Cropanzano and K.M. Kacmar (eds) *Organizational Politics, Justice, and Support: Managing Social Climate at Work*. Westport, CT: Quorum Press, 149–64.

Solomon, C.M. 1993: Working smarter: how HR can help. *Personnel Journal*, 72 (6), 54–64.

Stowell, D.M. 1994: Innovative approaches to quality and downsizing. *Quality Digest*, April, 46–52.

Struebing, L. 1997: Experts link customer satisfaction decline to downsizing. *Quality Progress*, 30 (8), 17–20.

Thorlakson, A.J.H. and Murray, R.P. 1996: An empirical study of empowerment in the workplace. *Group and Organization Management*, 21, 67–83.

Van Dyne, L. and LePine, J.A. 1998: Helping and voice extra-role behaviors: evidence of construct and predictive validity. *Academy of Management Journal*, 41, 108–19.

part III The New Career Reality

10 The New Employment Contract: Psychological Implications of Future Work

Paul R. Sparrow

INTRODUCTION

In analyzing the new employment contract, this chapter looks outside what is apparently happening within organizations and considers some of the implications of the unfolding drama surrounding the future of work. The formation of the new employment contract is proving to be a very emotionally charged process. Pascale (1995) puts the problem starkly. We are looking for a painless way out of dealing with the changes in self-esteem, community and social identity that work is now creating, yet many of the changes are inescapably painful. The individual and the organization cannot resolve these issues themselves – it has to be resolved at the level of society and policy. A new social context is necessary to legitimize the experiences associated with the loss and change to our working lives and make them acceptable. Researchers are now asking searching questions about the role of organizations, expectations of the employment contract, and behavior of employees. This chapter explores these questions and summarizes the emerging evidence for each of four possible consequences from changes in the employment contract.

What is meant by the "new" employment contract? Organizational sociologists call it the "new capitalism," arguing that it emerged from 1980 onwards. It is characterized by stiff international competition, state deregulation of industry, institutional ownership of firms, rapid technological change, smaller firm size, structural simplicity, and flexibility (Budros, 1997). For Cappelli (1999), a labor economist, the "traditional" relationship was ended by a variety of management practices that brought both the external product market and the labor market inside the organization. These included competitive pressures to cut time to market and an acceleration in the obsolescence of fixed investments in capital (including human capital). Information technology replaced the co-ordination and monitoring tasks of middle managers and enabled a large range of business functions to be outsourced. Financial arrangements made it possible to advance the interests of shareholders far ahead of other traditional stakeholders, increasing the squeeze of fixed costs. Finally, management techniques such as profit centers, external benchmarking, and core competences exposed every business process and employee to market pressures. Market principles have therefore quickly replaced the old behavioral rules of reciprocity, equity, loyalty, attachment, and long-term commitment. Cappelli (1999) notes that managers who believe that they can draw up a new employment contract that will deliver high performance based on lowered expectations and heightened individual responsibility for "employability" have some nasty shocks in store. There is a contradiction. The nature of most managerial work does not lend itself to market-based relationships and free agency legal contracts. It operates on the basis of open-ended relationships and adjusting obligations as the situation changes. The need to develop unique skills within the organization, and a degree of mutual commitment and trust are inevitable, he argues, yet there is pressure on organizations to shed obsolete skills and poach marketable skills from others. The new contract is an "uneasy dance" because "while both parties know that the relationship is unlikely to last forever, neither knows exactly when it will end, while either side can end it unilaterally when it so desires" (Cappelli, 1999, p. 3). There are new sets of winners and losers. In the 1980s and 1990s the employers were clear winners, but the return of tight labor markets in the US has created new bargaining power advantages for some employees. The "revenge effects" of employee behavior are also creating hidden cost calculations in the delivery of effective organizational performance.

Flexibility is a key word in the new employment contract. It has been a significant driver of change for several years, but it is the uneven burden of flexibility that creates most concerns. In the US in 1998 385,000 manufacturing jobs disappeared, but more than 3 million new jobs were created. Key growth occupations included software programmers, management consultants, amusement park workers, mortgage lenders and temporary employees. US unemployment is at its lowest level (below 4 percent) since the 1960s (Wall Street Journal, 1999) yet during the decade of the 1980s nearly a quarter of all US jobs created were part-time, and of these, 40 percent were involuntary (Appelbaum, 1992). Recent data suggest that the level of involuntary occupancy of peripheral work roles may have increased. Citing a US Bureau of Labor (1995) statistics survey of workers engaged in contingent and alternative work structures, Murphy and Jackson (1999) note that almost two-thirds of respondents worked in such roles involuntarily and would prefer a more traditional full-time employment contract.

Who owns the new employment contract? Who has bottom line accountability for its consequences? Who bears the social cost? Put simply, who pays if you are over-stressed? The trend has been for organizations to shift more social cost accountability onto the state or the individual, and to reduce the core of employees for whom they will be accountable. Freeman's (1996) economic analysis of the dangers of an apartheid employment contract reveals that the problem facing the US is not creating jobs, but making work pay. From 1910–73 the average employee enjoyed substantial gains in real earnings (wage increases of 2 percent per year leading to a doubling of generational income every 35 years) and leisure time. But from 1979 to the mid-1990s median earnings of male employees dropped by 13 percent. Inequalities grew in this period. If the $2 trillion increase in GDP from 1980–94 had been divided equally, each US family would have gained $2,000. Instead, median family income was stagnant. The proportion of aggregate income for the top 5 percent rose from 15 percent to 19 percent from 1980–93, while the proportion going to 80 percent of families fell. A decade of gains in GDP and in employment were accompanied by falling incomes for the bottom half of US families. The decline of trade unionism in the US from 30 percent to 11 percent of the private sector accounted for about one-fifth of the rise in inequality of earnings.

Some of the hidden costs in the new employment contract operate at the institutional level, and there is much instability in the economic structures that have driven the new employment contract. Managerial attitude surveys convey a sense of unease about the employment contract, and hint at limits in the capacity of many individuals to cope with the adaptations required. Two recent managerial surveys in the UK demonstrate the point. Based on a survey of a panel of 5,000 British Institute of Management members, Worrall and Cooper (1998) found that 52 percent of managers feared that their company had lost essential skills and experience – up from 45 percent of managers in 1997. Forty-one percent of managers referred to a poverty of communication and consultation about strategic change in their organization. Attitudes to longer working hours were ambivalent. Forty-five percent of senior managers thought working long hours was acceptable, but 22 percent of junior managers felt it unacceptable, but had no choice over the matter. Seventy percent of managers reported working over 40 hours a week, 53 percent regularly work in the evening, and 34 percent regularly work over the weekend. Seventy-two percent correctly sense that working long hours affected their relationship with their partner. Fifty-five percent perceive that long work hours damages their health, 55 percent feel it actually makes them less productive and 49 percent feel that they suffer from information overload.

Similarly, a Management Today/Ceridian survey of work-life balance of nearly 2,000 managers (Davis, 1999) examined attitudes about what bothered managers in the new employment contract, what they would most like to change, and what the perceived consequences were. The conclusion was that British managers faced a "strain drain" as a significant proportion of senior managers made sacrifices in their personal lives to keep up with the "rat race." Forty-nine percent thought morale in their organizations was low, 55 percent felt they faced frequent stress at work, 30 percent felt their health was suffering because of this, half felt they had no time to build relationships out of work, 20 percent admitting drinking to ease work pressure, and 8 percent had resorted to therapy. Such surveys are not statistically representative – but capture a mood that deserves further consideration. Forty percent were looking for a job over the next 12 months (whether they would get one is irrelevant, in their minds they were mobile). However, long work hours (12 percent), workload pressure (18 percent) and corporate culture (20 percent) were not the main drivers for this. Rather it was lack of challenge (44 percent), lack of recognition (37 percent), lack of money (36 percent) and poor work-life balance (35 percent). Although 81 percent responded that "I am very loyal to my organization," 71 percent would seriously consider an approach from a head-hunter.

PSYCHOLOGICAL PERSPECTIVES ON THE NEW EMPLOYMENT CONTRACT

Several writers now argue that new theories and approaches are needed in the field of organizational psychology (Hartley, 1995; Tetrick and Barling, 1995). Psychologists have looked at the changing employment contract principally through four "lenses":

1. changes in the nature of trust (see Bradach and Eccles, 1989; Clark and Payne, 1997; Miles and Creed, 1996);

2. changes in and breach of the psychological contract (see McLean-Parkes and Schmedemann, 1994; Morrison and Robinson, 1997; Robinson and Morrison, 1995; Robinson and Rousseau, 1994);

3. the content of, and perceived breach in, distributive, procedural, retributive and interactional forms of organizational justice (see Cropanzano, 1993; Greenberg, 1990; Sheppard, Lewicki, and Minton, 1992); and

4. the development of social exclusion within organizations (access to important resources, social networks, and intangible career opportunities) and related changes in organizational behaviour (see Barker, 1995).

This chapter concentrates on the psychological contract, but some comments about trust must be made as it is a central theme to recent psychological research. Tensions surrounding perceptions of trust will continue. American Management Association data show that 80 percent of US firms that downsized were still profitable at the point of downsizing, and that on the day of announcement of rationalization stock prices typically rose by 7 percent. Trust is actually a willingness to rely or depend on some externality such as an event, process, individual, group or system (Clark and Payne, 1997). It implies the ability to take for granted many features of the social order (Miles and Creed, 1996), and expect that actions will be beneficial rather than detrimental (Gambetta, 1988). Creed and Miles (1996) distinguish *three* different facets of trust:

*   *process-based* – personal experience of recurring exchanges which create ongoing expectations and norms of obligation about what is felt to be fair treatment;
*   *characteristic-based* – beliefs about another's trustworthiness that results from a perception of their expertise, intentions, actions, words, and general qualities; and
*   *institutional-based* – trust in the integrity and competence of informal societal structures.

All three facets have been challenged recently, but the HRM solutions to the breach and rebuilding of each facet are not as yet understood (Sparrow and Marchington, 1998). At an anecdotal level, it is easy to see growing levels of mistrust. Do people trust presidents, politicians or political processes? Do they trust major institutions such as the police or the independence of their judiciary? Do they trust key professions such as food scientists or medical doctors? Do they trust the quality of information they have to deal with at work? Media such as television or the Internet? There has always been distrust in the employment contract, a sense of us and them, but mistrust is highly evident again. The problem is that organizations are asking employees to trust *in* transition at the very time that the nature of employee trust *is itself in* transition (Sparrow and Cooper, 1998). The ability of organizations to re-establish high levels of trust has to be questioned.

THE PSYCHOLOGICAL CONTRACT AS AN ANALYTICAL CONSTRUCT

The psychological contract is viewed not as a construct *per se*, but as a perceived agreement between two parties, consisting of various contractual terms (Shore and Barksdale, 1998). Although highly idiosyncratic and situation-bound, it has been used to capture recent changes in the new employment contract (Shore and Tetrick, 1994). It has additional value over other constructs such as perceived organizational support and can help us describe, understand, and predict the consequences of changes in employment (Coyle-Shapiro and Kessler, 1999). The sense of mutuality implicit in the psychological contract has proved a useful vehicle to capture the consequences of perceived imbalances of exchange in the new employment contract. It represents an implicit and open-ended agreement on what is given and what is received and captures expectations of reciprocal behavior that cover a wide range of societal norms and interpersonal behavior. It is based on changing perceptions of the employer–employee balance of power and is very emotive – academics argue that you only know what the contract is when you breach it.

Because it is evidenced in an individual's mental models of the world, it is felt to act as a deep driver of careers, rewards, and commitment behavior. Positive employer contract behavior has been linked to outcomes such as: job satisfaction and organizational commitment (Coyle-Shapiro and Kessler, 1999; Guest et al., 1996; Robinson and Rousseau, 1994); organizational citizenship behavior (Robinson and Morrison, 1995); and employee performance (Robinson, 1996). These studies have demonstrated generic impacts on outcomes such as organizational citizenship behavior and commitment. Social exchange theory is used to argue that different employees appear to react similarly to contract violations or fulfilment. When fulfilled, employees are assumed to reduce their indebtedness by reciprocating with more effort directed at the source of the benefits. Breach of contract is seen through three primary reactions (Hirschman, 1970; Turnley and Feldman, 1998):

- *Exit behaviour*, where the individual is angered by the violation so seeks employment elsewhere,
- *Voice*, where the individual makes an attempt to correct the problem and salvage the employment contract, and
- *Loss of loyalty*, where the individual withdraws emotionally, displays less loyalty and lower organizational citizenship behavior.

Initially attention to the psychological contract associated with changes in the employment contract outlined the "old deal" and the "new deal." There is no consensus on the components of the new psychological contract (Cavanaugh and Noe, 1999) but the shift is seen in terms of a move from a paternalistic to a partnership relationship, and a move from relational aspects of the relationship to more transactional components. The old deal was stereotyped as one in which promotion could be expected, based on time-served and technical competence. As long as the company was in profit and you did your job then you had no cause to fear job loss. The organizational culture was paternalistic, and encouraged an exchange of security for commitment. Responsibilities were part of an instrumental exchange, but were progressively linked to the career hierarchy. Personal development was the company's responsibility. High trust was not widespread, but deemed possible. The new employment contract has been stereotyped in a different way. Change is seen to be continuous. There is less opportunity for vertical grade promotion and it is against new criteria. Anyway, isn't promotion only something for those who deserve it? Tenure cannot be guaranteed. In a globalizing economy you are "lucky to have a job." More responsibilities are encouraged, balanced by increased accountabilities. Status is based on perceived competence and credibility. Personal development is the employee's responsibility – individuals have to keep themselves employable whilst the organization offers employability (the opportunity to develop marketable skills). High trust is still deemed desirable, but organizations accept that employees are less committed to them, but more committed to the project they work on, their profession and their fellow team members. Organizations therefore build an attachment to proxies – such as the team – for whom employees will still perform. There is evidence that managers' loyalty to their employer has declined (Stroh, Brett, and Reilly, 1994) and commitment to type of work and profession appears to be stronger now than commitment to organization (Ancona et al., 1996).

There are many academic debates about the psychological contract (Guest, 1998). Research has mixed several psychological constructs – such as perceptions, expectations, beliefs, promises, and obligations – and has applied these processes to a range of outcomes – such as levels of commitment, job satisfaction, socialization, employer–employee fit, and organizational climate. On the positive side, the label "psychological contract" has captured complex changes in work in times of high uncertainty. It acts as an organization-wide frame of analysis – like culture or competencies – and uses a language – mindsets, frames of reference, schema, implicit deals, breach of trust and disengagement – that captures concerns over the new employment contract (Sparrow and Marchington, 1998). However, because it has been operationalized to include several different psychological facets, each of which bears an unknown relationship to the other, the contract has become an analytic nightmare (Guest, 1998). Employees are assumed to "input" various attributes to the "new deal," such as their work values and attitudes, motivational needs, and personal dispositions or competencies. Contract formation and breach processes (signals sent by the HRM environment about socialization, mutual exchanges, promises, and obligations) lie at the heart of most research. Attention is also turned to a series of "outputs" or outcomes, such as commitment, job satisfaction, trust, and organization citizenship behaviors.

Recent research is breaking the psychological contract down into a range of elements and examining the relationship between each element. For example, Coyle-Shapiro and Kessler (1999) make a distinction between perceived organizational support and the fulfilment of obligations in terms of the consequences on organizational citizenship behaviors and commitment. Perceived organizational support is defined as a general perception by the employee of the extent to which the organization values their general contribution and well-being (Eisenberger et al., 1986; Shore and Shore, 1995). This is an important distinction to make in terms of the new employment contract. An organization may not be able to offer jobs for life and may engage in more transactional relationships, but may be able to (or may be perceived as being able to) show high levels of personal support. Does perceived organizational support mediate the impact that the fulfilment of obligations and promises has on important psychological outcomes? Does the psychological contract account for useful additional variance in outcome behaviors? Survey data from 703 managers and 6,953 employees of a British public sector local authority found high levels of perceived breach of contract (89 percent felt that their employer had fallen short of valued transactional obligations and 81 percent felt it had fallen short of valued relational obligations). Psychological contract fulfillment did indeed account for unique and additional variance in explaining levels of commitment and organizational citizenship behavior.

Figure 10.1 Four different adaptation processes to the new employment contract

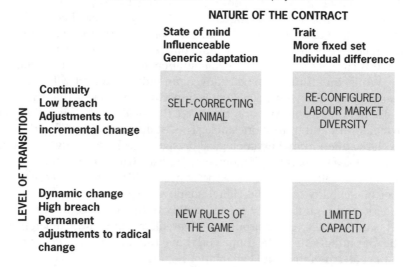

NATURE OF THE CONTRACT

	State of mind Influenceable Generic adaptation	Trait More fixed set Individual difference
Continuity Low breach Adjustments to incremental change	SELF-CORRECTING ANIMAL	RE-CONFIGURED LABOUR MARKET DIVERSITY
Dynamic change High breach Permanent adjustments to radical change	NEW RULES OF THE GAME	LIMITED CAPACITY

LEVEL OF TRANSITION

FOUR SCENARIOS ABOUT THE FUTURE PSYCHOLOGICAL CONTRACTS FACED BY ORGANIZATIONS

In an attempt to construct a framework for examining the impact on organizational HRM systems of different employment contract scenarios, Sparrow and Cooper (1998) reviewed published work on changes in the psychological contract. In order for the framework to have conceptual clarity the categories must have a consistent focus. The four quadrants in figure 10.1 describe and capture the *nature of adaptive responses* of individuals to the new employment contract. The framework can be used to question whether much of our current HRM knowledge is now redundant. The combination of people variety, and environmental complexity and change, will inevitably produce a range of different psychological contract scenarios. There are two sets of bi-polar conclusions we might draw from existing research on adaptation to the new employment contract. The first axis reflects the nature of the organizational environment and the scale of changes required in individual behavior and adaptation. It concerns the level of transition we are actually witnessing. This may be seen as low or high. Those who feel that the level of change in the psychological contract is currently low, will point to much continuity in the nature of the employment contract, low levels of breach of contract or an over-statement of breach of contract issue, and an incremental adjustment to change. Those who feel that the level of change in the psychological contract is high, point to very dynamic levels of change in employment, a more subjective view of insecurity, high levels of breach of contract, and some permanent changes in behavior. The second axis concerns the nature of the individual adaptive reaction to these levels of change, and the level of flexibility within the adaptation. Again, two contrasting positions can be taken. On the one hand, it can be argued that the contract is very much a state of mind – an attitude. As such, it is open to influence, and may be compensated for, perhaps by activity outside work (such as leisure or non-work activities). This state of mind, reflecting high flexibility to change within the individual adaptive response, is also seen to be generic. The flexibility applies to (most) all people. On the other hand, the psychological contract might be seen to operate more as an individual trait. The contracts that people form might be much more reflective of underlying individual differences – such as personality, career anchors. In this case, it will not be as open to influence as the level of individual flexibility is low. Whilst an attitude can be changed, an individual trait will reflect a much more resistant position for some people. It is important to be clear that the "state versus trait" distinction on this axis *does not reflect the traditional psychological view* that states are temporary and traits more stable. The "state versus trait" distinction therefore needs clarification from a psychological perspective. A state is by definition a less permanent (that is a temporary) phenomenon, whilst a trait is more stable. The framework here does not imply this sense of permanancy. Rather, it reflects the level of flexibility or malleability in the individual adaptive response. The state of mind pole reflects generic and high flexibility or malleability of the adaptive response. The trait pole reflects low flexibility based around more predictive individual difference factors. Each of the four quadrants in the framework have the same degree of permanence in capturing the pattern of individual adaptation.

The four different future scenarios are briefly outlined:

1. The *self-correcting animal* scenario is based on assumptions about the generic capacity of individuals to adapt to environments. The generic ability of individuals to manage in turn makes them more manageable from an HRM perspective.
2. The *reconfigured diversity* scenario implicitly hints at the nature of the situation facing organizations, but is intended to capture the pattern seen in the individual adaptive response. It is based on the assumption that although the majority of individuals are capable of adjusting to the new employment contract in terms of abilities, there are wide individual differences in terms of work motivation. These new and diverse work motivation responses will dominate the individual adaptation process. The diversity will be driven along unfamiliar lines. This will create immense difficulty for organizations in designing "workable" psychological contracts.
3. The *limited capacity* scenario also concerns the ability of people to adjust and adapt to their environment. Changes forced on individuals are seen to be more rapid and paradigm breaking. The capacity of individuals in adapting to this radical change is assumed to meet limits, and depending on a series of important individual differences, there is a failure to cope, at least for a significant amount of time. This fallability of certain individuals makes them unmanageable from the perspective of the organization.
4. The *new rules of the game* quadrant implicitly labels the type of organizational environment, but is intended to characterize the nature of the individual adaptive response. Again, the environment is not stable, but has changed radically. Individual differences (except perhaps across age or life-cohort) are less important in understanding the adaptive response. Rather, generic adaptations are seen in the way that people work out what, for them, are the new rules for playing the game. In this scenario it is the organization that might have limited capacities, rather than individuals, in that organizations will find it hard to

cope with the new behaviors and rule-sets that will govern the adaptive response of all employees.

These four scenarios are not alternative futures. Each scenario tends to reflect different findings that say much about the methodologies and assumptions made by the researchers, but no finite conclusions should be drawn about the superiority of one scenario over another. To some extent, different industrial sectors might see themselves facing different scenarios, given that they have traditionally employed different types of employee.

Self-correcting animals?

The first scenario suggests some generic but moderate consequences of breach in the psychological contract, but nonetheless far more stability in the employment contract than we might believe. This scenario is based around assumptions that there are low levels of breach in the contract, and that it operates as a state of mind, open to considerable influence. The following arguments or empirical evidence come to the fore:

Historical relativity

There have been periods of intense change in the employment contract before, with low levels of trust. We are seeing the demise of a post-war blip in employment and people are resilient. Indeed, despite his concerns about the new employment contract, Cappelli (1999) reminds us that the "traditional" employment contract in the US was a contractor system. Only the need to co-ordinate more complex organizations and safeguard the supply of large integrated operations (reinforced by war time controls) brought the workforce inside organizations and led to the development of longer-term relationships.

Multiple employment agents

There are several agents in the new employment contract – team members, supervisors, customers – and it is inevitable that one may have breached some facet of an individual's psychological contract (Guest, 1998). Single agent studies tend to overstate the amount and seriousness of breach of contract and the consequence might be insignificant.

Poor delineation of psychological reaction

Many studies have not truly measured the real psychological response. Turnley and Feldman (1998) distinguish four types of response: "no violation, the organization has fulfilled all promises"; "the organization never made any commitments in the first place"; "work might not be what I expected it to be, but this is just part of doing business, not a contract violation"; and finally "my contract has been seriously violated." Even in high change sectors (banking and state agencies) they found that whilst 25 percent of employees felt they had received less than they had been promised, only

25 percent felt their contracts had been violated. Researchers rarely distinguish between breach of contract – commonplace but inconsequential – and violation – more emotive with more serious psychological consequences.

Lack of structured samples

We have relied on anecdotal evidence, case studies in high change industrial sectors, and unrepresentative surveys. More reliable and representative surveys suggest there are far more limited levels of breach or violation of contract. Evidence from national surveys carried out by Guest et al. (1996) for the British Institute of Personnel and Development (IPD) show that deterioration in the psychological contract is restricted to around 20 percent of the workforce, mainly less educated employees in more peripheral jobs. Larger but unstructured surveys also tend to come up with this figure of from 20–30 percent highly dissatisfied individuals perceiving dysfunctional consequences to the new employment contract (Davis, 1999). For the majority, change is less stark than often suggested (Guest et al., 1996). The IPD surveys showed that 79 percent of UK employees said that they still trusted management a lot.

Stable labor market data

Measures of job tenure suggest it is not falling radically, nor is there yet an employee backlash and high levels of job turnover. In the 1970s the average length of job tenure in the UK was 6 years. It is currently around 5.5 years, having fallen to a low of 4.5 years in the early 1990s (Smith, 1997). Male job tenure has fallen 25 percent since 1976, but women now have 12 percent longer periods of tenure. Cappelli (1999) notes research into average rates of job tenure in the US in the mid-1990s produced contradictory results, but at face level initial reports suggested not much had changed.

Two things might be happening under this scenario. First, there may be a robust adjustment process in evidence. Although employees might be temporarily affected by downsizing and dislocations in employment, survivors are capable of re-imbuing the organization with a degree of trust. Second, the slow shift towards high commitment HRM practices might be paying off, moderating falls in average levels of commitment and re-engaging a sufficiently large proportion of the workforce.

Reconfigured diversity scenario

Continuing with a set of relatively low and incremental change assumptions, what if we now assume that the psychological contract operates more like an individual trait, with markedly different reactions to the changing employment contract. Much literature assumes a generic response to perceived breach of contract in terms of the impact on commitment and organizational citizenship behavior. Research in sectors that have undergone significant amounts of rationalization, such as financial services (see, for example, Hartley, 1995; Herriot and Pemberton, 1996; Sparrow, 1996) suggests a more individually-diverse response. These studies have teased out different attitudinal and contractual stances held by segments of the workforce as shown in table 10.1.

Sparrow (1996) studied a major change initiative aimed at understanding the "deal" sought by a structured sample of 200 employees in a large UK retail bank. Attitudes to

Table 10.1 Diverse contractual stance frameworks and exchange deals

Sparrow (1996) Contractual stances	Herriot and Pemberton (1996) Career contracts
Still ambitious: understood the realities of the new deal but felt that some advancement was still possible for them	*Development or core deal:* organization seeks high flexibility, high commitment and work hours involvement, added-value in the skills that the individual possesses. Individuals sign up to this deal in return for as much trust and security that the firm can offer, the provision of employability, and development of core skills.
Frustratedly mobile: had disengaged mentally and were hoping for and seeking a job elsewhere, but only because they were frustrated that their manager did not understand their needs	*Autonomy or project deal:* organization seeks specific but cross-organization skills for short time. Individuals capable of delivering high performance with low supervision or management. Individuals sign up to this deal in return for the provision of autonomy, freedom over how they design their work, and the provision of interesting and challenging work.
Passively flexible: expected to have to be more flexible in most areas, but had little enthusiasm for it or sense of agency in it	*Lifestyle or part-time deal:* organization seeks flexibility to match work and time pattern demands, part-time individuals with skills of a full-timer, and performance levels to match high levels of customer service. Individuals sign up to this deal in return for a willingness from their employer to balance their work with other lifestyle roles, and provision of work patterns matched to their lifestyle.
Lifers: respected the old deal, not impressed with performance pay, and thought that time-served and technical competence were a legitimate way to decide on advancement	
Buy me outers: had a price to buy them out of their job, waiting for the right deal to come along	
Guidance seekers: needed help and assistance to understand what the changes meant for their careers and future course of action	
Don't push me too fast: understood and would go along the changes, but felt it was happening too fast and being asked to change too soon	
Just pay me more: transactional outlook, would take on most flexibilities at a negotiated price	

pay, promotion, tenure, and flexibility were measured from the three attitudinal dimensions: what do you expect to happen, how do you feel about this, and what do you intend to do? Ninety-five percent of the workforce expected less opportunity for promotion, only 7 percent expected that promises about their career would be kept, 35 percent expected to actively seek out a new job outside the company, and 43 percent thought there was some possibility that they might be made compulsorily redundant in the future. When their expectations, feelings and intentions were factor analyzed, it became clear that there were eight different contractual stances within this workforce.

The important point about the contractual stances found by Sparrow (1996) is that they are not different people – but rather dimensions along which the attitudes held towards the new employment contract varied. In principle, an individual might hold several of these positions to varying degrees, might be disengaged now, but capable of redemption. The different contractual stances make it clear that a "one size fits all" brand of HRM, or the pursuit of high commitment practices, is not something that will suit all. The armoury brought to bear (cafeteria benefits, empowerment, performance-related pay, high involvement teams and so forth) will not work for many segments of this workforce – 31 percent of this workforce had disengaged in any event. The con-tractual stances were a source of major individual difference, and could not be pre-dicted significantly by traditional internal labor market segmenting variables. Age, length of service, sex, and grade level together accounted for generally no more than 16 percent of variance in contractual stances. Anyone could be a "buy me outer." Perceptions about the new employment contract are clearly relative, and responses highly variable. Hartley's (1995) survey analysis of 587 bank employees found marked differences in job satisfaction and trust (not commitment) between key-time employees who chose to join a union and those who did not. The least satisfied, least trusting employees were more inclined to join the union. They had least faith in the intentions of managers, in their abilities or competence. Contours of change in insecurity are not straightforward.

The contract may pattern in relation to telling individual differences. There is a long history of attention to diverse work orientations, career anchors and the desire of managers to disengage. Although changes are still seen as incremental and reflective of a long pattern of HRM change over the last decade, in some sectors breach is high and new individual patterns of behavior are developing as the new contours of the internal labor market emerge. Individual differences are expected to return as import-ant predictors of adaptive work behavior in the new employment contract. Some indi-viduals will pursue high intensity/variety patterns, others will seek the opposite. The strategies that organizations have to pursue in this scenario are to:

1. attend to the delivery of the basic mutualities of the contract to re-engage many employees, and to institute a process of individual dealing (Herriot, Manning, and Kidd, 1997);
2. predict new internal labor market groupings on the basis of the different "con-tractual stances" and develop different brands of HRM to suit the new internal labor markets (Sparrow and Marchington, 1998).

An understatement of the true level of transition?

A number of arguments suggest that the level of change and transformation being experienced is more radical and pervasive than that suggested above. They point to methodological shortcomings of research that reports a stable situation in terms of employee and labor market behavior, or argue that survey instruments and items are insensitive to underlying changes in cognitive structures and cause-and-effect reasoning. Change in deep cognitive and value structures is more important than employees saying "mustn't grumble" when answering surveys. Surveys may simply pick up employee naivety, or cognitive dissonance. Faced with the consequences of radical economic and structural transitions, individuals act as though it will happen to others but not to them.

Perceptual framing

Although affected by change and behaving differently, employees might report minor adjustments in their perceptions of what is happening. If times are tough, we adjust expectations downwards and report that things are not as bad as others make out. Many studies on full-time and part-time employees found that reported levels of job satisfaction are little different, despite significant differences in pay, rewards, and job design. Hulin and Glomb (1999) argue that this discrepancy is explained by different perceptual framing. If the employee's frame is anchored in a context of no work, even irregular work and income may be viewed positively. Survey findings that show reported levels of job satisfaction or trust that are little altered might be evidencing changes in the perceptual frame. If survey questions were asked more sensitively, or if qualitative data were gathered, valid changes might well be detected.

Incorrect assumptions about stable labor market behavior

In tight labor markets more workers quit but fewer are dismissed, and in loose markets the opposite happens. Cappelli's (1999) analysis of published data on voluntary and involuntary quits presents the following picture. In terms of attachment to an employer, then the overall length of time that the average employee stays with a given employer, whilst quite constant until the mid-1990s, has indeed now eroded. The percentage of the US workforce with long-tenure jobs (of ten years or more) declined slightly from the late 1970s to 1993, then fell sharply, and is now at its lowest level in 20 years of comparable data. This hides significant differences for specific employment groups, such as women being less likely to leave jobs voluntarily because of marriage or child-birth and older and less-educated males being more likely to have reduced tenure. Of interest too are generational cohort differences. Cappelli (1999) notes that in the US there has been a 10 percent increase in the number of job changes for younger workers. Evidence in the UK from the British Household Panel Survey shows the same situation emerging. Looking across generational cohorts, the percentage who have experienced only one employment status was only 28 percent for the 1920s cohort, rising to 37 percent for the 1930s cohort and peaking at 71 percent for the 1940s cohort. It fell away again to 53 percent for the 1950s cohort and 34 percent for the 1960s cohort. Clearly, the "traditional" employment contract was a historical blip, as noted by Cappelli (1999). However, something new is happening for the younger generation. The proportion of 15–30 year olds who have experienced four or more employment statuses has more than doubled from 8 percent of the 1920s cohort to 19 percent of the 1960s cohort. The key issue with such data is the focus of identity or commitment. Although average organizational tenure is falling, if we ask how frequently employees have changed occupations rather than employers, then the opposite has happened (Cappelli, 1999). If anything workers seem to be staying in the same occupation longer, paralleling the increase in occupational as opposed to organizational loyalty noted by Stroh, Brett, and Reilly (1994). As internal labor markets erode, then external labor market skill identities have become more evident. The role of such new identities should form a new focus for research career psychology.

Subjective impact of job insecurity

Perceptual definitions of job insecurity range may be narrow in scope (for example, anticipation of a potential termination of a job – Jacobson, 1987, 1991) or broad definitions (such as perceived powerlessness to maintain desired continuity of employment, or loss of subjectively important features of the job – Greenhalgh and Rosenblatt, 1984). The objective data covered earlier ignore changes and disruptions caused *within* internal labor markets. Downsized and delayered organizations, even if not reducing job tenure of survivors, alter the rules in terms of who gets promoted, how, and what promotion means. Subjective job insecurity includes assessments of expected risk and consequences of job loss. Shifts in the work of nations, international patterns of job creation, changes in employment conditions associated with social dumping, and changes in organizational power and autonomy over the employment contract suggest subjective insecurity has increased. Significant financial adjustments and psychological transitions associated with job loss arise because of: increased segmentation and structural nature of unemployment; increased duration of unemployment spells; political moves in societies towards "back to work" or "work-fare" philosophies; significant reductions in earning power of the re-employed; and reduced power of supportive institutions (such as trades union collective bargaining power and welfare systems). Employees are *more objective in their subjective assessment of insecurity* than external labor market and psychological outcome analysts may believe (Sparrow and Cooper, 1998). Those with good jobs hang on to them, whilst those in more dissatisfying environments see all options tarred with the same brush, and are in no hurry to move.

Limited capacities

The limited capacity scenario therefore suggests we will witness a reaction to new forms of work constrained by significant individual limits on flexibility and adaptability. Three streams of research support this scenario:

- average level of well-being, stress and reactions to long working hours;
- competency gaps associated with new organizational roles, and specific cognitive limits to new managerial work roles, such as information overload;
- cultural constraints to organizational behavior, level of adaptation and attraction to the new employment contract.

Deteriorating well-being and a long work hours culture

Does the fear and anxiety associated with the new employment contract impact motivation and well-being? Evidence of lasting effects on motivational processes has been summarized by Brockner et al. (1993). They examined the extent to which fear associated with layoffs was a positive incentive to motivation or not and found a complex interaction between levels of self-esteem, worry, threat of future layoff and motivation levels. Perversely, Brockner et al.'s (1993) data showed that survivors with the greatest level of motivation were those with the lowest self-esteem, high worry and high threat of future layoff. If ways can be found to ensure the commitment of these high threat/high motivation individuals, then organizations might be able to survive the transition with limited detriment in organizational behavior. Noting the possible health-related consequences of such a strategy, Daniels (1995) advanced an alternative hypothesis – in the field setting as opposed to experimental situation, the "fear" interaction only actually explained 3 percent of the variance in employee motivation in the Brockner et al. study. Psychologists have long considered the nature of anxiety (Warr, 1990) but have recently tackled the concept of "recession fatigue." Exposure to stressful stimuli leads initially to anxiety and worry, but prolonged exposure may force individuals to interpret events as uncontrollable. Anxiety is terminated as the employee adopts a "if it is going to happen, it will, so I might as well get on with my life" attitude. Although the fear element is reduced, depression tends to set in. Large scale survey studies with repeated measures tend to support this latter pattern of transition (Daniels and Guppy, 1993).

This issue of detrimental limits has been reflected in research examining the link between work hours and health. Evidence that employees are working longer hours to cope with increasing workloads, job insecurity, and pressures for improved or "stretched" performance is clear, but the success of many atypical forms of employment in terms of their impact on productivity and employee well-being has yet to be fully evaluated (Wallace and Greenwood, 1995). Reviews of the effect of shift work on health (Harrington, 1994) concluded that working hours in excess of 48–56 hours are harmful. Clear cut recommendations are not yet possible. Sparks et al. (1997) found a small but statistically significant link between working hours and health. The stress and well-being literature draws attention to limits to capacity evidenced through physical or psychological costs. The mean correlation between physiological and psychological health and work hours was 0.0636 and 0.1465 respectively. Sparks et al. (1997) argue that these correlations underestimate the true linkage. We assume linear relationships between work stressors and outcomes, but at certain levels we may see breakpoints and discontinuities in the work intensity–well-being relationship. However, existing studies apply insufficient experimental control and several factors will have a moderating influence on the work hours–well-being relationship.

Competency limits

Many organizations find themselves experiencing significant competency gaps, relying on a narrowing base of managers seen as capable of performing effectively in new managerial roles (Sparrow, 1999). The ability of organizations, indeed nations, to resource sufficient numbers of people skilled for the new employment contract cannot be assumed. Associated with this is the problem of individual cognitive limits. We are in danger of designing jobs, roles, and organizations that will impose a dysfunctional burden on employees, thereby bringing the problem of limits to capacity to the fore. Information overload (number and difficulty of decisions and judgments that information requires; time available to act; quality of required information processing; and predictability of information inputs) is now a significant issue. The ill-conceived actions of over-burdened managers generates potential for unjustified risk-taking and error. Expecting managers to improve their cognitive capabilities to cope with information overload seems a route to further chaos. Not all managers may be capable of development in important skills, organizations might not have enough depth of talent capable of development, and even competent managers have cognitive limits.

National culture as a limiting factor

National culture value orientations are relatively stable sources of individual difference, which though aggregated at national level, operate within the individual psychology of employees. Significant differences in contract formation and breach processes can be theorized (Sparrow, 1998). As stable sources of individual differences, values are predictive of much organizational behavior and many precepts of the new employment contract, such as high performance HRM, or rewards preferences. Individual level research provides evidence that cultural value orientations act as a factor that limit capacity to make the necessary adaptations (Schuler and Rogovsky, in press; Sparrow and Wu, 1998) with some people remaining hide bound by deep-seated cultural objections to changes in the employment contract.

CONCLUSIONS: NEW RULES OF THE GAME?

In conclusion, are there grounds to suggest a more radical scenario for the new employment contract – one in which high levels of transition and high levels of flexibility create new patterns of employee behavior? Evidence for the fourth and final scenario is as yet weak, but may be inferred from studies that:

1. examine whether employees' work experiences such as downsizing, restructuring, job loss and job change are related to adoption of new elements in the psychological contract;
2. find empirically, or question theoretically, the limited validity and transferability of previously held organizational behavior relationships in new organizational settings.

Research into job loss suggests affected employees adopt new beliefs or perceptions regarding careers (Leana and Feldman, 1994; Shore and Tetrick, 1994). Individuals who experience job loss believe all subsequent employment opportunities are less secure. However, are employees adopting new elements in their psychological contract? This has not been tested empirically, nor has the consequence of "new" psychological contracts for historically demonstrated links to key organizational behaviors. If revision of the contract does take place, we may see "new rules of the game" emerging. Cavanaugh and Noe (1999) investigated the relationship between work experience and adoption of beliefs or perceptions congruent with relational components of the new psychological contract. Some aspects of work experience explained elements of the new contract and alignment of employees' belief with relational elements of the new psychological contract translated into reduced organizational commitment and job satisfaction. Involuntary job loss was significantly related to adoption of personal responsibility for career development, voluntary job change was related to greater commitment for type of work (not organizational commitment), as was violation of psychological contract. Commitment to type of work was negatively associated with intentions to remain with current employer.

To test the proposition that victims of downsizing will be less likely to trust future employers than those who have not been laid off, Singh (1998) examined data from the 1993 General Social Survey. This assessed general disposition, satisfaction, happiness, racial attitudes, and political views of 500 to 800 individuals representative of the US public. Items related to trust, and self-interest versus organizational interest, were analyzed for those in full-time employment and those who had experienced being laid off. Victims represented over 6 percent of the general population, and were significantly less trustful and had attitudes more inclined to self-interest. The next research agenda is to identify demonstrable alterations to underlying cognitive schema of a wider set of individuals (not just direct victims of downsizing and related changes). For Rousseau (1995), cognitive schema form the base of psychological contracts. Which mindset changes are associated with alterations to which values, which of these value-changes lead to a solidification of (more negative or positive) attitudes, and what new linkages may arise down the attitude–intention–behavior–performance path of employee behavior?

We should be cautious applying the collective wisdom of some existing organizational behavior findings – based on research on the "old deal" post-war generation – to younger work cohorts. Some authors argue – whether from meta-theoretical perspectives of the "psychological contract" or on grounds of "moral exclusion" – that current models of socialization, commitment, and culture have limited utility for organizations that will have a greater reliance on the contingent workforce. Barker (1995) outlined the new behaviors generated by increasing differentiation between different "layers of citizenship" within an organization. Associated privileges and exclusions are embedded within each layer (for example access to facilities, training, or career enhancing experiences). Those with lower layers of citizenship accumulate deficits over their employment contract, and probably new value sets, that might shock those in the core: ". . . contingent work may be the solvent that dissolves older forms of workplace privilege" (Barker, 1995, p. 50).

Those who speculate about "new rules of the game" focus on the long-term implications of the creation at a societal level of a pool of labor lacking exposure to long-term and relational psychological contracts. Murphy and Jackson (1999) question what the impact of repeated exposure to people with transactional assumptions to their employment contract might be, either directly through their own experience, or indirectly through the experience of family, friends or peers. Work on the impact of layoffs on children's values (Barling, Dupre, and Hepburn, 1998) and on third-party perceptions (Skarlicki, Ellard, and Kelln, 1998) suggests that a shift to more transactional contracts in a broader range of people is now taking place. Murphy and Jackson (1999, p. 358) conclude that if there is continued and widespread erosion of the foundations of trust and relational expectations in the employment contract, then "at the societal level, such an effect could cause the psychological landscape of work to be so fundamentally altered that employment structures based on relational contracts may become increasingly difficult to retrieve."

The new rules of the game scenario might then result from changing psychology across generational cohorts, or might result from different psychological dynamics associated with structural changes in the workforce. Cappelli (1999) supports this conclusion. He outlines an *imaging inertia* theory, which assumes that altered perceptions endure throughout generational cohorts. This perspective argues that employees do not make decisions or judgments purely on the basis of a rational cost-benefit model. They rely on recalling previous experiences in similar situations – imaging – and base decisions on what happened then. People who experienced the hardships of the Great Depression felt insecure throughout their lives, even when they became wealthy. The generation that grew up assuming their employer was responsible for careers may never forget the waves of downsizing. Their children, the next generation of workers, may also never forget. A recent survey of US employees found that 94 percent saw themselves and not their employers as responsible for their employability (Towers Perrin, 1997). A fundamental reason why employers would find it difficult to go back to the old model is that the new generation of employees probably will not go back to the old model. Their images of work have been forever altered. They might be willing to let their employer make an up-front investment in their skills, but "it is hard to see what could make employees give that control and responsibility back to the employer" (Cappelli, 1999, p. 226).

Sparrow and Marchington (1998) raise issues that generational change in HRM behavior may pose for the employment contract. Consider the questions raised about just one policy area – that of rewards behavior. Are higher levels of insecurity associated with a shift in acceptable timeframe for rewards, for example more immediate reward and less deferred gratification? As employees exchange free time for consumerism, will they all exchange more free time for less pay? What will be the impact of the increasing attractions of, the cost of losing touch with, but desire to stay in touch with, a consumer society? Will increasingly productive households and processes of wealth creation outside employment (such as the value of housing, inheritance of wealth from previous generations) lead to strategies of income substitution and blunt the value and incentives created by rewards in the new employment contract? Will the pursuit of job-pauperizing economic growth mean that traditional careers, progression systems and rewards expectations become the interests of an ever narrower range of people? As young employees enter the organization later and older employees leave it earlier, and more job statuses are experienced, what will be the impact on processes of transition, socialization and learning? Is the pauperization of many areas of employment leading to large segments of the population forever estranged from traditional social expectations of advancement, and the historically valid exchange of financial security for compliance? In order to accommodate these potential shifts in behavior we will see calls for more inventive work sharing, new forms of wealth distribution, alternative forms of work organization and fundamental changes in work values. "New rules of the game" may yet come to influence our thinking about the new employment contract.

REFERENCES

Ancona, D., Kochan, T., Scully, M., Van Maanen, J.V., and Westney, D.E. 1996: *The New Organization*. Cincinnati, OH: South-Western College Publishing.

Appelbaum, E. 1992: Structural change and the growth of part-time and temporary employment. In V.L. duRivage (ed.) *New Policies for the Part-time and Contingent Workforce.* Armonk, NY: Sharpe.

Barker, K. 1995: Contingent work: research issues and the lens of moral exclusion. In L.E. Tetrick and J. Barling (eds) *Changing Employment Relations: Behavioural and Social Perspectives.* Washington: American Psychological Association.

Barling, J., Dupre, K., and Hepburn, C.G. 1998: Effects of parents' job insecurity on children's work beliefs and attitudes. *Journal of Applied Psychology,* 83, 112–18.

Bradach, J.L. and Eccles, R.G. 1989: Price, authority, and trust: from ideal types to plural forms. *Annual Review of Sociology,* 15, 97–118.

Brockner, J., Grover, S., O'Malley, M.N., Reed, T., and Glynn, M. 1993: Threat of future layoffs, self-esteem, and survivors' reactions: evidence from the laboratory and field. *Strategic Management Journal,* 14, 153–66.

Budros, A. 1997: The new capitalism and organizational rationality: the adoption of downsizing programs, 1979–1994. *Social Forces,* 76 (1), 229–50.

Cappelli, P. 1999: *The New Deal at Work: Managing the Market-driven Workforce.* Boston, MA: Harvard Business School Press.

Cavanaugh, M.A. and Noe, R.A. 1999: Antecedents and consequences of relational components of the new psychological contract. *Journal of Organizational Behaviour,* 20 (3), 323–40.

Clark, M.C. and Payne, R.L. 1997: The nature and structure of workers' trust in management. *Journal of Organizational Behaviour,* 18 (3), 205–24.

Coyle-Shapiro, J. and Kessler, I. 1999: Consequences of the psychological contract for the employment relationship: a large scale survey. *Journal of Management,* in press.

Creed, W.E.D. and Miles, R.E. 1996: Trust in organizations: a conceptual framework linking organizational forms, managerial philosophies and the opportunity costs of control. In R.M. Kramer and T.R. Tyler (eds) *Trust in Organizations: Frontiers of Theory and Research.* London: Sage.

Cropanzano, R. 1993: *Justice in the Workplace: Approaching Fairness in Human Resource Management.* Hillsdale, NJ: Erlbaum.

Daniels, K. 1995: A comment on Brockner et al. 1993. *Strategic Management Journal,* 16, 325–8.

Daniels, K. and Guppy, A. 1993: Reversing the occupational stress process: some consequences of employee psychological well-being. *Cranfield School of Management Working Paper SWP 19/93.* Cranfield University.

Davis, E. 1999: Does your life work? The Management Today Work Life Survey. *Management Today,* August, 48–55.

Eisenberger, R., Huntington, R., Hutchison, S., and Sowa, D. 1986: Perceived organizational support. *Journal of Applied Psychology,* 71 (3), 500–7.

Freeman, R.B. 1996: Toward an apartheid economy? *Harvard Business Review,* September–October, 114–21.

Gambetta, D. 1988: Can we trust trust? In D. Gambetta (ed.) *Trust: Making and Breaking Cooperative Relationships.* Oxford: Basil Blackwell.

Greenberg, J. 1990: Organizational justice: yesterday, today and tomorrow. *Journal of Management,* 16, 399–432.

Greenhalgh, L. and Rosenblatt, Z. 1984: Job insecurity: toward a conceptual clarity. *Academy of Management Review,* 9, 438–48.

Guest, D. 1998: Is the psychological contract worth taking seriously? *Journal of Organizational Behaviour.* 19, Special Issue, 649–64.

Guest, D., Conway, N., Briner, R., and Dickmann, M. 1996: The state of the psychological contract in employment. *Issues in People Management No. 16.* London: IPD.

Harrington, J.M. 1994: Shift work and health – a critical review of the literature on working hours. *Annals of Academic Medicine (Singapore),* 23, 699–705.

Hartley, J. 1995: Challenge and change in employment relations: issues for psychology, trade unions and managers. In L.E. Tetrick and J. Barling (eds) *Changing Employment Relations: Behavioral and Social Perspectives.* Washington: American Psychological Association.

Herriot, P. and Pemberton, C. 1996: Contracting careers. *Human Relations,* 49 (6), 757–90.

Herriot, P., Manning, W.E.G., and Kidd, J.M. 1997: The content of the psychological contract. *British Journal of Management,* 8 (2), 151–62.

Hirschman, A.O. 1970: *Exit, Voice and Loyalty: Responses to Decline in Firms, Organizations and States.* Cambridge, MA: Harvard University Press.

Hulin, C.L. and Glomb, T.M. 1999: Contingent employees: individual and organizational considerations. In D.R. Ilgen and E.D. Pulakos (eds) *The Changing Nature of Performance: Implications for Staffing Motivation and Development.* San Francisco: Jossey-Bass.

Jacobson, D. 1987: A personological study of the job security experience. *Social Behaviour,* 2, 143–55.

Jacobson, D. 1991: The conceptual approach to job insecurity. In J.F. Hartley, D. Jacobson, B. Klandermans, and T. Van Vuuren (eds) *Job Insecurity: Coping with Jobs at Risk.* London: Sage.

Leana, C.R. and Feldman, D.C. 1994: The psychology of job loss. In G.R. Ferris (ed.) *Research in Personnel and Human Resource Management, Volume 12.* Greenwich, CT: JAI Press.

McLean Parks, J. and Schmedemann, D.A. 1994: When promises become contracts: implied contract and handbook provisions on job security. *Human Resource Management,* 33, 403–23.

Miles, R. and Creed, D. 1996: Organizational forms and managerial philosophies: a descriptive and analytical review. In L.L. Cummings and B.M. Staw (eds) *Research in Organizational Behavior, Volume 17.* Greenwich: JAI Press, 333–72.

Morrison, E.W. and Robinson, S.L. 1997: When employees feel betrayed: a model of how psychological contract violation develops. *Academy of Management Review,* 22 (1), 226–56.

Murphy, P.E. and Jackson, S.E. 1999: Managing work role performance: challenges for twenty first century organizations and their employees. In D.R. Ilgen and E.D. Pulakos (eds) *The Changing Nature of Performance: Implications for Staffing Motivation and Development.* San Francisco: Jossey-Bass.

Pascale, R. 1995: In search of "the new employment contract". Paper for the 20th Anniversary Euroforum Conference, 15–16 September, Strategic Leadership Programme, London Business School.

Robinson, S.L. 1996: Trust and breach of the psychological contract. *Administrative Science Quarterly,* 41, 574–99.

Robinson, S.L. and Morrison, E.W. 1995: Psychological contracts and organization citizenship behaviour: the effect of unfulfilled obligations on civic virtue behaviour. *Journal of Organizational Behaviour,* 16, 289–98.

Robinson, S.L. and Rousseau, D.M. 1994: Violating the psychological contract: not the exception but the norm. *Journal of Organizational Behaviour,* 15, 245–59.

Rousseau, D.M. 1995: *Psychological Contracts in Organizations: Understanding Written and Unwritten Agreements.* Thousand Oaks, CA: Sage.

Schuler, R.S. and Rogovsky, N. in press: Understanding compensation practice variations across firms: the impact of national culture. *Journal of International Business Studies.*

Sheppard, B.H., Lewicki, R.J., and Minton, J.W. 1992: *Organizational Justice: The Search for Fairness in the Workplace.* Lexington, MA: Lexington Books.

Shore, L.M. and Barksdale, K. 1998: Examining degree of balance and level of obligation in the employment relationship: a social exchange approach. *Journal of Organizational Behaviour,* 19, Special Issue, 731–44.

Shore, L.M. and Shore, T.H. 1995: Perceived organizational support and organizational justice. In R.S. Cropanzano and K.M. Kacmar (eds) *Organizational Politics, Justice and Support: Managing the Social Climate of the Workplace.* Westport, CT: Quorum Books.

Shore, L.M. and Tetrick, L.E. 1994: The psychological contract as an explanatory framework in the employment relationship. In C.L. Cooper and D.M. Rousseau (eds) *Trends in Organizational Behaviour, Volume 1*. Somerset, NJ: John Wiley.

Singh, R. 1998: Redefining psychological contracts with the US work force: a critical task for strategic human resource management planners in the 1990s. *Human Resource Management*, 37 (1), 61–70.

Skarlicki, D.P., Ellard, J.H., and Kelln, B.R. 1998: Third-party perceptions of a layoff: procedural, derogation, and retributive aspects of justice. *Journal of Applied Psychology*, 83, 119–27.

Smith, D. 1997: Job insecurity and other myths: the employment climate. *Management Today*, May, 38–41.

Sparks, K., Cooper, C., Fried, Y., and Shirom, A. 1997: The effects of hours of work on health: a meta-analytic review. *Journal of Occupational and Organizational Psychology*, 70 (4), 391–408.

Sparrow, P.R. 1996: Transitions in the psychological contract in UK banking. *Human Resource Management Journal*, 6 (4), 75–92.

Sparrow, P.R. 1998: Re-appraising psychological contracting: lessons for employee development from cross-cultural and occupational psychology research. *International Studies of Management and Organisation*, 28 (1), 30–63.

Sparrow, P.R. 1999: Strategy and cognition: understanding the role of management knowledge structures, organizational memory and information overload. *Creativity and Innovation Management*, 8 (2), 140–8.

Sparrow, P.R. and Cooper, C.L. 1998: New organizational forms: the strategic relevance of future psychological contract scenarios. *Canadian Journal of Administrative Sciences*, 15 (4), 356–71.

Sparrow, P.R. and Marchington, M. 1998: *Human Resource Management: The New Agenda*. London: Pitman/Financial Times.

Sparrow, P.R. and Wu, P.C. 1998: How much do national value orientations really matter? Predicting HRM preferences of Taiwanese employees. *Employee Relations: The International Journal*, 20 (1), 26–56.

Stroh, L.K., Brett, J.M., and Reilly, J.H. 1994: A decade of change: managers' attachment to their organizations and their jobs. *Human Resource Management*, 33, 531–48.

Tetrick, L.E. and Barling, J. (eds) 1995: *Changing Employment Relations: Behavioral and Social Perspectives*. Washington: American Psychological Association.

Towers Perrin 1997: *Towers Perrin Workplace Index 1997*. New York: Towers Perrin.

Turnley, W.H. and Feldman, D.C. 1998: Psychological contract violations during corporate restructuring. *Human Resource Management*, 37 (1), 71–83.

US Bureau of Labor 1995: Contingent and alternative employment arrangements. *Bureau of Labor Statistics Report No. 900*. Washington, DC: US Department of Labor.

Wall Street Journal 1999: The outlook: the blessings of low unemployment. *Wall Street Journal*, 233 (55), p. A1.

Wallace, M. and Greenwood, K.M. 1995: Editorial: twelve hour shifts. *Work and Stress*, 9 (2/3), 105–8.

Warr, P. 1990: The measurement of well-being and other aspects of mental health. *Journal of Occupational Psychology*, 63, 193–210.

Worrall, L. and Cooper, C. 1998: *The Quality of Working Life – The 1998 Survey of Managers' Changing Experiences*. Institute of Management/UMIST.

11 Down but Not Out: Career Trajectories of Middle-aged and Older Workers after Downsizing

Daniel C. Feldman

INTRODUCTION

The large-scale layoffs which occurred after the recession of 1973 and the market crash of 1987 have reawakened interest in the topic of unemployment and its aftermath. Researchers have extensively investigated such topics as employees' psychological reactions to job loss (Payne and Hartley, 1987), the adverse effects layoffs have on employees' health (Cobb and Kasl, 1977), the disruptions layoffs cause in family dynamics (Newman, 1988), the problems of colleagues who "survive" layoffs (Brockner et al., 1987), and the economic upheaval in regions where layoffs and unemployment are widespread (Leana and Feldman, 1992). Taken together, this research highlights the acute, short-term negative effects of downsizing and restructuring on laid-off employees, their co-workers, their families, and even their communities.

What has received much less attention, though, has been the long-term consequences of downsizing and restructuring on the subsequent career paths of laid-off employees. There are three major ways in which the post-layoff career trajectories of middle-aged and older workers may differ considerably from the career paths they pursued before downsizing.

First, after older employees have experienced this major violation of their psychological contract, they are more likely to change their career strategies in the future (Rousseau, 1996; Turnley and Feldman, 1998). Having lost their jobs once, downsized employees appear to manage their careers more defensively (Feldman, 1996; Hirsch, 1987). For example, employees who have already lost a job may be more likely to choose subsequent career paths where the chances of future layoffs are much lower or the chances of quick re-employment, if they are laid off, are much higher. Indeed, even employees who have not been laid off themselves and new entrants into the labor force who have never worked at all are becoming much more security-conscious in their choice of occupations and organizations (Feldman and Turnley, 1995; Feldman and Weitz, 1991).

Second, the issue of the quality of "replacement jobs" (that is, the jobs laid-off employees take after they have been downsized) has been largely ignored by organizational researchers. As Leana and Feldman (1995) note, most of the research on job loss has taken as its end point the attainment of re-employment; that is, once laid-off workers get new jobs, they typically cease to be the focus of further research. As a result, little is known about the quality of the replacement positions laid-off employees obtain or the extent to which laid-off workers drop out of the workforce altogether. However, there is evidence that many middle-aged and older workers end up leaving the labor force permanently after layoffs (Doeringer, 1990) while others end up underemployed in jobs which do not fully utilize their previous education, experience, and training (Feldman, 1996; Leana, Feldman, and Tan, 1998).

Third, there is good reason to believe that, as a consequence of having been downsized, employees' subsequent work-centeredness decreases and their preference for personal life activities increases. Having seen first-hand the lack of payoff heavy investment in their careers has brought them so far, many downsized employees in their 40s and 50s re-evaluate their priorities about work and its centrality in their lives (Stephens and Feldman, 1997). Thus, although replacement jobs may be "object-ively" worse in terms of compensation or hierarchical level, they may be experienced as "subjectively" better because they provide greater satisfaction of individuals' non-work-related needs (Hall, 1976).

In this chapter two career trends among middle-aged and older workers that have become more pronounced in the aftermath of downsizing are explored: (1) increased acceptance of early retirement incentives and bridge employment options; and (2) increased pursuit of entrepreneurial ventures and self-employment. The focus here will be on the factors which give rise to these trends, the extent to which these replace-ment jobs represent satisfactory re-employment or underemployment, and the ways in which these career paths allow employees to rebalance their priorities between work life and personal life. For each of these career trends, directions for future theoretical and methodological research are outlined as well.

EARLY RETIREMENT AND BRIDGE EMPLOYMENT

As organizations began to consider alternatives to widespread layoffs, the idea of offer-ing early retirement incentives to older workers to shrink their workforce gained greater currency (Greenhalgh, McKersie, and Gilkey, 1986; Perry, 1986). These "open window programs" offer employees economic incentives to voluntarily leave the organization. For example, if employees accept the early retirement offer, they can retire at the same level of pension benefits they would receive if they continued to work five more years and/or were five years older (Gustman and Steinmeier, 1991). The rationale behind this strategy is that if more older employees can be enticed to withdraw from the workforce voluntarily, fewer other employees will have to be laid off involuntarily.

A second human resource program which often complements early retirement incentives provides opportunities for "bridge employment" to early retirees. Bridge employment refers to jobs which individuals take *after* they "retire" from long-term positions but *before* they fully withdraw from the workforce altogether (Doeringer, 1990; Ruhm, 1990). While many older workers are quite happy to retire early with increased benefits, others are reluctant to stop working on tasks which they find inter-esting, with colleagues whom they find enjoyable, and in settings they find familiar.

Thus, organizations began to offer older workers some opportunities for "bridge employment" after retirement (usually for a fixed period of 2–5 years) so they could make the transition out of work gradually rather than abruptly (Atchley, 1989).

Extent of early retirement incentives and bridge employment

There are intriguing new trends in the employment patterns of older workers. Individuals aged 65 and older now account for 12.5 percent of the population as a whole, up from 6.9 percent of the total population in 1940. Moreover, US Bureau of Census estimates suggest that by the year 2030 at least 20 percent of the US population will be 65 or older (US Bureau of the Census Population Projections, 1996). On the other hand, despite this increase in life expectancy, the percentage of workers who are still working full-time at age 65 is declining. Over 2.5 million people in the US are retiring annually, and only 54 percent of the men and 33 percent of the women aged 60–64 are employed in full-time jobs (Andrews, 1992; Herz, 1995). Thus, it is clear that workers are retiring at an increasingly early age.

However, there are two other trends which are interesting to note here as well. First, the percentage of firms offering early retirement incentives appears to be declining somewhat after several years of widespread use. In the private sector, the percentage of firms offering early retirement incentives has dropped over the past five years from 13.2 percent to 10.8 percent; in the public sector, the drop off has been even more noticeable, from 27.9 percent to 16.5 percent (LaRock, 1996). A second trend, though, is equally visible: the percentage of workers who accept these incentives, when offered them, has increased substantially. In 1991, 32.7 percent of eligible employees accepted early retirement incentives; in 1995, that number jumped to 42.4 percent (LaRock, 1996). Consequently, while the percentage of employees eligible for early retirement incentives is declining, the percentage of eligible employees accepting these offers is increasing.

The data on bridge employment also suggest that this form of labor market participation is increasing as well. Although older workers are retiring from their long-term jobs at an earlier age, they are still continuing to participate in the labor market in some form after their "retirement." Indeed, while 50 percent of US workers have left their career-long jobs by age 60, only 11 percent have fully withdrawn from the workforce by that time (Ruhm, 1990). While it is often assumed that bridge employment occurs in the same industry or company as the last full-time job, 75 percent of all bridge jobs involve a change in occupation or industry and almost half involve changes in both occupation and industry (Doeringer, 1990).

Factors influencing acceptance of early retirement incentives and bridge employment opportunities

Among the variables which influence the acceptance of early retirement incentives and bridge employment opportunities, the financial status of older workers is a primary factor. In general, the economic research on early retirement suggests that older workers' decisions are greatly influenced by their expectations of future streams of income. Employees do not want to withdraw from the workforce if they expect that their life in retirement will require them to dramatically cut back on their standard of living (Quinn, Burkhauser, and Myers, 1990).

Consequently, the higher an individual's salary, the less likely he/she is to accept an early retirement offer, since that individual will lose a greater sum of money by exiting the workforce (Ruhm, 1990). Conversely, the lower an individual's salary, the more likely he/she is to accept bridge employment, since such employment will provide a needed financial supplement to family income (Kim and Feldman, 1999). Following the same logic, the higher a retiree's potential pension benefits, the more likely he/she is to accept early retirement; the lower a retiree's actual pension benefits, the more likely he/she is to accept bridge employment (Kim and Feldman, 1999; Ruhm, 1990).

Health and age also play significant roles in individuals' decisions to retire early and to accept bridge employment. Previous research suggests that poor physical health contributes to the acceptance of early retirement decisions and the decline of bridge employment opportunities (Kim and Feldman, 1998; Muller and Boaz, 1988). Major illnesses (such as cancer) and severe functional impairment (such as deafness) make it very difficult for older workers to remain in the workforce in any capacity. Age is also positively related to early retirement decisions but negatively related to acceptance of bridge employment opportunities, since individuals' health tends to decline along with age (Anderson and Burkhauser, 1985; Colsher, Dorfman, and Wallace, 1988).

Two other factors have attracted some research attention in this area as well: current work productivity and job satisfaction. The research suggests that the lower the older workers' performance the more likely they are to accept early retirement offers, both because they do not expect large pay raises in the future and because they are getting social pressure from co-workers to quit (Creswell, 1989; Chronister and Kepple, 1987; Kim and Feldman, 1998). To date, there are no data linking current work productivity to acceptance of bridge employment opportunities, although one could reasonably hypothesize that job dissatisfied older workers would be less likely to accept bridge employment. The findings on the relationships between job satisfaction and acceptance of early retirement incentives and bridge employment have been consistent across research studies (cf. Beehr, 1986; Feldman, 1994). That is, the more older workers enjoy their jobs, the less likely they are to accept early retirement and the more likely they are, once retired, to accept bridge employment (Schmitt and McCune, 1981).

Extent of underemployment

The research on underemployment among bridge employees is fairly recent. Most of that research has focused on the extent to which employees pursue bridge employment within the same organization (or occupation) and the extent to which employees are forced to accept bridge employment outside their organization (or occupation). In much of the economics research on this topic, bridge employment outside the occupation has been considered underemployment because most bridge employees taking such positions are employed in lower paying jobs and in smaller, less prestigious firms (cf. Doeringer, 1990).

However, as Christensen (1990) and others have noted, one cannot simply equate bridge employment in the same organization or same occupation with satisfactory re-employment. A recent study by Kim and Feldman (1999) suggests some reasons why such an assumption may be invalid. Their study suggests that, for older workers who are performing poorly on their pre-retirement jobs and feel pressured to quit them, opportunities for a fresh start are highly attractive; these workers do not feel underemployed in their new bridge jobs. Moreover, many bridge retirees who return to work at their former employers are struck by the extent to which they are now treated as "second class citizens." Thus, even though they may be performing jobs requiring their skills, they feel significant relative deprivation from their pre-retirement work experiences.

Rebalancing work and family

As the result of increased pre-retirement counselling, more and more middle-aged and older workers are considering the impact of retirement on their family relationships before accepting early retirement offers (Rosen and Jerdee, 1989). Three findings emerge fairly consistently in this research area.

First, highly successful, work-centered managers and professionals appear to have greater difficulty coping with retirement (Bradford, 1979; Sonnenfeld, 1988). Because so much of their self-identity is tied up with work, the loss of their positions is devastating to their self-esteem and self-confidence. Moreover, many of the retirees' spouses, long used to their partners' absence from the home and long involved in their own activities, resent the retirees' constant desire for companionship.

Second, there is substantial evidence that older workers try to time their retirement to occur at the same time as their spouses' retirement (Erdner and Guy, 1990). Older workers appear to be less likely to retire if their spouses are working because they do not want to give up their day-to-day interactions at work if there will be no companionship for them at home. Moreover, some of the activities retirees might anticipate with pleasure – such as travel – would be less feasible if spouses were still in the workforce full-time (Feldman, 1994).

Third, family status impacts on both early retirement and bridge employment decisions. When workers still have financially dependent children to support, they are less likely to accept early retirement and are more likely, when retired, to accept bridge employment (Kim and Feldman, 1998). In both cases, financial need plays a key role in these employment decisions; having more people to support raises the financial hurdle for total withdrawal from the workforce.

Directions for future research

Previous research results have been particularly inconsistent on the effects of gender. Some studies suggest women may retire later than men because they experience more "career disorderliness" (Kilty and Behling, 1985). That is, women have more frequent absences from the workforce; consequently, they are less bored with long-term jobs and have fewer accumulated savings on which to retire. On the other hand, women may retire earlier because they are married to older men, who want their companionship at home in retirement even if their younger wives still want to work (Erdner and

Guy, 1990; Feldman, 1994). Moreover, the effects of gender on older workers' retirement decisions are somewhat confounded by marital status, since married employees'
retirement decisions are based not only on their own financial assets but on their partners' financial assets as well (Feldman, 1994). Thus, further research on the role of
gender, marital status, and family finances is clearly needed to fully understand employees' early retirement decisions and acceptance of bridge employment opportunities.

Another area in which more research is needed is the role of repeated early retirement incentive offers on employees' decisions. Ironically, the more successive early
retirement incentive programs an organization runs, the less likely eligible employees
will be to accept their offers (Kim and Feldman, 1998). In part, this is because employees
who are undecided about whether they would like to retire feel no pressure about
accepting any given offer because they expect others to come along in the future. In
part, too, older employees know that companies often "sweeten the deal" in subsequent offers, so there may be some economic benefits of staying on the job as long as
possible. How early retirement incentive programs are structured, particularly in combination with how bridge employment opportunities are structured, also needs to be
investigated further.

The research in the organizational sciences on bridge employment is in its infancy,
and much more work is needed here. To date, underemployment in bridge jobs has
been assessed either by salary measures or by whether bridge employment occurs in
the same organization or occupation. However, as noted above, individuals' perceptions of bridge jobs as underemployment may be far different from objective measures
of underemployment like a drop in income. For example, a retired CEO who takes over
the management of a small, not-for-profit organization may be objectively underemployed on every tangible measure yet feel highly challenged, stimulated, and excited
by the new assignment. Consequently, we need to discover how older workers themselves interpret their bridge employment as satisfactory or underemployment, and
why subjective judgments about quality of re-employment differ from objective meas-
urements of underemployment (Feldman, 1996).

Another important research question, particularly relevant to workers in their 50s,
is the effectiveness of pre-retirement counselling on adjustment to retirement and/or
acceptance of bridge employment opportunities. Most of the research on this topic has
examined the effects of such counselling on intentions to retire, using a dichotomous
measure of pre-retirement counselling (received or did not receive) as the independent
variable. However, there is enormous variance in the length of such programs, the
focus of such programs (financial aspects exclusively or comprehensive in nature),
and the level of participation of spouses in such programs (Rosen and Jerdee, 1989).
Consequently, much more careful evaluation research is needed to understand the
impact of pre-retirement counselling on adjustment to retirement and acceptance of
bridge employment opportunities. To date, the results show small positive outcomes
associated with pre-retirement counselling, but the measurement of that counselling
is often inadequate.

Finally here, the research on early retirement and bridge employment would be
greatly facilitated by increased use of archival data and longitudinal designs. While
more and more researchers are incorporating archival data into their studies, even
greater efforts are needed in this direction since employees' self-reports on such variables
as health, income, and intentions to retire are often distorted by social desirability

response bias (Muller and Boaz, 1988). In addition, the research on early retirement decisions, participation in bridge employment, and adjustment to retirement has largely been conducted by three separate groups of researchers with three very different samples. Consequently, very little research has followed older workers from consideration of early retirement through bridge employment and on to full retirement. Such research is essential to discover the empirical links among these theoretically linked topics.

SELF-EMPLOYMENT, SMALL BUSINESS, AND ENTREPRENEURSHIP

As the downsizing trend has continued, the pursuit of self-employment, small business proprietorships, and entrepreneurship as alternative career paths has increased as well. At the simplest level, self-employment entails working as an independent consultant, contractor, or service provider. Small business proprietors manage local or regional businesses with a limited number of staff and with no real goal of major expansion. At the entrepreneur level, individuals invest their own capital and seek investments from venture capitalists to build new enterprises into major corporate powers (Case, 1992). For many middle-aged and older workers, new careers in self-employment, small business proprietorships, and entrepreneurship are attractive alternatives to searching for new jobs in other corporations where they may face layoffs yet again (Dennis, 1996).

Growth in self-employment, small business, and entrepreneurship

By all accounts, labor force participation in self-employment, small business proprietorships, and entrepreneurship has increased significantly over the past several years. Dun & Bradstreet reports that annual new business incorporations have risen from 685,572 in 1987 to 789,126 in 1997. In fiscal year 1996 alone, the US Small Business Administration made 45,878 government-guaranteed loans totalling $7.75 billion. Over the past five years, the amount of venture capital invested in entrepreneurial start-up firms has increased from $4 billion to $10 billion (Alsop, 1997). Across the board, then, entry into these three career paths has accelerated dramatically over the past decade.

Individuals who have lost their jobs through downsizing have contributed to this growth spurt in self-employment, small business proprietorships, and entrepreneurship. This has been particularly true for women and minorities, who view such career paths as a way of circumventing discrimination in existing organizations. Over a five-year period, the number of women-owned sole proprietorships, partnerships, and small businesses has increased from 4.1 million to 5.9 million, an increase of 43 percent. During the same time period, the number of minority-owned small businesses has grown from 1.3 million to 2.1 million, an increase of 60 percent (Mehta, 1997).

Even middle-aged and older white males appear to be seeking self-employment in larger numbers after layoffs, as they, too, face the unpleasant reality of age discrimination in trying to find satisfactory "replacement jobs" (Leana and Feldman, 1992). For example, Dennis (1996) reports that unemployed workers are about twice as likely to start new businesses as employed workers.

Factors influencing entry into self-employment, small business, and entrepreneurship

The research on factors influencing entry into these kinds of career paths has taken two distinct directions. One set of researchers has examined the demographic differences and personality traits which are associated with entry into self-employment, small business, and entrepreneurship. The other set of researchers has examined the macroeconomic and structural factors which affect the pursuit of these kinds of career paths.

In terms of demographic differences, males currently constitute 67 percent of the ownership of small businesses, but the percentage of women entering these independent employment career paths is rising steadily, as noted above (Mehta, 1997). The predominance of males in these positions has been frequently attributed to greater incomes earned by males, and hence their greater initial capital to invest in such enterprises. However, as females become a greater percentage of the workforce, self-employment activities become more attractive to them as a means of balancing work and family demands (Stephens and Feldman, 1997).

Along the same lines, about 33 percent of small business proprietors are aged 50 or older, again largely because of the savings needed to begin these ventures. However, widespread downsizings have made the climb up the corporate ladder less attractive to new business school graduates, so that more and more young adults are trying to become entrepreneurs or start small businesses too (Feldman and Turnley, 1995). Perhaps surprisingly, self-employment is more prevalent among older workers with less education. It appears that these older workers view self-employment as a means of improving their economic status outside of large corporations, which typically rely heavily on formal education credentials for selection and promotion (Carr, 1996; Case, 1992).

A wide variety of personality traits have been investigated in the context of entry into entrepreneurship. Some of the personality traits most commonly associated with these career paths are need for achievement, need for control, and tolerance for ambiguity (cf. Dyer, 1994; Kolvereid, 1996). More recently, Feldman and Bolino (1997, 1999) examined the "career anchors" of entrepreneurs. These career anchors represent the stable sets of interests, abilities, and motivations which individuals develop after several years in the workforce (Schein, 1990). This research suggests that entry into self-employment, small business, and entrepreneurship is significantly associated with high needs for autonomy, security, and creativity.

A variety of approaches have been taken in investigating the macro-level factors influencing entry into these career paths. Dyer (1994) suggests that periods of economic growth give rise to greater new business creation. Having parents and family members in small businesses is also highly correlated with entry into these career paths, both because of inheritances of these businesses and because of better access to relevant networks of investors and customers (Bregger, 1996; Carroll and Mosakowksi, 1987). As noted earlier, institutional barriers to advancement due to gender and race are also associated with entry into self-employment, small business, and entrepreneurship (Carr, 1996; Mehta, 1997).

Extent of underemployment

There has been very little research on underemployment among the self-employed, small business proprietors, and entrepreneurs. Taking a labor economic approach to underemployment, Carroll and Mosakowski (1987) examined the effects of self-employment and family-business employment on subsequent career stability and compensation. Their results suggest that rather than being associated with unstable or risky employment, self-employment actually leads to more job stability. That is, once individuals enter self-employment, they are unlikely to do much job changing thereafter or leave this career path except when their business fails. Moreover, the results of Carroll and Mosakowski (1987) reflect no significant wage differences between pre-self-employment and post-self-employment positions. Their research, then, suggests that individuals entering self-employment and family businesses are not more underemployed (either in terms of salary or job stability) than their conventionally employed counterparts.

Using data from a national sample of self-employed individuals, Feldman and Bolino (1999) examined self-employed workers' own perceptions of their underemployment. Their results suggest that individuals who are pursuing self-employment out of a desire for autonomy and independence report the highest levels of skill utilization and intent to remain self-employed. Thus, these individuals, as a group, do not view themselves as underemployed.

Feldman and Bolino (1999) also found that individuals who are pursuing self-employment out of a desire for greater creativity and challenge have somewhat lower levels of skill utilization, but the highest levels of job satisfaction, psychological well-being, and overall life satisfaction. These individuals, then, do not feel fully utilized in terms of their skills and work experience, but nonetheless find their positions fulfilling in other ways.

In contrast, those individuals who entered self-employment to maximize security and stability systematically had the lowest levels of both skill utilization and job attitudes. While they reported that the insecurity associated with self-employment was less aversive to them than the thought of going through another downsizing, they also had significant concerns about the financial risks of self-employment, the high costs of fringe benefits and health care insurance premiums, and the vulnerability of small businesses to market shifts and macroeconomic downturns.

Using Case's (1992) typology of self-employed workers, Feldman and Bolino (1999) also examined whether underemployment was more prevalent among particular groups. Their results suggest that the "job creators" (that is, those who were hoping to grow their businesses into major ventures over the next five years) were typically not underemployed, earned the most money, and had the most positive job attitudes. By way of contrast, the results suggest that "traditional" small business owners (that is, those who owned small restaurants and small retail stores) and "solo" self-employed workers (that is, those who were consultants or freelance professionals) were the most underemployed and had the poorest attitudes toward their jobs and their careers. For these individuals, the biggest sources of their underemployment were the daily grinds of recruiting and training new employees, dealing with taxes and government regulations, "cold calling" and developing new clients, and dealing with angry or unpleasant customers.

Rebalancing work and family

It is clear that entry into self-employment, small business proprietorships, and entrepreneurship is viewed as a desirable method of balancing work and family demands. A recent study by Dennis (1996) suggests that 54 percent of new entrants into self-employment rate "gaining greater control over my life" and "building something for my family" as very important determinants of their career choice. Carr (1996) notes that the increase in self-employment among women is largely attributable to "occupational drift"; that is, women enter this career path due to its scheduling flexibility (in terms of number of hours worked, where they work, and when they work). In fact, Bregger (1996) suggests female participation in small businesses may be considerably understated, since many wives are unpaid for their contributions to their husbands' businesses. Certainly, then, entry into these career paths is generally viewed positively in terms of balancing work and family demands.

However, many new entrants into these career paths – while generally acknowledging the greater flexibility for dealing with family issues – also notice some unexpected negative consequences of these new career paths for their personal lives. For example, self-employed workers in the Feldman and Bolino (1999) study commented that the job autonomy which came with self-employment also brought greater social isolation, particularly for those self-employed individuals working out of their homes or who travelled extensively. In some cases, spouses of new entrants into these career paths actually had to increase their working hours to help make ends meet in the short-run and to ensure continued health care coverage for their families. For many new small business owners, their increased scheduling flexibility was partially offset by the need to always be "on call" and their decreased ability to take extended vacations and consecutive days off. Thus, the benefits of flexible scheduling for the self-employed are counterbalanced by some new (and often unexpected) constraints in their lives (Feldman and Bolino, 1999).

Directions for future research

Surprisingly, there has been very little empirical research on the pursuit of self-employment, small business proprietorships, and entrepreneurship in the aftermath of downsizing. Both in terms of theory development and research methodology, much remains to be done in this area.

First and foremost, more theoretical and empirical research is needed on the distinctions among these various forms of self-employment. Across research projects, these terms are sometimes used interchangeably or synonymously, often resulting in confusing or misleading statistics. For example, are part-time freelancers self-employed workers, small business proprietors (if they incorporate), entrepreneurs, or simply contingent workers? How the terms are defined, to a great extent, determines the results of a particular research project. Case's (1992) four-category typology ("traditionalists," "job creators," "soloists," and "minimalists") appears to be a promising start for a useful taxonomy.

Second, greater focus is needed on the motivations for entry into self-employment (broadly defined) in the aftermath of downsizing. While there are some existing research studies on the number of individuals who enter self-employment from unemployment, the motivations, expectations, and needs of these individuals have largely gone unexamined. For instance, middle-aged, laid-off executives may enter these career paths with far greater capital but far less enthusiasm. The whole issue of underemployment among the self-employed needs greater attention, then, and longitudinal and panel studies will be needed to address these questions.

Third, particularly in investigating self-employment among middle-aged and older workers, greater attention needs to be paid to family issues. For example, what is the impact of entry into self-employment or small business upon the labor force participation rates of spouses? Conversely, how does a spouse's income and savings enable an individual to take (or inhibit an individual from taking) the risk of entering self-employment? What is the impact of working at home on marital and parent–child relationships? Similarly, little research has been done on the "hidden economies" of non-paid relatives in family businesses. In this research area, more data from members of the entrepreneur's network of family and friends are needed as well.

Finally here, much more research is needed on the outcomes of entering self-employment, small business proprietorships, and entrepreneurial ventures for those pursuing these career paths in the aftermath of downsizing. In general, there are very few studies which examine the effects of entry into these career paths on compensation, not to mention on job satisfaction, attitudes toward's one's career, and overall life satisfaction. Moreover, the specific effects of downsizing on rates of entry into these career paths have not been studied, nor have the differences between those who enter self-employment "voluntarily" or "involuntarily" after downsizing. As the trends toward both downsizing and entry into self-employment grow, these research issues take on even greater significance.

CONCLUSION

For a variety of reasons, including widespread downsizing, middle-aged and older workers are leaving long-time jobs to take early retirement, to accept bridge employment, or to enter self-employment, small business, or entrepreneurial ventures. The research focus on the aftermath of downsizing, then, is changing from individuals' short-term reactions to unemployment to their longer-term strategies for managing careers outside the boundaries of traditional organizations. Concomitantly, the research on laid-off employees has expanded from the study of attainment of new jobs to include the study of the quality of those replacement jobs.

What makes these career trajectories so interesting is that they bring into question the role of work in middle-aged and older workers' lives. As individuals mature, the centrality of work in their lives may lessen – making the loss of jobs during downsizing no less traumatic but potentially freeing older workers to re-evaluate and redirect their careers in more fulfilling ways. Moreover, bridge employment and self-employment opportunities let older workers better integrate work and family demands, allowing them to reconnect more fully with their spouses before total withdrawal from the workforce. Perhaps most importantly, these career trajectories may actually provide some middle-aged and older workers with greater, rather than fewer, opportunities for skill utilization. The role of these career trajectories after downsizing, then, is of critical importance to academics and practitioners alike. As this chapter suggests, even after downsizing, older workers may be down but not out of the workforce.

REFERENCES

Alsop, R.J. (ed.) 1997: *The Wall Street Journal Almanac*. New York: Dow Jones & Company.

Anderson, K.H. and Burkhauser, R.V. 1985: The retirement-health nexus: a new measure for an old puzzle. *Journal of Human Resources*, 20, 315–30.

Andrews, E. 1992: Expanding opportunities for older workers. *Journal of Labor Research*, 13, 55–65.

Atchley, R. 1989: A continuity theory of aging. *Gerontologist*, 29, 183–90.

Beehr, T.A. 1986: The process of retirement: a review and recommendations for future investigation. *Personnel Psychology*, 39, 31–56.

Bradford, L.P. 1979: Can you survive your retirement? *Harvard Business Review*, 57, 103–9.

Bregger, J. 1996: Measuring self-employment in the United States. *Monthly Labor Review*, 199, 3–9.

Brockner, J., Grover, S., Reed, T., DeWitt, R., and O'Malley, M. 1987: Survivors' reactions to layoffs: we get by with a little help from our friends. *Administrative Science Quarterly*, 32, 526–41.

Carr, D. 1996: Two paths to self-employment? *Work and Occupations*, 23, 26–53.

Carroll, G.R. and Mosakowski, E. 1987: The career dynamics of self-employment. *Administrative Science Quarterly*, 32, 570–89.

Case, J. 1992: How to survive without a job. *Inc.* (June), 32–44.

Christensen, K. 1990: Bridges over trouble water: how older workers view the labor market. In P.B. Doeringer (ed.) *Bridges to Retirement*. Ithaca, NY: Cornell University ILR Press, 175–207.

Chronister, J.L. and Kepple, T.R. 1987: *Incentive Early Retirement Programs for Faculty: Innovative Responses to a Changing Environment* (ASHE-ERIC Higher Education Report No. 1). Washington, DC: Association for the Study of Higher Education.

Cobb, S. and Kasl, S.V. 1977: *Termination: The Consequences of Job Loss*. Washington, DC: National Institute for Occupational Safety and Health, Report No. 76-1261.

Colsher, P.L., Dorfman, L.T., and Wallace, R.B. 1988: Specific health conditions and work-retirement status among the elderly. *Journal of Applied Gerontology*, 7, 485–503.

Creswell, J.W. 1989: *Faculty Research Performance* (ASHE-ERIC Higher Education Report No. 4). Washington, DC: Association for the Study of Higher Education.

Dennis, W.I. Jr. 1996: Self-employment: when nothing else is available? *Journal of Labor Research*, 17, 645–61.

Doeringer, P.B. 1990: Economic security, labor market flexibility, and bridges to retirement. In P.B. Doeringer (ed.) *Bridges to Retirement*. Ithaca, NY: Cornell University ILR Press, 3–22.

Dyer, W.G. Jr. 1994: Toward a theory of entrepreneurial careers. *Entrepreneurship Theory and Practice*, 19, 7–21.

Erdner, R.A., and Guy, R.F. 1990: Career identification and women's attitudes towards retirement. *International Journal of Aging and Human Development*, 30, 129–39.

Feldman, D.C. 1994. The decision to retire: a review and conceptualization. *Academy of Management Review*, 19, 285–311.

Feldman, D.C. 1996: The nature and consequences of underemployment. *Journal of Management*, 22, 385–409.

Feldman, D.C. and Bolino, M.C. 1997: Careers within careers: reconceptualizing the nature of career anchors and their consequences. *Human Resource Management Review*, 6, 89–112.

Feldman, D.C. and Bolino, M.C. 1999: Career patterns of the self-employed: motivations for entry and career outcomes.

Feldman, D.C. and Turnley, W.H. 1995: Underemployment among recent college graduates. *Journal of Organizational Behavior*, 16, 691–706.

Feldman, D.C. and Weitz, B.A. 1991: From the invisible hand to the gladhand: understanding the nature of a careerist orientation to work. *Human Resource Management*, 30, 237–57.

Greenhalgh, L., McKersie, R.B., and Gilkey, R.W. 1986: Rebalancing the work force at IBM: a case study of redeployment and revitalization. *Organizational Dynamics*, 14, 30–47.

Gustman, A.L. and Steinmeier, T.L. 1991: The effects of pensions and retirement policies on retirement in higher education. *American Economic Review*, 81, 111–15.

Hall, D.T. 1976: *Careers in Organizations*. Pacific Palisades, CA: Goodyear Publishing.

Herz, D.E. 1995: Work after early retirement: an increasing trend among men. *Monthly Labor Review*, 118, 13–20.

Hirsch, P.M. 1987: *Pack your own Parachute*. Reading, MA: Addison-Wesley.

Kilty, K.M. and Behling, J.H. 1985: Predicting the retirement intentions and attitudes of professional workers. *Journal of Gerontology*, 40, 219–27.

Kim, S. and Feldman, D.C. 1998: Healthy, wealthy, or wise: predicting actual acceptances of early retirement incentives at three points in time. *Personnel Psychology*, 51, 623–42.

Kim, S. and Feldman, D.C. 1999: Working in "retirement": the antecedents and consequences of bridge employment.

Kolvereid, L. 1996: Organizational employment versus self-employment: reasons for career choice intentions. *Entrepreneurship Theory and Practice*, 20, 23–31.

LaRock, S. 1996: Early retirement incentives in 1995: more takers for fewer offers. *Employee Benefit Plan Review*, 51, 54–6.

Leana, C.R. and Feldman, D.C. 1992: *Coping with Job Loss: How Individuals, Organizations, and Communities Respond to Layoffs*. New York: Macmillan/Lexington Books.

Leana, C.R. and Feldman, D.C. 1995: Finding new jobs after a plant closing: antecedents and outcomes of the occurrence and quality of reemployment. *Human Relations*, 48, 1381–1401.

Leana, C.R., Feldman, D.C., and Tan, G.Y. 1998: Predictors of coping behavior after a layoff. *Journal of Organizational Behavior*, 19, 85–97.

Mehta, S.N. 1997: Women entrepreneurs and minority entrepreneurs. In R.I. Alsop (ed.) *The 1998 Wall Street Journal Almanac*. New York: Ballantine Books, 232–6.

Muller, C.F. and Boaz, R.F. 1988: Health as a reason or a rationalization for being retired? *Research on Aging*, 10, 37–55.

Newman, K.S. 1988: *Falling from Grace: The Experience of Downward Mobility in the American Middle Class*. New York: Vintage Books.

Payne, R. and Hartley, J. 1987: A test of a model for explaining the affective experience of unemployed men. *Journal of Occupational Psychology*, 60, 31–47.

Perry, L.T. 1986: Least-cost alternatives to layoffs in declining industries. *Organizational Dynamics*, 14, 48–61.

Quinn, J.F., Burkhauser, R.V., and Myers, D.A. 1990: *Passing the Torch*. Kalamazoo, MI: W.E. Upjohn Institute of Employment Research.

Rosen, B. and Jerdee, T.H. 1989: Retirement policies: evidence of the need for change. *Human Resource Management*, 28, 87–103.

Rousseau, D.M. 1996: Changing the deal while keeping the people. *Academy of Management Executive*, 10, 50–61.

Ruhm, C.J. 1990: Career jobs, bridge employment, and retirement. In P.B. Doeringer (ed.) *Bridges to Retirement*. Ithaca, NY: Cornell University ILR Press, 92–107.

Schein, E.H. 1990: *Career Anchors: Discovering your Real Values*. San Diego, CA: Pfeiffer & Company.

Schmitt, N. and McCune, J.T. 1981: The relationship between job attitudes and the decision to retire. *Academy of Management Journal*, 24, 795–802.

Sonnenfeld, J. 1988: *The Hero's Farewell*. New York: Oxford University Press.

Stephens, G.K. and Feldman, D.C. 1997: A motivational approach for understanding work versus personal life investments. In G.R. Ferris (ed.) *Research in Personnel and Human Resources Management*, 15, 333–78.

Turnley, W.H. and Feldman, D.C. 1998: Psychological contract violations during corporate restructuring. *Human Resource Management*, 37, 71–84.

12 Organizational Crisis and Change: The New Career Contract at Work

John F. McCarthy and Douglas T. Hall

INTRODUCTION

Intense market forces and widespread turbulence have spawned an environment of sustained instability and uncertainty throughout the business world. The heightened pace and depth of organizational change dramatically upset ongoing working relationships and traditional notions of careers and career development. Careers and job patterns for most have been forced to become increasingly "protean," shifting and changing in concert with this new landscape. Consequently, new mindsets, expectations, and very different modes of preparation are necessary to forge a contemporary career. This chapter summarizes the changing market forces, their impact on careers, and a new viewpoint on the altered psychological contract between individuals and organizations to deal more effectively with these new organizational realities. The resulting career development challenges are also outlined.

CHANGING TIMES

The current organizational environment is characterized by violent change, turbulence, chaos and confusion. Intense global competitive forces have substantially hastened the pace and heightened the complexity of decision making throughout all areas of organizational life (Drucker, 1998; Kanter, 1995). Instability and unpredictable shifts are the norm, and "every organization has to prepare for the abandonment of everything it does" (Drucker, 1998, p. 79). Rapid technological change and simultaneous diffusion intensify the already dizzying information-driven market dynamics (Davis, 1998). Old skills and tools no longer work.

In the face of such a punishing climate, organizations have responded with countless sorties of strategic initiatives. Recent press tells of massive restructuring at such bellweather names as Boeing, Levi Strauss & Co., Dell, Sony, Raytheon, and many others, where thousands of jobs are being eliminated in each organization. Over the past ten years – a decade of downsizing – an estimated 3 million jobs per year have been eliminated from major US companies (Mishra, Spreitzer, and Mishra, 1998). In addition to restructuring, consolidation, and delayering, a myriad of other ongoing change initiatives are also in play, such as creating dispersed virtual organizations, building new and different alliances, and spinning webs of interconnected work teams. All of this change has brought about wider, flattened organizations with fewer support systems than ever before and a stunned workforce grappling with constant instability and uncertainty, totally redefining working relationships and careers.

Adult Development and Careers

The changing nature of work is a driving factor in any discussion of adult development and careers. Stability, in the form of a job-for-life in any organization is clearly a relic of the past (Hall and Moss, 1998; Mirvis, 1992). Gone, too, is the sense of identity derived from the permanency of work and the context of place in an organization on a particular trajectory or career path. Roles within organizations have accordingly shifted from relational to transactional (Hall and Mirvis, 1996); separation is often sudden and unanticipated, dampening loyalty. Work must now be viewed in much more of a *portfolio* sense (Handy, 1989), shifting frequently and intermittently between varied dimensions of paid work and free work.

These organizational changes are occurring at the same time as major demographic (US) shifts; the workforce has matured to the point where the majority of the post-war baby boom have now reached middle age (that is ages 35–45), and women and minorities now comprise a significant proportion of professional positions. These factors have particular career ramifications for both men and women. For men, mid-life traditionally marks a key transition point in the *individuation* process, denoting "changes in a person's relationship to himself and to the external world" (Levinson, 1978, p. 195), whereby one takes stock in accomplishments, shortfalls and with mortality. For women, many of whom may have entered, or re-entered, the workforce later than their male counterparts, mid-life may signify (in addition to individuation) a "catching up" time when children are more on their own and previously subordinated career drives can be more engaged, despite still facing a difficult "glass ceiling" to penetrate (Gallos, 1989; Sekaran and Hall, 1989). In addition, women and men of color may also be reaching management levels after years of challenge as minority members of the workforce (Thomas and Gabarro, 1999).

At the same time, for both men and women, relational learning and mentoring are essential developmentally, but much harder to arrange due to the faster pace and more frequent turnover (Kram, 1988; Kram and Hall, 1995). Organizational relationships in every direction are increasingly fragile. Consequently, at a stage of life when varying degrees of career success have traditionally been achieved, the bottom is pulled out – in terms of a predictable or stable career path – for many managers and executives.

This has all resulted in the widespread redefinition and restructuring of psychological contracts, the unwritten reciprocal relationships between employees and organizations (Rousseau, 1995). Historical "promises" of organizational tenure and opportunity in response to services and diligence have become completely unrealistic; mutual loyalty will be solely based on performance. As a result, individuals have been forced to adopt a "protean" career (Hall and Mirvis, 1996; Hall and Moss, 1998), marked by constant adaptation, and where the individual must take responsibility for career trajectory in a boundaryless sense. Individuals must also develop the inner meta-competencies of identity growth and adaptability to respond to the changed organizational dynamics (Hall and Mirvis, 1996; Hall and Moss, 1998), becoming fully aware of one's own "career anchors" (Schein, 1992). Lifelong learning, particularly the not-so-obvious component of "learning how to learn," is seen as a core competency, as opposed to the traditional notions of skills or occupations (Hall and Mirvis, 1996). People will, in fact, work in wide ranging capacities in many organizations, and will likely have dozens of "mini-careers," with broader roles of shorter duration in a wider variety of organizational settings.

Some individuals, however, may be able to approach this new terrain with the positive outlook of seeking a life balance that was often absent in the traditional career path, particularly for executives rising to high level leadership positions. Executives have traditionally been driven to career success by ever-increasing levels of commitment and dedication to the organizations. In one sense, "organizations provide a context, a medium, in which individuals pursue their aspirations" (Hall and Mirvis, 1996, p. 21). In another sense, the traditional structure of power and authority has also been disrupted by the changing organizational realities; historically, organizations commanded authority through various control or reward systems (Etzioni, 1961) or hierarchically top-down through setting priorities and providing opportunities (March and Simon, 1958; Perrow, 1986). Today, the unshackling of the career contract may be double-edged: individuals will increasingly focus on personal growth opportunities while organizations may still offer only remunerative and extrinsic inducements (Schneider, Gunnarson, and Niles-Jolley, 1994), further widening the imbalance between individual and organizational needs. In these cases, individuals with a strong interdependent internal model of authority (Kahn and Kram, 1994) will be confident to explore employment options or work configurations elsewhere. In this vein, the broken career contract and loss of control may ultimately have a freeing effect on those individuals able to successfully respond or adapt and move on to better situations. Those that do not have – or do not develop – more adaptive relational skills will fall even further behind.

New Loyalties?

Some research indicates that the basic nature of organizational loyalty has also changed as a result of continued corporate restructuring (Heckscher, 1995): here the paradoxical effect was noted where strong loyalty to the organization by managers was *not* seen to be a factor in the performance, attitude or success following restructuring; instead, a strong link was found in how well managers understood the business itself. Managers who were well informed about ongoing operational and strategic issues (before and after restructuring) maintained realistic notions – and generally positive attitudes – about the company's potential and future. Conversely, even when restructuring and change were handled with great care and communication, managers who did not feel they had an active role in the company's development or a good sense about the underlying business conditions tended to be pessimistic and exhibited greater anxiety about change and the future.

In "dynamic" organizations – those exhibiting adaptive capabilities and optimistic views of the future – managers seem to have forged a way of working together around a "community of purpose" (Heckscher, 1995). New loyalties today seem to be more tied to negotiating and striking a balance between individuals and the organization on the basis of tasks or mission. Here, cooperation and creativity are provided by employees without any promise of long-term security. In fact, it is often explicit and understood that the relationship is temporary and will only exist to the extent that both parties benefit: where the individual has the opportunity to learn and can build, enhance or develop particular desired skill sets, *and* the organization gains expertise and com-mitments toward ongoing projects and initiatives. In these settings, strong informal networks develop, and open dialogue and two-way understanding between indi-viduals and the organization are essential. This is seen as a mutual contribution-based relationship driven by *shared purpose*. Where old loyalties fostered stability and, often, subordination, such purpose-driven loyalty encourages adaptability and acceptance of "open ended change" (Heckscher, 1995). Managers increasingly view themselves as coaches and resource coordinators, giving rise to a "new professionalism," governed by shared purpose and opportunistic relationships. These managers display initiative and a real sense of cooperation with their colleagues and with the organization – bound by a temporary but firm epoxy of *purpose*.

It is, at the same time, important to recognize that, despite the mutual consequences of organizational change, individuals typically remain very much at the receiving end of these new deals; strategic decisions are made at the executive level within com-panies to restructure or consolidate, and employees are subsequently forced to react. The degree of surprise, anxiety, or even anger, in response to the changes depends upon each individual's personal make-up, marketability inside and outside the company, family situation, dependence on current income stream, commitment to the organiza-tion and community, as well as a host of other factors. But, for most, these changes are often sudden, unanticipated, and very unsettling at both a personal and professional level. Following restructuring, the individuals who seem most prepared for change – and who possess the most positive perspective going forward – are those employees who view the new situation as an opportunity to learn new things and to accomplish more than in the past (Mohrman, 1999). Again, the new loyalty and new relationship are based on the opportunity to learn and grow while working, however temporary, toward common goals and mutual gain.

THE NEW PSYCHOLOGICAL CONTRACT

It is clear that dependencies and expectations have been dramatically changed. Indi-viduals must recognize these changes and take a far greater share of the responsibility for charting and piloting their career course. Understanding one's own capabilities is a critical ongoing process, gained and maintained through feedback and reflection. The details of the new psychological contract between employees and organization will constantly change; the strongest contracts will, like the US constitution, be constructed upon a framework that allows for sufficient contingent interpretation, but steered by firmly held guiding principles.

Figure 12.1   Career contract dynamics

Old versus New Career Contract Dynamics

	Old Contract	*New Contract*
Environment	Stable, Strategic Growth	Turbulence, Chaos
Competition	Domestic, Multinational	Global
Workforce	Majority Rule	Diverse
Tenure Expectations	Long Term, Lifetime?	Short Term
Organizational Role	Relational	Transactional
Hiring Rationale	"fitting in"	"adding value"
Organizational Loyalty	Subordination	Purpose-Driven
Career Path	Step-wise Trajectory	Protean
Career Goals	Hierarchical	Opportunistic
Success Measure	Ascension	Psychological success, Autonomy
Job Attractiveness	Responsibility, Power	Opportunity to Learn
Core Competencies	Job-Specific Knowledge, Skills, and Abilities	Metacompetencies: Adaptability, Identity growth
Identity Source	Organization	Occupations, Interests
Working Relationship	Explicit, Understood	Contingent, Tacit, Evolving

The changing dynamics of the new career contract are summarized in figure 12.1. A fundamental tenet of the new career is that a key driver is the new economy, a turbulent, highly competitive, global economy, in which diverse skills and quick adaptation are critical to survival and success. Organizations and individuals must possess the "3F" qualities: fast, flexible, and facile (that is, smart, quick-witted) (Hall, 1994). The sense of time has shifted from a long-term relational contract between employer and employee to a shorter-term transactional one ("what have you done for me lately?"). As opposed to the earlier notion of organizational socialization, in which fitting into the new role was the initial step toward success (Feldman, 1976), now even very early in the relationship the person must demonstrate the ability to add value to the enterprise (O'Connell, 1998). The employee's expectations of the transaction focus on purpose, a sense that this is a place where he or she can do meaningful work and be fairly rewarded for it, where the career rewards include learning and opportunities for growth for a "protean" (self-directed) career. The measure of success is autonomy and psychological success (achieving one's own most important goals, fulfilling one's most prized values).

Meta-competencies

To be successful in the future global economy, the employee will have to demonstrate more than a set of currently required skills and competencies; the profile simply changes too quickly to provide any real security. What is really key for a person is to possess two *meta-competencies*, which enable one to *learn how to learn*. The two most important qualities for career survival are *identity growth* and *adaptability*. Adaptability is the ability to sense quickly and respond appropriately to signals from the environment. It means recognizing the need to change early enough so that one can be "ahead of the curve" and change in a way that is smooth and proactive, as opposed to crisis-driven. But adaptability without an inner sense of direction is only reaction, blind learning in the operant sense.

Adaptability must be coupled with a strong sense of one's own desired path and sense of identity – which leads us to the second metacompetency. Identity growth is the ability to learn about oneself, to ask for, understand, and accept personal feedback, and to act on it, with the result of coming to see oneself and value oneself in a new way. This sense of identity comes from inside the person, based on interactions with the environment, rather than directly from the organization's socialization, as it did under the old contract. And as the person develops, this view of the self becomes increasingly complex, with the ability to see the self in relation to the world from multiple perspectives and with more complicated interrelationships (Kegan, 1982, 1994).

Put together, all of this means that the new career contract is very subtle: tacit, continuously changing, and contingent on the simultaneous satisfaction of the two parties. This is in contrast to the past contract, which was often governed by explicit factors, such as seniority, rank, and clear, stable relational norms.

A transactional relationship?

But let us complicate this picture a bit, lest the reader think the whole "new deal" is as simple as figure 12.1 would indicate. We are also seeing some paradoxical trends as organizations try to re-establish employee loyalty in a tight labor market, with a "war for talent," as McKinsey & Co. has called it. First, although it is now understood that there are no lifetime employment arrangements, the pendulum seems to be swinging back to a valuing of long-term, continuing relationships. Reicheld's (1996) research has shown that the longer the length of service of the average employee, the stronger are the firm's financial results. (The same positive effect of longevity holds for owners and customers.) We are seeing employers recruiting people with the claim that we can provide an environment for growth and learning, a place where you can have a real *career*. There is an implicit suggestion of something long term, a hope that things will work out well so that you can have a long-term career here – while acknowledging that all we can really promise is the *ingredients* for career growth: challenging assignments, training and development, and good management, resources, and relationships. Thus, the resultant of the two is *contingent loyalty*.

Another paradox, then, is that we are again talking about a *relational* experience, while acknowledging that it is still at its heart a *transaction*. We all know this could end in a heartbeat, but we will act *as if* we were going to have a career-long relationship. What is important is that both parties value an ongoing relationship and would prefer, if things work out well, to stay together as opposed to having either job-hopping (by the employee) or rapid churn (by the employer). So, the resultant of the two is a *transactional relationship.*

This, then, is the theory of the new protean career contract. But to really understand this "new deal," we have to see it in practice. Let us first expand upon this framework and then turn to some real organizations and see how it operates.

Figure 12.2   Career resilience map

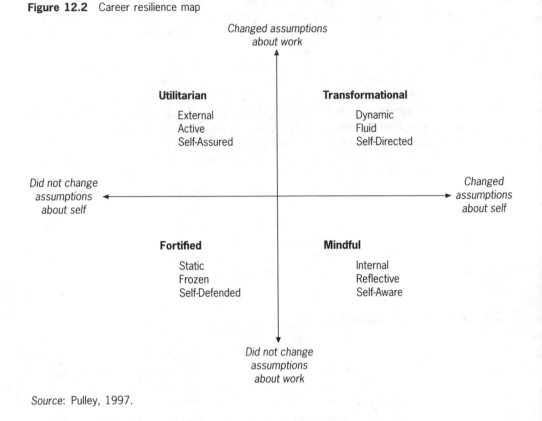

Source: Pulley, 1997.

FINDING RESILIENCY

Thinking about protean careers and the new career contract in terms of adaptability and identity growth may seem fairly abstract. The challenge then is to operationalize these concepts in ways that make more sense out of the many different organizations, personalities and situations facing us today. Building a two-by-two model can often be a helpful way to visualize varied characteristics across changing dimensions; we have found Pulley's (1997) Career Resilience Map, as shown in figure 12.2, to be useful in further sketching out these ideas. (The notion of resilience was first identified by London, 1983, based on research on AT&T's early assessment centers.)

In this research (Pulley, 1997), people who had involuntarily lost jobs were studied and found to express attitudes about the impact of change along two primary dimensions: changed assumptions about work and changed assumptions about oneself. The degree to which one's assumptions change – and possibly accept and adapt to – the changing career landscape can signify varying levels of *career resiliency*. Figure 12.2 is intended to depict different types of responses to change and job loss, with the vertical axis showing work-related attitude changes, versus changing assumptions about oneself along the horizontal dimension. The top half of the model reflects acknowledgment of the changing career contract, with increasing levels of recognition and acceptance toward change as one moves upward and to the right in the model (that is, greater ability to examine oneself, adapt and "bounce back" from a job loss situation equates to higher career resiliency). Individuals who possess such heightened resiliency exhibit more optimism and readiness to deal with additional changes, tend to be more realistic about themselves and the changing marketplace, and are much more likely to plan and act accordingly. Those lacking resiliency seem less prepared for and more defensive about ongoing change.

Segmenting this into quadrants based on high and low assumption changes across the two dimensions (self versus work) results in four archetypes to categorize the range of responses to the changing environment, broadly summarized below (Pulley, 1997):

1. The *fortified* quadrant (lower left) reflects people who change very few assumptions about either themselves or the workplace, despite being displaced and disrupted by restructuring. People here have difficulty seeing themselves doing much differently in the future and, although they may brace for oncoming change, do little to adapt or prepare for these changes. Unfortunately, many individuals exhibiting this profile are seen as being "frozen" and are locked out of changing future job opportunities as well; they will look for new jobs in the same old ways and, not surprisingly, come across the same types of jobs and situations – starting the cycle all over again.

2. The *mindful* quadrant (lower right) is comprised of people who seem to be very self-aware and introspective after losing their job. They are able to reflect and develop personal insights that may lead to changed attitudes and behavior. As Pulley reports (1997, p. 111), "Not only did [mindful] people change or clarify their values, they also changed some assumptions about themselves. Many learned to separate their identity from their work role. This is what [an interviewee] referred to when he said, 'I had to come to the realization of who I was, and that there's a difference between who I am and what I do.' [Another person] echoed a similar sentiment when she said, 'My job is important to me . . . but it's not who I am.'" Mindful people are less likely, however, to come to grips with the changed career contract in the marketplace. As a result, although they often have a heightened sense of self-worth and a better focus on their priorities and values after experiencing major change, these people may find themselves equally unprepared for the next restructuring or wave of organizational changes. (This quadrant would describe people who have acquired the metacompetency, described earlier, of identity learning.)

3. The *utilitarian* quadrant (upper left) is the opposite image of the mindful profile. Utilitarian people are very externally focused and explicitly acknowledge changed work assumptions, but are not introspective about what *they* need to do differently to ready themselves for change. People here can be very active in preparing for future changes, but principally direct their energy to gaining increased control on their career path, typically by becoming more self-employed and engaging in more consulting and independent contractor relationships. Utilitarian people seek out ways to gain, or regain, elements of control – or at least the feeling of being in control – of their career trajectory. One person reported (Pulley, 1997, p. 107) that, "Before my career was something I had to put up with to get a paycheck, and now it's a vehicle to get me where I want to go. It's a tool to open doors instead of something to go fight and get paid for." They adapt to the marketplace by changing their approach and position, but not their underlying attitude or skill sets.

This quadrant would represent people who have acquired the career metacompetency of adaptability, the ability to sense and respond effectively to weak signals in the external environment. But people in this quadrant, who possess adaptability without the other metacompetency, identity learning, are blindly reacting to the environment. They are adapting, but the adaptation is to the demands of others, not to their own values and needs. They are not aware of their own "path with a heart."

4. Finally, the *transformational* quadrant (upper right) reflects the most dynamic and adaptive profile. People here acknowledge the changed career contract and recognize the need to be open to change themselves. These individuals are seen to be highly resilient, able to generate profound changes in themselves and are open to ongoing changes in the nature of work. Pulley reports (1997, p. 136) that people who undergo transformative change forge a strong sense of self and build successful relationships to weather crisis and change; they "were able to make significant changes in their lives and they had the support for doing so. Rather than responding to their job loss by holding on to what they had or were in the past, they used the loss as an opportunity to experiment with new possibilities. Instead of clinging to what they'd lost, they ended up feeling much better about what they found." They seem more ready for change and more able to execute and adapt to these changing conditions – in short, they appear to be far more resilient.

Again, relating these quadrants to the metacompetencies described earlier, a person in the transformational cell would possess both adaptability and identity learning. This person is aware of the signals from the environment and is able to act on them, but is adapting in a way that meets not only the environment's demands but also is congruent with his/her own values and needs. Thus, this transactional quadrant represents an alignment of the person and the environment.

So, as we continue to refine our understanding of the changing career contract, examples and situations may be conceptually plotted along the above dimensions. In this way, some progression toward increased career resilience can be identified and mapped. Perhaps, more importantly, individual shortcomings and opportunities for additional development may be targeted and identified early enough to take action – possibly preventing derailment and being able to enhance career and individual growth.

ILLUSTRATIONS AND APPLICATIONS

A new era at AT&T

It is certainly not Ma Bell's phone company anymore. This massive bureaucracy had led a regal 100+ year privileged corporate life, and was the world's largest corporation in the mid-1980s. Widespread concerns about antitrust from AT&T's telecommunications monopoly grew to a roar for restructuring; after years of legal maneuvering and massive litigation expenses, the company finally agreed to shear the company – through "trivestiture" – into three pieces in 1995: (1) gladly spinning off its underperforming computer business under the previously-acquired NCR moniker; (2) the

Bell Labs equipment and research organization – the company's crown jewel – was reborn with much fanfare as Lucent Technologies; and (3) the remainder of the organization, which principally continues to provide business and residential long distance telephone service, lived on as AT&T (Rudolph, 1998). Where the company's strength – and soul – had been forged from a century of predictability, stability, and an understood way of life, a new landscape of change and turbulence emerged. The company is now known more for its break-up and restructuring than for its rich history.

As Rudolph (1998) recounts, the downsizing of AT&T resulted in $19 billion in restructuring charges from 1988–96. More significantly, between 1984 and 1995 roughly 120,000 people "disappeared" – through voluntary as well as involuntary reductions – from the company payroll. AT&T was transformed from a monopolistic exemplar of lifetime employment, often across generations of employee families, to a market-driven competitor, with countless painful vignettes of the new corporate order. Rudolph's presentation of six case studies, representing "life histories" of individuals who were downsized out of AT&T in the mid-1990s, prominently raises the interconnected themes of broken loyalties and changed identities. Some representative tales of survival and adjustment from those downsized, all former long term AT&T employees, acknowledging the new career contract, follow:

"I don't assume that any corporate environment is static. Markets, industries and technologies all shift. You have to be prepared to pick yourself up and move with them. You have to depend, finally, on yourself" (Rudolph, 1998, p. 95).

"Before, I'd say to people, 'I'm an operator.' Now I'm not exactly sure what I am. It's not something I focus on" (Rudolph, 1998, p. 134).

"What's in it for me? That's my new ideology. I am not looking for a job that will make me, quote, more secure. I don't believe in it and I won't fool myself into thinking that it exists. Any job that I take, I'm going to ask, 'What is this doing for me now? Does it make sense for me to stay?' And if I doesn't, I will move, fast" (Rudolph, 1998, p. 138).

"At this point, I don't expect to find personal validation in my work. Have I always been a fish out of water in the corporate world? Perhaps. I will do my job responsibly, but I will not look to any organization to reassure me of my self worth, to tell me who I am" (Rudolph, 1998, pp. 41–2).

These stories speak too of the contemporary coda of individual responsibility and adaptability. Today, organizations and individuals come together far more opportunistically than ever before, each cautiously eyeing the other for value-adding experiences and attributes. Careers are built in many phases and stages – with many unpredictable fits, swerves and starts – on a foundation of change and shifting identity. Rudolph concludes (1998, p. 199):

"Emerging from the shadow of their loss, these men and women have been forced to reconsider the meaning of work in their lives. For all of them it was a process of scaling back, of dismantling earlier-established expectations that work would bring them personal validation . . . For all of us in corporate America, the bond between company and employee has become a more nebulous connection, something that shifts according to circumstances."

Starbucks: the new loyalty[1]

How does an organization create the kind of person-firm alignment that is represented by the transformational quadrant in figure 12.2? Today's employees can develop a high degree of loyalty to an organization that is committed to them and with whose purpose they can identify. In fact, we would argue that this kind of commitment to a higher, valued purpose is precisely what many young people are seeking today. And these loyal, committed employees will, in turn, produce loyal, committed customers. Consider the fast-growing Starbucks' Coffee organization, run by entrepreneur Howard Schultz, who purchased it in 1987 as a local Seattle business that sold coffee beans. He envisioned an empire of stores "based on the notion that even though the term 'coffee break' is part of the vernacular, there's traditionally been no place to enjoy one, 'An extension of people's front porch,' as he puts it." The firm is now the largest coffee-bar chain in the United States – and growing rapidly worldwide – with a very loyal clientele.

To implement his strategy of having Starbucks' stores become "an extension of people's front porch," he takes care of employees first, so that they will in turn take care of customers. "The customer does not come first, the employee does. It's sort of the corporate version of 'I'm O.K., You're O.K.'." Starbucks was the first company in the US to grant full health-care benefits and stock options to its part-time workers (who make up 65 percent of its workforce). As Schultz described his mission, "I always saw myself wanting to be deemed successful and good at the same time . . . Service is a lost art in America. I think people want to do a good job, but if they are treated poorly they get beaten down . . . We want to provide our people with dignity and self-esteem, and we can't do that with lip service. So we offer tangible benefits. The attrition rate in retail fast food is between 200 and 400 percent a year. At Starbucks, it's 60 percent."

Interviews with the manager and employees at a recently-opened store in Cambridge, MA, illustrated the clear ambitions and satisfaction of Starbucks' employees. Serving coffee can be difficult work, but the workers seem satisfied with their positions. Between the medical benefits and the option of a free pound of coffee every week, the employees feel well compensated. And then there is the issue of upward mobility: the manager of the store has only worked for Starbucks for 10 months and has no previous experience in the food service industry. A fairly new employee we talked to seems to be inspired by the manager, commenting, "I hope to be managing my own store in not too many months" (Witchel, 1994, p. c1).

Founder Howard Schultz described the origin of his management philosophy in very personal terms:

"My father didn't finish high school, and what I remember most was the way he was treated in his adult life, which beat him down. He didn't have the self-esteem to feel worthy of a good job. So, I try to give people hope and self-esteem through a company that respects them. Dad never had that opportunity . . . Every one of our actions have to be compatible with the quality of our coffee. It never lets you down."

When asked about the secret of his success, Schultz looked a bit embarrassed and reflected, "Maybe I wasn't jaded. I always wanted to do something to make a difference.

Maybe people gravitated to that." Starbucks' performance seems to be an example of the notion that in business "you can do well by doing good."

Other new contract employers

In their study of the new career contract, Hall and Moss (1998) identified a group of companies in which, although there is definitely a new contract, employees never felt that the old contract had "broken." Instead, the new set of mutual expectations changed gradually over the years, in a continuous learning process. The continuous learning firms identified in this study included Hewlett-Packard, Beth Israel Hospital (Boston), Hannaford Brothers (a food retailer), Polaroid, and Xerox. Although these firms have faced difficult times over the years, they were generally able to remain competitive, in part because of strong organizational learning and employee involvement processes.

A core element in creating this alignment between employee and organization in all of these organizations is a core value of respect for the individual – both the employee and the customer. This value provides important continuity between the old and new contracts. This close link between taking care of employees and taking care of customers was described by an employee of Beth Israel Hospital, describing how the changes in her workplace have evolved:

> "Dr. Rabkin came in as President in 1966. He was keen on the subject of personalized care and established it as a clear philosophy. He felt that the patient and employees are on an equal footing. Both people ought to be treated with respect and dignity by Beth Israel . . . The underlining commitment to the employee was evident several years ago as the private doctors' cafeteria was discarded back in the 1960s . . . Even during rapid growth, the diverse workforce was taken into account. The culture and the philosophy of the hospital have a very narrow gap between them" (Hall and Moss, 1998, p. 28).

Note that there are no guarantees of long-term employment security here. The security for the employee is in her constant learning, self-awareness, and always current skills and in the business success and respect for the individual of the organization. Thus, both parties possess the metacompetencies of identity awareness and adaptability.

How does this new "no-guarantees" career contract look in Hewlett-Packard? Brad Harrington, H-P's manager for management development, has identified some of the ways the work environment has been made more flexible, to accommodate both changing business needs and changing employee circumstances (Hall and Harrington, 1998):

- telecommuting;
- job sharing;
- temporary and contract work;
- downshifting (for example, cutting back on work hours);
- managing excess staffing.

Harrington described how his own career was marked by many twists and turns, including a stint in the UK as quality manager, entering a two-career marriage, and juggling issues of job location, parental care, a doctoral program, and, later, child care. In 1999 he had a job that was based in California, and the company set up a home office so that he could telecommute from Winchester, MA. In all of these matters, he reported needing – and receiving – support from his bosses and from top management for his continuous development, a concern for balance (even when it was not necessarily delivered, and a sense of *mutuality* (that is, "we're both committed to this work relationship"). And, above all, there is a sense of flexibility.

How does it all shake out? He describes the "balance sheet" as follows:

• "My work is more varied"	*but*	"I need to 'job hunt' more often"
• "I am doing work that I feel adds value"	*but*	"I'm always explaining what I'm doing"
• "I often do work which is more interesting"	*but*	"I often feel vulnerable, no real anchor"
• "I am driven by the work, not by the status"	*but*	"I'm not as secure (or high status) as I once felt" (Hall and Harrington, 1998).

PROBLEMS AND ISSUES WITH THE NEW CONTRACT

Before we get too carried away with the potential and opportunities of the new contract, let us consider some of the questions and problems that it raises (some of which are suggested by the *buts* in Brad Harrington's balance sheet above). In the same way that the current global economy presents many inequities and has caused much suffering in the world, so too has the new career contract which has been created by this new economy. We will consider some of the more important issues here.

Growing gap between "haves" and "have-nots"

The new career contract is based on the ability to learn. And this requires that the person has a certain level of education, a certain level of confidence or self-esteem, a certain level of (positive) past experience with self-generated learning, and access to resources that support learning, such as challenging work and supportive relationships (Hall and Associates, 1996; Arthur and Rousseau, 1996). All of these qualities represent a degree of *privilege* that may not be widely shared in the world. People who are less well educated, people who are poor, people who are at a survival level of existence, especially those in poor countries, older people who may feel threatened or discriminated against in relation to protean learning, and people who are not connected to a support network, and people who lack access to technology, to name a few, may be most at risk from the new career contract. (See, for example, Kossek, 1996 for a discussion of the working poor and the new contract.) These are serious issues, and we are just beginning to focus on them.

A "me first," "winner take all" mentality

Related to the issue of privilege mentioned above is the mindset that can potentially develop in those in the advantaged group – that they are entitled to these advantages, that they have worked for them, and that they have achieved their rewards in life through independent effort. And furthermore, the mindset goes, those who are less privileged are therefore in that condition because of their own laziness and moral shortcomings. The fact is that those in the privileged group, even those who "worked their way up", generally had critical advantages, such as a good education, loving and supportive parents, inborn qualities such as initiative, intelligence, interpersonal skills, and resilience.

Can the metacompetencies be developed?

This point also relates to the notion of privilege. If the metacompetencies are in effect the "DNA" that sets the code for one's ability to learn, to what extent are they developable? Can a person become more adaptable through conscious development? Or is this a function of personality dimensions such as flexibility and hardiness? And what about identity? A review of the relevant literature suggests that a lot of the variance in adaptability is accounted for by fairly stable individual differences, although there are some environmental and experiential inputs that can affect it as well (Morrison and Hall, 1999). Although there is evidence that levels of consciousness of identity can develop (Kegan, 1986), it is also clear that the development of one's identity is a difficult process (Kegan, 1994).

Does this give downsizers free rein?

One problem with celebrating the autonomous and self-directed protean career is that it can have the effect of taking the employing organization off the hook regarding formal development activities. "People are self-directed now; that's the new career. People can develop themselves. The firm doesn't have a responsibility here." This could be the thinking of some executives now. Worse, it could help legitimize downsizing and layoffs, via the attitude that employees are now resilient and can fend fine for themselves. This is wrong, especially if the organization has not been supporting employee learning up until this point. In a company like Hewlett-Packard, which promotes "employability" by keeping employees trained and continuously learning through challenging job assignments, if they have to lay a person off, that person is equipped to be mobile. But if that person were doing one job for 20 years, with no training, there would be no way he or she would be equipped to make a good self-directed change.

How to juggle work, family, and self?

Don't look now, but the protean career just made the issue of work/life balance much more complicated. By putting responsibility for career choices inside the person, the protean career has moved work/life conflict inside as well. The struggle is no longer between the employee and the employer or co-workers; it is a tussle between the employee and himself. Or it is between the employee and those he or she loves the most. It is wonderful when a person enjoys the work, does it well, and the work provides a strong sense of purpose and meaning. But that high involvement can often show up as late nights or weekends at the office (or in the home office), with the resulting internal and family conflicts that this lack of home presence can create. A key question here is how can the protean careerist learn to create and maintain good boundaries, within the self, to allow work and life to get along well together?

DEVELOPMENT IMPLICATIONS AND STRATEGY

When we consider the nature of the protean career contract, as well as some of the issues just discussed, the career development ramifications are many. For example, the individual and the organization must take into account the lack of permanency in any organization (*development must occur real-time*), content is unpredictable (*not knowing what will develop*), career paths move laterally, vertically and often (*hierarchical boundaries are confused*), and selection and retention of "key" employees has become a vital but truly monumental challenge (*not knowing whom to retain, why or when*). Furthermore, developmental efforts must, of course, be viewed by the organization as being cost-effective, in light of competitive economic pressures (Hollenbeck and McCall, 1998). Traditional notions of career progression have become irrelevant, and executive development must incorporate the current organizational dynamics.

Identifying high-potential young managers for executive development will be increasingly difficult. The concept of "high-potential" is typically conceptualized by past successes – and previous accomplishments are less relevant and less predictive of future success (McCall, 1998). Technical knowledge, skills and ability are also less relevant to potential upcoming tasks; "competency" itself is therefore problematic to measure (Hollenbeck and McCall, 1998) and may even create a "false sense of security" (Briscoe and Hall, 1999).

Some organizations have developed leadership models which consistently contain more *relevant* competencies (Schaffer, 1994; Sontag, 1996): learn continuously, think strategically, create a climate for success, champion change, lead with confidence, promote shared values, and inspire a shared purpose. Overall, however, the most critical leadership development areas are *relational skills*, the *ability to learn and adapt*, and *learning how to learn from experience* (Hollenbeck and McCall, 1998). In addition, it is also universally agreed that a strong *link to real business problems* is the most effective executive development path. In fact, on-line experience is clearly considered to be the best "classroom for leadership" (McCall, 1998). Finally, the highest "competency for learning" is evidenced by people who *seek out* opportunities to learn and develop an openness to *learning by doing* different things (McCall, 1998), taking steps and being self-aware (Briscoe and Hall, 1999), consistent with Argyris' (1992) notion of generative Model II "double-loop" learning. In *learning from action* the organization and the individual will develop and grow together (Baird, 1997).

In summary, a *combination* of initiatives that build identity and adaptability will be the most effective to enhance individual development and generate organizational learning (Briscoe and Hall, 1999). These efforts must be integrated into the corporate culture, actively promoted and supported, be as individualized as possible, and be focused on specific business needs. The new career contract requires new ways of thinking about career development.

TOWARD THE HORIZON: SOME CONCLUSIONS

This, then, is the new psychological career contract at work. The critical protean elements of adaptability and identity are key metacompetencies that are drivers at the individual level. As we saw in Brad Harrington's experience the mutual commitment to the relationship is critical at the organizational level. And, as we saw with AT&T, Starbucks, and Beth Israel Hospital, where the new contract works well, new loyalties are based on continuous learning and opportunistic development forged on a foundation of shared purpose – temporary in nature but strong in proportion to the mutual value gained. Finally, the new contract is a mixed blessing. Although it represents greater individual freedom and meaning, it does create more of a feeling of living "on the edge." Not everyone has equal access to the opportunities it provides, and not everyone has the personal qualities necessary to thrive in this more uncertain and demanding environment. Career development can be challenging under such conditions. It is incumbent on employing organizations to provide the conditions – a deep respect for the individual, continuous learning, mutual commitment to making the relationship work, and flexibility – that can permit employees to create their own skill-based security as they pursue their paths with a heart.

NOTE

1. The material on Starbucks is adapted from Hall and Moss (1998).

REFERENCES

Argyris, C. 1992: *On Organizational Learning*. Malden, MA: Blackwell Publishers.

Baird, L. 1997: *Learning faster than the speed of change*. Presentation to the Executive Development Roundtable, Boston University.

Bennis, W. and Townsend, R. 1995: *Reinventing Leadership: Strategies to Empower the Organization*. New York: William Morrow.

Briscoe, J.P. and Hall, D.T. 1999: Using "competencies" to groom and pick leaders: are we on the right track? *Organizational Dynamics* (in press).

Davis, S. 1998: *Blur: The Speed of Change in the Connected Economy*. Reading, MA: Addison-Wesley.

Drucker, P. 1998: *Managing in a Time of Great Change*. New York: Truman Talley Books.

Etzioni, A. 1961: *A Comparative Analysis of Complex Organizations*. Glencoe, IL: Free Press.

Feldman, D. 1976: A contingency theory of socialization. *Administrative Science Quarterly*, 21 (3), 433–52.

Gallos, J. 1989: Exploring women's development: implications for career theory, practice and research. In M. Arthur, D. Hall, and B. Lawrence, (eds) *Handbook of Career Theory*. Cambridge: Cambridge University Press.

Hall, D. 1994: The new "career contract": wrong on both counts. Boston, MA: Executive Development Roundtable, Boston University School of Management, Report # 9403.

Hall, D. and Mirvis, P. 1996: The new protean career. In Hall, D. (ed.) *The Career is Dead: Long Live the Career*. San Francisco: Jossey-Bass.

Hall, D.T. and Harrington, B. 1998: The new protean career contract. Presentation to the Boston Human Resource Association. Newton, MA.

Hall, D. and Moss, J. 1998: The new protean career contract: how organizations and employees adapt. *Organizational Dynamics*, 26 (3), 22–36.

Handy, C. 1989: *The Age of Unreason*. Boston: Harvard Business School Press.

Heckscher, C. 1995: *White-Collar Blues: Management Loyalties in an Age of Corporate Restructuring*. New York: Basic Books.

Hollenbeck, G. and McCall, M. 1998: Leadership development: contemporary practice. In A. Kraut and A. Korman (eds) *Changing Concepts and Practices for Human Resource Management: Contributions from Industrial/Organizational Psychology*. San Francisco: Jossey-Bass.

Kahn, W. and Kram, K. 1994: Authority at work: internal models and their organizational consequences. *Academy of Management Review*, 19 (1), 17–50.

Kanter, R. 1995: *World Class: Thriving Locally in the Global Economy*. New York: Touchstone.

Kegan, R. 1982: *The Evolving Self*. Cambridge, MA: Harvard University Press.

Kegan, R. 1994: *In Over Our Heads: The Mental Demands of Modern Life*. Cambridge, MA: Harvard University Press.

Kram, K. 1988: *Mentoring at Work: Developmental Relationships in Organizational Life*. Lanham, MD: University Press of America.

Kram, K. and Hall, D. 1995: Mentoring in a context of diversity and turbulence. In S. Lobel and E. Kossek (eds) *Human Resource Strategies for Managing Diversity*. London: Blackwell.

Levinson, D., with Darrow, C., Klein, E., Levinson, M., and McKee, B. 1978: *The Seasons of a Man's Life*. New York: Knopf.

London, M. 1983: Toward a theory of career motivation. *Academy of Management Review*, 16, 507–21.

March, J. and Simon, H. 1958: *Organizations*. New York: John Wiley.

McCall, M. 1998: *High Flyers: Developing the Next Generation of Leaders*. Boston: Harvard Business.

Mirvis, P. 1992: Job security: current trends. In L. Jones (ed.) *The Encyclopedia of Career Change and Work Issues*. Phoenix: Oryx Press.

Mishra, K., Spreitzer, G., and Mishra, A. 1998: Preserving employee morale during downsizing. *Sloan Management Review*, 39 (2), 83–95.

Mohrman, S. 1999: Top management viewed from below: a learning perspective on transformation. In J. Conger, G. Spreitzer, and E. Lawler (eds) *The Leader's Change Handbook: An Essential Guide to Setting Direction and Taking Action*. San Francisco: Jossey-Bass.

Morrison, R.F. and Hall, D.T. 1999: Examining adaptability: can it be developed? Technical Report, Executive Development Roundtable, Boston University School of Management.

O'Connell, D. 1998: Just sitting in: The navigation of tenuous work circumstances by contingent workers. Unpublished doctoral dissertation. Boston University School of Management.

Perrow, C. 1986: *Complex Organizations: A Critical Essay*. 3rd edn, New York: McGraw-Hill.

Pulley, M. 1997: *Losing your Job – Reclaiming your Soul: Stories of Resilience, Renewal, and Hope*. San Francisco: Jossey-Bass.

Reichheld, F. 1996: *The Loyalty Effect*. Boston: Harvard Business School Press.

Rousseau, D. 1995: *The Psychological Contract in Organizations*. Thousand Oaks, CA: Sage.

Rudolph, B. 1998: *How Six People from AT&T Discovered the New Meaning of Work in a Downsized Corporate America*. New York: Free Press.

Schaffer, G. 1994: Competency-based managerial and leadership development. *Proceedings of the National Conference on Using Competency-based Tools*, Boston. (In Hollenbeck and McCall, 1998.)

Schein, E. 1992: *Organizational Culture and Leadership*. San Francisco: Jossey-Bass.

Schneider, B., Gunnarson, S., and Niles-Jolley, K. 1994: Creating the climate and culture of success, *Organizational Dynamics*, 23 (1), 17–29.

Sekaran, U. and Hall, D. 1989: Asynchronism in dual-career and family linkages. In M. Arthur, D. Hall, and B. Lawrence (eds) *Handbook of Career Theory*. Cambridge: Cambridge University Press.

Sontag, L. 1996: The evolution of competencies at Chase: lessons learned. Presentation to the Executive Development Roundtable, Boston University (In Hollenbeck and McCall, 1998).

Thomas, D.A. and Gabarro, J.J. 1999: *Breaking Through: The Making of Minority Executives in Corporate America*. Boston: Harvard Business School Press.

Witchel, A. 1994: By way of Canarsie, one large cup of business strategy. *New York Times*, pp. C1, C8.

13 Eroding Organizational Social Capital among US Firms: The Price of Job Instability

Carrie R. Leana and Harry J. Van Buren III

INTRODUCTION

The job market in the United States is in a state of flux. The US employment rate is currently at a 30-year low and employers regularly complain about labor shortages in both manufacturing and service industries. At the same time, downsizing rates at US firms are at record highs and large-scale employee cuts are announced virtually every day in the business press (Weinstein, 1999).

It is unclear how long either of these trends will continue but the effects of such job instability over the long term are expected to be profound. Many writers have pointed to the "sea change" in how jobs and employment are defined in the United States (Arthur and Rousseau, 1996; Leana, 1996). No longer can employees count on job stability, regardless of the quality of the work they produce, and no longer can employers count on loyalty and commitment from their workforce. Both parties have a short-term perspective and rely more on transactional arrangements rather than implicit relationships in negotiating both day-to-day practices in the workplace and larger employment policies.

These trends are visible and receive a good deal of attention by business writers and academics, perhaps because they diverge so radically from traditional employment practices established over the last 50 years in the US. Yet at the same time there is a counter-movement in the US that extolls the economic and social virtues of stability in the workplace as in other parts of life (Fukuyama, 1995; Sennett, 1998). Due in part to the adverse consequences of employment practices like downsizing and contingent work (Leana, 1996; Leana and Feldman, 1992), increasingly business writers and academics – as well as firms themselves – are realizing the costs of instability and beginning to explore the benefits of shared community, mutual trust, and stability in employment relations (for example, Fukuyama, 1999; Leana and Rousseau, 2000; Rousseau et al., 1999).

In this paper we discuss the concept of organizational social capital – the value to an organization and its members of relationships formed for the purpose of engaging in collective action. To be built and maintained, organizational social capital requires trust and shared responsibility. We argue that current trends in US employment are undermining organizational social capital to the detriment of both the long-term competitiveness of US firms and the long-term stability of individuals and the society as a whole. We conclude with some recommendations on how firms and individuals can build organizational social capital and realize what Leana and Rousseau (2000) have labeled "relational wealth."

ORGANIZATIONAL SOCIAL CAPITAL

Organizational social capital is the glue that binds employers and employees together, as well as employees to one another. It is a resource that can benefit both employee and employer and creates value by facilitating successful collective action. Organizational social capital reflects the character of social relations within a firm and can be contrasted to other sources of capital such as financial resources (financial capital), plant and equipment (physical capital), and the skills and experience of the workforce (human capital). Organizational social capital is jointly "owned" by the organization and its members, while human capital is owned by individuals and financial and physical capital by the organization. Organizational social capital is therefore a public rather than a private good. As we will discuss in a subsequent section, rational individuals will not invest in actions that build and maintain organizational social capital unless they believe that they will benefit, even if indirectly and in the long run.

As we have described in a recent paper (Leana and Van Buren, 1999), organizational social capital has two primary components: (1) associability; and (2) shared trust. Associability describes how willing and how able organizational members are to subordinate their individual goals and associated actions to the goals and actions of the collective. Associability combines elements of sociability (the ability to interact socially with others) with a willingness to prioritize group objectives over individual desires. Associability has both an affective component (for example, collectivist feelings) and a skill-based component (for example, the ability to coordinate activities). Some level of associability is necessary if individuals are to agree upon and effectively coordinate their common activities.

The second component of organizational social capital is trust. Researchers generally agree that trust requires a willingness to be vulnerable (Rousseau et al., 1998). Trust is necessary for people to work in an organization, even if only to the extent that employees believe they will be compensated in full and on time. According to Ring and Van de Ven (1992), trust can be fragile (that is, based on risk-reward calculations) or resilient (based on on-going norms and values of reciprocity). Organizations strong in social capital will have members who share resilient rather than fragile trust both between the organization and its employees, and among employees themselves.

Trust can also be dyadic or generalized (Leana and Van Buren, 1999). Dyadic trust describes trust between parties who have direct knowledge of, or interaction with, one another. Generalized trust does not require this direct knowledge and/or interaction. Instead, it is based on affiliation and reputation. Thus, organizational members may trust one another without much direct information or previous interaction simply by virtue of being in the same social network. Organizations strong in social capital will be characterized by generalized trust. Thus, they will exhibit resilient trust, even among individuals connected generally rather than personally. Organizations weak in social capital are characterized by fragile trust (if any), even among members who know one another well.

How Organizations Create and Maintain Social Capital

Organizational social capital is largely managed through the firm's employment practices (Leana and Van Buren, 1999). The most obvious way that firms can build and maintain organizational social capital is by engaging in employment practices that promote stability and associability among organizational members. Typically this is done by making investments in training, job security, and team-building, and minimizing the use of practices such as downsizing and contingent work. Organizational social capital can also operate through norms whereby employees are selected in part for their ability and appreciation for working together cooperatively. Socialization systems can also be used to promote reciprocity norms, as can the organization's reward systems in the form of promotions and compensation. Employment practices that encourage stable job tenure and reinforce associability and trust enhance an organization's stock of organizational social capital, with a parallel benefit to the organization's ability to organize collective action.

The organizational social capital model implicitly treats employees – and their relationships within and outside their workgroups – as assets rather than costs. As Pfeffer (1998) has noted, however, many US firms are acting in ways that emphasize short-term, transactional arrangements through the use of contingent workforces, performance-based pay for individuals, an emphasis on employability (see Waterman, Waterman, and Collard, 1994), and downsizing. In a subsequent section, we discuss how the loss of organizational social capital associated with such practices is harmful to firms. In this next section, we look at some of the factors that are contributing to a decline in social capital in US firms.

Factors Contributing to the Decline of Social Capital in US Firms

In contrast with many other countries, the United States generally does not have a regulatory tradition of job property rights (Lansing and Van Buren, 1993; Pfeffer, 1998). Rather, most employment relationships are governed by the "employment-at-will" concept: in the absence of a regulatory restriction (like firing a person based on his or her race or sex) or a prior employment contract, an employment relationship can be terminated at any time by either employer or employee (Radin and Werhane, 1996). The regulatory bias in favor of not interfering with the ability of employers to dismiss employees at will differentiates the US from other countries. As a variety of academic (Cohany et al., 1998) and popular (*The New York Times Special Report*, 1996) writers have suggested, employment practices that emphasize short-term relationships are prominent in the US context. Such practices afford organizations a certain kind of flexibility. At the same time, however, they contribute to the decline in the social capital of US firms. Four factors are contributing to this decline: (1) pressures to maintain short-term profitability lead to the use of transactional employment relationships; (2) organizations value human capital more highly than social capital; (3) the changing nature of the psychological contracts that employees have with employers; and (4) the growth of a market-focused ideology in the US.

The effects of short-term profitability pressures

One phenomenon that has been widely noted by a variety of observers of US corporations is the pressures that corporate managers face to enhance short-term profitability. Indeed, news of a downsizing is often treated as positive by market observers – at least initially (Sloan, 1996), although a study by Worrell, Davidson and Sharma (1991) reported more mixed evidence about the effects of downsizing announcements on stock price. If reducing labor costs indeed translated into increased profitability, then employment practices like downsizing and the use of contingent workers might be seen as a valuable tool for managers facing pressures for increased short-term profitability. But the empirical evidence for this proposition is mixed; Cascio, Young, and Morris (1997) found that pure downsizings (unaccompanied by asset restructurings) were not linked to increased profitability. There has not yet been extensive empirical work done on organizational-level outcomes *vis-à-vis* the use of contingent workforces, but there is evidence that such practices are becoming more popular as organizations seek to reduce the number of core workers (Cohany et al., 1998).

Short-term profitability pressures may lead managers to think of workers as costs to be reduced rather than assets to be maintained. When a company announces that it is laying off workers or outsourcing work, it might seem logical to assume that the organization is becoming more efficient. But labor costs are often a small portion of total costs (Pfeffer, 1998), and it does not – for reasons that we will discuss in the next section – follow that reducing labor costs makes the organization more efficient.

Organizations value human capital more highly than social capital

The second reason for declining organizational social capital in US firms is the emphasis that organizations are placing on procuring human capital. Many employment markets are marked by the "winner-take-all" phenomenon (Frank and Cook, 1995) in which disproportionate rewards accrue to individuals with talents deemed to be scarce. Organizations will focus, for example, on attracting and remunerating a chief executive officer with the talents and abilities that are thought to be the missing element needed to make the organization successful.

Such practices emphasize the contributions that individuals – specifically individuals at the apex of organizations – make to organizational success. But it is well known that structural effects, like the personal social capital of CEOs, explain variance in remuneration over and above performance differences (Belliveau, O'Reilly, and Wade, 1996). Further, compensation schemes that emphasize individual contributions are generally inappropriate in contexts where team productions occurs (Campbell, Campbell, and Chia, 1998). Because organizational social capital is intangible and thus difficult to quantify, it is devalued by organizations in ways that human (and both financial and physical capital) are not. Organizations in general pay more attention to human rather than social capital when devising human resources policies and practices. As we will argue in a subsequent section, however, an organization's stock of social capital can either unleash or retard the positive effects of human capital on organizational success.

The changing nature of the psychological contracts that employees have with employers

The changing nature of the psychological contract between employers and employees can undermine organizational social capital. A psychological contract is defined as an individual's beliefs about the terms and conditions of a reciprocal exchange agreement between that person and another party (Rousseau, 1995). Considerable attention has been given to the effects of psychological contract breaches on employee commitment and future trust in the firm (see, for example, Robinson, 1996). Less attention, however, has been given to the content of particular psychological contracts between individuals and their organizations.

A recent exception is the work of Cavanaugh and Noe (1999), who have developed a scale for what they term the "new psychological contract." The new psychological contract emphasizes personal responsibility for career development, commitment to a particular kind of work rather than a particular organization, constant organizational change rather than stasis, expectations of job insecurity, and careers that will unfold over the course of interactions with a number of organizations. We have noted that many organizations have signaled to employees that they should not expect job security; rather, the new psychological contract is based on employability obligations of employers to employees. In short, employees can reasonably expect employers to help them remain competitive on the labor market (whether within or outside the firm) by providing opportunities for personal growth.

If the new psychological contract accurately describes the trend in US employment practices – and many writers, both pro and con, maintain that it does – it is easy to see how it would be inconsistent with an organizational social capital perspective. Rational individuals who perceive this sort of psychological contract would not invest in firm-specific skills except to the degree necessary to do their current projects. Further, time spent on engaging in extra-role behavior like organizational citizenship behaviors – consistent with norms of associability – would be better used to maintain personal networks that will help an employee find his or her next job. Firms that see the "new psychological contract" as a good way to structure the employment relationship should not be surprised when employees act in ways consistent with it. In a subsequent section, we take up the issue of how employment practices that seemingly emphasize flexibility may not allow for the flexible organization of work, but we note here that there is little room for norms of reciprocity, resilient trust, or associability in a psychological contract that emphasizes employees' ability to maintain their skills so that they will be ready at any time to find work with another organization.

Market-based ideology

A final contributing factor to the demise of organizational social capital within US firms is the prevalence of market-centered ideology in the US. The market as an arbiter of individual worth is a strongly held value in the United States. Moreover, as more Americans invest in capital markets through their retirement plans and savings, they become more attached to the rise and fall of the stock market as a prime indicator of their personal well-being. As recently noted by Cox (1999), the market and the neoclassical economic assumptions that underlie its operation, are often discussed as if they were a form of religion rather than a system of exchange. The market has assumed a sort of deification in the writings of the business press that is seldom questioned or critiqued. Government involvement in the operation of financial or labor markets in the United States is looked upon with suspicion and generally discouraged as a form of "interference" that only constrains the national benevolence of a market left to Adam Smith's "invisible hand." This market-based ideology also values independence and mobility for all sorts of capital – physical, financial, and human – over stability and interdependence (Sennett, 1998), further contributing to a decline in stable employment and reliance on any particular employer.

THE COSTS OF DECLINING ORGANIZATIONAL SOCIAL CAPITAL

Organizational social capital represents the value to an organization and its members of relationships formed for the purpose of engaging in collective action. A decline in the stock of organizational social capital, therefore, should have deleterious effects on an organization's ability to engage in successful collective action. We discuss three potential costs of declining organizational social capital: (1) individuals in organizations with low social capital are less committed to their organizations than to the particular work they do; (2) a decline in organizational social capital can paradoxically make the goal of flexible work organization harder rather than easier to achieve; and (3) low social capital organizations are less successful in managing collective action.

Individuals in organizations with low social capital are less committed to their organizations than to the particular work they do

The employability perspective on jobs (Waterman, Waterman, and Collard, 1994) emphasizes a new arrangement between employees and employers whereby the organization cannot ensure continued employment or a career ladder, but it will provide its employees with the work experiences and training necessary to maintain their ability to procure employment, whether inside or outside of the organization. Employability arguments can be critiqued on a variety of grounds; one might, for example, look at the ethical duties posed by such arrangements (Van Buren, 1999). For the present analysis, it is helpful to think about what it is that organizations that emphasize employability are signaling to their employees (see Spence, 1973, for a discussion of signaling in employment).

Organizations that use employability as the dominant frame for work relationships are in effect encouraging employees to think of themselves as independent contractors who are free to leave at any time. Those employees with the scarcest human capital – and who are most highly sought in the external labor market – are constantly scanning the external environment for other opportunities. Such employees are likely willing to extend fragile and dyadic trust at the expense of resilient and generalized trust. Further, they are encouraged to think of themselves as "professionals" in the traditional sense of that term – people who define themselves by the work that they do rather than by the organizations of which they are (temporarily) members. The organization that emphasizes employability rather than stable employment is therefore betting that it will be able to assemble the human capital it needs on a contingent basis.

Two points are important here. The first is that organizations are more than conglomerations of human capital. A corporation like General Electric, for example, does have talented people who would be highly sought after in the external labor market. But GE's success can be ascribed as much to the norms and shared understandings of the organization as to the collective talents of its individual employees (Byrne, 1998). An organization can be greater or less than the sum of its parts.

The second point is related to the first: employment strategies that emphasize buying labor on an as-needed basis are not likely to be sources of competitive advantage. Pfeffer (1998) asks the provocative question of whether normal employment practices can ever be the source of abnormal (positive) returns. When a firm's employees are encouraged to think of themselves as maintainers of personal employability rather than as long-term employees, they are less likely to make the investments in firm-specific knowledge (including norms and habits of practice) that are a critical source of sustained competitive advantage.

The organizational social capital model suggests a contrary view of the relationship between human capital and organizational success. Organizational social capital provides the trust, associability, and reciprocity norms that make collective action possible, thus unleashing the collective value of a firm's human capital. Organizations with large stocks of social capital will therefore be able to deploy human capital in ways that ensure individuals are not working at cross-purposes – or even worse, working on developing skills and personal networks that benefit the individual first and the organization only secondarily, if at all. A "career-resilient workforce" that has learned to expect that their career ladders will unfold over the course of a variety of interactions with many different firms will not be likely to invest very much in the success of any one organization. While individuals in the contemporary employment environment should define themselves in part by the work they do, it is in an organization's interest to get its employees to define themselves by their membership in that organization as well. Eroding organizational social capital makes that task more difficult.

Declining social capital makes flexible work organization harder rather than easier to achieve

It might seem paradoxical to propose that declining organizational social capital might make flexibility in work organization harder rather than easier to achieve – especially given the prevalence of employment practices that emphasize transactional contracts designed to maintain flexibility. Recent research into what have been called "high-performance work practices," however (see Ichniowski et al., 1996), illustrates why organizational social capital might well bring about the flexibility that organizations are increasingly seeking.

We noted that associability and trust are the primary components of organizational social capital. Work practices that emphasize employee involvement, cross-functional training, flexible employment, and labor-management cooperation all require some level of associability and trust to operate effectively. These practices also have been linked to improved productivity, cost savings, and quality improvement. Pil and MacDuffie (1996), for example, suggest that durability in relationships is an important predictor of the adoption of high-performance work practices in the automobile industry because of the need for cooperation and trust. Scully and Preuss (1996) found that elements of social capital were present in workgroups that engaged in task rotation and team meetings but not in workgroups that operated under transactional employment relationships and formalized rules. Because of the uncertainty posed by any change in work practices, employees will be more likely to adopt them if they are willing to extend resilient trust to their organizations. Kramer (1999) proposes that the inculcation of trust in organizations requires time to develop, but such trust can break down quickly upon violation. Organizations that engage in employment practices that emphasize short-term, transactional relationships encourage reliance on fragile rather than resilient trust; resilient trust, however, is necessary for workers to feel comfortable participating in high-performance workplace practices.

This might seem surprising, given the trend in US employment practices, but both theory and empirical findings make the connections between organizational social capital and flexible workplace practices quite clear. Flexible workplace practices rely on collective identity and generalized trust rather than the formal monitoring and control mechanisms associated with more traditional ways of organizing work. Employment practices that emphasize transactional arrangements and human capital at the expense of social capital, therefore, may retard rather than enhance flexibility. As Pfeffer (1998) has properly pointed out, just because an organization undertakes a particular employment policy doesn't mean that it is logical or sensible to do so. To the extent that flexible workplace practices require informal norms for workgroup governance and resilient, generalized trust, an organizational social capital perspective on the employment relationship is necessary.

Low social capital organizations are less successful at managing collective action

Thus far we have focused on stable employment relationships as a means of building and sustaining organizational social capital, while critiquing more temporary, transactional employment arrangements. Much of the economics literature on transactions costs (Coase, 1937; Williamson, 1985) postulates that organizations are potential solutions to the costs of transacting. Employees who perceive their employment relationships to be stable are more likely to invest in firm-specific knowledge and skills that in turn make collective action possible. In high social capital organizations, informal norms of associability, trust, and reciprocity make extensive monitoring less necessary, reducing the costs of transacting and increasing the likelihood that employees' interests will be aligned with the organization's. Human resources policies that emphasize transactional arrangements, in contrast, require formalized monitoring and incentives mechanisms – which ironically make flexible work arrangements harder to sustain because employees in transactional arrangements will want to also renegotiate the terms of the exchange relationship when the organization does.

Employment practices that emphasize the building and maintenance of organizational social capital can enhance the organization's ability to manage collective action because organizational social capital can be a substitute for agency concepts of incentives and formalized monitoring. Consider the use of outsourcing as a strategy for reducing the number of core employees, which is thought by many organizations to increase flexibility. The outsourcing decision does not eliminate the collective action or monitoring problems associated with constructing such tasks in-house; rather, outsourcing can not only replicate these problems but also deprives the organization of recourse to shared organizational norms. The organization that is doing the outsourced work may share the focal organization's values, or it may not. Outsourced work may be done in accordance with the strategy of the organization contracting for it, or it may not. In short, while the outsourcing decision may allow work to be done by an organization that is more efficient, the benefits of outsourcing must be weighed against the monitoring and contracting costs of such a relationship.

An organizational social capital perspective on employment does not mean that an organization would never engage in downsizing or the use of contingent work, but it does focus an analysis of such decisions within a social context. The organizational social capital model extends the agency and transactions costs perspectives on the management of collective action by offering shared norms and relationships as a means by which collective action can be more efficiently managed. Employment decisions that cause a loss of social capital may unintentionally lead to the loss of resilient, generalized trust and the diminution of associability and reciprocity norms. In seeking the goal of greater flexibility and lower labor costs, many organizations implicitly devalue organizational social capital and therefore do not achieve either goal.

BUILDING ORGANIZATIONAL SOCIAL CAPITAL IN US FIRMS

We have discussed the dangers of eroding social capital in US firms and the costs of such erosion. Now we turn our attention to how organizational social capital can be built and maintained. Here we have several recommendations regarding the behavior of the firm and its managers, as well as some suggestions about the financial and legal environment in which US firms operate.

Firm investments in organizational social capital

As we noted earlier, firms can have the greatest impact on organizational social capital through their employment practices. Practices that build trust, stability, and associability can foster organizational social capital. Practices such as downsizing and the use of contingent workers destroy trust and undermine stability, thus eroding organizational social capital. The following is a partial list of employment practices that promote organizational social capital:

- Job security provisions or at least an understanding that practices like downsizing are a last resort rather than a first strike method of cost cutting.
- Socialization practices that encourage collective goal setting and attainment.
- Firm- or group-based incentive compensation systems rather than incentive compensation based on individual performance.
- Compensation and promotion practices that reward social capital-enhancing behavior, particularly among managers.
- Compensation practices that do not over-reward a few individuals strong in human capital at the expense of the collective social capital of the workforce as a whole.
- Selective hiring so that individuals who join the firm have an aptitude for, and appreciation of, behaviors that encourage organizational social capital.
- Long-term partnerships between labor and management rather than adversarial contract-based exchanges.

Encouraging patient capital

The structure of financial markets has influenced many of the incentives US firms face, including those relating to employment and job stability and thus organizational social capital. Financial capital in the US has become increasingly "impatient": investors are holding onto their investments for shorter periods of time, managers of firms face increasing pressure to produce short-term financial performance results, and mutual and investment funds are turning over their investments more quickly. Day trading is becoming a popular avocation and vocation for an increasing share of American investors (Vinzant, 1999). At the same time, the rate of CEO turnover is also increasing, due in part to shareholder pressure for short-term financial performance. Vesting periods for executive stock options are also getting shorter to correspond to the shorter tenure of the executives themselves (Lederer and Weinberg, 1999).

Patient capital refers to "long-term investments focused upon creating economic value by levering the complex of resources that requires time to build" (Leana and Rousseau, 2000). Organizational social capital requires such long-term investment as its pay-offs to the firm are often not immediately tangible. Capital markets that will not wait for such long-term investments cannot offer US firms the advantage of workforce relations that are hard for international competitors to replicate.

Focusing managerial attention on social capital

As the preceding discussion suggests, one reason that US managers have devalued organizational social capital is that they are focused on increasing short-term profitability. There is a tendency among US managers to conflate "financial management" with "management." The statement "what gets measured gets managed" illustrates the operating environment of many US corporations; a corollary to this statement might well be "what gets measured is the basis for remuneration." As a result, managers concentrate on doing what they can to increase short-term profitability, despite any damage to organizational social capital.

Why should managers focus on organizational social capital and on creating what Leana and Rousseau (2000) label "relational wealth"? Simply put, all the other forms of capital – physical, human, and financial – can be procured from external sources. But organizational social capital is a resource that cannot be bought and cannot be duplicated; rather, it is the result of shared trust and successful collective action that creates a virtuous circle. US firms often try to trade off organizational social capital for increased short-term profitability through such measures as workforce reductions, curtailed expenditures on training, or outsourcing core business functions. Just as an organization can temporarily increase profitability by deferring needed maintenance on plant and equipment, it can achieve a similar result by the use of human resource practices that may save money in the short term but harm organizational social capital in the long term. If organizations are measuring and remunerating managers on the basis of year-to-year (or even quarter-to-quarter) profitability, then it should not be surprising that managers act in ways that damage organizational social capital and by extension limit the organization's ability to generate relational wealth. Changing such an orientation requires changing the incentive structure for managers to direct their attention toward the long-term as well as the short-term health of the firm, and on the relational as well as the financial components of wealth creation.

Regulatory environment that fosters employment stability

Finally, the United States differs from many of its international competitors in the manner and extent to which employment practices are regulated by government. As noted earlier, employment-at-will is the legal axiom underlying most employment relations in the United States. In general, the US has been willing to set a legal floor on particular employment practices such as minimum wages, child labor, and occupational health and safety requirements. It has also set out restrictions on employers in terms of the actions they can take regarding employees' rights to union representation. These regulations have been inconsistently enforced, however, and in general the United States has not had an activist stance with regard to government regulation of employment. This may have the effect of enhancing employer flexibility in terms of issues like hiring and firing workers, but, as we have already stated, it may limit flexibility in terms of fostering a cooperative and inimitable workforce and work environment.

CONCLUSION

In this paper we discuss organizational social capital – a resource reflecting the character of social relations within the firm. We note that organizational social capital appears to be particularly undervalued by US firms. This, in turn, has cost American firms a potentially powerful advantage over their competitors. At the same time, employees of American firms assume the risks of a volatile labor market as well as a challenge to their character by an employment system that is indifferent to them as individuals (Sennett, 1998). We offer here an analysis of these trends and costs, as well as some direction for correcting their course.

REFERENCES

Arthur, M. and Rousseau, D. 1996: *The Boundaryless Career: A New Employment Principle for a New Organizational Era*. New York: Oxford University Press.

Belliveau, M.A., O'Reilly III, C.A., and Wade, J.B. 1996: Social capital at the top: effects of similarity and status on CEO compensation. *Academy of Management Journal*, 39, 1568–93.

Campbell, D.J., Campbell, C.M., and Chia, H. 1998: Merit pay, performance appraisal, and individual motivation: an analysis and alternative. *Human Resource Management*, 37, 131–46.

Cascio, W.F., Young, C.E., and Morris, J.R. 1997: Financial consequences of employment change decisions in major US corporations. *Academy of Management Journal*, 40, 1175–89.

Cavanaugh, M.A. and Noe, R.A. 1999: Antecedents and consequences of relational components of the new psychological contract. *Journal of Organizational Behavior*, 20, 323–40.

Cohany, S.R., Hipple, S.F., Nardone, T.J., Polivka, A.E., and Stewart, J.C. 1998: Counting the workers: results of a first survey. In K. Barker and K. Christensen (eds) *Contingent Work: American Employment Relations in Transition*. Ithaca, NY: ILR Press.

Cox, H. 1999: The market as God: living in the new dispensation. *The Atlantic Monthly*. March, 18, 20, 21, 23.

Frank, R. and Cook, P. 1995: *The Winner-Take-All Society*. New York: Free Press.

Fukuyama, F. 1995: *Trust: The Social Virtues and the Creation of Prosperity*. New York: The Free Press.

Fukuyama, F. 1999: *The Great Disruption: Human Nature and the Reconstitution of Social Order*. New York: The Free Press.

Ichniowski, C., Kochan, T., Levine, D., Olson, C., and Strauss, G. 1996: What works at work: overview and assessment. *Industrial Relations*, 35, 299–333.

Kramer, R.M. 1999: Trust and distrust in organizations: emerging perspectives, enduring questions. *Annual Review of Psychology*, 50, 569–98.

Lansing, P.A. and Van Buren III, H.J. 1993: Downsizing: is there an ethical dimension to a partial plant closing? *Labor Law Journal*, 44, 697–706.

Leana, C. 1996: Why downsizing won't work. *Chicago Tribune Magazine*. April 14, 14–16; 18.

Leana, C. and Feldman, D. 1992: *Coping with Job Loss: How Individuals, Organizations, and Communities Cope with Layoffs*. Lexington, MA: Lexington Press.

Leana, C. and Rousseau, D. 2000: *Relational Wealth: A New Model of Competitive Advantage*. New York: Oxford University Press.

Leana, C. and Van Buren, H. 1999: Organizational social capital and employment practices. *Academy of Management Review*, 24 (3), 538–55.

Lederer, J. and Weinberg, C. 1999: Largess oblige. *Chief Executive*. September, 127, 138–55.

The New York Times Special Report 1996: *The Downsizing of America*. New York: Times Books.

Pfeffer, J. 1998: *The Human Equation: Building Profits by Putting People First*. Boston: Harvard Business School Press.

Pil, F. and MacDuffie, J.P. 1996: The adoption of high-performance workplace practices. *Industrial Relations*, 25, 423–55.

Radin, T.J. and Werhane, P.H. 1996: The public/private distinction and the political status of employment. *American Business Law Journal*, 34, 245–60.

Robinson, S.L. 1996: Trust and breach of the psychological contract. *Administrative Science Quarterly*, 41, 574–99.

Rousseau, D.M. 1995: *Psychological Contracts in Organizations*. Thousand Oaks, CA: Sage.

Rousseau, D., Sitkin, S., Burt, R., and Camerer, C. 1998: Not so different after all: a cross-discipline view of trust. *Academy of Management Review*, 23, 393–404.

Scully, M. and Preuss, G. 1996: *Two Faces of Trust: The Roles of Calculative and Relational Trust in Work Transformation.* Working paper No. 3923-96, Massachusetts Institute of Technology, Cambridge, MA.

Sloan, A. 1996: The hit men. *Newsweek*, February 26, 44.

Spence, M. 1973: Job market signaling. *Quarterly Journal of Economics*, 87, 355–74.

Van Buren III, H.J. 1999: Boundaryless careers, respect for persons, and the obligation of making employees employable. Paper presented at the annual meeting of the Society for Business Ethics, Chicago.

Vinzant, C. 1999: The world of the hard-core day traders. *Fortune*. February 16, 196–7.

Waterman, R.H., Waterman, J.A., and Collard, B. 1994: Toward a career resilient workforce. *Harvard Business Review*, 94, 87–95.

Weinstein, M. 1999: Cream in labor market's churn: Why job losses are rising amid job hunters' nirvana. *The New York Times*. July 22, C1, C10.

Worrell, D.L., Davidson III, W.N., and Sharma, V.M. 1991: Layoff announcements and stockholder wealth. *Academy of Management Journal*, 34, 662–78.

part IV
Renewal and Revitalization: Best Practices

14 Leading Organizations through Survivor Sickness: A Framework for the New Millennium

David Noer

INTRODUCTION

This chapter presents a practitioner's perspective of the issues and challenges involved in leading organizations through the trauma of downsizing. It is based both on field research and my own experience working with a large number of organizations attempting to put the pieces together after mergers, cost-cutting, and re-engineering. The presenting symptom of the trauma experienced by these organizations was downsizing. The underlying disease was a pervading sense of violation which triggered employee feelings of fear, anger, and anxiety. These feelings, in turn, resulted in reduced organizational creativity, productivity, and a decrease in employee self-esteem. I coined the term "layoff survivor sickness," to describe this process (Noer, 1993).

Layoff survivor sickness is not limited to the stereotypical North American, for-profit organization. The organizations I have worked with represent significant diversity in terms of mission, geographical orientation, and industry. They have encompassed, public, private, for profit, not-for-profit, religious, military, and governmental missions and structures. Their geographical orientation has included North and South America, Europe, Asia, and the Middle East. Industries have included high technology, manufacturing, health care, petrochemical, and public utilities. For all their diversity, these organizations share two remarkably similar characteristics. The first is the need to create new organizational cultures that shed outdated concepts of loyalty, motivation, and employee commitment. The second is the difficulty they have letting go of their old cultures. Almost every organization underestimates the intensity of the struggle, and many have what amounts to an institutional death grip on assumptions that are no longer valid. It is clear that the roots of what has been called the old psychological contract (Tornow and De Meuse, 1990) run deep and will continue into the new millennium. It is also increasingly apparent that a different, more relevant, paradigm is necessary for organizations to grow and thrive in the future (Kraut and Korman, 1999). This chapter will articulate the problem and offer some practical strategies to facilitate the necessary change for both the organization and the individual.

ONE ORGANIZATION: THREE PERSPECTIVES

At the individual level, employee reaction to organizational trauma varies by such factors as tenure, marketable skills, willingness to relocate, position in the hierarchy, and organizational cultural conditioning. Organizations need processes to both help employees respond to the trauma of layoff survivor sickness, and, at the same time, to develop cultures that attract and retain the scarce and valuable employees that will assure their future competitiveness. The most effective of these cultures attract these key, scarce, and marketable employees, not by maintenance factors such as pay or benefits, but by connecting them with relevant work that builds their self-esteem and sense of purpose.

Helping employees cope with the symptoms of survivor sickness and developing an organizational culture that attracts scarce human resources is a complex and demanding leadership task. In order to illustrate how these dynamics operate in the "real world," I am including an example of different employee reactions from a recent merger. What follows are condensed and slightly paraphrased extractions from three individual interviews with employees whose organization was "merged" with another:

- A 52-year-old male administrative middle manager who I'll call Joe, working in the headquarters of the company being acquired:

  "I feel like the bottom has dropped out! I know they have a whole department doing what I'm doing here. They have a different information system – different accounting system – we can't keep running different systems! It's only a matter of time before they pick one system and it's not going to be ours! I've worked here since college – done whatever they've asked. Now what have I got for all that loyalty? I know I make more money than some of the young guys there. I hear all this happy talk about the new team and that we're all important, but I don't believe it. I'm 52 years old with experience that works here – I'm not so sure it fits anywhere else. How can I duplicate my salary outside? I can't. When I hear all those speeches – those pep talks – I feel like asking what about us old guys – what are you going to do for us? We're the ones who hung in there all those years. It's only a matter of time before they ease me out. How can they expect me to be positive?"

- Betty, a 28-year-old female information systems analyst from the same organization:

  "I think the acquisition is exciting. I really mean that – exciting! Exciting from a professional, geographic, and market viewpoint. First of all we should stop calling it a 'merger.' That's just the politically correct word. We all know they have taken us over – it's an acquisition. They own us and when push comes to shove, they'll make the hard decisions. I'm looking forward to learning about them – the way they do business – why they are doing so well – how they are different than us. I like the international travel, too. We were too US oriented in our strategy – it will be very different now that we are owned by a truly global organization. I've already been involved in some European integration meetings and I'm learning a lot. The way I look at it this has a tremendous upside potential for my career and learning. Let's face it, they have better systems and a much bigger market. The only negative is that it may not work out for me – there may not be a fit. Frankly, that's OK, too. I can always find another job."

• Harry, a 63-year-old senior vice president of the same organization:

> "No one should worry about their job because of this merger. There will be plenty of opportunities for everyone. I'd be very disappointed if people left, thinking they had no opportunity. This company was built on loyalty. Our people work hard for us and we take care of them. That won't change because of the merger. Our bond with our employees is what holds this organization together. It was that way when I started as an accounting clerk 40 years ago and it is that way today!"

THREE PERSPECTIVES: FOUR LEARNING POINTS FOR THE NEW REALITY

The interviews from which these excerpts were taken took place three years prior to the development of this chapter. With the benefit of hindsight, they provide some important new reality learning points for both individuals and organizations. Here are four lessons.

Those who have skills and perspectives that are of value to only one organization are in trouble

These employees are not only vulnerable to layoff survivor sickness, they are the most likely to lose their jobs in a downsizing and the least likely to rebound in similar roles in other organizations. Joe was right to worry – he did lose his job along with most of those in his department. After a long period of unemployment, he has recently resurfaced as a salesperson in a department store, earning about half the income he enjoyed at his previous employer. The lesson to all the Joes in organizations is that, whatever the pain and discomfort, they need to develop marketable skills and not trust that the organization will take care of them throughout their career. The lesson for organizations is that it is good business to insist that employees keep their skills honed so that they are valued by the external market. They will feel better about working for you and will be more productive, knowing they have other options and stay by choice, not fear. It is a positive, rather than a negative, motivation. Organizations won't have the handicap of attempting to compete in a global economy with workforces crippled by survivor symptoms. Marketable employees who choose to stay because of the work and the challenge are staying for the right reasons, not because they are afraid to leave. In today's world a dependent employee is a liability, not an asset.

Employees with valuable skills will be attracted by the work, not the organization where the work is performed

Good working conditions, pay and competitive benefits will be a given. They represent what Herzberg (1964) calls hygiene factors: not having them will demotivate, possessing them will not result in motivation. Challenging, stimulating work and the opportunity to learn, are what will attract and retain the scarce human resources who will create a competitive advantage. Slogans, corporate trinkets that reward tenure, and subjective calls for loyalty to the organization in the abstract, are clichés of the old paradigm.

SMART employees are the currency of the realm in the new reality

Betty was single and mobile with very marketable technical skills. She was one of a very important category of emerging new millennium human resources, what I call SMART employees: Self-directed, Motivated by their work, Adaptive, Relocatable, and Technically competent. Self-directed employees respond to their own sense of purpose and relevance, not external slogans, trinkets, or abstractions. Employees who are motivated by their work invest their human spirit and creativity in their work and that work is seen as different than managing others or climbing the corporate ladder. Adaptive employees value learning and are not trapped by one dimensional thinking. Employees who are relocatable are willing, often anxious, to move (organizationally, geographically, culturally) in order to learn and contribute. Technically competent employees are more than computer literate, they understand and are able to harness the explosion of information technology, and, often have a specific set of scarce technical skills.

Betty exhibited a number of SMART employee traits. She rejected what she called the "politically correct" spin the organization was putting on what clearly was not a merger but an acquisition. She saw the acquisition as an opportunity to learn and grow – that's why she stayed. She relocated and now holds a key technical position with the parent company. She will stay there as long as she can continue to grow and perceive her work as challenging and relevant. If that changes, she, true to SMART behavior patterns, will leave.

The lesson for organizations is the necessity of discovering ways to attract and motivate SMART employees. If I were running a business, I'd much rather have SMART employees like Betty who came to work because what they did stimulated their creativity and harnessed their human spirit, than people like Joe, whose main motivation was security and, and in his situation, the valid fear that he didn't have the requisite skills necessary to compete in the open market. The examples of Joe and Betty illustrate the two, very different, challenges faced by organizations of the new millennium. The first involves dealing with the past; finding ways to revitalize entrenched and overwhelmed employees. The second looks toward the future and requires strategies that attract, motivate, and retain SMART employees. This second, future oriented, challenge often hooks and angers organizational leaders whose perspectives and values in regard to loyalty, motivation, and committment were forged in the old reality.

Relevant new reality leadership requires discarding what worked in the past

Harry illustrates the problem many senior managers have in discarding the values and assumptions that got them where they are and replacing them with those that fit the new reality and will keep their organizations moving forward. People like Harry are devastated and overwhelmed by the facts of life in the new reality: that blind loyalty, trust that the organization will take care of employees, selfless obedience to hierarchical wisdom, and strategies that tie employees to the organization and create dependency, no longer fit either the needs of the organization or the employee. These new realities often stimulate a powerful dissidence that results in anger and shooting the messenger. The underlying issue is that managers like Harry face the ego-damaging truth that the beliefs and values that caused them to rise to the top are no longer valid. This realization often causes a deep sense of violation and a stubborn death grip on the past. They may be able to accept the new reality in their heads, but they reject it in their hearts. In my experience, top management resistance to the reality of the new paradigm has often been a significant deterrent to sustained growth and profitability. In Harry's situation, in spite of his uninformed optimism, his organization was downsized by nearly 20 percent, and the new organization has still not come close to their pre-merger productivity and market share goals. Although Harry, himself, received a lucrative golden parachute, he left a bitter man. Had his cultural conditioning from the old reality not filtered out the messages of the new, he could have left a much better legacy and helped the new organization achieve the necessary transition.

In order to be relevant to the needs of the new reality, leaders like Harry need to drop their assumptions that motivation and commitment are linked to lifetime employment, loyalty to the organization, and fitting in. They need to discard past human resource strategies that tie employee self-esteem to employment continuity, and advocate that employees put all of their social and emotional eggs in the organizational basket. It is necessary that they accept the new reality that loyalty to self, profession, and a career management strategy that includes other organizations, does not diminish employee commitment or contribution.

Survivor Sickness: The Symptom

As the result of field research, I used the term "layoff survivor sickness," to describe the symptoms of people who remained in organizations after downsizing. These symptoms broke down into four clusters of feelings: fear, insecurity, and uncertainty; frustration, resentment, and anger; sadness, depression, and guilt; and injustice, betrayal, and distrust.

Survivors coped in ways that were not good for them or the organization. They were reluctant to take personal or organizational risks. At the very time they needed the courage and drive to re-assess their career and seek new opportunities either inside or outside their current organization, they were paralyzed and took no action. From an organizational perspective, risk averse survivors demonstrated reduced innovation and productivity. Although articulated differently, the symptoms of survivor sickness are described in a variety of research settings (for example Brockner et al., 1994; Cameron, Freeman, and Mishra, 1991; Jick, 1985; Marks, 1994).

Time does not appear to heal the wounds. In many cases the symptoms seem to intensify with time. As is the case with other survivors of human trauma, help is necessary before moving forward is possible. As much as macho-oriented individuals and organizations would like it to go away, toughing it out without external assistance just won't work.

What emerges is a compelling scenario for leadership action. Downsizing leads to a set of debilitating feelings that, in turn, lead to decreased risk taking and productivity that ultimately result in organizations not achieving the very goals that triggered the reductions in the first place. Since the symptoms of survivor sickness do not seem to go away on their own, this downward, negative spiral will tend to continue until someone does something – an intervention takes place.

Although the initial research focused on for-profit organizations that were involuntarily reducing staff for cost-cutting economic purposes, the effects of layoff survivor symptoms can be found in a variety of settings. Organizations that have experienced mergers, re-engineering, privatization, and deregulation are prime candidates for survivor sickness. The common denominator is a deep and pervasive sense of violation. The reason many organizations continue to resist the necessary interventions is that they repress and fail to deal with the basic issue: underlying and often repressed perceptions of violation.

VIOLATION: THE ROOT CAUSE

The reason most efforts to help transform and revitalize organizations run into difficulty and often fail, is that they jump too quickly to a quick fix technique without dealing adequately with the root cause: violation. I am continually surprised at the degree to which otherwise competent management consultants and effective leaders move to their favorite analytical technique, organizational structure, or team development process, without first coming to grips with this basic issue.

There appear to be three reason for this knee jerk escape into technique. First, many organizational decision makers repress and deny their own survivor sickness. They have been conditioned into viewing feelings and emotions as something they leave at the door on their way into the office. Confronting their own feelings is often counter-cultural and seen as a sign of weakness. Secondly, this institutional norm against authenticity results in a repression and denial of true feelings. This denial leads to an impatience with "touchy-feely" interventions which is grounded in a personal fear of vulnerability. Finally, technique sells. Even though many programs and processes are solutions looking for problems and bypass the root issue, they are seen as taking action, doing something. This is much more palatable to many organizations than the necessary pain of forcing a confrontation with repressed feelings of violation. Difficult as it may be, the first step in leading organizations away from the grip of survivor sickness involves dealing with the underlying violation. I have found that there are three, often overlapping, types of violation:

Violation caused by the broken psychological contract

The essence of the old psychological contract between employee and employer was, "Give us your complete loyalty and trust and we will take care of you for life." Historically a modern manifestation of feudalism, this old psychological contract flourished and fully bloomed in post World War II North America, Western Europe, and parts of Asia; prototypically, Japan. The old psychological contract took particularly deep roots in large, hierarchically arrayed, bureaucratic organizations. Organizations developed human resource strategies to tie employees into the organization over time. Old contract organizations had benefits, compensation plans, status symbols, and recognition programs that rewarded tenure. Although in locations such as Japan, the old psychological contract was somewhat narrow in scope (male, Japanese, professional and managerial employees), in other cultures it was much more extensive, covering virtually all levels and types of employees.

The implicit strategy was to entice employees to put all of their social and emotional eggs in the organizational basket. The strategy worked very well. In many organizations employees' sense of identity and self-esteem was based on their organizational affiliation. Who they were was where they worked. If who you are is where you work, when your job is threatened there is a lot more at risk than just a paycheck. When organizations dropped the basket (instituted involuntary staff reductions) and some of the eggs broke, the perception of violation was triggered among those who remained.

The new reality, or the new psychological contract, began in the late 1970s and reached epidemic proportions during the 1980s. Employees were no longer long-term assets to be developed over time: they were short-term costs to be managed and, hopefully, reduced. Long-term employees found themselves with inflated salaries and skills that were not valued outside their organization. Middle managers, heretofore the purveyors of the culture and the source of bureaucratic wisdom, found themselves devalued and obsolete. For many employees, the rules had changed, the contract had been violated. The result was an epidemic of layoff survivor sickness. The victims were not just older, longer tenured employees. The fear, anger, and depression also extended to those newer workers who had been seduced by the apparent security and predictability of the old psychological contract. Younger employees in government agencies, privatized institutions, and deregulated utilities were particularly stricken.

Violation triggered by changed corporate cultures

Corporate cultures shape behavior through norms that establish the way things "ought" or "ought not" to be. I recently worked with a small, high technology, organization in California that was acquired by a large financial services firm on the east coast. The California organization was informal, casual, non-bureaucratic, and had few rules and policies. The acquiring organization was formal, control-oriented, and valued structure and procedures. Many of the employees had joined the California organization because of the laid back, informal culture. As the financial services firm gradually imposed their norms – their sense of how things ought to be – the morale of the California employees dropped and their anger increased. Their sense of how things ought to be was violated. As the anger and frustration increased, productivity decreased. Many of the best left, and, although there was no layoff, those who remained experienced the classic symptoms of survivor sickness. Mergers and acquisitions are fertile breeding grounds for survivor sickness. They are usually planned by financially oriented deal makers who either completely ignore or seriously underestimate the effects of cultural incompatibility on organizational performance.

Another example of cultural violation as a stimulus for survivor sickness is the Canadian Federal government. Many employees in Federal agencies perceived their role as providing a service to the population. Their "ought to" was that a government employee should provide a first-class service to the taxpayers. Their survivor symptoms were caused by mandated cost cutting and downsizing. For many, the anger, frustration, and guilt was fueled more by their inability to provide what they perceived as a necessary service to the public, than by the threat of their own job loss. The same dynamic holds true for formerly regulated organizations such as telephone companies whose previous cultural "ought to" was customer service, and is now cost cutting and fiercely competitive, aggressive market behavior. A classic example is the health care industry where the major culturally imposed "ought to" was first-class patient care. Now it is *cost effective*, first-class, patient care. Despite economic realities, many health care providers experience a deep sense of violation when they are forced to factor costs into patient care decisions.

The violated self-concept

The third dimension of violation cuts across the other two and involves individual perceptions of violated purpose and relevance. Here are three representative examples from my practice:

1. Bill is a physician who was a partner in a small, suburban, family-oriented practice. He really cared about his patients and spared no expense to provide them with the best quality health care available. He was an exceptional physician, but, like many good scientists, was neither interested in, nor very adept at administration. Because of turnover and his seniority, Bill assumed the role of managing partner in his practice. Soon thereafter, following the national trend in the US, his private practice became part of a much larger managed care organization. Today Bill is sad, frustrated, and often angry. He feels the quality of his practice is compromised by the financial controls of his parent organization, and that he is spending more time "doing paperwork than practicing medicine." The core of his problem is a sense of personal violation: his sense of purpose, relevance, and contribution is not congruent with his current role.

2. Ellen worked her way up from the clerical ranks in a large public utility. She sacrificed a great deal, going to school at night, and neglecting her family. Her goal was a management position. From her perspective, power, control, and status were epitomized in the management role. When she finally made it and became a middle manager, the organization "privatized," which resulted in a significant reduction in staff. The hardest hit population segment was middle management. Positions were slashed, levels were reduced, spans of control were increased. Ellen ended up with a manager's title but a non-supervisory administrative role. Middle management positions have changed and are not very respected in the downsized organization: they are seen as "paper shufflers," and don't have any real power. Ellen is bitter and angry. What she worked so hard to achieve has changed, and she feels violated.

3. Malcom was promoted to president of a UK consumer products firm. The firm had a tradition of keeping presidents in their role for a few years and then promoting them to chairman when the incumbent retired. The role of the president was to manage the financial controls and maintain market share. It also involved a great deal of external public relations and internal employee motivational activities. However,

soon after Malcom's appointment, it became clear that the organization was in deep trouble. For the first time in the organization's history it had to reduce staff, consolidate locations, and struggle for its continued existence. The president's role radically changed and primarily focused on downsizing and cutting costs. After making some particularly painful reduction decisions, Malcom tearfully confided in me, "I didn't sign up for this. This is not the way I want to spend my time. Why did this have to happen during my watch?"

A FRAMEWORK FOR INTERVENTION

Individuals and organizations require help in order to overcome their sense of violation and shed the symptoms of survivor sickness. In my experience this help is best delivered through a combination of internal leadership and coaching and external consulting and facilitation. My four level intervention model has served a wide variety of organizations and is offered here, not as the only model or the perfect solution, but as one example of a framework for dealing with the issues.

Level one: process interventions

There has been a fair amount of research on the relationship of the way reductions take place to the feelings and perceptions of those who stay (for example Brockner, 1992; Davy and Tansik, 1986). Perceptions by those who stay concerning the fairness and inclusiveness of the process, adequate prior notice, openness and honesty of communication, and respect and the preservation of dignity for those who leave, are all important for the morale of those who remain. These interventions which deal with the process of reduction will not cure layoff survivor sickness, but they will make the cure easier by facilitating and blocking resistance to deeper levels of intervention. Here are some examples of level one interventions that have proven effective.

Celebrate departures

Don't escort people to the door on Friday afternoons. Don't put out terse, sterile, announcements. Don't keep planned departures a secret. In the new reality people will come and go much more often. Secrecy and assuming that those who leave will somehow contaminate those who stay, cloaks the entire process in unnecessary guilt and secretiveness. Find ways to hold rituals – luncheons, employee communication events, informal cake and coffee gatherings – to celebrate and sanction departures. Even if the people leaving are reluctant to participate, help them understand that the purpose is as much for those who stay as for them.

Tell the truth

Even if the truth is that you don't fully know what is going on it is much better to own up to your own vulnerability than to attempt to fake it. For the leader, shutting down, attempting to pretend things are under control and OK when they are not, sabotages his or her own credibility as a boss and erodes their authenticity as a human. Faking it hurts both the leader and the employees. Robert Lifton, a psychiatrist who has studied human reaction to many forms of human trauma states that we have one of two options to violation: we can either "shut down," or "open out" (1993, p. 82). The way to help yourself and others through the trauma of downsizing is to open out and tell the truth.

Communicate by leading with the heart, not the head

Wounded employees, caught in the grips of survivor sickness are not interested in "objective" facts and figures, they need someone to acknowledge and respond to their emotions. Most corporate communication programs emphasize the logic and rationale for restructuring, re-engineering, and downsizing. This communication helps the senders, not the receivers. If you are angry, depressed, and fearful, understanding facts and figures concerning ROI, earnings per share, or sterile and abstract strategic key indicators, does not respond to your needs. The most effective leaders in times of stress and transition listen and respond to employee feelings and emotions. They begin by owning up to their own feelings, then attend to those of their employees. Communicating with employees during change, transition, and downsizing is much more than reading the corporate script, playing the video of top executives explaining the new vision, or explaining the logic and rationale for hard decisions. It involves meeting employees where they are: in the warm, messy, and unpredictable plane of feelings and emotions. My clients always describe their best boss as a person who was the best listener, who didn't try to "fix" their feelings, but simply heard and acknowledged them. Conversely, they describe their worst boss as one who "wasn't real," who was aloof, hid behind the company script, and devalued them by telling them they should not have felt the way they felt.

Level two: grieving interventions

Level two interventions move beyond helping employees through the process of downsizing. They deal with the underlying issues of violation and help survivors deal with their repressed feelings and emotions. These interventions are, thus, critical to the catharsis necessary for letting go and moving forward. It is a basic principle of mental health that debilitating feelings and emotions cannot be left to fester under the surface: they need to be dealt with before an individual can move forward. Many organizations find themselves in a bind in this regard. They have strong norms that imply that feelings and emotions – especially negative ones such as those found in survivor sickness – have no place in the workplace, and that articulating these feelings is a sign of weakness and disloyalty. At the very time employees have a need to articulate and externalize their survivor anger and guilt, organizational norms block them. The result of these organizational norms against authenticity is that things get worse: grieving goes underground and turns bitter, productivity suffers, trust erodes, rumors mushroom, and customer service declines.

Organizations need to find ways to legitimize grieving and catharsis. Without dealing with the fundamental emotional blockage, programmatic fixes are doomed to failure.

This is why many organizational attempts at quality programs, work redesign, performance management, 360-degree feedback, re-engineering, or any one of a multiplicity of other programmatic fixes don't seem to work. They put the cart before the horse. The emotional damage needs to be dealt with first. Using programs and flavor of the month management gimmicks as band aids for repressed survivor violation is a shallow and useless activity trap. Here are some examples of ways organizations have dealt with the issue.

Venting sessions

Many organizations have utilized structured group sessions to facilitate employee "venting." These can be a very helpful way of validating and sanctioning employee anger and frustration. The trick is to make these sessions authentic enough to conjure up authentic grieving while eliminating harmful blaming. The difference between those sessions that work and those that break down into mean spirited destructiveness lies in careful planning and facilitation. For this reason, it is recommended that a professionally trained and experienced facilitator be involved.

Team coping meetings

These are versions of team building sessions and are often called by that, more politically correct, name. They, however, focus on helping team members externalize their feelings and emotions and articulate their sense of violation. Skillful facilitators focus on the process and usually don't use labels such as "violation." The essence of these sessions is the externalization of repressed feelings of violation, and working on ways to help the team move forward. These have proven very helpful for many organizations. They are often a guerrilla effort and publicized as "normal" team building in order to overcome corporate norms against truth telling and dealing with emotions.

Training line managers in helping skills

Most managers got where they are because of their technical, analytical, or administrative skills. These are not the skills necessary to help employees through the trauma and anxiety of survivor sickness. In times of transition, effective and relevant management is a helping, not a controlling, function. Several organizations have had success in conducting brief (two to three day) workshops for line managers in empathetic listening, reflecting feelings and emotions, and giving and receiving feedback in non-evaluative and non-defensive ways. Participants have then been required to meet with each of their employees one-on-one in order to listen to, and respond to their feelings and emotions. In every case this process has been met with initial skepticism and doubt, but has resulted in an exceptionally powerful intervention. In my experience, the most stilted but genuine line management effort to enter into a helping relationship with a direct report is much more effective and authentic than a similar session with a skilled outsider who is not part of the system. Additional benefits are that the manager begins to understand and deal with his own issues through the training, and the employee interaction creates a bond of trust and authenticity.

Coaching, counseling, and mentoring

Many employees seek help on their own through friends, family, community, or religious resources. Some seek professional therapy or counseling. Senior executives are particularly vulnerable, and many of my "executive coaching" assignments have initially involved working through deep and previously unexpressed feelings of violation. Trusted internal colleagues and, in those organizations that have them, formal mentors are also good resources. The key point is that all employees need to find a way to externalize their feelings of violation. It does not have to be a formal therapeutic relationship, but does require skilled listening and non-judgmental respect. A small amount of grieving facilitation goes a very long way. Lack of dealing with repressed feelings of violation is the primary reason many revitalization efforts fail.

Level three: breaking organizational codependency

The concept of codependency began in the treatment of alcoholism (Beattie, 1987). If a significant other's self-esteem is contingent on an alcoholic staying dry, they are codependent with the alcoholic's addiction. Organizational codependency occurs when an employee's sense of reverence, contribution, and self-esteem is contingent on remaining employed by a specific organization. Many employees are seduced into codependency by old psychological contract strategies that provide benefits, services, and status symbols that reward and reinforce dependence. In the new reality, a codependent relationship is neither good for the individual, nor the organization. An employee who places all his or her social and emotional eggs in the organizational basket is preconditioned for survivor sickness and ends up staying for the wrong reasons – security and dependence – as opposed to the right reason – relevant work that is a manifestation of his or her human spirit. From an organizational perspective, dependent, risk averse, employees are not the human resources necessary to create competitive advantage in the new millennium. Here are some ideas for fostering non-codependent employee relationships.

Organizations need to be clear on the psychological contract and stop giving mixed messages

Most organizations are operating within a cultural lag from the old psychological contract. They want the flexibility of the new reality, yet they maintain artifacts – systems, career paths, benefits, communications patterns – of the old reality. It is not unusual for organizations who advocate the short-term, customer focused, continually and mutually renewable nature of the new reality, to have benefits, pay plans and status symbols that are based on tenure. When I interview organizational leaders, I get a very different articulation of the operant psychological contract by level: the top describes the old contract, the middle isn't sure, and first line supervision outlines the new reality. Organizations need to be clear on the mutual obligations that constitute the psychological contract and not be afraid to communicate them in an unambiguous manner.

Employees need to invest their human spirit in their work, not where they perform that work

Investing your self-esteem in your work, not in where you do that work, provides a structural immunity to layoff survivor sickness. Work on developing valued skills and abilities so that you can be an outstanding engineer, secretary, accountant, salesperson – whatever your profession. Ground your self-worth in your work. That way when you lose your job, that is all you will lose. Your sense of identity and purpose will stay with you. It takes two things to develop this perspective. The first is the courage to go against the grain, to resist the subtle corporate efforts to connect your identity and self-esteem to an organizational entity. The second is to be ruthless in keeping your skills tuned to the market place. You need to devote whatever time and energy is necessary to develop skills that are valuable to organizations other than your current employer.

Organizations need to develop a job-content pull

The only way organizations will be able to attract and retain the SMART employees who are critical to their future success, will be to create jobs that attract and challenge them. Dependency and abstract, long-term, corporate loyalty won't work with mobile, technically competent, scarce human resources. What attracts these crucial employees is meaningful, important work that gives them the opportunity to learn and develop. Organizations that want to attract the competent, skilled employees who will insure their future, need to discard strategies that create codependence and replace them with strategies that insure meaningful and relevant work.

Level four: systems interventions

Level four interventions are systems within organizations that reinforce the new reality. They provide a structural foundation for level three interventions. Here are a few examples.

Align reward and recognition systems with the new reality

Unfortunately, many organizations that articulate the short-term, task-focused, orientation of the new reality, have reward and recognition systems that focus on tenure and fitting into the bureaucracy. Compensation systems should be grounded on projects, customer satisfaction, and measurable task accomplishment. Too often, they are based on years of experience, irrelevant administrative competencies, and pleasing the boss as opposed to the customer. Many organizations that emphasize short-term performance and project management, give out trinkets celebrating years of service. While there is nothing inherently wrong with giving out trinkets and celebrating employees remaining in the organization for five, ten, fifteen, and twenty or more years, organizations need to equally celebrate short-term task achievement and customer satisfaction. Benefits and services that increase with tenure can often entice employees into remaining for the wrong reasons. If organizations want a flexible, task-focused, non-codependent work force, they need to develop compensation and benefits plans that don't reinforce the opposite behavior. They need to put their money where their mouth is and truly pay for performance, not tenure or conformity.

De-emphasize distinctions between categories of employees

The full-time permanent employee is an endangered species in many organizational systems. In the new reality we are all temporary employees regardless of our classification. The effective organization of the new millennium will be made up of a combination of full-time, part-time, temporary, and contract employees along with several varieties of consultants. Organizations that have sharp status or pay differentiations between these various categories create artificial distinctions which create disharmony and confusion. In order to create the flexible, responsive workforce of the future, organizations should minimize distinctions and make it easier to move between categories, not create artificial barriers.

Eliminate paternalism

In the old reality, organizations took care of employees and employees developed a dependency relationship. In the new reality, employees are empowered and trusted to take care of themselves and develop an interdependent relationship with their organization. This does not mean that organizations should not provide competitive benefits and help employees develop new skills. It does mean that employees need to be given responsibility for planning, co-paying, and deciding levels of service in regard to benefits, and that they be given primary responsibility for skill and career development.

THE COMPLEXITY OF RELEVANT LEADERSHIP

Leading organizations through the trauma and transition of the past and into the new millennium is an exceedingly complex task. It requires leaders who are capable of moving in two, often opposite, directions at the same time. It also requires leaders who have the courage and ability to deal with their own issues while helping their organization.

Helping the violated while attracting SMART employees

Organizational leaders are confronted with two very different tasks. The first involves devising strategies to help violated employees shed their survivor sickness and regain their creativity and productivity. The four-level intervention model provides a general frame of reference for this task. I have also found that employees respond to change and transition in four ways. These response types, and the related research, are outlined in my book *Breaking Free* (Noer, 1996). Each of these response patterns requires a different set of leadership behaviors. The four response types are:

  1. *The overwhelmed.* Employees who exhibit the overwhelmed response type are beaten down by change and transition. They don't learn from their experience and

simply hope that things will improve without taking any responsibility for changing. They require leadership that will deal with their symptoms of depression and fear while gradually rebuilding their self-esteem.

2. *The entrenched.* Entrenched employees react to change by working harder at previously successful behavior. They equate activity with learning and growth and operate out of a strategy that if they hunker down long enough things will return to normal. Leading the entrenched requires coaching and role modeling behavior that allows employees to take risks and experiment with new, more relevant ways of working.

3. *The BS response type.* This response pattern confuses bluff, bluster, and activity with learning and direction. Employees who respond in this manner are often uninformed optimists who have never come up against a problem they couldn't *sell* their way out of. In the new reality they have to *learn* their way out of the past and they revert to bluff and misguided activity. The core leadership task involves moving them toward self-awareness, vulnerability, and learning.

4. *The learning response.* Learners have learned how to learn from change. They are optimistic and find ways to help themselves and the organization move forward. SMART employees are learners. Leading learners involves protecting them from burning out by over-reaching and attempting to be all things to all people as well as devising strategies to retain them and leverage their talents.

The second overall leadership task involves creating an organizational environment that will attract and retain SMART employees. This requires a focus on meaningful, challenging work, fostering empowerment and employee autonomy, and establishing a coaching and facilitating leadership role. Attracting SMART employees and helping employees overcome their repressed violation are two very different and opposite leadership tasks. Leaders are required to do both at the same time and this is why leading organizations into the new millennium is such a complex task. When organizations are accused of "hiring in the front door, and firing out the back door," they are often performing the difficult balancing act required by these two necessary, but, very different, tasks.

Working simultaneously on self and system

Effective leaders of the new millennium face the difficult process of working on their own perspective and values while simultaneously devising strategies to help their organizations. Old paradigm perspectives of motivation, loyalty, and commitment require re-examination by leaders who seek to be effective in the new reality. This is neither an easy, nor a painless task. The most effective leaders I have known have gone through the necessary agony of discarding values and perspectives which have served them well in the past but didn't translate into the future.

Organizations that seek to grow and prosper in the new millennium require leaders at all levels with the courage and ability to develop new, more relevant, values and perspectives. They must then apply their energies and talents to the dual tasks of helping their fellow employees overcome repressed feelings of violation, and, at the same time, create cultures that attract and retain those SMART employees who will insure innovation and organizational growth.

REFERENCES

Beattie, M. 1987: *Codependent No More: How to Stop Controlling Others and Start Caring for Yourself.* San Francisco: Harper-Collins.

Brockner, J. 1992: Managing the effects of layoffs on others. *California Management Review*, Winter, 9–27.

Brockner, J., Konovsky, M., Cooper-Schneider, R., Folger, R., Martin, C., and Bies, R. 1994: Interactive effects of procedural justice and outcome negativity on victims and survivors of job loss. *Academy of Management Journal*, 37, 397–409.

Cameron, K., Freeman, S.J., and Mishra, A.K. 1991: Best practices in white-collar downsizing: managing contradictions. *Academy of Management Executive*, 5, 57–73.

Davy, J.A. and Tansif, D. 1986: Procedural justice and layoff survival: preliminary evidence for the effects of voice and choice and survivors' attitudes and behavior. Unpublished manuscript, Arizona State University, Tempe.

Herzberg, F. 1964: The motivation-hygiene concept and problems of manpower. *Personnel Administration*, 27 (1), 3–7.

Jick, T.D. 1985: As the axe falls: budget cuts and the experience of stress in organizations. In T.A. Beer and R.S. Bhaget (eds) *Human Stress and Cognition in Organizations: An Integrated Perspective*. New York: Wiley, 83–114.

Kraut, A.I. and Korman, A.K. 1999: The "DELTA Forces" causing change in human resource management. In A.I. Kraut and A.K. Korman (eds) *Evolving Practices in Human Resource Management: Responses to a Changing World of Work*. San Francisco: Jossey-Bass, 3–22.

Lifton, R.J. 1993: *The Protean Self: Human Resilience in an Age of Fragmentation*. New York: Basic Books.

Marks, M.L. 1994: *From Turmoil to Triumph*. New York: Lexington Books.

Noer, D. 1993: *Healing the Wounds: Overcoming the Trauma of Layoffs and Revitalizing Downsized Organizations*. San Francisco: Jossey-Bass.

Noer, D. 1996: *Breaking Free: A Prescription for Personal and Organizational Change*. San Francisco: Jossey-Bass.

Tornow, W.W. and De Meuse, K.P. 1990: The tie that binds has become very, very frayed. *Human Resource Planning Society*, 13 (3), 203–12.

15 Values-based Management: A Tool for Managing Change

Todd D. Jick

INTRODUCTION

The "re" words are found everywhere in management circles today: reinvention, re-engineering, restructuring, revitalizing, rejuvenating, renewal, etc. With unprecedented pressures and opportunities, most organizations are in motion, experiencing multi-faceted change. Nothing is stable, it seems, and "change is the only constant" has become the mantra.

Nevertheless, or perhaps as a result of all this volatility, companies are also searching for some moorings, just as explorers of old used the stars to guide them through wilderness and uncharted territory. And for today's organization, those stars indeed are often emerging in the form of corporate values, that is norms, behaviors, and standards – explicitly identified – which are designated to be the desired way of "how we behave here." They are to be constantly and consistently lived.

Their constancy gives people reassurance in the midst of turbulence, anchoring the organization to certain unwavering beliefs and ways of doing things. In addition however, the values typically identified by companies today are ones that if lived on a consistent basis would themselves stretch the organization to new behaviors required to be effective in their marketplace (similar to what Kotter and Heskett, 1992 called "adaptive cultures"). For these and other reasons, planned efforts to introduce a code of values (sometimes labeled "operating principles", for example) are increasingly commonplace.

And yet, implementing values in an organization successfully is no easy task. Many companies have tried and failed, leaving a residue of cynicism and superficiality. After all, restructuring provides tangible, often immediate and visible results, whereas trying to influence the mindset and daily habits of people is time-consuming, often invisible, and less tangible. And values seem so soft in contrast to the financial focus of so much change. Finally, there are a wide range of implementation pitfalls which are the ones typically associated with introducing any large-scale organizational and behavioral change (Kanter, Stein, and Jick, 1992). Thus, the biggest challenge for organizations is not to identify the values they want to live by, but rather to live by the values they've identified and to embed them in the organization's "genetic code."

252 – 268.   chp 15.

values based managent - A tool 4 Managing change

This chapter will focus on why companies are turning to values, on the challenges and techniques for implementing them effectively over time, and some of the key success ingredients. To highlight these issues, this chapter will feature a case study of how values were implemented in one company, Seagram. Finally, this chapter will close with some observations about values-based management for researchers and for reflective practitioners.

THE VALUE OF VALUES

A fundamental task of all organizations is to develop their mission, purpose, and values. This becomes the foundation of what they stand for and how they will operate. Successful organizations, in particular, become "built to last" (Collins and Porras, 1994) by aligning their core characteristics with the way everything gets done and with all management practices.

Moreover, the explicit articulation of values provides a very pragmatic use. The demands of today's fast-paced marketplace and the flattening of organizational hierarchies has entrusted more people in the company with decision-making responsibilities. In these circumstances it is no longer practical or possible for management to control the activities of subordinates. Consequently, values serve the purpose of setting parameters (indeed, soft controls) within which people can take initiative and make decisions. This is all the more necessary in global, geographically dispersed companies.

This need only becomes greater during periods of turbulence, especially in the throes of restructuring. In the midst of change, it is common for employees to question not only the strategy and business processes but also whether the cultural norms and habits of the past are still functional and relevant for the future, or whether they need to be redefined. For an organization to move forward in the right direction and achieve its goals, it needs to ensure that its values and strategy are aligned.

At such times values can serve as an integrating force to bring people together to pursue and achieve common goals and objectives. Values-based management serves this need by establishing a common language and setting expectations of behaviors for the management team and the entire organization.

In short, values can serve multiple functions for an organization:

1. They make explicit a desired culture and a code of conduct.
2. They serve as a common basis for decisions, whether day to day, or in crisis.
3. They provide a "rock of Gibraltar" in the midst of change.
4. They ultimately can help to distinguish what is special about a company.
5. And finally they serve as an impetus to change by creating explicit, and typically high aspirations and standards.

There are many companies today, from all industries, which have developed an explicit set of values and benefited from one or more of the purposes above – including Intel, AT&T, Johnson and Johnson (J&J), Intuit, General Electric (GE), British Petroleum, and Hewlett Packard. Each has tried to codify their cultural expectations and aspirations to provide people with a roadmap. Interestingly, many of these companies and others are considered to be very hard-nosed and bottom line oriented.

The values in these companies can be seen to be treated seriously when they play a visible role in times of crisis and change. The famous Tylenol incident experienced by J&J benefited from the J&J credo which enabled quick and decisive action to remove the drug from all stores in short order – because it was simply the "right" thing to do based on their values. Similarly, GE's list of values includes "Reality – describe the environment as it is, not as we hope it to be . . ." and GE has been renowned for making change before it was needed and having a high sense of urgency in their decision making. Lastly, when Intuit's basic business model was challenged by the prolific use of the Internet and required a major transformation, people instinctively turned to their "customer focus" value as a framework for thinking through, and implementing, a series of strategic and operational changes (Dillon, 1998).

With all these rather public examples, there are all too many values statements buried in company archives, or mounted vacuously on company walls, or cheapened in slogans and on coffee mugs. For those, there is a legacy as well – one of cynicism and frustration, of wasted efforts and costs, and of course unmet expectations. In most instances, the downfall was not the values themselves – the words and their intent – but rather the half-hearted efforts to implement them and bring them alive.

Shifting to values-based management does not happen overnight. It is a multi-phased initiative that requires a firm-wide commitment and full-throttled execution. Values can be neither imported nor imposed. Organizations must define, communicate, implement and manage their own values. These values should be aligned with the organizational culture and be the product of a shared effort. Organizations that take this process seriously can experience significant pay-offs, both short term and long term. What follows is a full-blown illustration of an effort to reap those benefits, and one that exemplifies the planful, systematic steps required to inculcate values into an organization as both a stimulus to needed change, and as a foundation for weathering through change in the future.

THE SEAGRAM CASE ILLUSTRATION

Joseph E. Seagram and Sons, Inc., traditionally a major player in the world-wide beverage industry and more recently in the entertainment industry as well, represents an example of a company that implemented a values-based management program in conjunction with a major re-engineering effort. The case study below outlines the circumstances for doing so, and the nature of their initiative through the second half of the 1990s.

The challenge to change

In February 1995, Edgar Bronfman Jr, President and CEO of Joseph E. Seagram and Sons, Inc., told 200 senior managers that his vision for Seagram was to be the "best managed beverage company":

> "I have a vision and a belief that we will be best managed. We will be focused on growth, we will be fast and flexible, customer and consumer oriented. We will honor and reward teamwork; we will lead, not control. We will be willing to learn. We will develop, train

and motivate our people. We will be honest with ourselves and each other. We will manage based on the values we articulate and share."

To realize this vision, Seagram would have to transform itself, its strategy and its way of doing things internally. Ultimately it required major strategic repositioning, process re-engineering, and, quite importantly, a lot of change in how people behaved on a daily basis.

Bronfman's statement stimulated major change and transformation at Seagram. The company was already attempting to increase profits through global expansion, re-engineering, and diversification. Seagram recognized, however, that it could not ultimately succeed without changing its culture and work processes. One key to this was the creation and introduction of "Seagram Values." Despite initial skepticism by many employees that this was nothing more than the "flavor of the month," Bronfman was determined to prove that values "will not go away" and those who live the values "will be rewarded."

Over the following years, the values played an increasingly central role in implementing and shaping Seagram's priorities and new culture. A once proud and successful culture of individualism, entrepreneurship, authority, functional pride, and personal relationships, was "in transition" to a new culture built around new values such as teamwork, innovation, and consumer focus. Indeed the value of innovation would become very dramatic as major strategic changes – multi-billion dollar acquisitions into the entertainment industry – were later to emerge as strong evidence that change was needed. But first, let us examine how the need for change itself emerged.

The history of Seagram was a classic example of a company whose founding values and implicit practices seemed outmoded and counterproductive in the face of significant marketplace challenges. The Seagram Company was founded in 1924 with a single distillery in Canada, and became a major player in the beverage industry for more than 70 years. Seagram developed a loyal consumer following with premier products and premier brands such as Chivas Regal, Glenlivet, and Mum Champagne. Primarily operating in North America and Europe, Seagram successfully positioned itself in these growth markets for decades.

By the late 1980s, however, these markets matured and Seagram began to diversify. In 1988 it acquired Tropicana products (fruit juice and juice beverages). This was the first of many steps taken in recognition of the maturing and the eroding of Seagram's core markets. It grew to 14,000 employees by the mid-1990s.

Indeed, the operating income growth of Seagram's core spirits and wine business had stalled in the US. The entire $16 billion industry faced harsh new realities: the "new sobriety" of the 1990s, increased taxes on liquor, the early 1990s recession, increased government regulation, and social criticism of spirits marketing. Liquor sales spiraled down, and it was predicted that the decline would continue for several years.

Bronfman and the Seagram executives recognized the need for strategic repositioning and a redefinition of the company's competitive advantage. Bronfman declared over and over that Seagram would "not be able to achieve business results with business as usual." Thus, Seagram:

- expanded its spirits business into China and other countries in Asia Pacific;
- acquired a global fruit juice business from Dole Food Company, Inc;

- redeemed 156 million of its DuPont shares for $8.8 billion;
- purchased 80 percent of MCA Inc. from Matsushita Electric Industrial Co., Ltd. for $5.7 billion (adding 15,000 employees);
- purchased Polygram Music and divested Tropicana orange juice to Pepsi.

Seagram's success in the future would derive from this very different portfolio of businesses and a far more global enterprise. And its young, vibrant, and visionary CEO had visibly taken significant risks and made major new bets for the company. To succeed would require aggressive development of their brands, products, and people to exploit their new businesses and improve old ones. But as the plans for reinventing Seagram were fashioned, it became more and more clear that Seagram had to change every aspect of the way they had managed. Indeed, it was then that Bronfman set the goal of being the "best managed" company, and a growth goal of 15 percent per year – both highly aggressive targets.

Re-engineering the company

Towards that end, Seagram engaged the Boston Consulting Group in the mid-1990s to assist them in a major re-engineering effort. The goal was to manage more effectively Seagram's business processes and operation, and reduce costs. The re-engineering task involved hundreds of employees throughout Seagram, organized into teams to redesign and streamline key business processes such as: business planning, MIS (management information systems), finance, customer fulfillment, marketing, and manufacturing.

Under the leadership of senior executives, this effort quickly engulfed the energies of people across the company. With a mix of enthusiasm and trepidation, the business processes were subjected to careful scrutiny and a wide variety of efficiencies and cost savings were identified. In addition, by examining the best practices of other companies and determining the true needs of their customers, Seagram began to break out of its internally directed culture. After six to nine months of self-examination, the opportunities for improvement were huge.

Yet, there was also increasing recognition that significant barriers to progress also existed. The new processes required numerous changes in how people behaved and interacted with each other – indeed a new culture. Seagram would have to unlearn its old culture typified by silos, risk aversion, hierarchy, and limited communication. And it would have to learn how to be more innovative, cooperative, communicative, and customer-focused.

Values: the missing link

Bronfman personally articulated that business processes would only change if behavior changed – and to change behavior required a new set of underlying values. He was convinced that "living the values would allow them to behave in ways that *were* new and better at Seagram." And as he told one group of managers in the mid-1990s:

> "Performance is not 'fine' right now, otherwise we would already be growing 15 percent a year. If we were doing fine and living the values, there wouldn't be the level of frustration there is at Seagram."

Bronfman personally drafted ten governing values to present to his top 200 managers for discussion, debate, and revision at a management meeting in February 1995. This began a nine-month process of creating and agreeing upon Seagram's new corporate values. Seagram engaged in an intensive top down *and* bottom up process to reach agreement on the right wording and the right implementation.

Thus, the output of the management conference was refined and redrafted by the top 15 executives. This in turn was reviewed and critiqued by over 300 employees through eight to ten person focus groups. These employees represented a vertical cross-section of the entire company – all businesses, all functions, all levels were represented. Not only were they asked to give feedback on the values draft, but also to identify the behavioral examples of the values in action, and suggestions as to how to introduce and communicate the values. The employee version was much simpler, shorter and easier to understand by all levels and all cultural backgrounds. These inputs were then fed back to the top executives who once again redrafted the values. With this draft, the company appeared ready to finalize the values: consumer and customer focus, respect, integrity, teamwork, innovation, and quality (see figure 15.1). Along with the values, there also was a summary of "Values in Action," a checklist of behavioral examples for living the values (see figure 15.2), and there was a strong view that the values had to be measurable in order to be practiced.

Bronfman also developed a framework, which he constantly referenced, to reinforce the link between the values and the business performance:

Values
↓
Behaviors
↓
Business Processes
↓
Results: Growth

In essence, his message was that in order to achieve growth, business processes had to be revamped. However, this was not just a structural exercise. The processes would change when and if people's habits and behaviors changed. However, these behaviors would only change if people subscribed to the underlying beliefs and values. Thus, values served as a foundation for the growth of the business and one would not occur without the other.

Introducing the values

A plan was developed to introduce the values, which included: (1) a personalized communication cascade; (2) a 360-degree feedback process for the senior executives; and (3) a training program for equipping the top 1,200 managers.

When it came to communicating the values, focus group participants had sent a strong message that:

> "this should not be just another program of the month. No hype, no t-shirts, no hats, and no video conference with Bronfman announcing the values to the whole company."

Figure 15.1 Seagram's values

As Seagram Employees We Commit to the Following Values:

Consumer and Customer Focus
Everything we do is dedicated to the satisfaction
of present and future consumers and customers.

Respect
We treat everyone with dignity, and we value different backgrounds, cultures, and viewpoints.

Integrity
We are honest, consistent and professional in every facet of our behavior.
We communicate openly and directly.

Teamwork
We work and communicate across functions, levels, geographies,
and business units to build our global Seagram family.
We are each accountable for our behavior and performance.

Innovation
We challenge ourselves by embracing innovation and creativity,
not only in our brands, but also in all aspects of our work.
We learn from both our successes and failures.

Quality
We deliver the quality and craftsmanship that our consumers and
customers demand — in all we do — with our products, our services and our people.

By Living These Values,
we will achieve our growth objectives, and we will make
Seagram the company preferred by consumers, customers,
employees, shareholders and communities.

Figure 15.2 Seagram values in action

Consumer and Customer Focus	⇨ We demonstrate through our actions that consumers and customers have top priority in our daily work. ⇨ We treat each person we deal with as a customer. ⇨ We work continually to understand our consumer and customer's requirements and anticipate future needs.
Respect	⇨ We seek ideas and contributions from people, regardless of their level. ⇨ We have a climate where issues are openly discussed and resolved. ⇨ We have a balance between our professional and private commitments.
Integrity	⇨ We deliver what we promise. ⇨ We disclose facts even when the news is bad. ⇨ We make decisions based on what's best for the company, rather than personal gain.
Teamwork	⇨ We share across borders, across affiliates and across functions to learn from one another. ⇨ We work together to achieve consistent, shared goals ⇨ We consider the impact our activities have on other areas of Seagram.
Innovation	⇨ We create an atmosphere where continuous improvement and creative thinking are encouraged. ⇨ We look for new ways to remove layers of bureaucracy to enable speed and action. ⇨ We have patience with new ventures and recognize there will be failures.
Quality	⇨ We produce results that consistently meet or exceed the standards of performance our consumers and customers expect. ⇨ We consistently improve our processes to better serve our customers. ⇨ We get the job done accurately and on time.

In the spirit of the values, Seagram senior management heeded the advice of their "customers" (that is their employees) and decided to try a new technique – a cascade of personal communication meetings. Each manager met with his or her direct reports to discuss the values and what it meant to live them in their specific business environment. The communication plan was initiated by Bronfman himself who held a two-hour meeting with his direct reports to discuss the values. Next, the top 15 executives met with their direct reports who, in turn, met with their direct reports, and this was repeated all the way down through the company – discussing the values, until all employees at Seagram had participated in a "cascade" meeting.

Second, focus group participants had also said, "people are waiting to see if management is really serious about living the new values themselves." As a result, a 360-degree feedback tool based on the six values was developed. The survey questions were directly derived by asking focus group participants to identify key behaviors required for living the values. (See figure 15.3 for an illustration of the 360-degree tool.) Historically, Seagram managers provided little feedback to employees except through an annual top down review.

Given this lack of experience and lack of trust, the 360-degree process was carefully implemented, using the help of professional coaches, a third-party data processor, and clearly defined developmental, not evaluative, purposes. Initially, Bronfman himself and the top 15 executives participated in the 360-degree feedback process. Next, the top 200 senior managers were evaluated and personally coached during the training program. Each manager was encouraged to share the findings with those who gave them feedback and to develop an action plan for personal improvement in modeling the values.

Figure 15.3 Sample questions from Seagram's 360–degree survey

Respect

Value Total		
Total	4.14	
Supervisor	4.57	
Peers	3.96	
Dir Rpts	4.21	
Self	4.71	

6. This executive is approachable and friendly.

(9) Total	4.67	
(1) Supervisor	5.00	
(4) Peers	4.75	
(4) Dir Rpts	4.50	
(1) Self	5.00	

1. This executive seeks ideas from people regardless of their level in the organization.

(9) Total	4.44	
(1) Supervisor	4.00	
(4) Peers	4.50	
(4) Dir Rpts	4.50	
(1) Self	4.00	

3. This executive is careful to consider another person's idea before accepting or rejecting it.

(9) Total	4.11	
(1) Supervisor	4.00	
(4) Peers	3.75	
(4) Dir Rpts	4.50	
(1) Self	5.00	

4. This executive explains issues and answers questions when communicating.

(9) Total	4.11	
(1) Supervisor	4.00	
(4) Peers	3.75	
(4) Dir Rpts	4.50	
(1) Self	5.00	

5. This executive treats people fairly when they make a mistake.

(9) Total	4.11	
(1) Supervisor	5.00	
(4) Peers	3.75	
(4) Dir Rpts	4.25	
(1) Self	5.00	

2. This executive supports people in their efforts to balance their professional time with their private lives.

(9) Total	3.78	
(1) Supervisor	5.00	
(4) Peers	3.75	
(4) Dir Rpts	3.50	
(1) Self	5.00	

7. This executive provides periodic feedback to tell others where they stand in terms of performance.

(9) Total	3.78	
(1) Supervisor	5.00	
(4) Peers	3.50	
(4) Dir Rpts	3.75	
(1) Self	4.00	

Finally, the third ingredient for introducing the values was through training. To this end, Seagram, assisted by an outside consulting firm (the Center for Executive Development in Cambridge, MA, USA), designed two values training programs of four days' duration. The first program, *Leading with Values* targeted Seagram's top 200 managers, while the second program, *The Seagram Challenge*, reached approximately 1,000 middle managers. Each program focused on the meaning and application of the six values in everyday Seagram life and best practice standards from other companies. Participants discussed mini case studies of Seagram situations in which the values were effectively put to a test.

In addition, each participant received 360-degree feedback about their own behavior related to each value, was provided with a coach to discuss their findings, and was encouraged to develop personal action plans. Finally, each value was assessed on a companywide basis in terms of the perceived amount of "talk" about it, and the perceived amount of "walk." Participants were asked to summarize their recommendations for improvements for the company to close the gap between the walk and the talk, as well as the gap between "today's walk" and the desired amount of "walk." These recommendations were presented and discussed with one or two senior executives, often Edgar Bronfman himself, during the last half day of each training program.

These programs were conducted over 12–18 months, and by the end, over 1,500 people (approximately 10 percent of the employees) participated. Successfully received, it served as one of the building blocks of cultural change.

Deepening the new culture: Phase II of implementation

Together, the three steps described above helped to launch Seagram's culture change. Indeed expectations for the company to change – and for executive behavior itself to change – rose considerably. By the second year after the values were created, Seagram executives faced numerous issues in ensuring that the values would indeed be reinforced and institutionalized. These issues were most typically crystallized at the concluding day – typically, Friday – of each values training program. Over and over in the discussions with senior executives, a series of challenges and issues kept emerging:

1. *What will be done with the various recommendations for action raised by participants in the programs?* At the close of each training program, recommendations for action were presented by participants to a senior executive. However, there was no clear mechanism for implementation and follow-up. Some actions could be taken by participants, while others required senior management support. Participants often wondered aloud "What will be done with all these good ideas?"

2. *Are the values violators going to be punished?* If management was serious about the values, many argued, the values "violators" should be demoted or fired. Many pointed to a dramatic diagram that Bronfman often referenced – in a "2 × 2" format – labeling those who violated the values while still getting good results, as "former heroes" (see figure 15.4). This decision tree, derived from Jack Welch at GE, set out a clear message that anyone violating the values in a significant, and/or ongoing fashion, would not be tolerated. Seagram employees seemed buoyed by this management practice. However, some were concerned that such actions might violate the value of "respect." Moreover, it was not agreed how much time people would be afforded to change.

Figure 15.4 The 2 × 2 of personnel actions

	Inappropriate Values	Appropriate Values
Make the Numbers	Type I Former Heroes	Type II New Heroes
Miss the Numbers	Type IV Newly Unemployed Executives	Type III Potential Heroes

3. *How will the values champions be recognized and rewarded?* Managers often stated that people who behaved consistently in line with the values should be recognized and rewarded. Some argued that those who "live" the values should be given financial bonuses and/or recognition. But others said that people should not be paid *extra* to live the values – it is expected of everyone. In any case, participants pointed to the performance management and incentive system and looked for changes.

4. *How will the momentum and attention on values be sustained? What should be done to institutionalize the values deeper and wider across Seagram? How should the awareness and commitment to the values be extended to the entire employee population?* By the "Friday session" of the values training where enthusiasm typically reached its peak, participants searched for ways to sustain the values-based management approach. They asked about (a) training that extended beyond the top 1,500 to the 15,000; (b) opportunities for "alumni" gatherings; and (c) communication support to keep the spotlight on values. No clear plans for any of these were initially set.

With senior and middle managers feeling challenged and hopeful about the values as one critical ingredient of the changes needed at the company, there emerged a common desire to bring the message, and the expectations of behavior, to all levels of employees at the company. But how to reach the approximately 13,500 other employees was not obvious.

Leadership response

There was a full plate of challenges – and no shortage of opinions about what should be done. In effect, the real commitment to the culture change effort, and to a critical ingredient of the reinvention of the company, was being tested. A series of actions was put into place over years 2 and 3 to address the four issues above, and each will be described below.

Extending the awareness and momentum

A pair of action learning initiatives were created to extend the awareness and commitment to the values. The first, called *Living the Values*, was a two-day training program designed for the broad population of Seagram employees. These were delivered by a combination of internal and external facilitators at local workplaces. In addition to learning the basics about the values, each group developed an action plan to improve upon one or more of the values, as well as visible communication and graphics to be posted in their offices and plants. The *Living the Values* program provided a forum to maintain enthusiasm for the values and openly discuss and commit to ways to "live" the values.

Three years into the values initiative, Seagram realized that although their efforts thus far had built awareness, attendees from original values programs sought to be refreshed in the values and to identify specific links to business challenges they were facing. This was the objective of *Seagram Discovery*, to apply the values to a business context. *Seagram Discovery* targeted new recruits in addition to employees who could not attend one of the original values programs. It was cross-cultural, targeting middle and senior managers across different businesses, geographies, levels and functions. This was a journey of self-discovery for attendees, to get them to see how people view them as individuals and as part of a team. Over the course of the three and a half day program, participants learned about growth and performance in the context of people, brands and values. As their Vice President of Organization and Leadership Development recounted:

> "Values by themselves won't change the company. What *Seagram Discovery* aimed to do is apply the Values where relevant to people's jobs, while permitting them to step back and look at themselves, learn from each other and, by looking outside, explore different ways of achieving better performance and growth."

Ronny Vansteenkiste, Head of Organizational Learning and Change, and the designer of *Seagram Discovery*, said, "This program forced people to put on a different lens and see things from other angles. We needed to expose people to this if we are going to become innovative. They needed to see the bigger picture."

Both of these formal programs, *Living the Values* and *Seagram Discovery*, were supplemented by informal communication from managers who had attended the earlier programs as well. What seemed to happen, most often, was that there were always new people being energized and refreshed on the values at any point in time. And these people naturally kept challenging the company and their colleagues to "walk the talk." This proved to be very effective for keeping the spotlight on the values and for keeping the momentum going.

Deepening the ownership for implementing the values through business objectives and measures

Although the various training efforts helped to raise awareness and build commitment, the day-to-day business objectives had not yet been supplemented to include the values. A business leader's credibility for "preaching the values" relied heavily on the extent to which the business included values into its explicit plans, measurement and commensurate rewards. To address this issue, each business unit head was tasked by Edgar Bronfman to include "implementing the Seagram values" as one key element of their annual business plan.

As a result, business heads focused more extensively on such measures and indicators as employee survey results, the number of people attending values training, business improvement initiatives focusing on values such as innovation, customer focus, and quality, and the creation of structures and processes which encouraged teamwork. By including values in the annual business planning exercise, the importance of values in their scorecard became unmistakable.

Leaders "walking the talk": 360 round II

The success of the 360-degree feedback process in the first year made it easy for Seagram executives to continue the process thereafter, but with some important twists. First, each executive committed to having a 360 done on an annual basis, and with the coaching help of a third party outside. However, whereas in the first year the results were only shared with the coach (and in some cases, voluntarily shared with a boss, direct reports, or peers), in the second round, it was agreed that all feedback would be shared with each individual's boss and that a dialogue between them would occur. This added more of an evaluative component then to the 360 process. In the subsequent years, moreover, the 360 results would be factored into an individual's annual appraisal review and compensation.

In addition, the 360 was extended on an informal basis to a wider population in the company – beyond the top 1,500 managers. This helped to create a more common vocabulary for development and appraisal discussions, and clearly served to reinforce the sense that values had become an important measuring stick of one's success.

Rewarding the stars, punishing the values violators: awards and management turnover

Although there was considerable and articulate debate as to whether there should be extra special awards for people who "live the values" (since some argued that this was merely a condition of employment), the majority agreed that some kind of visible annual award would help to send loud signals throughout the company that the values were indeed "valued." Accordingly, a *Values in Action* quarterly awards program was created to recognize those individuals within Seagram who best embodied the Seagram values in their work. Criteria were created and then publicized, nominations submitted, and recipients selected by a cross-business unit committee.

However, there were also actions taken to sanction individuals who were demonstrably violating the values. These individuals were given feedback – either through the 360 or in their performance reviews – and provided with coaching and a timetable for improvement. This process was considered to be fair and "respectful" while at the same time was a clear signal that they were in a period of probation. Ultimately, some managers in key positions were either demoted or fired, and it was public knowledge that their values violations were a major factor in taking such action.

Together, these visible symbols of the rewards for exemplary values behavior and the costs of values violations were crucial actions to reinforce and sustain the values. While there were always disagreements as to who truly deserved an over and above award, or who deserved to be fired, the signal was sent that there would be consequences to living or not living the values.

Communication of values in action

Finally, the corporate and business unit communications managers developed communication plans to highlight the values in executive speeches, corporate magazines, off-site conferences, annual reports, and letters from the CEO. For example, the quarterly corporate magazine called *Premiere*, included stories of successful values in action – highlighting one or two values in each of their editions. Even as times and individuals changed, terms such as "Team Seagram," "consumer focus" and "innovation" appeared regularly through the end of the 1990s decade.

What happened? Outcomes and results

- New genetic code
- New business strategy
- Stock price up and a new spirit
- Challenge of integration of values with a new corporate sub-culture (entertainment)

There was no formal evaluation of the impact of the values culture change, but there are a variety of data points – qualitative and quantitative – which together add up to a qualified success overall. What follows are comments made by Seagram executives in interviews:

> "Re-engineering did not just spot gaps in our knowledge and processes, it also discovered a host of hidden talents, roles and capabilities. We are already reaping the benefits of re-engineering, in terms of improved business practices and working culture as well as cost savings as part of a continuous drive towards excellence" (Donard Gaynor, Re-engineering leader).

> "Cultural change was crucial to us improving our performance as we seek to be flexible, innovative and fast-to-market. For this to happen people need a common denominator and clear reference points for behavior, hence our values-in-action program" (Steven J. Kalagher, President and CEO, Seagram Spirits and Wine Group).

> "Regarding teamwork, there has been more cross-departmental cooperation. Employees from sales and manufacturing areas have come together in workshops and learned about one another's job challenges and responsibilities which has led to a greater respect among and across departments" (Seagram manufacturing manager).

> "Our surveys of customers have shown that Seagram's external consumers are more satisfied, validating our commitment to the value of Customer and Consumer Focus" (Seagram marketing manager).

> "Some of the traditional, militaristic methods that were a common complaint among employees have been replaced by flex-time options and casual work day attire. This is a big part of what the Respect value is all about" (Seagram employee).

In addition to these comments, one can point to some quantitative factors of success. Customer satisfaction surveys, training workshop evaluations, and the innovative acquisition of new businesses all point to marked improvements in Seagram's performance. The values have served as a critical impetus for all these initiatives. Indeed, the overall growth rate of the company – attributable to many more factors than the values of course – has increased in the late 1990s. Finally, all the values workshops and discussions have sparked enthusiasm in a group of employees who have the potential to become future leaders and/or key contributors.

But expectations have been raised, and by no means always met. Despite some of the positive changes which have occurred in Seagram since implementation of the values, there remained some underlying skepticism among some employees. Despite the fact that this four-year initiative – continuing to date – has been the longest in Seagram history, employees still question if their managers are truly living the values. Conflicts in day-to-day behaviors and decisions with some of the Seagram values continued to exist and understandably send demotivating messages within the organization.

For example, to some of the old guard at Seagram, the value of "respect" means keeping your mouth clean and your head down and treating those who rank above you with respect. To some of the newer, younger and more innovative thinkers, they interpret respect differently and feel themselves to be disrespected by their elders. Another value which is subject of some criticism is the value of teamwork. For some the existing bonus system still essentially says, "rank still has its privileges." And as a result, "team Seagram," which is meant to cut across vertical and horizontal boundaries feels unachieved – as yet.

In summary, the experience to date with the values and the re-engineering has created a lot of good results, but with some obvious gaps still remaining. The reinvention of Seagram's business strategy and business processes are palpable. It has become both a beverage and an entertainment company. It has transformed numerous fundamental business processes through re-engineering. But, as to the creation of a new "genetic code," labeled as the values, there is still work to be done. Indeed this is hard work which takes many years to occur, and Seagram has seen undeniable progress to date.

But as was stated at the outset of this chapter, it is easier to focus on the restructuring, the buying and selling of businesses, and the cost-cutting efficiencies, than it is to change the daily work habits and attitudes of thousands of employees. However, the long-lasting results of change will only occur when the values are indeed the instinctive habits of the new company and, as such, institutionalized.

DISCUSSION AND IMPLICATIONS OF THE SEAGRAM CASE STUDY

Seagram's example provides an in-depth look at implementing values-based management as a critical component in a restructuring and/or reinvention effort. The process details were provided because it is in the details that the success or failure of an effort is determined. What are the general lessons from all this? There are two ways to put this case example in perspective – one for the pragmatic practitioners and the other for the reflective practitioners.

What differentiates successful from unsuccessful values-based management? What is common to companies that succeed and to those that fail? The way a company implements its values program is a critical determinant of whether the program fails or succeeds. If executed properly a values program can become the very essence of a company. If not, it can become the subject of mockery and make the shortcomings of the company only more glaring.

Successful values-based management efforts tend to share similar characteristics. Values systems cannot be imported; they have to be home-grown. In doing so, first and foremost, a company must make sure its values are aligned with its strategy, and be seen as a vehicle to help a company build competitive advantage. Values are typically balanced between "soft" and "hard" issues which is important to ensure values are linked to real business and customer issues. This requires a subtle combination of top down and bottom up involvement, typically done through focus groups with employees from all levels of a company becoming involved, eliciting a shared creation and understanding of the values. Proposed values are discussed in detail and their relevance to the company are debated. If employees contribute to the process they are far more likely to support and live the values. Richard Pascale in *Managing on the Edge* (1991) supports these observations as well:

> "Experience teaches us that an effective statement of vision, values, and guiding principles cannot be hammered out by the public relations staff or the human resources personnel department. Nor do they blossom from crash efforts of an executive task force. Values are truly a 'no pain, no gain' proposition. If top management doesn't agonize over them and regard them as a psychological contract between themselves and employees and society, such statements are little more than empty words. But if hewn from discussion and introspection, values come to be internalized as honored precepts of behavior. They serve like the North Star – valuable guiding lights that orient an organization and focus its energies."

Once agreeing to a set of values and aspirations, people must be equipped, trained, coached and reinforced to live the values. In the case of Seagram, there was clear evolution of training efforts to help reinforce the values. In the beginning there was the *Leading with Values* and *Seagram Challenge* programs which were designed to create awareness and build commitment. Then the *Living the Values* program was instituted to provide a forum for employees to talk about values and later the *Seagram Discovery* program emerged to address specific "how to's."

In addition, it is absolutely critical to see visible examples of the values in practice. In most companies, where skepticism abounds, tangible actions consistent with the values – and linked to the business – must be visible to all. Executives and local leaders need to become personally involved and take initiative in encouraging future leaders to embrace values-based behaviors and actions. Behavioral indicators need to be present to determine who is and is not living the values in day-to-day behaviors. Finally, a successful values program must include a system for recognizing and rewarding those who have embraced the values. Companies must also make sure measurement and reward systems are aligned with the values. Employees must see symbolic actions at all levels which encourage and reinforce values-based behaviors.

In putting all these elements together, one can see that the implementation of values-based management ultimately requires a broad repertoire of change levers, all of which are aligned and all of which are crucial. Figure 15.5 summarizes the key

Figure 15.5 Values management levers

elements discussed here, and serves as a roadmap for change practitioners. The exact sequence and obviously the specific details vary company by company. However, it is in the effective use of these levers, and the disciplined execution, that the success or failure of values-based management is determined.

Finally, for the reflective practitioner of change management, the Seagram example raises an important question of what is meant by success. Is it when the values are generally being lived or is it when the values are continually being challenged and even changed? Seagram's effort to reinvent itself seems to be within the time frame generally found in studies of organizational change. Reinventing a company – with culture change as a key goal – takes five to seven years according to a review of best practice (Jick, 1995).

But companies today want to measure quickly, change quickly, and typically move on, and one year seems like a long time. Moreover, one of the mantras today is to stay adaptable and continually change. But is this also to include values? How often are they to change? In other words, is the work of values-based management more in the category of an "initiative" with a beginning, middle, and an end, or is it more of the "journey" variety?

There are different schools of thought on the longitudinal nature of values-based management. Collins and Porras (1994) argued that companies built to last adhere to an unchanging code of rules; Schein's (1992) work on organizational culture argued that an organization should adopt two sets of values, a core set that essentially never changes and a "peripheral" set that changes with the times; Peters (1987) advocated continuous change and presumably that includes adapting values; and Kotter and Heskett (1992) found that successful companies include adaptability as a core value itself.

The companies that have been engaged in values-based management the longest, such as Johnson and Johnson, have shown that it is indeed a combination of balancing the effort to reinforce with an effort to reinvigorate. Every few years, J&J has engaged in a companywide exercise to challenge and improve its credo of corporate values. The words ironically seem to end up largely the same, but the dialogue that occurs serves to refresh and reinvigorate and thereby enable people to recommit to the values. Thus, there emerges a delicate but effective balance between preserving what people believe to be critical standards of behavior and decisions while continually challenging how to improve them.

Thus, ironically, values-based management can both help to create change in organizations, as was stated at the outset of this chapter, and itself be subject to change and challenge. For most companies, the challenge of instituting and living values is itself formidable. But the ultimate challenge for the most successful companies is how to keep the values alive through refreshers, reinterpretations, renaming, and reiterating. Thus, the "re" words are just as applicable to values-based management as they are to the companies that themselves are facing change pressures and opportunities.

REFERENCES

Collins, J.C. and Porras, J.I. 1994: *Built to Last: Successful Habits of Visionary Companies*. New York: HarperCollins.

Dillon, P. 1998: *Conspiracy of Change*. Fast Company, October.

Jick, T.D. 1995: *Accelerating Change for Competitive Advantage*. Organizational Dynamics, American Management Association.

Kanter, R.M., Stein, B.A., and Jick, T.D. 1992: *The Challenge of Organizational Change*. New York: The Free Press.

Kotter, J.P. and Heskett, J.L. 1992: *Corporate Culture and Performance*. New York: Free Press.

Pascale, R.T. 1990: *Managing on the Edge: How the Smartest Companies Use Conflict to Stay Ahead*. New York: Touchstone.

Peters, T. 1987: *Thriving on Chaos*. New York: Alfred A. Knoff.

Schein, E.H. 1992: *Organizational Culture and Leadership*. San Francisco: Jossey-Bass.

16 Coping with Mergers and Acquisitions

Susan Cartwright and Sarah-Louise Hudson

INTRODUCTION

Mergers and acquisitions (M&As) are an extensive worldwide phenomenon. In 1997, there were over six thousand M&As in Europe alone. The collective value of which exceeded 300 billion dollars (*Acquisition Monthly*, February 1998). In financial terms, many M&As prove disappointing. Conservative estimates suggest that at least half of all mergers fail to achieve the expected synergies and economies of scale (Cartwright and Cooper, 1996; Marks and Mirvis, 1986). In behavioral terms, M&As are associated with a range of factors which adversely affect productivity and organizational performance, for example high labor turnover and the departure of key personnel (Walsh, 1988), increased absenteeism, employee apathy and job dissatisfaction (Altendorf, 1988; Cartwright and Cooper, 1996). As the gains to be derived from M&A have increasingly become dependent upon the successful integration of personnel, technical systems, and organizational cultures, the role of human factors in determining merger outcomes has assumed greater prominence. Characteristically, the problems for human resource management inherent in M&A situations concern dealing with employee uncertainty and stress, maintaining morale and motivation and overcoming resistance to change.

In particular, research studies have highlighted the stressful and costly potential of such a major change event (Cartwright and Cooper, 1996; Siu, Cooper, and Donald, 1997). In a recent study, individuals' satisfaction with a merger was associated with many factors including their view of their supervision, the future of their career and their agreement with the acquiring company's mission statement (Covin et al., 1996). Whilst for some individuals, M&As may provide opportunities and be positively appraised (Brockner et al., 1993), the more commonly reported response is one of anxiety and threat.

A qualitative study (Schweiger, Ivancevich, and Power, 1987) found that employees reported ulcers, migraines and eating problems as a result of merger. In a study of Chinese workers at a merged television company, Sui, Cooper, and Donald (1997) found that high levels of stress were associated with poor mental health. Similarly, evidence from a merger in the financial sector (Cartwright and Cooper, 1993) of its health effects on middle managers, found that an unusually high percentage of managers scored higher than psycho-neurotic outpatients on all six scales of the Crown–Crisp inventory (Crown and Crisp, 1966). In extreme cases, individuals have been reported to commit suicide on hearing that their company has been acquired (Magnet, 1984).

Practical advice to organizations wishing to reduce the stress of M&A has tended to emphasize the importance of "overcommunicating" (Offerman and Gowing, 1990) and the presentation of realistic merger previews (Schweiger and DeNisi, 1991).

Transformational leaders are also suggested to be a valuable resource during mergers (Dunphy and Stace, 1990), in that their people skills may help to communicate that the organization is committed to its employees. Human resource professionals have also been encouraged to actively select the type of leaders needed and identify appropriate change agents in advance of the merger, as this may alleviate perceptions that redundancies and reorganization are arbitrary (Gall, 1986). Although the introduction of stress management programs and employee counseling services (Ivancevich et al., 1990) is likely to have value in reducing experienced stress, in practice employees may be reluctant to participate in such activities out of fear of exposing their inability to cope at a vulnerable stage in their work career.

Much of the advice recommended to organizations has been at a relatively generic level and has treated the M&A event and process as if it was similar to any other form of restructuring and downsizing. In contrast, few studies have focused on the real life experience and ways in which individuals actually cope with M&As and used such information to identify what in fact are adaptive coping mechanisms.

This chapter considers the potential sources of stress associated with M&As and the ways in which individuals cope with experienced stress. It presents the results of a recent study involving the transnational merger between three insurance broking companies. In drawing on the evidence of the UK experience, it discusses the implications for M&A management.

Sources of M&A Stress

Researchers have suggested that the M&A event and the ensuing integration process, may expose employees to a plethora of potential stressors. Some of these stressors may be relatively temporary, for example vulnerability to redundancy, others may be of a more enduring nature, such as ambiguity and cultural change, dependent upon the speed of integration.

The occupational stress literature more generally has identified six broad categories of workplace stress (Cooper, Cooper, and Eaker, 1988). These are described as factors intrinsic to the job, role in the organization, relationships, career development, organizational structure and climate and home/work interface. M&As can be considered to be exceptionally stressful in that they are likely to impact simultaneously upon all six broad categories of stressors in a more acute way than major restructuring (Shaw et al., 1993).

Research based largely on interviews with acquired or merger employees (for example Cartwright and Cooper, 1996; Schweiger and Ivancevich, 1985) has highlighted a number of merger specific stressors. The main ones are discussed below.

Stress associated with survival

From the outset, M&As mobilize employee fears about their continued personal survival and the financial effects which redundancy might have on their quality of life (Magnet, 1984; Schweiger and Ivancevich, 1985). If they remain in employment, employees may be required to relocate or accept a position with reduced status, pay or responsibility. Their role may change, sometimes involving reduced levels of control. Their future career path may be adversely affected (Fried et al., 1996; Hambrick and Canella, 1993).

Research evidence (Schweiger, Ivancevich, and Power, 1987) has also highlighted the stress associated with the seemingly arbitrary nature of such decisions and the lack of positive regard with which they are often implemented.

Stress associated with loss of identity and uncertainty

The loss of identity and concomitant feelings of detachment and bereavement emerge as strong themes within the M&A literature (Marks, 1988; Schweiger, Ivancevich, and Power, 1987). Uncertainty and delayed change contribute to create a state of organizational "limbo" which is likely to be stressful. In a commentary on mergers, Van de Vliet (1997) suggests that proceeding too slowly is a common mistake in merger management. Schweiger, Ivancevich, and Power (1987) similarly observe that acquisitions often take a long time to "unfold." In a longitudinal study of the privatization and reorganization of a utilities company, Nelson, Cooper, and Jackson (1995) found that job satisfaction, and mental and physical health worsened during the privatization process and only started to improve after the reorganization had taken place.

Managers may have difficult decisions to make about the information that should be communicated and that which should be withheld. Thus, some employees may experience a dearth of information that leads to uncertainty and others may experience information overload (Schweiger, Ivancevich, and Power, 1987).

Stress associated with changed working arrangements and relationships

Relationships with others may be a source of stress during mergers due to increased political maneuvering and power games. Failure to replace experienced, departing personnel may increase the workload of those who remain. Changes in staffing arrangements invariably means that employees have to adapt to new peers and supervisors who are likely to have different work methods. An influx of new work colleagues can catalyze change in social norms and employees may have to learn different methods of earning rewards. Colleagues may also be the source of conflicting and negative rumors which induce stress (Ashford, 1988; Cartwright and Cooper, 1993; Marks, 1982; Nadler, 1982).

Acculturation stress

Finally, the degree of cultural compatibility between the two combining organizations has continued to emerge as an important factor in determining merger outcomes (Gertsen, Søderberg, and Torp, 1998). Acculturative stress refers to the disruptive tension that is experienced by members of one culture when they are required to interact with another culture and adopt its ways (Nahavandi and Malekzadeh, 1988). Some researchers (Schneider and DeMeyer, 1991; Very, Calori, and Lubatkin, 1993) have suggested that the problem is more pronounced among cross-national than domestic M&As as there is a double layered acculturation process (Barkema, Bell, and Pennings, 1996; Malekzadeh and Nahavandi, 1998).

Coping Responses and Resources

The exact nature of the relationship between coping and the stress response remains imprecise and is the subject of a variety of theoretical models (Edwards, Baglioni, and Cooper, 1990). These models describe the different ways that coping responses and resources may affect the potential of stressors to lead to stress. They explore the possibility that coping responses and resources may have a direct, mediating or buffering effect.

Lazarus and Folkman's (1984) cognitive model of coping is probably the most popular conceptualization and has been used as a basis for much research. This model suggests that an individual conducts a primary appraisal of a situation or event to determine whether or not it poses a threat and is perceived as stressful. Dependent upon the emotions experienced, the individual may then conduct a secondary appraisal which involves the question "what can I do?" and determines the coping responses that are utilized to deal with the emotions experienced. This model suggests that coping strategies are situationally dependent and contrasts with the trait approach (Moos and Billings, 1982) which suggests that individuals generally use one type of coping response in most situations. According to Lazarus and Folkman (1984) there are two broad foci of coping. Problem-focused coping (pfc) involves efforts to solve the problem. Whereas emotion-focused coping (efc) is directed towards changing the intensity of the emotion. Emotion-focused coping is suggested to be most appropriate when the individual cannot control the environment, while pfc is appropriate for environments that can be controlled (Forsythe and Compas, 1987).

In the context of M&As the literature has been "curiously silent" (Ashford, 1988) and few studies have examined the effectiveness of different coping responses to reduce the stress associated with mergers (Terry, Callan, and Sartori, 1996). According to Schweiger and Ivancevich (1985), the event is likely to be negatively appraised by most affected employees and because it is an essentially unique and unfamiliar experience, employees are unlikely to have developed an appropriate coping strategy to deal with the situation. In a study of a recently merged airline company (Terry, Callan, and Sartori, 1996) found that efc was associated with lower job satisfaction and poorer mental well-being than pfc. Yet evidence from a study of employees involved in a major reorganization indicates that efc was associated with better adjustment and lower levels of stress (Ashford, 1988).

Given the high level of M&A activity over the last ten years, it could be argued that the event has become more commonplace and that a significant proportion of the workforce, particularly in certain business sectors, for example pharmaceuticals, banking and insurance, have now experienced multiple mergers. It would appear that no empirical research has been conducted regarding the effect of past experience on an individual's ability to cope with a subsequent merger.

Research in other fields provides inconclusive findings regarding the effect of past experience on coping. For example, a study was conducted regarding the post-war emotional health of World War II veterans. It was found that younger men were more likely to experience emotional problems except when they had had previous experience of wartime combat and leadership. This would suggest that prior experience had helped them to cope and avoid emotional problems (Hastings, 1991).

However, in a different study, the stress levels of cancer patients' "significant others" were examined (Hart, 1987). In this case, stress levels were higher among the significant others who had prior experience of coping with the cancer of a loved one. This would suggest that prior experience did not enable them to cope more successfully and was in fact detrimental.

The study which follows seeks to investigate the relationship between coping and stress in a merger situation. In particular, it examines the influence of previous merger experience as a potentially useful source of information to guide future merger management.

BACKGROUND TO THE STUDY

Eversure is a large, US owned, multinational organization.[1] Its core business activity is the provision of insurance broking and risk management services. Recognizing that it was a comparatively small player in a rapidly consolidating UK market, Eversure has recently pursued an aggressive strategy of growth by acquisition. In a period of less than 18 months, it initiated not one, but three mergers to form the largest insurance broking company in the UK. Whilst a merger is generally conceived as involving two parties, this combination brought together four separate employee groups and their different organizational cultures.

The sample which forms this study comprises employees based at two UK locations. At Location 1, physical, procedural and socio-cultural integration had occurred soon after the third merger. In contrast, at Location 2, the operations of the constituent parts of the merged company had yet to be physically integrated almost 11 months after the third merger.

Methodology

Three methods of data collection were used. A questionnaire survey was administered to the total population at the two locations of 292 employees. Interviews and diary keeping exercises provided supplementary qualitative information. Interview data were collected prior to the questionnaire distribution and the information was used to generate additional items which were incorporated in the standardized measures used.

Questionnaire

The questionnaire comprised the Pressure Management Indicator (PMI) devised by Cooper and Williams (1994).

Seven sections from the PMI were used in the study. These sections measured:

- sources of pressure (40 items);
- personal influence and control (15 items);
- organizational security and organizational commitment (20 items);
- job satisfaction and organizational satisfaction (12 items);
- state of mind, resilience and confidence level (12 items);
- physical symptoms and energy level (9 items).

Additional items ($n = 21$) relating to merger specific stressors identified from the qualitative data were included. Sample items related to the degree of perceived stress experienced from "difficulty in combining the different cultures of the merged organizations," "rumors," "maintaining a high standard of client service," and "adjustment to new colleagues or supervisors." All responses were made on a six-point Likert-type scale.

The questionnaire also included a 54 item adaptation of the Ways of Coping Questionnaire (WOCQ: Lazarus and Folkman, 1984). In its original form, the WOCQ consists of 67 items relating to pfc, efc, and avoidance coping. Items generated from the qualitative data relating to merger-specific coping responses were added to the WOCQ. Sample items included: "I drew on my past experience of mergers"; "I sought information through informal sources" (such as rumors), and "I focused on factors that I could control." As these additions resulted in some unnecessary repetition, some existing items were removed. Responses to the WOCQ were made on a four-point Likert scale.

Procedure

Questionnaires, covering letters and return envelopes were distributed by internal mail. Of the 292 questionnaires distributed, 155 usable questionnaires were returned to the University. This represents a 53 percent response rate. There were 68 respondents from Location 1 that had integrated rapidly and 84 from Location 2 that had experienced a delay. The age range was 18–55 years. In terms of previous experience, individuals had experienced between zero and eight mergers, with a mean of 2.67 mergers (SD 1.67).

Results

Stressor scale

The responses to the sources of stress section of the PMI were factor analyzed. Factors were extracted using Principal Component Analysis and were rotated orthogonally

Table 16.1 Descriptive statistics of the stressors

Stressor sub-scale	Range of scores	Mean score	SD of score	Mean of each item in sub-scale
Recognition and relationships	8–48	26.14	8.53	3.25
Communication	3–18	5.57	3.82	3.25
Other's merger coping responses	3–18	9.34	3.75	3.13
Future concerns	2–12	6.18	2.78	3.09
Daily hassles	3–18	8.59	3.36	2.87
Change	4–21	11.37	4.07	2.84
Role stressors	6–36	16.00	6.37	2.65
Work-home	14–80	34.15	14.22	2.42
Managerial stressors	3–17	5.57	3.02	1.87

using Varimax. Seventeen iterations were required to produce the rotated factor solution. All factors had an eigen value of more than 1 and scree charts were consulted to determine how many factors should be retained. Loadings of less than 0.5 were suppressed. A ten factor solution was obtained which explained 68 percent of the variance (see table 16.1).

Scores on the stressor scale were arranged whereby a score of 1 was very definitely not a source of stress and a score of 6 was very definitely a source of stress. Recognition and relationships and communication issues received the highest scores but overall scores were not particularly elevated.

Stress outcomes

The mean scores on the physical and mental well-being and job satisfaction scales were comparative to normative data ($n = 4,946$). However, t tests showed a significant difference ($p < 0.05$) in the organizational satisfaction mean for the sample ($x = 18.07$ SD 4.56) compared to normative data ($x = 19.34$ SD 4.65) with individuals in the sample reporting lower levels of organizational satisfaction. Surprisingly, the sample reported significantly ($p < 0.05$) higher levels of organizational security ($x = 16.65$ SD 3.17) compared to normative data ($x = 16.08$ SD 3.96) and comparable levels of organizational commitment. Individuals in the sample also reported significantly less ability to control and influence events.

Coping

The responses to the Ways of Coping Questionnaire were similarly factor analyzed using Principal Component Analysis. This produced a six factor solution which explained 46 percent of the variance (see table 16.2).

Table 16.2 The intercorrelations between the Ways of Coping sub-scales and the reliability of each sub-scale

	Efc	Future	Change	Pfc 1	Pfc 2	Supp. & Info.
Efc	(0.80)					
Future	0.14	(0.66)				
Change	0.25	0.37	(0.68)			
Pfc 1	0.63	0.25	0.54	(0.86)		
Pfc 2	0.45	0.11	0.29	0.57	(0.72)	
Supp. & Info.	0.28	0.23	0.39	0.45	0.21	(0.68)

Future = thinking about the future
Change = changing something
Supp. & Info. = seeking support and information
Sub-scale reliabilities are in parentheses.

Table 16.3 Descriptive statistics of the coping responses

Coping response	Range of scores	Mean score	SD of score	Mean of each item in sub-scale
Efc	0–21	11.14	4.72	1.60
Pfc 1	0–26	11.52	6.48	1.06
Thinking about future	0–9	2.92	2.52	0.73
Pfc 2	0–11	2.73	2.54	0.69
Support and information	0–19	6.02	4.44	0.66
Change something	0–13	2.47	2.78	0.35

Items loaded on two separate pfc factors. There were no differentiating characteristics between these two types of pfc. However, they were not combined as each scale had high levels of reliability. Intercorrelations between the scales and the reliability of each scale is also shown in table 16.2.

Table 16.3 shows the mean of all the items in the subscale. A score of 1 indicates that the coping response was used somewhat; a score of 3 indicates that it was used a lot. The most used strategy was emotion-focused coping.

Speed of integration

Whilst there were no significant differences in the overall mean health scores between employees at Location 1 and Location 2, speed of integration was related to resilience and to job satisfaction. Individuals at the location that had experienced delayed integration (Location 2) reported significantly higher levels of resilience (Location 1 mean score = 16.60 SD 3.65; Location 2 mean score = 17.77 SD 3.36). Speed of integration was also linked. Individuals at Location 2 which experienced delayed integration reported significantly higher levels of job satisfaction (Location 1 mean score = 20.81 SD 6.02; Location 2 mean score = 23.44 SD 5.23; $p < 0.01$). Furthermore, the levels of job satisfaction at Location 1 were significantly poorer compared to normative data (mean = 22.60 SD 5.39; $p < 0.05$).

The direct effect of prior merger experience on coping with the current merger

Three separate multiple regression analyses were used to test the direct effects model for each of the four outcomes (mental well-being, physical well-being, satisfaction and attitude towards the organization). First, the outcomes were regressed on stressors, secondly on coping responses (control and personal influence) and thirdly, they were regressed on coping resources (efc, thinking about the future etc.). Due to the large number of independent variables, the coping resources and responses were entered as a set (Callan, 1994). The nine types of stressors were also combined to produce a measure of the total stressors.

The stressors were negatively related to all of the outcomes and the coping resources were positively related to the outcomes. In terms of coping responses, problem-focused coping was positively related to mental and physical well-being. "Thinking about the future" and "seeking support or information from others" were negatively related to mental and physical well-being (see table 16.4).

These results indicate that those reporting fewer stressors were more likely to have better mental and physical health, be more satisfied and have a more positive organizational attitude. Individuals who perceived that they had high levels of control and personal influence also exhibited more positive outcomes. Those who extensively used pfc, sought little support and information from others, and thought little about the future, were more likely to have better mental and physical well-being.

To ascertain the direct effects of previous merger experience, an additional multiple regression analysis was conducted with outcome regressed on the number of mergers experienced. The number of mergers was found to have a positive relationship with physical and mental well-being (table 16.5) suggesting that prior experience was related to better health.

Further analyses were conducted to more fully investigate the effect of prior experience and to ascertain whether previous merger experience has a mediating effect on perceived stressors (table 16.6). There was found to be no significant relationship between stressors and number of mergers. However, a negative relationship was found between "number of mergers" and the coping response "thinking about the future" and a positive relationship with the coping resource "personal influence."

These results suggest that individuals who had previous merger experience did not perceive the stressful potential of the merger any differently from those without prior experience. Rather, they were less likely to use the maladaptive coping response "thinking about the future" and more likely to perceive higher levels of personal influence. In turn, they were likely to have better mental and physical health.

These results do not support the mediating effect of previous merger experience on perceived stressors; instead they suggest that previous experience has a direct effect on coping responses, coping resources, and outcomes.

Table 16.4 Direct effects model

Independent variable	Dependent variable	β	t value	R^2	R^2 Adj.	ΔR^2	F change
Stressors	Mental well-being (mental)	−0.35	−4.23***	0.12	0.17	0.12	17.87***
Stressors	Physical well-being (physical)	−0.37	−4.52***	0.14	0.13	0.14	20.46***
Stressors	Satisfaction	−0.26	−2.94***	0.07	0.06	0.07	8.67***
Stressors	Attitude to organization (attitude)	−0.30	−3.46***	0.09	0.08	0.09	11.98***
Resources	Mental			0.19	0.18	0.19	15.99***
Control	Mental	0.32	4.11***				
Personal influence (Influence)	Mental	0.25	3.17**				
Resources	Physical			0.14	0.13	0.14	11.28***
Control	Physical	0.30	3.77***				
Influence	Physical	0.19	2.33*				
Resources	Satisfaction			0.32	0.31	0.32	31.28***
Control	Satisfaction	0.41	5.62***				
Influence	Satisfaction	0.35	4.83***				
Resources	Attitude			0.30	0.28	0.30	27.04***
Control	Attitude	0.40	5.34***				
Influence	Attitude	0.33	4.38***				
Responses	Mental			0.24	0.21	0.24	7.06***
Pfc 1	Mental	0.41	3.20**				
Think about future (Future)	Mental	−0.37	−4.54***				
Seek support and information (Supp. & Info.)	Mental	−0.25	−3.16**				
Efc	Mental	0.04	0.37				
Change something	Mental	−0.04	−0.42				
Pfc 2	Mental	−0.09	−1.00				
Responses	Physical			0.26	0.23	0.26	7.96***
Pfc 1	Physical	0.46	3.78***				
Future	Physical	−0.33	−4.18***				
Supp. & Info.	Physical	−0.31	−3.66***				
Efc 2	Physical	−0.09	−0.89				
Change something	Physical	−0.01	−0.13				
Pfc 2	Physical	0.001	0.07				
Responses	Satisfaction			0.07	0.03	0.07	1.68
Pfc 1	Satisfaction	0.07	0.46				
Future	Satisfaction	−0.15	−1.65				
Supp. & Info.	Satisfaction	0.05	0.51				
Efc	Satisfaction	0.17	1.46				
Change something	Satisfaction	−0.04	−0.36				
Pfc 2	Satisfaction	0.04	0.38				
Responses	Attitude			0.07	0.02	0.07	1.45
Pfc 1	Attitude	0.11	0.73				
Future	Attitude	−0.16	−1.76				
Supp. & Info.	Attitude	0.04	0.41				
Efc	Attitude	0.14	1.24				
Change something	Attitude	−0.01	−0.67				
Pfc 2	Attitude	0.03	0.26				

*$p < 0.05$, **$p < 0.01$, ***$p < 0.001$

Table 16.5 The direct effect of prior merger experience on outcomes

Independent variable	Dependent variable	β	t value	R^2	R^2 Adj.	ΔR^2	F change
No. of Mergers	Mental	0.33	3.79***	0.11	0.10	0.10	14.36***
No. of Mergers	Physical	0.28	3.24**	0.08	0.07	0.08	10.48**
No. of Mergers	Satisfaction	0.00	0.03	0.00	−0.01	0.00	0.00
No. of Mergers	Attitude	0.08	0.89	0.01	0.00	0.01	0.78

*$p < 0.05$, **$p < 0.01$, ***$p < 0.001$

Table 16.6 The mediating effect of previous merger experience

Independent variable	Dependent variable	β	t value	R^2	R^2 Adj.	ΔR^2	F change	F
No. of Mergers[a]	Mental	0.25	2.93**	0.39	0.34	0.06	8.56**	7.62***
No. of Mergers[b]	Mental	0.25	2.90**	0.40	0.35	0.05	8.41**	7.04***
No. of Mergers[a]	Physical	0.18	2.03*	0.39	0.33	0.03	4.10*	7.50***
No. of Mergers[b]	Physical	0.17	2.00*	0.40	0.35	0.03	4.01*	7.11***
No. of Mergers[a]	Satisfaction	−0.03	−0.30	0.30	0.24	0.03	0.92	7.51***
No. of Mergers[a]	Attitude	0.00	0.03	0.28	0.22	0.00	0.00	8.21***
No. of Mergers	Stressors	0.04	0.41	0.00	−0.01	0.00	0.16	
No. of Mergers	Efc	0.04	0.42	0.00	−0.01	0.00	0.18	
No. of Mergers	Future	−0.18	−2.08	0.03	0.03	0.03	4.33*	
No. of Mergers	Change	−0.08	−0.89	0.01	0.00	0.01	0.79	
No. of Mergers	Pfc 1	0.16	1.77	0.03	0.02	0.03	3.12	
No. of Mergers	Pfc 2	0.00	0.00	0.00	−0.01	0.00	0.00	
No. of Mergers	Supp. & Info.	−0.15	−1.65	0.02	0.01	0.02	2.74	
No. of Mergers[c]	Mental	0.24	2.73**	0.37	0.34	0.05	7.46**	13.76***
No. of Mergers[c]	Physical	0.25	2.77**	0.31	0.28	0.06	7.68**	10.83***
No. of Mergers[c]	Satisfaction	−0.14	−1.59	0.39	0.37	0.02	2.54	13.78***
No. of Mergers[c]	Attitude	−0.03	−0.38	0.38	0.35	0.00	0.15	15.28***
No. of Mergers	Con.	0.03	0.37	0.00	−0.01	0.00	0.137	
No. of Mergers	Inf.	0.30	3.45**	0.09	0.08	0.09	11.87**	

[a] Controlled for stressors and coping responses
[b] Controlled for stressors and coping responses and occupation
[c] Controlled for stressors and coping resources
*$p < 0.05$, **$p < 0.0$, ***$p < 0.001$.

DISCUSSION

Overall, the study found that the stress levels and health of merged employees did not differ significantly from the general working population. However, there was evidence to suggest that the experience may have resulted in organizational dissatisfaction and that rapid integration may result in reduced job satisfaction and resilience. As the last merger occurred 11 months prior to data collection, it would appear that the merger environment might have stabilized. It has been suggested that stress-related mental ill-health might last for up to four years after a significant organizational transition (Cooper and Payne, 1988). These results indicate a more rapid recovery; perhaps because of the high number of respondents who had already been through and presumably survived, a previous merger experience.

Counter intuitively, employees reported above average levels of organizational security. There are a number of possible explanations for these findings. First, there had already been a number of redundancies in the company, individuals may therefore feel secure because they had survived the redundancy process and did not anticipate any future job losses. Secondly, in tending to positively cope with events by not thinking about the future and adopting a more "here and now" approach, individuals did not entertain or consciously think about the possibility of future mergers and redundancies. Or thirdly, employees were suppressing their fears and felt that to admit low levels of organizational security would be an admission of vulnerability.

The most interesting finding of the study relates to the impact of prior experience. Prior experience would not appear to immunize employees against the stressful potential of M&A but rather help employees to cope more effectively and reduce the strain of the experience.

The study found evidence to suggest that "thinking about the future" and seeking social support and information were maladaptive coping strategies in M&As and were associated with poorer physical and mental well-being. In the general coping literature, social support is widely regarded as a positive coping resource (Kahn and Byosiene, 1992). However, it has been suggested (Terry, Callan, and Sartori, 1996) that employees who seek social support from their colleagues during mergers may become highly involved in informal networks which excessively expose them to inaccurate and anxiety-provoking rumors and the potentially dysfunctional nature of "collective grief." Tentatively, the evidence from this study would seem to confirm this.

Limitations of the study

The application of a rigorous and robust methodology to the study of M&As is problematic and the retrospective nature of this study is an obvious limitation. There were some discrepancies between the qualitative and quantitative methods of data collection in terms of the intensity of the negative experiences expressed. Again, this appears to be typical of M&A research (Cartwright and Cooper, 1996) and suggests that individuals may minimize their negative experiences in responding to a questionnaire survey to appear "merger fit"; whereas in an interview situation, they express more emotionality and negative affect.

As a measure of coping, the Ways of Coping Questionnaire has been increasingly criticized, particularly in relation to its unstable factor structure (Oakland and Ostell, 1996). Efforts were made to incorporate an alternative way of exploring coping by asking individuals to keep a diary or stress log over a period of time in which they enter details of stressful events experienced and the way in which they coped with them. Unfortunately, due to the considerable time commitment required on behalf of the participants, few usable diaries were returned and the data was limited in terms of its value and representativeness.

Implications for merger management

Despite its limitations, evidence from this study should indicate that those with previous merger experience can be a useful resource and source of information to M&A

management. It may be advantageous for merging/acquiring companies to retain such individuals as role models and more directly involve them in the integration process. Their previous experience could be most helpful in encouraging individuals to adopt more adaptive methods of coping with M&As. In particular, employees need to be discouraged from engaging in too much speculative thinking about what may happen and focus more on addressing problems as and when they occur. It could be argued that it is "thinking about the future" which drives individuals to seek social support and information from others. This method of coping becomes so unsatisfactory in that it so increases anxiety (the collective "fear the worse" syndrome) that it becomes a stressor of itself. This would emphasize the importance of continual and consistent organizational communication about merger-related issues. Again, previous M&A survivors may be useful "ambassadors" in the communication process.

Finally, the study reinforced the importance of perceived personal influence. This suggests that M&A management needs to actively consult and involve employees in the integration process, such as the formation of task groups at all levels. Aside from increasing employee perceptions of control, the formation of task groups or working parties will also provide merging employees with a superordinate goal which will positively focus their attention on solving a current problem rather than perhaps worrying and coping poorly with a future problem that may never even happen.

NOTE

1. For confidentiality reasons, the company has been assigned a fictitious name.

REFERENCES

Altendorf, D.M. 1988: When cultures clash: a case study of the Texaco Takeover of Getty Oil and the impact of acculturation on the acquired firm. August 1986, Dissertation, Faculty of Graduate School, University of Southern California.

Ashford, S.J. 1988: Individual strategies for coping with stress during organizational transitions. *Journal of Applied Behavioral Science*, 24 (1), 19–36.

Barkema, H.G., Bell, J.H., and Pennings, J.M. 1996: Foreign entry. *Cultural Barriers and Learning Strategic Management Journal*, 17, 151–66.

Brockner, J., Wiesenfeld, B.M., Reed, T., Grover, S., and Martin, C. 1993: Interactive effects of job content and context on the reactions of layoff survivors. *Journal of Personality and Social Psychology*, 64, 187–97.

Callan, V.J. 1994: Coping resources, coping strategies and adjustment to organizational change: direct or buffering effects? *Work and Stress*, 8, 372–83.

Cartwright, S. and Cooper, C.L. 1993: The psychological impact of merger and acquisition on the individual: a study of building society managers. *Human Relations*, 46 (3), 327–47.

Cartwright, S. and Cooper, C.L. 1996: *Managing Mergers, Acquisitions and Strategic Alliances: Interpreting People and Cultures*. Oxford: Butterworth-Heinemann.

Cooper, C.L., Cooper, R.D., and Eaker, L. 1988: *Living with Stress*. London: Penguin.

Cooper, C.L. and Payne, R. 1988: *Causes, Coping and Consequences of Stress at Work*. New York: John Wiley & Sons.

Cooper, C.L. and Williams, S. 1994: *Creating Healthy Work Organization*. Chichester: John Wiley & Sons.

Covin, T.J., Sightler, K.W., Kolenko, T.A., and Tudor, R.K. 1996: An investigation of post-acquisition satisfaction with the merger. *Journal of Applied Behavioral Science*, 32 (2), 125–42.

Crown, S. and Crisp, A.H. 1966: *Manual of the Crown-Crisp Experiential Index*. London: Hodder & Stoughton.

Dunphy, S. and Stace, D. 1990: *Under New Management: Australian Organization in Transition*. Sydney: Addison-Wesley.

Edwards, J.R., Baglioni, A.J., and Cooper, C.L. 1990: Stress, Type-A, coping and psychological and physical symptoms: a multi-sample test of alternative models. *Human Relations*, 43 (10), 191–5.

Forsythe, C.J. and Compas, B. 1987: Interaction of cognitive appraisals of stressful events and coping: testing the goodness of fit hypothesis. *Cognitive Therapy and Research*, 11, 473–85.

Fried, Y., Tiegs, R.B., Naughton, T.J., and Ashforth, B.E. 1996: Manager's reactions to a corporate acquisition: a test of an integrative model. *Journal of Organizational Behavior*, 17, 401–27.

Gall, A.L. 1986: What is the role of HRD in a merger? *Training and Development Journal*, 18–23.

Gertsen, M.C., Søderberg, A.M., and Torp, J.E. (eds) 1998: *Cultural Dimensions of International Mergers and Acquisitions*. Berlin: Walter de Gruyter.

Hambrick, D.C. and Canella, A.A. 1993: Relative standing: a framework for understanding departures of acquired executives. *Academy of Management Journal*, 36 (4), 733–62.

Hart, K. 1987: Stress encountered by significant others of cancer patients receiving chemotherapy. *Omega: Journal of Death and Dying*, 17 (12), 151–67.

Hastings, T.J. 1991: The Stanford-Terman study revisited: post-war emotional health of World War II veterans. *Military Psychology*, 3 (4), 201–14.

Ivancevich, J.M., Matteson, M.T., Freedman, S.M., and Phillips, J.S. 1990: Worksite stress management. *American Psychologist*, 45, 259–61.

Kahn, R. and Byosiene, P. 1992: Stress in organizations. In M. Dunnette and L. Hough (eds) *Handbook of Industrial and Organizational Psychology* (2nd edn). Palo Alto, CA: Consulting Psychologists Press.

Lazarus, R.S. and Folkman, S. 1984: *Stress, Appraisal and Coping*. New York: Springer.

Magnet, M. 1984: Help! My company has just been taken over. *Fortune*, July 9, 44–51.

Malekzadeh A.R. and Nahavandi A. 1998: Leadership and culture in transnational strategic alliances. In A.C. Gertsen, A.M. Søderberg, and J.E. Torp (eds) *Cultural Dimensions of International Mergers and Acquisitions*. Berlin: Walter de Gruyter.

Marks, M. 1982: Merging human resources: a review of current research. *Mergers & Acquisitions*, 38–44.

Marks, M. 1988: The merger syndrome: the human side of corporate combinations. *Journal of Buyouts and Acquisitions*, January–February, 18–23.

Marks, M.L. and Mirvis, P.H. 1986: The merger syndrome. *Psychology Today*, 20 (10), 36–42.

Moos, R.H. and Billings, A.G. 1982: Conceptualizing and measuring coping resources and processes. In L. Goldberger and S. Breznitz (eds) *Handbook of Stress*. New York: Free Press.

Nadler, D.A. 1982: Managing transitions to uncertain future states. *Organizational Dynamics*, Summer, 37–45.

Nahavandi, A. and Malekzadeh, A.R. 1988: Acculturation in mergers and acquisitions. *Academy of Management Review*, 13 (1), 79–90.

Nelson, A., Cooper, C.L., and Jackson, P.R. 1995: Uncertainty amidst change: the impact of privatization on employee job satisfaction and well being. *Journal of Occupational and Organizational Psychology*, 68, 57–71.

Oakland, S. and Ostell, A. 1996: Measuring coping: a review and a critique. *Human Relations*, 49 (2), 133–56.

Offerman, L.R. and Gowing, M.K. 1990: Organizations of the future, changes and challenges. *Journal of Personality and Social Psychology*, 46, 655–68.

Schneider, S.C. and DeMeyer, A. 1991: Interpreting and responding to strategic issues: the impact of national culture. *Strategic Management Journal*, 12 (4), 307–20.

Schweiger, D.L. and DeNisi, A.S. 1991: Communication with employees following a merger: a longitudinal field experiment. *Academy of Management Journal*, 34, 110–35.

Schweiger, D.L. and Ivancevich, J.M. 1985: Human resources: the forgotten factor in mergers and acquisitions. *Personnel Administrator*, 30, 47–61.

Schweiger, D.L., Ivancevich, J.M., and Power, F.R. 1987: Executive actions for managing human resources before and after acquisition. *Academy of Management Executive*, 1, 127–38.

Shaw, J.B., Fields, M.W., Thacker, J.W., and Fisher, C.D. 1993: The availability of personal and external coping resources: their impact on job stress and employee attitudes during organizational restructuring. *Work and Stress*, 7 (3), 229–46.

Siu, O., Cooper, C.L., and Donald, I. 1997: Occupational stress, job satisfaction and mental health among employees of an acquired TV company in Hong Kong. *Stress Medicine*, 13, 99–107.

Terry, D.J., Callan, V.J., and Sartori, G. 1996: Employee adjustment to an organizational merger: stress, coping and inter-group differences. *Stress Medicine*, 12, 105–22.

Terry, D.J. and Callan, V.J. 1997: Employee adjustment to large scale organizational change. *Australian Psychologist*, 32 (3), 203–10.

Van der Vliet, A. 1997: When mergers misfire. *Management Today*, June, 40–2.

Very, P., Calori, R., and Lubatkin, M. 1993: An investigation of national and organizational cultural influences in recent European mergers. In P. Shrivastava, A. Huff, and J. Dutton (eds) *Advances in Strategic Management*. London: JAI Press, 323–43.

Walsh, J. 1988: Top management turnover following mergers and acquisitions. *Strategic Management Journal*, 9, 177.

17 Organizational Restructuring: Identifying Effective Hospital Downsizing Processes

Ronald J. Burke and Esther R. Greenglass

The early 1990s were characterized by economic slowdown, plant closings, layoffs, and budget cutbacks (Gowing, Kraft, and Quick, 1998). This mood of austerity has affected private and public sector organizations alike, and is expected to continue through the early 2000s and beyond. More organizations are working toward balanced budgets and fiscal responsibility; they are becoming "leaner and meaner" (Burke and Nelson, 1998).

WHY DOWNSIZE OR RESTRUCTURE?

Downsizing refers to the voluntary actions of an organization to reduce expenses. This is usually, but not exclusively, accomplished by shrinking the size of the workforce. But the term covers a whole range of activities from personnel layoffs and hiring freezes to consolidation and mergers of units. Downsizing refers to an array of initiatives implemented by an organization in response to a decision to reduce head count.

Wrenching changes have forced organizations to look for ways to compete. The globalization of the marketplace, sweeping technological advances, and changes to a service-based economy are but a few of these forces. Global benchmarking, in particular, has led companies to compare their overhead costs with those of global competitors, and to cut their payrolls in response. It must also be acknowledged that downsizing is sometimes the price paid for mismanagement and strategic errors at the top of the organization (Kets de Vries and Balazs, 1997).

The outcomes that organizations seek from restructuring may include increased productivity, improved quality, enhanced competitive advantage, and potential regeneration of success (Hoskisson and Hitt, 1994). In addition, organizations hope to achieve lower overheads, less bureaucracy, more effective decision making, improved communication, and greater innovativeness.

Although we might like to think that the reasons for downsizing are well thought out, many of the reasons are purely social ones. McKinley, Sanchez, and Schick (1995) proposed that three social forces that precipitate downsizing efforts are constraining forces, cloning forces, and learning forces. Constraining forces place pressures on executives to do the "right thing" in terms of legitimate managerial actions. Managers are expected to reduce their workforces, and those who make drastic cuts are often cast in the media as heroes. Cloning forces are the result of imitation or benchmarking. Reacting to uncertainty, managers want to display that they are doing something to address the decline. They look to other organizations within their industries to demonstrate some initiative, and then they follow suit. Learning, the third social force that brings about downsizing efforts, takes place through educational institutions and professional associations. Cost accounting methods encourage downsizing as a legitimate business activity. Organizations thus choose to downsize for a variety of reasons, some of them economic and some of them social. The rationale for downsizing is an integral part of the issue of whether downsizing efforts are effective, or whether they fail.

In the United States between 1980 and 1985, about 2.5 million jobs were lost each year, most of these blue-collar. From 1985–8, a different pattern occurred. Over one-third of the Fortune 1,000 companies reduced their workforces by 10 percent each year. They were reducing their workforces not because the company was losing money, but because they aimed to increase productivity and cut costs. Hourly workers in manufacturing still are the hardest hit, suffering about 50 percent of the job losses; the rest are spread fairly evenly over the other organizational levels. The experts believe that downsizing, now seen as an organizational initiative to increase profitability, will continue through the early 2000s. White-collar workers now are as vulnerable as blue-collar workers. Job loss will continue to be a problem and will quite likely worsen (Cascio, 1995).

Cascio (1993) drew several conclusions from an exhaustive literature review and interviews with managers having downsizing experiences. He pointed out that downsizing would continue as overhead costs remain non-competitive with domestic and international rivals. He also pointed out that there were risks for the employer, for former employees, and for employees who stayed on the job, which needed to be addressed. In view of this evidence, we conclude that downsizing is likely to be followed by more downsizing. The experiences of many companies (for example, IBM, Xerox, TRW, Digital Equipment, Kodak, Honeywell) bear this out.

Many companies say they turn to layoffs only as a last resort. The facts indicate otherwise. Right Associates, in surveys of 1,204 and 909 organizations that had downsized, reported that only 6 percent of employers had tried cutting pay, 9 percent used vacations without pay, and 14 percent had developed job sharing plans. Yet 80 percent of respondents in a Time/CNN survey indicated that they would rather see all employees of their firm take a 10 percent wage cut than lay off 10 percent of the workers to cut expenses and stay in business.

Various levels of government have also focused their attention in recent years on balancing their budgets and reducing the size of their financial deficits. They have done this, in part, by reducing the levels of financial support provided to the health care system. This has resulted in considerable change to hospitals and the health care system in general. These efforts have been associated with hospital restructuring, mergers and closures as the health care system has had to provide the same levels of service with fewer resources. In the US, between 1979 and 1993, 454,000 public service jobs were lost (Uchitelle and Kleinfield, 1996). As with most tax-funded government services, restructuring and downsizing is being imposed on the health care system. Hospitals are restructuring, merging or closing. In the US, 828 hospitals closed between 1980 and 1992 (Godfrey, 1994).

In Canada, government-sponsored medicare has been drastically cut. Since 1992, health care institutions have had to manage with a reduction of government allocation. As a result of severe cutbacks in federal funding to the provinces, the equivalent of $2.5 billion was expected to be cut from health care in 1996–7 (Canadian College of Health Services Executives, 1995). The government of Ontario is planning to close ten hospitals in Toronto, downgrading two others to outpatient clinics, merging programs and downloading a whole host of services onto municipalities, a strategy expected to save $430 million annually in health care costs. As a result, it has been estimated that 10,000 workers could lose their jobs. As hospitals have closed, merged or restructured, hospital workers, and in particular nurses, are at risk of losing their jobs. In the last few years more than 3,700 full-time equivalent registered nurses have lost their jobs in Ontario (Davidson, 1994). It is estimated that another 15,000 may also be at immediate risk (Doyle-Driedger, 1997).

The impact on nurses of these sweeping changes has been considerable and far-reaching. With fewer qualified staff to care for patients, the workload for nurses has significantly increased. Not only are there less staff, but on the whole the hospital population is sicker than in the past since it takes longer to get them into hospital, so when they do get in, they are more ill and require more care. With early discharge of patients, there is an increased rate of re-admission of patients needing intensive care, thus increasing the workload of severely ill patients. According to a recent survey of Ontario nurses, patient care is suffering under health care reforms (Dialogue on Health Reform, 1996). Eighty-one percent of 20,000 members of the Ontario Nurses Association believe that understaffing due to budget cuts and downsizing has reached the point that unsafe conditions exist for patients. Ninety-four percent believe the health-care system needs reform.

Do Downsizing Efforts Work?

Evidence for the effectiveness of downsizing is not impressive. Many efforts produce results that are dismal, and unintended consequences that are devastating. Two-thirds of firms that downsized during the 1980s were behind industry averages for the 1990s. Despite lower unit labor costs, less than half the firms that downsized in the US in the 1990s improved profits or productivity. Seventy-four percent of managers in downsized companies said that morale, trust, and productivity dropped following downsizing, and half of the 1,468 firms in still another survey reported that productivity suffered after downsizing (Henkoff, 1994). A majority of organizations that downsized in another survey failed to realize desired results, only 9 percent indicating an improvement in quality. Evidence suggests that quality, productivity, and customer service often decline over time, and financial performance, while often improving in the short run following downsizing because of promised savings and lower costs, diminish over the long run.

A four-year study of downsizing that attempted to identify best practices demonstrated a significant negative relationship between organizational effectiveness and downsizing accomplished through layoffs (Freeman and Cameron, 1993). Another study of 1,005 firms showed that less than half of these firms had reduced expenses, one-third increased profits, and one-fifth increased productivity. Two-thirds of the firms reported that morale was seriously affected by the downsizing (Bennett, 1991).

Cascio (1998) provided recent evidence that underscores these findings in a study of 311 companies that downsized employees by more than 3 percent in any year between 1980 and 1990. He concluded that the level of employee downsizing did not lead to improved company financial or stock performance. A pure downsizing strategy, then, is unlikely to be effective.

In a study of 281 acute care hospitals, morbidity and mortality rates were 200–400 percent higher in hospitals that downsized in the traditional head count reduction, across-the-board way (Murphy, 1994). That is, patient deaths were significantly higher when downsizing occurred by targeting head count reductions as the chief approach to downsizing, and when reductions occurred in an imprecise fashion. Moreover, the cost savings associated with downsizing dissipated in 12–18 months, and the costs rose to pre-downsizing levels in a relatively short time.

Organizational memory and valued skills and experience are often eroded following downsizing (Burke, 1997). In organizations that downsize as a response to decline, the most competent people are the first to leave. They do not want to be associated with a failing organization, and seek opportunities elsewhere. Because their skills are marketable, they leave, and the organization is left with a crew of individuals who are less competent, or less mobile. This early departure of the most qualified employees may leave the organizations suffering from the "cesspool syndrome" in which less qualified employees rise to the top (Bedeian and Armenakis, 1998).

The human costs of downsizing are immense and far-reaching. Acquisitions, downsizing, restructuring, re-engineering, culture change and leadership succession have left workers saturated with changes (Marks, 1994). Victims and survivors witness destroyed careers and career paths. Psychological contracts between organizations and individuals are destroyed. Cynicism is up, and trust in organizational leadership is down (O'Neill and Lenn, 1995). Survivors are forced to work harder with fewer rewards. Waves of downsizings are seen over a few years. Employees see no end in sight, and feel powerless to influence the "permanent whitewater" of change.

Organizational downsizing is a strong stress-inducing factor that has a powerful effect on the attitudes and work behavior of remaining employees (Greenberg, 1990). These stressors include increased uncertainty and ambiguity, feelings of loss of mastery and control over one's environment, and threats to one's self concept (Cameron, Whetten, and Kim, 1987).

Studies that examine survivors' attitudes in the aftermath of corporate layoffs consistently indicate that their job attitudes such as job satisfaction, job involvement, organizational commitment, and intention to remain with the organization become more negative (Brockner et al., 1992; 1994; 1995; Hallier and Lyon, 1996). These negative reactions, combined with the fact that survivors must do more with few resources, make the aftermath of layoffs difficult to deal with.

Noer (1993) offered a vivid description of the state of layoff survivors. Individuals who survive cutbacks must deal with their own feelings as they develop a new relationship with their organization in which they are more empowered and less dependent. Managers must help other survivors through a painful but irrevocable change in the psychological contract between employees and employer. Employees need to develop a more autonomous and less dependent link with the organization, and should not assume job security. Unlike discarding machines, discarding people has an effect on those who remain (Gottleib and Conkling, 1995).

Some organizations, however, have seen benefits from downsizing. There can be a healthy side to restructuring and downsizing. Some organizations were bloated: they needed to rightsize by eliminating unnecessary work. In a Canadian study of 1,034 organizations by Axmith (1995), 85 percent cut costs, 63 percent improved earnings, 58 percent improved productivity, and 36 percent reported improved customer service. Cameron (1999) found, contrary to expectations, that downsizing of one military command was associated with favorable results. First, there were considerable cost savings ($90 million in three years). Second, on-time delivery and order processing time decreased. Third, quality of products delivered also improved. Fourth, employee grievances dropped. Fifth, customer complaints dropped while their satisfaction improved. In short, substantial improvement took place on a variety of objective performance indicators over this three-year period. When questionnaire measures of the process dimensions of downsizing, the general approach to downsizing and the effects of downsizing were compared at the start and at the end of the three-year period, the responses were significantly more favorable at the end of this period. The command was seen as more effective and downsizing was seen as a contributor to this improvement.

The majority of evidence suggests, however, that most downsizing efforts fall short of meeting objectives. Despite its dismal track record, downsizing remains a strategy of choice for organizations faced with excess capacity, bloated employee ranks, sky-high costs, and declining efficiency. In order to learn from the experience of downsizing, the many failures and few successes must be examined.

IDENTIFYING EFFECTIVE HOSPITAL DOWNSIZING PROCESSES

We undertook a study to examine nursing staff reactions to the ways Ontario hospitals managed and implemented their downsizing and restructuring efforts. A literature review suggested that five factors were likely to improve downsizing and restructuring initiatives: the development of a vision of the future; staff participation; active and open communication; fairness of sacrifice; and concrete efforts to rebuild morale during the downsizing and restructuring process. Would the presence of these implementation processes reduce the negative consequences associated with organizational downsizing and restructuring?

A research model was developed to guide the selection of variables to be considered as well as the data analysis (see figure 17.1). Predictor variables were organized in blocks which followed a particular order. The first block of predictors were personal demographic characteristics (for example, age, marital status, level of education). The second block of predictors were situational characteristics (for example, size of hospital, years with present hospital). The third block of predictors considered the extent of hospital restructuring. The fourth and final block of predictors involved the five dimensions of hospital restructuring and downsizing processes experienced by respondents. Outcome variables included a variety of work satisfaction and individual well-being measures.

Figure 17.1 Research framework

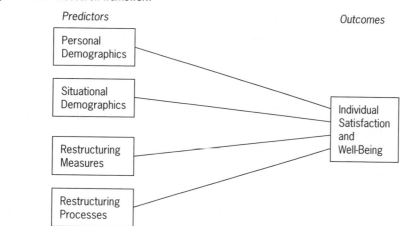

Study procedure

Data were collected using a confidential and anonymous mail-out questionnaire which was sent to about 3,900 hospital nurses in Ontario who were members of the nurses union. Respondents were randomly chosen from all hospital nurses in their membership (about 45,000). The sample ($N = 1,363$) represented a 35 percent response rate. Completed questionnaires were returned to a university address in a stamped addressed envelope that was provided.

Respondents

There was considerable diversity on most demographic items. Respondents were mainly women (95 percent), about one-half worked full-time, about half had some type of supervisory duties, over 80 percent had an RN degree – either college or hospital based – about 80 percent were married or living with a partner and about three-quarters had children. On average, respondents had been employed in their current units about 9 years and in their current hospital about 15 years. The average age of respondents was 42. Respondents lived and worked in communities and hospitals of various sizes. Finally, respondents worked in a variety of nursing units, with about two-thirds in medical/surgical, intensive care/coronary, emergency and obstetrics.

MEASURES

Hospital restructuring and downsizing process

Five aspects of the implementation and management of the hospitals' restructuring and downsizing efforts were assessed.

Vision

The existence of a vision of a desired end-state was measured by three items ($\alpha = 0.86$). "I have a clear sense of where the hospital will be headed following the restructuring."

Staff participation

The extent to which nursing staff participated in the planning and implementation of hospital restructuring was measured by three items ($\alpha = 0.62$). "I feel like I have 'had a voice' in the hospital restructuring and downsizing process."

Communication

Efforts by senior management to inform staff about the restructuring initiative were assessed by three items ($\alpha = 0.77$). "The hospital provided in-service sessions, bulletins and lecture rounds to inform and educate staff about the restructuring initiatives."

Fairness

Nursing staff views about the fairness of decisions and actions taken during restructuring were assessed by three items ($\alpha = 0.56$). "The approach taken by senior management to cutting costs has been fair to all staff."

Revitalization

Efforts by the hospital to be sensitive to and rebuild nursing staff morale and commitment were assessed by three items ($\alpha = 0.92$). "During restructuring the hospital has made efforts to rebuild staff morale."

Personal and situational characteristics

A number of personal and situational characteristics were measured by single items. These included: age, sex, marital status, size of hospital, full or part-time employment status, and hospital tenure.

Restructuring and downsizing efforts

Two different but related features of the hospitals' restructuring and downsizing efforts were considered.

Extent of restructuring

Respondents indicated whether each of 16 restructuring initiatives ($\alpha = 0.69$) had taken place in their hospital during the last year (yes/no). Items included: staff layoffs, units closed, overtime restrictions, hiring freezes, and early retirement incentives.

Work stressors

Three work stressors specifically addressed to hospital restructuring and downsizing were included.

Workload

This measure had three items ($\alpha = 0.69$) and determined the extent to which hospital restructuring had influenced nursing staff jobs. "The changes in my unit have made my job more demanding."

Use of generic workers

This two item measure ($\alpha = 0.69$) assessed how efforts being made to make greater use of less skilled, lower paid "generic" hospital workers affected nursing performance. "The use of generic workers to perform nursing duties has resulted in a deterioration of patient care."

Staff bumping

The effects of staff bumping, the movement of nursing staff throughout the hospital as a function of their seniority, on nursing practice was measured by three items ($\alpha = 0.57$). "Changes in staff in my unit as a result of bumping (one nurse replacing another due to greater seniority) have caused some problems."

Work outcomes

Three work outcomes were included.

Job satisfaction

Job satisfaction was measured by a five item scale ($\alpha = 0.82$) developed by Quinn and Shepard (1974). A sample item was "All in all, how satisfied would you say you are with your job (1= not at all satisfied, 4 = very satisfied)."

Intent to quit

Intent to quit was measured by a two item scale ($\alpha = 0.30$). "Given your present situation in the hospital, would you quit your job it were possible? (1 = no, 3 = yes)."

Absenteeism

Two items ($\alpha = 0.87$) measured absenteeism. "How many days of scheduled work have you missed in the past month."

Psychological well-being

Two areas of psychological well-being were considered: psychosomatic symptoms and psychological burnout.

Psychosomatic symptoms

Respondents indicated, for 30 specific troubles and complaints ($\alpha = 0.92$), how frequently they experienced them during the past three months ($5 =$ never, $1 =$ extremely often). Items included: headaches, faintness or dizziness, poor appetite, heart pounding or racing and crying easily (Derogatis et al., 1979).

Psychological burnout

Three dimensions of psychological burnout were assessed using the General Burnout Questionnaire (Leiter, Schaufeli, and Kalimo, 1995).

Emotional exhaustion

Emotional exhaustion was measured by a five item scale ($\alpha = 0.90$). Respondents indicated how frequently they experienced particular job-related feelings ($0 =$ never, $6 =$ every day). Items included: "I feel emotionally drained from my work. Working all day is really a strain for me."

Professional efficacy

Professional efficacy was measured by six items ($\alpha = 0.73$). "I feel I am making an effective contribution to what this organization does."

Cynicism

Cynicism was assessed by five items ($\alpha = 0.82$). "I have become more cynical about whether my work contributes anything."

Hospital effectiveness

Impact of restructuring

Impact of restructuring (7 items) indicated the extent to which hospital restructuring had negative effects on the delivery of health care programs and services and staff morale ($\alpha = 0.78$). "The restructuring and budget cuts this hospital is undertaking has lowered the quality of health care provided to patients."

ANALYSIS PLAN

A series of hierarchical regression analyses were undertaken in which predictor variables were entered in blocks in a specified order (see figure 17.1). The first block entered were personal demographic characteristics ($N = 6$). The second block entered were situational characteristics ($N = 5$). The third block entered was either the measure of the extent of restructuring and downsizing ($N = 1$) initiatives or the measure of work stressors ($N = 3$). The fourth block entered were the measures of implementation and management of the hospital restructuring process ($N = 5$). The important question was whether the inclusion of the fourth block would indicate a significant increment in explained variance on a particular dependent variable.

Table 17.1 presents the results of hierarchical regression analyses in which eight work and individual well-being outcomes were regressed on the four blocks of predictors. In these analyses, organizational restructuring was measured by the number or extent of restructuring initiatives undertaken by their hospital. The restructuring and downsizing process panel of variables accounted for significant increments in explained variance on six of the eight outcome measures; restructuring and downsizing processes had no relationship with levels of absenteeism or professional efficacy. In all cases, nursing staff reporting more favorable restructuring processes (for example, more staff participation, more communication) also reported more positive work outcomes (such as a less adverse impact of hospital restructuring, more job satisfaction, less emotional exhaustion).

Specific restructuring and downsizing processes also had significant and independent relationships with the work and individual well-being outcomes. Fairness of the restructuring and downsizing process had a significant and independent relationship with all six outcomes that showed significant restructuring and downsizing process effects. Greater use of revitalization efforts by hospitals had significant and independent relationships with five of these six outcomes; followed by greater communication efforts, two of six; and greater staff participation in the restructuring and downsizing activities, one of six. The presence of an organizational vision for the restructuring and downsizing effort was not related to any of these six outcomes.

Table 17.2 presents the results of hierarchical regression analyses in which eight work and individual well-being outcomes were regressed on the four blocks of predictors. In these analyses, the three work stressors served as measures of the restructuring and downsizing impact. Restructuring and downsizing processes accounted for significant increments on six of these eight outcomes, controlling for individual and situational characteristics and work stressors. These six outcomes were also predicted by the restructuring processes measures when extent of restructuring initiatives was using the restructuring measure. Once again, restructuring processes were not related to absenteeism or professional efficacy. In all cases nursing staff reporting more favorable restructuring processes (such as more fairness of sacrifice) also reported more positive outcomes (for example, job satisfaction), controlling for personal and situational characteristics and work stressors.

Particular restructuring and downsizing processes also had significant and independent relationships with work and individual well-being outcomes. Fairness of the restructuring and downsizing effort had significant and independent relationships with two outcomes; communication and presence of a future vision for the exercise each had significant and independent relationships with one outcome; greater hospital use of revitalization efforts had significant relationships with three outcomes. Staff participation in restructuring efforts was not related to any of these six work outcomes.

Previous writing on organizational downsizing and restructuring has indicated that many organizations undertake these efforts both ineffectively and unsuccessfully (Cameron, 1999). This seemed to be the situation described by this sample of staff nurses.

Table 17.1 Restructuring implementation and outcomes: restructuring initiatives

	R	R^2	$\blacklozenge R^2$	P
Impact of restructuring (N = 1,113)				
Demographic characteristics	0.18	0.03	0.03	0.001
Situational characteristics	0.21	0.04	0.01	NS
Restructuring initiatives	0.33	0.11	0.07	0.001
Restructuring processes	0.48	0.23	0.12	0.001
Fairness (−0.21)				
Revitalization (−0.11)				
Communication (−0.12)				
Job satisfaction (N = 1,134)				
Demographic characteristics	0.12	0.01	0.01	0.05
Situational characteristics	0.14	0.02	0.00	NS
Restructuring initiatives	0.18	0.03	0.02	0.001
Restructuring processes	0.34	0.12	0.08	0.001
Revitalization (0.17)				
Fairness (0.09)				
Absenteeism (N = 1,094)				
Demographic characteristics	0.04	0.00	0.00	NS
Situational characteristics	0.24	0.06	0.06	0.001
Restructuring initiatives	0.25	0.06	0.00	NS
Restructuring processes	0.27	0.07	0.01	NS
Intent to quit (N = 1,136)				
Demographic characteristics	0.22	0.05	0.05	0.001
Situational characteristics	0.28	0.08	0.03	0.001
Restructuring initiatives	0.32	0.10	0.03	0.001
Restructuring processes	0.38	0.14	0.04	0.001
Fairness (−0.09)				
Revitalization (−0.08)				
Communication (−0.07)				
Exhaustion (N = 1,130)				
Demographic characteristics	0.13	0.02	0.02	0.01
Situational characteristics	0.24	0.06	0.04	0.001
Restructuring initiatives	0.30	0.06	0.04	0.001
Restructuring processes	0.39	0.15	0.06	0.001
Revitalization (−0.17)				
Fairness (−0.09)				
Professional efficacy (N = 1,100)				
Demographic characteristics	0.09	0.01	0.01	NS
Situational characteristics	0.14	0.02	0.01	0.05
Restructuring initiatives	0.14	0.02	0.00	NS
Restructuring processes	0.17	0.03	0.01	NS
Cynicism (N = 1,121)				
Descriptive characteristics	0.11	0.01	0.01	0.05
Situational characteristics	0.13	0.02	0.01	NS
Restructuring initiatives	0.18	0.03	0.02	0.001
Restructuring processes	0.31	0.10	0.06	0.001
Revitalization (−0.12)				
Fairness (−0.09)				
Participation (−0.09)				
Psychosomatic symptoms (N = 1,032)				
Demographic characteristics	0.05	0.00	0.00	NS
Situational characteristics	0.14	0.02	0.02	0.01
Restructuring initiatives	0.19	0.04	0.02	0.001
Restructuring processes	0.26	0.07	0.03	0.001
Fairness (−0.12)				

NS = not significant

Table 17.2 Restructuring process and work outcomes: work stressors

	R	R^2	$\blacktriangle R^2$	P
Impact of restructuring (N = 1,010)				
Demographic characteristics	0.18	0.03	0.03	0.001
Situational characteristics	0.20	0.04	0.01	NS
Work stressors	0.63	0.40	0.36	0.001
Workload (0.40)				
Generic (0.17)				
Bumping (0.16)				
Restructuring processes	0.66	0.43	0.03	0.001
Fairness (0.11)				
Communication (−0.08)				
Vision (−0.06)				
Job satisfaction (N = 1,014)				
Demographic characteristics	0.12	0.02	0.02	0.05
Situational characteristics	0.14	0.02	0.00	NS
Work stressors	0.41	0.17	0.15	0.001
Workload (−0.33)				
Restructuring processes	0.45	0.20	0.03	0.001
Revitalization (0.12)				
Absenteeism (N = 983)				
Demographic characteristics	0.05	0.00	0.00	NS
Situational characteristics	0.24	0.06	0.06	0.001
Work stressors	0.26	0.06	0.01	NS
Restructuring processes	0.27	0.07	0.01	NS
Intent to quit (N = 1,016)				
Demographic characteristics	0.21	0.04	0.04	0.001
Situational characteristics	0.26	0.07	0.02	0.001
Work stressors	0.37	0.14	0.07	0.001
Workload (0.19)				
Restructuring processes	0.40	0.16	0.02	0.001
Exhaustion (N = 1,010)				
Demographic characteristics	0.13	0.02	0.02	0.01
Situational characteristics	0.23	0.05	0.04	0.001
Work stressors	0.49	0.24	0.19	0.001
Workload (0.37)				
Bumping (0.06)				
Restructuring processes	0.51	0.26	0.02	0.001
Revitalization (−0.11)				
Professional efficacy (N = 985)				
Demographic characteristics	0.11	0.01	0.01	0.05
Situational characteristics	0.16	0.02	0.01	0.05
Work stressors	0.19	0.03	0.01	0.05
Restructuring processes	0.21	0.04	0.01	NS
Cynicism (N = 1,003)				
Demographic characteristics	0.11	0.01	0.01	NS
Situational characteristics	0.14	0.02	0.01	NS
Work stressors	0.33	0.11	0.09	0.001
Workload (0.23)				
Restructuring processes	0.37	0.13	0.03	0.001
Revitalization (−0.09)				

Table 17.2 *(cont'd)*

	R	*R²*	♠*R²*	*P*
Psychosomatic symptoms (N = 924)				
Demographic characteristics	0.05	0.00	0.00	NS
Situational characteristics	0.14	0.02	0.02	0.01
Work stressors	0.27	0.07	0.05	0.001
Workload (0.15)				
Bumping (0.09)				
Restructuring processes	0.30	0.09	0.02	0.01
Fairness (−0.08)				

NS = not significant

Respondents reported the implementation and management of hospital efforts as unilateral, top-down, somewhat unfair, not guided by a vision of clear and positive end state or characterized by efforts to rebuild staff morale.

Those staff nurses reporting favorable perceptions of the processes used by their hospitals in implementing downsizing and restructuring also reported more positive work outcomes (greater satisfaction, less intent to quit) and emotional well-being (fewer psychosomatic symptoms, less emotional exhaustion, less cynicism) and better organizational performance. Nursing staff reported less adverse impact of restructuring and downsizing on hospital effectiveness when implementation and management of these efforts involved high levels of these processes. These findings were consistent with those of previous researchers (Cameron, 1999; Cascio, 1993; Noer, 1993). This body of work sheds considerable light on both the importance of the planning and implementation process in organizational restructuring and downsizing, as well as the critical role of particular processes in the implementation and management of those efforts.

WHAT ORGANIZATIONS CAN DO

Considerable guidance is now available to senior organizational managers on how best to implement organizational restructuring and downsizing (Burke and Nelson, 1997; Nelson and Burke, 1998). Handled properly, we propose that revitalization can re-energize tired workers and heighten their aspirations, shift the organization's focus to future opportunities, strengthen the pay-for-performance link, increase investment in training and development, encourage innovation, improve communication, and produce a clearer mission. Downsizing may, in fact, be part of the revitalization process, but only a part.

There is no quick fix

One of the reasons for the failure of many downsizing efforts was an overly simplistic approach. Senior management equated downsizing with cutting costs through staff reduction. This approach has often been short-sighted, focusing on perceived internal efficiencies rather than examining the way the organization conducts its business.

Simply cost cutting is unlikely to improve the competitive position of most organizations over the long haul in the global marketplace. Kets de Vries and Balazs (1997) suggest that companies that implemented downsizing seem to be more concerned with their past than their future; long-term investments are postponed to realize short-term gains. They propose instead that downsizing be reframed "as a continuous process of corporate transformation and change, a way to plan for the continuity of the organization" (p. 11). In its broadest sense, downsizing can mean changing the firm's fundamental business practices, and even its corporate culture. Responsible restructuring focuses on how to use the current people more effectively, and as part of continuous improvement efforts, constitutes a more effective approach. A wider definition serves to place downsizing under the umbrella of continuous corporate renewal.

A THREE-STAGE APPROACH TO REVITALIZATION

We propose that organizations approach revitalization efforts within the framework of comprehensive organizational change (Burke and Nelson, 1997; Nelson and Burke, 1998). Large-scale changes can be recast within the three-stage framework of initiation, implementation, and institutionalization. A careful examination of the literature on downsizing and restructuring yields guidance for managers in each of the three stages. We offer a summary of organizational actions based on our review in table 17.3.

Initiation: planning revitalization efforts

Planning is an essential element in any change process. Graddick and Cairo (1998), note the importance of up-front planning. This includes the establishment of time frames, goals and objectives for the restructuring, the establishment of deadlines to monitor progress and the establishment of principles to ensure consistency and integrity of the process. Reframing the restructuring in a broader way offers a more constructive way of viewing the process. This new mindset opens up possibilities for learning and novel solutions to performance, productivity, and cost concerns.

Attempts to revitalize organizations should begin with a goal, and should be part of a long-term strategy rather than a quick fix. It is possible to downsize without layoffs. If the reasons for reducing the workforce are cost related, managers should consider cutting costs elsewhere. Process improvements may be more effective than reducing head count. In addition, a thorough organizational diagnosis should be conducted, and specific areas of inefficiency should be targeted. Employees should be given information about the financial state of the business, and when they are informed they can draw their own conclusions about actions that need to be taken. The individuals affected can provide input on cutting costs if they are made aware of the need to do so. When employees understand that the organization's performance affects them personally, they respond by helping to improve that performance (Burke and Nelson, 1997).

If downsizing is deemed a necessity, there are several short-term alternatives to be considered, each with advantages and disadvantages. Such options include attrition, hiring freezes, wage containment, limits in work hours, and alternative forms of termination (Knowdell, Branstead, and Moravec, 1994). Interestingly, Cameron (1998)

Table 17.3 A three-stage guide for managing revitalization efforts

Initiation: planning and preparing for the transition
- Integrate the change with business strategy
- Begin with a goal in mind
- Frame the process positively, in terms of opportunities
- Communicate extensively, and involve affected employees
- Consider alternatives to layoffs (attrition, hiring freezes, voluntary retirements)
- Determine the criteria for downsizing
- Establish empowered teams for managing the transition
- Develop timetables for enhancing predictability

Implementation: moving toward change
- Involve employees in all aspects of the implementation effort
- Communicate extensively
    Tell the truth
    Use a two-way process
    Overcommunicate
- Provide support to managers, survivors and victims
    Give news face-to-face
    Allow for grief and goodbyes
    Treat all parties with dignity and respect
    Be generous and fair to displaced employees
- Monitor the transition efforts
    Be vigilant for signals of distress and burnout
    Don't expect immediate positive results

Institutionalization: healing and refocusing
- Focus on the future and why changes are needed
- Clarify expectations and responsibilities
- Celebrate accomplishments
- Implement support groups for survivors
- Invest in retraining and development
- Establish the new psychological contract
- Evaluate the effectiveness of revitalization efforts
- Maintain individual and organizational health

found that the type of downsizing tactics used (such as use of layoffs, early retirement, severance packages, transfers, demotions) was unrelated to command effectiveness or performance improvements following downsizing. In addition, other factors such as salary or hiring freezes, number of management levels reduced, or amount of outsourcing undertaken had no effect on these closures.

Whatever option is taken, managers must clearly explain the criteria for workforce reductions.

The decision of what method to use requires in-depth analysis and careful forethought. This explanation must be characterized by open communication, candor, and repetition. Multiple methods of communication should be used, but face-to-face communication may be most effective. In addition, managers should be trained on how to effectively communicate the downsizing (Mishra, Spreitzer, and Mishra, 1998). Managers must be prepared to give bad news with empathy and be prepared to deal with the emotional reactions of employees.

Implementation: the change is underway

The way in which the transition plan is executed has a dramatic effect on the long-term success of the affort, and particularly affects the victims' and survivors' reactions to the process. Adkins (1998) advocated the use of broadly based change management teams in describing the military base closure. Graddick and Cairo (1998) concur with this point, and propose that transition teams formed in the planning stage be heavily involved in implementing the change process. Participation in the implementation of change gives employees a sense of control over their destinies and a means of influencing events that threaten their livelihoods and well-being.

Communication during the implementation stage is essential. Managers must tell the truth, and overcommunicate (Mishra, Spreitzer, and Mishra, 1998). Managers should carefully and thoroughly explain the criteria for layoffs, and clarify the role of performance valuations in the layoff process (Leana and Feldman, 1992). Using a procedure that is perceived as fair can build employee trust, especially when the outcome is negative, as in a layoff (Brockner, Wiesenfeld, and Martin, 1995). The communication process must be two-way; employees must be engaged in communication to determine their reactions to the process and their level of understanding.

Providing support to all affected employees is critical. All employees must be treated with respect and dignity. Providing laid-off employees with honest information and social support can help them face the future with more confidence. Also, employees should be given the bad news in person by someone they know rather than via mail or by someone they do not know. Laid-off workers and survivors should be allowed to grieve, and to say goodbye to each other. Generosity to those departing will benefit both victims and survivors. Providing clear explanations and treating people with respect while implementing a layoff are actions that are not costly in economic terms, but add to the perceptions of procedural fairness. Managers should provide laid-off workers with fair recommendations to future employers. Providing outplacement assistance for employees is a critical part of managing the transition process. These services can be provided by company career centers, or can be outsourced. One outplacement intervention that has been demonstrated to be helpful to displaced employees is stress management training. Participants in a stress management training program were able to maintain effective coping resources and minimize increases in distress and strain, while members of the control group either increased their distress levels or decreased their use of coping skills (Maysent and Spera, 1995). The program was also evaluated by participants, who indicated that one of the informal benefits of the training was the forum it provided for sharing their own frustrations and concerns about the job search process.

Continuous monitoring of progress during the implementation stage will help the organization assess its efforts and spot trouble early. Monitoring processes can help the transition teams adjust the plan along the way. The emotions and well-being of employees should be monitored as well, and managers should be especially vigilant for signals of distress and burnout (Graddick and Cairo, 1998). In conjunction with the monitoring process, managers should not expect immediate payoffs. Cameron (1998), in describing the downsizing of the military command, indicated that one factor that differentiated this case from typical downsizing efforts was an expectation of temporary downturns during the process, and subsequent moderate-term recovery.

Institutionalization: revitalization and renewal

If downsizing is required, then revitalization of the organization is a key third step in the transformation process. In their study of the trivestiture of AT&T, Graddick and Cairo (1998) distilled seven lessons learned about revitalization:

1. Avoid ignoring past accomplishments and qualities, but emphasize why changes are required for future success.
2. Ensure that employees understand the new business direction, opportunities for growth, and how they can contribute to these. Clarify requirements for change, including new skills and competencies, culture changes, and leadership behaviors.
3. Celebrate and recognize important accomplishments.
4. Drive process improvements so that the smaller, downsized workforce does not end up doing the same amount of work as the pre-downsizing workforce had done.
5. Communicate the new employment contract between employees and the company (that is, clarify mutual expectations).
6. Align goals throughout the organization and clarify roles and responsibilities.
7. Realign human resources processes and programs (for example, compensation, workforce planning, education and training, performance management, leadership development) with the new business direction.

These suggestions are in accordance with the view of downsizing as part of organizational redesign and systemic changes in organizational cultures.

Helping survivors cope with the trauma of the transition should be a major part of revitalization efforts. Layoff survivors' symptoms do not go away, and some even intensify over time. These symptoms include an increase in resignation, fear, and depression, deepening sense of loss of control, and heightened, more focused anger (Noer, 1993). Survivors' social support systems have been disrupted or destroyed, they are confused about role expectations, and fear the overload of work that will be passed along to them. They may suffer feelings of guilt from wondering "Why not me?" Managers must allow for a period of grieving and disruptions in productivity, and treat survivors gently following the transition (Leana and Feldman, 1992). Support groups can help employees feel safe in expressing their feelings.

Investment in the retraining and development of survivors is important because some organizations want to demonstrate some immediate improvements in bottom line from the downsizing efforts (Gutknecht and Keys, 1993). The new organizational reality, however, dictates that new strategies and even new organizational cultures be passed along through training and development efforts. It cannot be assumed that survivors will understand how to carry out their new jobs after downsizing. They will need new skills to tackle the work left behind by former colleagues. Adkins (1998) suggested that education and training efforts should include job training, transition skills, personal change, and stress management. Training can help the survivors to feel more competent and empowered in the throes of uncertainty (Mishra, Spreitzer, and Mishra, 1998).

Downsizing may necessitate a movement from the old employment contract, focused on long-term tenure and codependency, to the new employment contract, which views employees as self-employed entrepreneurs (Noer, 1993). Rather than emphasizing lifetime employment, the new psychological contract emphasizes employability. Workers are trained in transferable skills. Whereas long-term career planning was a part of the old psychological contract, the new environment requires career management programs for survivors that focus on opportunities for growth and development rather than advancement (Feldman, 1996). Providing survivors with growth opportunities that allow them to develop portfolios of transferable skills is an important support mechanism. It signals that the company believes in investing in human resources.

Conclusion: Leadership is Vital

A major theme that can be gleaned from the studies of successful revitalization efforts is that effective leadership is a critical element in the transformation process. The competence, knowledge, dynamism, and accessibility of senior managers and their ability to articulate a vision that provides motivation for the future increases the likelihood of positive outcomes. Consistent, strong, effective leaders must develop and communicate a new vision and motivate employees to embrace this vision. Changes in leadership are likely to affect the process adversely particularly if trust – a key ingredient – is jeopardized.

The behavior of senior management, particularly their treatment of survivors, is an important determinant of the success or failure of the downsizing process. The way senior managers handle layoffs has a major impact on survivor's attitudes and work behaviors. Many senior managers underestimate the importance of little details in the downsizing and restructuring process implementation on the productivity of those remaining. It is also a mistake to tell those that remain they should consider themselves fortunate and they should work hard since they still have jobs.

Acknowledgments

Preparation of this manuscript was supported in part by the School of Business, York University and the Department of Psychology, York University. The research would not have been possible without the cooperation of the Ontario Nurses Association. Graeme Macdermid assisted with data analysis and Louise Coutu prepared the manuscript. Finally, our thinking in this area has benefited from our work with our colleague Debra L. Nelson.

References

Adkins, J.A. 1998: Base closure: a case study in occupational stress and organizational decline. In M.K.L. Gowing, J.D. Kraft, and J.C. Quick (eds) *The New Organizational Reality: Downsizing, Restructuring and Revitalization*. Washington, DC: American Psychological Association, 111–42.

Axmith, M. 1995: *1995 Dismissal Practices Survey*. Toronto: Murray Axmith.

Bedeian, A.G. and Armenakis, A.A. 1998: The cesspool syndrome: how dreck floats to the top of declining organizations. *The Academy of Management Executive*, 12, 58–67.

Bennett, A. 1991: Downscoping doesn't necessarily being an upswing in corporate profitability. *The Wall Street Journal*, June 4, B-1, B-4.

Brockner, J., Grover, S., Reed, T., and DeWitt, R. 1992: Layoffs, job insecurity, and survivors work effort: evidence of an invented-relationship. *Academy of Management Journal*, 35, 413–25.

Brockner, J., Konovsky, M., Cooper-Schneider, R., Folger, R., Martin, C., and Bies, R. 1994: Interactive effects of procedural justice and outcome negativity on victims and survivors of job loss. *Academy of Management Journal*, 37, 397–409.

Brockner, J., Wiesenfeld, B.M., and Martin, C.L. 1995: Decision frame, procedural justice, and survivors' reactions to job layoffs. *Organizational Behavior and Human Decision Processes*, 63, 59–68.

Burke, W.W. 1997: The new agenda for organization development. *Organizational Dynamics*, 26, 6–20.

Burke, R.J. and Nelson, D.C. 1997: Downsizing and restructuring: lessons from the firing line for revitalizing organizations. *Leadership and Organization Development Journal*, 18, 325–34.

Burke, R.J. and Nelson, D.L. 1998: Mergers and acquisitions, downsizing and privatization: a North American perspective. In M.K. Gowing, J.D. Kraft, and J.C. Quick (eds) *The New Organizational Reality: Downsizing, Restructuring and Revitalization*. Washington, DC: American Psychological Association, 21–54.

Cameron, K. 1998: Strategic organizational downsizing: an extreme case. In C.L. Cooper and D. Rousseau (eds) *Trends in Organizational Behavior*. New York: John Wiley, 5, 185–229.

Cameron, K.S., Whetten, D.A., and Kim, M.U. 1987: Organizational dysfunctions of decline. *Academy of Management Journal*, 30, 126–37.

Canadian College of Health Services 1995: *Special Report – External Environmental Analysis and Health Reform Update*, summer.

Cascio, W.F. 1993: Downsizing: What do we know? What have we learned? *Academy of Management Executive*, 7, 95–104.

Cascio, W.F. 1995: Whither organizational psychology in a changing world of work? *American Psychologist*, 50, 928–39.

Cascio, W.F. 1998: Learning from outcomes: financial experiences of 311 firms that have downsized. In M.K. Gowing, J.D. Kraft, and J.C. Quick (eds) *The New Organizational Reality: Downsizing, Restructuring and Revitalization*. Washington DC: American Psychological Association, 55–70.

Davidson, J. 1996: Cited in D. Bell. Costing the cure. *CA Magazine*, September, 28.

Derogatis, L.R., Lipton, R.S., Rickets, K., Uhlenhuth, E., and Covi, L. 1979: The Hopkins Symptom Checklist (HSCL): a self-report symptom inventory. *Behavioural Science*, 19, 1–15.

Dialogue on Health Reform 1996: Toronto: Ontario Nurses Association.

Doyle-Driedger, S. 1997: The nurses. *MacLean's*, 106, 24–7, April 28.

Feldman, D.C. 1996: Managing careers in downsizing firms. *Human Resource Management*, 35, 145–61.

Freeman, S.J. and Cameron, K.S. 1993: Organizational downsizing: a convergence and reorientation framework. *Organization Science*, 4, 10–29.

Godfrey, C. 1994: Downsizing: coping with personal pain. *Nursing Management*, 25, 90–3.

Gottleib, M.R. and Conkling, L. 1995: *Managing the Workplace Survivors: Organizational Downsizing and the Commitment Gap*. New York: Quorum Books.

Gowing, M.K., Kraft, J.D., and Quick, J.C. 1998: *The New Organizational Reality: Downsizing, Restructuring and Revitalization*. Washington, DC: American Psychological Association.

Graddick, M.M. and Cairo, P.C. 1998: Helping people and organizations deal with the impact of competitive change: an AT&T case study. In M.K. Gowing, J.D. Kraft, and J.C. Quick (eds) *The New Organizational Reality: Downsizing, Restructuring and Revitalization*. Washington, DC: American Psychological Association, 77–98.

Greenberg, E.R. 1990: The latest AMA survey on downsizing. *Compensation and Benefits Review*, 22, 66–71.

Gutknecht, J.E. and Keys, J.B. 1993: Mergers, acquisitions and takeovers: maintaining morale of survivors and protecting employees. *Academy of Management Executive*, 7, 26–36.

Hallier, J. and Lyon, P. 1996: Job insecurity and employee's commitment: managers reactions to the threat and outcomes of redundancy selection. *British Journal of Management*, 7, 107–23.

Henkoff, R. 1994: Getting beyond downsizing. *Fortune*, January 10, 58–64.

Hoskisson, R.E. and Hitt, M.A. 1994: *Downscoping: How to Tame the Diversified Firm*. New York: Oxford University Press.

Kets deVries, M. and Balazs, K. 1997: The downside of downsizing. *Human Relations*, 50, 11–50.

Knowdell, R.L., Branstead, E., and Moravec, M. 1994: *From Downsizing to Recovery: Strategic Transition Options for Organizations and Individuals*. Palo Alto, CA: Cpp Books.

Leana, C.R. and Feldman, D.C. 1992: *Coping with Job Loss*. New York: Lexington Books.

Leiter, M.P., Schaufeli, W., and Kalimo, R. 1995: The General Burnout Questionnaire. Paper presented at the APA/NIOSH Work Stress Conference, Washington, DC, April.

Marks, M.L. 1994: *From Turmoil to Triumph*. New York: Lexington Books.

Maysent, M. and Spera, S. 1995: Coping with job loss and career stress: effectiveness of stress management training with outplaced employees. In L.R. Murphy, J.J. Hurrell Jr., S.L. Sauter, and G.P. Keita (eds) *Job Stress Interventions*. Washington, DC: American Psychological Association, 159–70.

McKinley, W., Sanchez, C.M., and Schick, A.G. 1995: Organizational downsizing: constraining, cloning, learning. *Academy of Management Executive*, 9, 32–42.

Mishra, K.E., Spreitzer, G.M., and Mishra, A.K. 1998: Preserving employee morale during downsizing. *Sloan Management Review*, 39, 83–95.

Murphy, E.C. 1994: *Strategies for Health Care Excellence*. Washington, DC: American Society for Work Redesign.

Nelson, D.L. and Burke, R.J. 1998: Lessons learned. *Canadian Journal of Administrative Sciences*, 15, 372–81.

Noer, D. 1993: *Healing the Wounds: Overcoming the Trauma of Layoffs and Revitalizing Downsized Organizations*. San Francisco: Jossey-Bass.

O'Neill, H.M. and Lenn, J. 1995: Voices of survivors: words that downsizing CEOs should hear. *Academy of Management Executive*, 9, 23–4.

Quinn, R.P. and Shepard, L.J. 1974: *The 1972–73 Quality of Employment Survey*. Ann Arbor, MI: Institute for Social Research, University of Michigan.

Uchitelle, L. and Kleinfield, N.R. 1996: The price of jobs lost. In The New York Times Special Report (eds) *The Downsizing of America*. New York: The New York Times Company Inc., 37–76.

Index